The GREAT AMERICAN Ale Trail

THE CRAFT BEER LOVER'S GUIDE TO THE BEST WATERING HOLES IN THE NATION

by Christian DeBenedetti

Running Press
PHILADELPHIA · LONDON

For Mom and Chuck—the "Traveling Companions," and Dad.

Books published by Running Press are available at special discounts for bulk purchases in
the United States by corporations, institutions, and other organizations. For more information,
please contact the Special Markets Department at the Perseus Books Group, 2300 Chestnut
Street, Suite 200, Philadelphia, PA 19103, or call (800) 810-4145, ext. 5000, or e-mail
special.markets@perseusbooks.com.

ISBN 978-0-7624-4375-8
Library of Congress Control Number: 2011931109

E-book ISBN 978-0-7624-4476-2

9   8   7   6   5   4
Digit on the right indicates the number of this printing

Cover design by Ryan Hayes
Interior design and illustration by Ryan Hayes
Edited by Jennifer Kasius
Typography: Garage Gothic, Fenway Park Gotham, and Chronicle

Running Press Book Publishers
2300 Chestnut Street
Philadelphia, PA 19103-4371

Visit us on the web!
www.runningpress.com

Contents

Preface

WHEN THE BOARDING PASS EMERGED FROM THE WHIRRING MACHINE AT

Helsinki-Vantaa Airport, I had to admit that I was relieved. I hadn't intended things to turn out this way, but this is what always happens, and I really should have known better. Only seven hours previously, I'd been at the pub—St. Urho's Pub, to be precise—a slightly grubby watering hole in one of lesser-known districts of Helsinki, Finland. Finns speak a language intelligible to no one else on Earth, but that has never slowed them down, especially when it comes to socializing. So now here I was, with Markku, Jussi, Kari, and a few others, telling improbable stories. I pinged my pal Matt on Facebook and told him I was drinking his beer in Helsinki. He picked up in England and pinged me back within minutes, asking how it was holding up. The beer was beautiful, and it was a fine evening—all about the ebullient company, and the company was all about the beer. St. Urho's has more than a dozen taps, all flowing with excellent beers, lovingly kept. I didn't mean to stay until 3:00 A.M., but that's what you do, and the reindeer pizza really *was* excellent.

I've been lucky enough to experience many evenings like this over the years. I started in the early 1980s in London, where I first fell in love with cask-conditioned British ale. I continued across Europe, racking up epic evenings in Germany, Belgium, and the Czech Republic. In those days, there was one country where great beer was not to be found, and that was the United States. I got back home from a year abroad in 1984 and found that we Americans had nothing to drink. Somehow the United States—once home to 4,000 breweries and the most exciting and varied beer culture in the world—had lost its way among the great brewing nations. Our breweries fell prey to a form of "progress" that involved removing all the flavor from one of the world's diverse and fascinating drinks. Like many future craft brewers, I started making my own beer at home—not because I wanted to *make* beer, but because I wanted to *drink* beer. Slowly but inevitably, beer took over my life, the slope became slippery, and I slid into the mash tun. I bobbed to the surface and never looked back.

Today, out of nothing, we have built everything. The United States is now the undisputed beer capital of the world, home to the most vibrant beer culture anywhere. It is difficult to overstate how unlikely this seemed twenty years ago. A newly minted craft brewer, I traveled to Europe frequently, and when I told people that I was an American brewer, the scorn was palpable. *Yes, we've heard of your American beer*, they sneered. I protested that Americans were making very flavorful beers now, but heads shook with disbelief. Slowly, however, over the late 1990s and into the 2000s, it dawned on the rest of the world that Americans had woken up to beer, and once awake we'd gotten mighty busy.

While some built breweries, others built restaurants, bars, bowling alleys, and movie theaters around great beer. Not only did we have our own beer—we had everyone else's beer too. The complex beers of Belgium, the fruity ales of England, the malty, bracing lagers of Bavaria, all began to flow from America's taps. Great restaurants, once content with lengthy fine wine lists and dismissive gas-station beer lists, started to realize that industrial beer was an insult to their food and to their beer-savvy patrons. Today I can find the best beers of Belgium faster in a twenty-minute walk from my front door in Brooklyn than I could walking from Grande Place in Brussels.

Do you know beer places and beer people? You should, because beer brings on a sort of fellowship that wine rarely inspires. When you get off a plane and head into an American town, do you know where to find the best of everything, places where people speak your language? Frankly, despite having been all over the world, I can't say that I do. But that's okay, because we have Christian DeBenedetti to show the way. I've read many beer books, of course, but none that capture the spirit, the philosophy, the people, and the feeling of the American beer scene the way that *The Great American Ale Trail* does. This book will tell you what you really want to know—where to go, why you want to go there, how the place came to be, what kind of food they serve, what types of beers you can enjoy with it, and who's going to be sitting next to you at the bar. At the same time, you'll read the stories of men and women who turned their backs on lucrative careers, mortgaged their houses, and put everything on the line to follow their passions and build the kinds of places where they'd want to spend their time. Occasionally, just *occasionally*, until 3:00 am. So read this book, follow Christian's well-laid path, and build your own ale trail. You'll have your own epic evenings with good people and the world's most exciting beverage. And if you should miss your plane, don't worry. Another one will leave soon, and in the meantime, there is some awfully nice beer at the airport bar.

—Garrett Oliver

Garrett Oliver is the brewmaster of The Brooklyn Brewery and the author of the award-winning book, The Brewmaster's Table. *He is also editor-in-chief of* The Oxford Companion to Beer *(2011), and has hosted more than seven hundred beer events in ten countries.*

Introduction

★ ★ ★

THE MOUNTAINS AHEAD ARE BRUSHED WITH CALIFORNIA CHAPARRAL

and piñon juniper, bathed in low angle sunlight, but I'm pulling over in the quiet little town of Alpine, California—a forty-minute drive into the Coast Range foothills outside of San Diego-to visit Alpine Brewing Company. Now the sweet, earthy smells of steeping grains and the tang of hops envelop me. There Pat McIlhenney, a former full-time fire captain with a handlebar mustache, is leading a tour of his handmade brewhouse built in an old TV-repair shop. His operation has been racking up accolades in global competitions. "I cannot make beer fast enough," he says, handing out samples.

Those beers are among the finest I've tasted anywhere: his balanced but tangy "Duet" is full of the fresh, citrusy flavors of Simcoe and Amarillo hops and a grainy, toasty backbone. Even without a bar or taproom, a stream of visitors—beer pilgrims—comes in to meet McIlhenney and buy fresh-brewed beers to go. It's a scene I find again and again across the United States, in cozy beer bars and small-batch breweries, even anodyne cul-de-sacs. I have to wonder: Where are they going next?

There's a genuine revolution happening in America, and I have just spent a year traveling through America to document it. Sure, the big breweries still dominate the cooler aisle, but make no mistake: small-batch "craft" beer (a term related to a brewery's modest size and independent ownership) is roaring back. After The Great Mistake ended in 1933, only the most aggressive, consolidated companies were able to survive; beer drinkers paid the price in flavor and selection. But from the nadir of just 44 breweries by the end of the 1970s, there are now more than 1,700 from Anchorage to the Big Apple, Kona to Kentucky, approaching half the 4,000 breweries of one hundred twenty-five years ago. Meanwhile beer bars from coast to coast are bursting with selections and seasonally driven food to go with them. Bottle shops and groceries are stocking 1,000-strong lists. Simply put, we're in the midst of a new golden age of American beer.

There's a simple reason for this comeback: good beer is part of a good life. The late British beer writer Michael Jackson once said, "You wouldn't walk into a restaurant and order 'a plate of food,' so why would you do the same with your beer?" Craft beer is about originality, flavor, and complexity derived from the many malts, hop varieties, yeast strains, water sources, even oak barrels a brewer can use, no matter where they live.

A wonderful thing happens when you travel with beer in mind: the world opens up in a more friendly way. During my travels, I met hundreds of dedicated, inspiring American brewers, barkeeps, chefs, and beer lovers, every one in love with the art and science of brewing. There's a bit of luck and joy in all this, but a *lot* of hard work: it's impossible to keep up, because new kettles are boiling in almost every single state.

Think of this book as a mere starting point, a preview of what's out there for you to discover. Wander, but bring a map, too: in this book, spots are organized in clusters, generally speaking, but not always. And talk to people: in every single one of the places in this book, you're going to meet pilgrims hitting the road for the love of beer. You're not likely to meet warmer and more friendly people. And along the way, I hope *The Great American Ale Trail* will help posit a new definition of craft beer: The growing love of artisan-made brews isn't because beer is becoming more like wine. It's becoming more *beer*-like. Brewing goes back to our Founding Fathers, and eons earlier, when Sumerians recorded beer batches as prayers in clay tablets. We're tapping into something ancient, something necessary. To the lucky ones who know, it makes perfect sense. And I hope that with this book, you'll begin your own search. The only question is: Where to go first?

—Christian DeBenedetti
Portland, OR, 2011

Oregon

★ ★ ★

THANKS TO A BAND OF BOLD BREWING PIONEERS STARTING IN THE

late 1970s and early 80s, the entire state is blessed with hoppy wonders, with Portland as its shining beer capital. Today, there are no less than forty breweries and counting in the small city of 600,000 known to many as Beervana. Some say it's the rain driving drinkers indoors; others point to the tough, timber-country ingenuity and independent spirit ingrained in the gene pool. Either way, craft beer is so popular throughout the state, you can pick up an artisan brew at the gas station.

The history of this good-beer revolution is well documented, but suffice it to say that Portland embraced craft beer early, becoming the brewing epicenter of the Northwest—and arguably the entire United States and even the world—by being both aggressively provincial and always innovative. With access to top-quality grain and regionally grown hops (and relatively inexpensive real estate), brewers thrived amid a population that loves to drink beer as much as it loves to climb, ski, surf, roast fair-trade coffee, build exotic bikes (and ride them around naked—why not?), and forage for mushrooms. It didn't hurt that in the 1970s and 80s the Oregon wine country emerged as a world-class destination amid the stirrings of Oregon's gourmet-inclined Slow Food movement. Throughout the state, from tiny upstarts to established regional and national brands like Widmer, there's no town too small for an excellent brewpub these days. With snowy peaks, smart cities, and verdant forests, what other excuse do you need to visit?

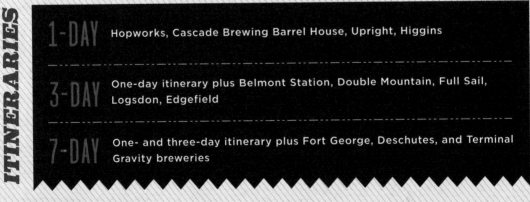

ITINERARIES

1-DAY Hopworks, Cascade Brewing Barrel House, Upright, Higgins

3-DAY One-day itinerary plus Belmont Station, Double Mountain, Full Sail, Logsdon, Edgefield

7-DAY One- and three-day itinerary plus Fort George, Deschutes, and Terminal Gravity breweries

APEX

1216 SE Division St. • Portland, OR 97202
(503) 273-9227 • apexbar.com • Established: 2010

SCENE & STORY

Built in a small industrial garage-like space by former New Belgium Brewing sales representative Jesse McCann, Apex is a squeaky-clean beer bar, which perfectly captures the lifestyle of Portlanders circa 2012: single-speed bike parked out front, barrel-aged Belgian ale in hand. Smoking? *Never—that's so last year.* Table service? Nope, stretch those legs. (Dogs, kids, and credit cards are also ixnayed.) But lest the scene sound too doctrinaire, it's ideal on a sunny day when you can bike there (you can even borrow a lock from the bar's own stash), grab a taco from the little place next door (no food is sold at the bar), and maybe shoot some pinball. Easy does it, except for the blaring heavy metal.

PHILOSOPHY

Serious about beer—intense, even, but not joyless. "I've been told I keep my beer too cold," says McCann, speaking of scolds, with a wry chuckle. But there are beers that *are* simply better cold—*ice cold*—especially when it's 95 degrees in the shade (rare in Portland, but not unheard of). So, thank heavens for one little nod to an older, less uptight mode of beer drinking: amid the list of esoteric brews is a lone "Cheap, Cold" Hamm's can for $2.50—a nice, if ironic, touch.

KEY BEER

McCann brings in bonafide rarities and displays an impressive forty-two-tap selection on a flat screen TV over the bar, so simply peruse the fast-changing list, try some samples, and engage the beer experts at work behind the bar. There are beers here no other bar in Portland can even think about getting, like Moonlight's Working for Tips, a garnet-colored 5.5% ABV ale spiced with redwood tips instead of hops that's only seldom spotted outside of the Bay Area.

HORSE BRASS PUB

4534 SE Belmont St. • Portland, OR 97215 • (503) 232-2202
horsebrass.com • Established: 1976

SCENE & STORY

It was with heavy but grateful hearts that thousands of fans (present company included)—including some from abroad—turned out for the wake to honor Horse Brass founder Don Younger in January of 2011 when he died at age 69 from complications related to being a wise, hard-drinking old buzzard. To hear the gray-bearded, long-haired, raspy-voiced Don tell it between puffs on his ever-present smoke, he woke up one day smarting from a big night of beer (and whiskey, which he loved dearly) and discovered he had bought the bar with his brother Bill, the late Bill Younger.

What happened next helped make Portland the great beer town it is. Bringing in scores of rare and hard-to-find beers, and championing the first efforts of the brewers in town, the Youngers' Horse Brass became one of the most famous and respected beer bars in the land. While Don drove a gray '72 Rolls around town, he did it in a T-shirt. And there was something else about Don: without fanfare, he loaned or simply gave money to a number of earnest young Portlanders trying to get a leg up in beer, in life—Duane Sorenson, founder of Portland's famous Stumptown Coffee Roasters, for one—and never made a fuss about it.

PHILOSOPHY

Generous and communal. The motto of the Horse Brass ("If it were any more authentic, you'd need a passport . . .") is apt, because it looks as if it were airlifted stick by stone out of old London. But Don also loved to say something a bit cryptic, too, something worth considering only with a beer in hand. "It's not about the beer. It's about the beer," he'd say, and then order you another round—on the house.

KEY BEER

There are fifty taps and seventy-five bottled selections, but before you drink anything else, order Younger's Special Bitter on cask (Y.S.B.), named for Bill, who died first, and raise a toast to the Youngers.

DETOUR → OREGON BREWERS FESTIVAL

Summer is the ultimate season here, and no weekend says it better than the one known locally as "brewfest"—the OBF, or Oregon Brewers Festival, at the end of July—when upwards of 60,000 revelers gather in the city's sprawling Tom McCall Waterfront Park under massive, beer-filled open-air tents, and, every ten minutes or so, spontaneously start cheering like fans at the Super Bowl, glasses held high. 2012 marks the festival's 25th year.

Chalk the good cheer up to the setting: With the city and its Willamette River as a backdrop, some eighty breweries from around the country show up to pour their latest. Live bands jam on stages as local-fave restaurants like Horn of Africa proffer healthy, spicy, beer-friendly fare. Trading wooden nickel tokens for tastes, imbibers mingle good-naturedly, old friends reunite, and, as the sun goes down, those cheers grow longer and louder, and, well, a heck of a lot more infectious. When the kegs run dry—*sic transit gloria mundi*—downtown taprooms fill with beer lovers celebrating the bounty until the wee hours. (www.oregonbrewfest.com)

THE GREEN DRAGON BISTRO & BREWPUB

928 SE 9th Ave. • Portland, OR 97214 • (503) 517-0660
pdxgreendragon.com • Established: 2007

SCENE & STORY

The Green Dragon (named for Boston's historic public house frequented by Paul Revere and his fellow Sons of Liberty) is a curious beast with a few tricks up its sleeve. There's brewing equipment in the back, but it's rarely steaming; (part of it is reserved for infrequent, pub-only beers and part for local home brewers when they have the time).

On its third owner—Oregon's Rogue Ales (a large Oregon brewing company) took over a few years ago—the Dragon's inner southeast Portland location and claim to one of the largest walk-in coolers in Oregon (ask for a tour, especially if glow-in-the-dark stars on the wall and rows of cold kegs set your heart racing) was an attractive purchase. Adjacent to an army green Quonset hut with bar offices (and a secret mini-arcade with pinball machines), the interior is a roomy warehouse-like space with two bars and an all-ages dining area. The entire place is supplied with beer from the "front" and "back" bars comprising fifty taps in all (there are forty-nine bottled beers for sale as well). But weather permitting, the place to be is the huge patio, strung with lights and shaded by a big tree. The beers aren't all from Rogue, either, and the selection changes daily. Count on a solidly contemporary mix of craft brews from around the country and sometimes Europe. When hunger hits, the best eats on the menu are the french fries (ask for a side of mac-and-cheese sauce) and buffalo blue meatballs (deliciously deep-fried upon special request).

PHILOSOPHY

As Samuel Johnson said, "Where secrecy begins, vice or roguery is not far off." Hmm—is that a bad thing?

KEY BEER

Twirling your mustache, ask about Tap 19, the "secret" tap, always reserved for rare beers (like Cantillon Lou Pepe kriek), and never advertised. But it's so secret, the servers may not even know what's on it. *Delicious.*

CASCADE BREWING BARREL HOUSE

939 SE Belmont • Portland, OR 97214 • (503) 265-8603
cascadebrewingbarrelhouse.com • Established: 2010

SCENE & STORY

Pucker up, Portland. To the truly devoted beer geeks, tart, barrel-aged beers are the next IPAs, and brewer Ron Gansberg—a veteran of the wine industry and residencies with both BridgePort Brewery and Portland Brewing Company—is Stumptown's master sourpuss. His award-winning wine-, whiskey-, and port-barrel-aged Belgian-style brews crackle with acidic notes and woody tannins that blur stylistic lines (and go nicely with cheese).

In the summer of 2010, Gansberg opened this 6,000-square-foot facility with barrel-aging rooms and sixteen taps, including at least two directly from the barrels. It was the country's first bar dedicated to sour beers, which begged the question: In the land of hops, wouldn't an IPA bar make more sense? Not so fast. Despite an uninspired food menu (so far) the bar is normally busy if not packed, and a May 2011 Saison Fest kicked off another new tradition for beer festival-packed Portland.

PHILOSOPHY

"Bring your A-game," says Gansberg. "If a beer isn't really making a statement, then it's really hardly worth our time to brew."

KEY BEER

Cascade Apricot (usually around 8.5% ABV) is a crisp, tart ale that goes through sixteen months of lactic fermentation and then spends four months resting on Washington State apricots in French oak wine barrels. Cascade has a huge lineup of beers, but this is consistently the best.

HAIR OF THE DOG BREWING CO.

61 SE Yamhill St. • Portland, OR 97214 • (503) 232-6585
hairofthedog.com • Established: 1993

SCENE & STORY

Once housed in a pub-less, ramshackle warehouse space in deep southeast Portland, the venerable Hair of the Dog operation has a new house. Its new home is much more user-friendly: the inner southeast industrial district, a chic mixed-use area of start-ups, farm-to-table eateries, and loft spaces in converted meatpacking and produce warehouses. There, founder Alan Sprints and family have set up shop in an airy space brightly painted in hues of teal, gray, and green around a polished eight-tap central bar. Off to the right side of the room is a little open kitchen where Sprints (a trained chef) himself does a lot of the cooking, like a recent dish of beer-braised beef served with whole grain mustard and spring greens.

PHILOSOPHY

Innovative and community-minded, Sprints was among the first brewers in the country to adopt the use of bourbon and whiskey barrels to age his beers, some of which are variations of long-forgotten styles like *adambier,* a type of strong aged ale from Dortmund, Germany. Sprints got the idea from legendary Portland beer writer Fred Eckhardt, who happily scored the first bottle.

KEY BEER

Sprints made his name with Adam and Fred (named for Eckhardt) and other big, boozy brews numbered for the purpose of cellaring; vintage bottles are available at the taproom (batch #1 of Adam is $75 for 12 ounces). But today his Blue Dot double IPA is setting a lot of tongues (or tails?) wagging. It's 7% ABV and often near perfect, with waves of sweet, grapefruity hops and a crackingly dry, bitter finish.

HOPWORKS URBAN BREWERY

2944 SE Powell Blvd. • Portland, OR 97202 • (503) 232-4677
hopworksbeer.com • Established: 2007

SCENE & STORY

San Francisco native Christian Ettinger found his beer inspiration in Cologne, Germany, touring the city's famed *Kölsch* producers and hanging out in atmospheric *bierstubes* during college. Back in the states, he attended brewing school through the Vermont-based American Brewers Guild, and then honed his skills in a Eugene brewpub and Portland's Laurelwood Public House.

Ettinger opened his kid- and bike-friendly brewpub in Southeast Portland (often called simply H.U.B.), using organic grains and innovative green-brewing practices like biodiesel to fuel the kettles, eco-friendly building materials, and both CO_2 and heat recycling. Recently, Ettinger has embarked on a fairly extensive barrel program at the brewery, opened a new bar in northeast Portland (Bikebar, summer 2011), and continues to sponsor a hugely popular party, Biketoberfest, at the brewery in September.

PHILOSOPHY

Ettinger keeps it simple. "Any [one] can throw a wall of ingredients at something and come up with a bold flavor, and some people will like it. I love simplicity. If it isn't simple, skip it."

KEY BEER

An homage to the birthplace of the Pilsner style, the ample but not heavy Czech-style H.U.B. Lager (5.1% ABV). "It's the most rewarding beer to make," says Ettinger, "because it's so simple and so stark. There's little body to hide behind; there's no formidable hop character to hide behind. That beer has to be made perfectly every time." So far, so good.

SOUR POWER 101

INSIDE THE ART *of* SOUR, BARREL-AGED BEERS

To speak beer-ese in Portland, or just about anywhere else these days, you've got to know what makes sour beers pop the way they do. Simply put, they're made by fermenting beer with a complex grain bill (for long, slow, layered fermentations) with *Lactobacillus* and/or other super active yeasts (sometimes wild rather than lab-cultured) and aging them in oak barrels that once contained wine, port, sherry, absinthe, rum, whiskey, or bourbon, occasionally with certain fruits or nuts added. After a period of three months to three years in the wood, the acidified brews are blended with one another in a stainless steel tank to taste, at which point fresh fruit additions or special brewers' sugars are occasionally added again. Lastly, they're kegged or bottled like Champagne, with a cork and wire cage. Executed well, these acid-forward ales echo the heft of certain big wines (meaty tannic reds, bright whites, and tawny old ports), and pair well with rich foods like cheese, charcuterie, and pork belly. One look at the beer lists in Portland's top restaurants confirms: sour is the new black.

LAURELWOOD PUBLIC HOUSE & BREWERY

5115 NE Sandy Blvd. • Portland, OR 97213 • (503) 282-0622
laurelwoodbrewpub.com • Established: 2001

SCENE & STORY

Now with a handful of convenient locations (including the Rose Garden, where the Portland Trail Blazers play, and the Portland International Airport's concourses A and E), Laurelwood was Portland's first certified-organic brewery, and also made a smart business decision in a town with big numbers in the stroller department: kids' areas. Ingenious! The adults found the beer irresistible (still do), and three years after opening, Laurelwood landed the coveted Best Small Brewpub and Best Brewer Award at the World Beer Cup 2004 and the second annual National IPA competition in 2009. These are not easy awards to win.

The main location is an old converted dinner theater; instead of floor lights, stainless conditioning tanks light up the room, and the food is filling, a mix of pub favorites like nachos and garlic fries with healthier options like wraps and spinach salads.

PHILOSOPHY

Green, but not obnoxiously so, and actively kid-focused: young parents themselves, founders Mike De Kalb and his wife made sure to put quality play spaces in all their properties.

KEY BEER

The tasty, pungent Workhorse IPA was the big winner in 2009, and it's still pouring on the hops, with three separate dry hop additions in the fermenter (7.5% ABV). Also, don't miss the coppery flagship beer, Free Range Red.

BELMONT STATION

4500 SE Stark St. • Portland, OR 97215 • (503) 232-8538
belmont-station.com • Established: 1997

SCENE & STORY

Founded by Carl Singmaster and the late, legendary publican Don Younger of The Horse Brass in that bar's tiny adjacent alleyway in southeast Portland, Belmont Station was an idea far ahead of its time. With thousands of imported beers, glassware, and other beer-related gifts, it was a hit with locals who would wander in after a pint and perhaps a chat with the irascible, inimitable owner Don Younger, who died in 2011. (Disclosure: By the good graces of Younger, I worked at Belmont Station briefly in its earliest days, helping ship beer, which it no longer does. I was enormously grateful for the gig.) Since then, the shop has moved a block north to Stark Street and has expanded to include its own bar with 16 taps, 1,200-plus bottles stored behind UV-filtered light, regular tastings, and brewmaster appearances. They even hold their own festival in July: Pucker Fest is a weeklong celebration of sour beer.

PHILOSOPHY

Know thy beer. Belmont Station's employees know a ton about beer and are glad to share their wisdom, *sans* attitude.

KEY BEER

The best beer is the one you taste fresh off one of the twenty taps as you wander the aisles, which is a lot of fun. Simply put, the selection here is incredible: up to date, varied, well cared for, and organized.

UPRIGHT BREWING CO.

240 N. Broadway, Ste. 2 • Portland, OR 97227
(503) 735-5337 • uprightbrewing.com • Established: 2009

SCENE & STORY

You know you're in a serious craft beer town when NBA fans cram into your subterranean taproom for every home game and sip barrel-aged beers before heading to the stadium. Alex Ganum's Upright Brewing Company is located a few paces from the Rose Garden arena, home of the Portland Trail Blazers. Ganum moved to Portland (he's from Michigan originally) for culinary school but fell in love with the beer scene instead. After an internship at the celebrated Ommegang brewery in Cooperstown, New York, he drew up plans for Upright, and these days his beers are all over town, and his brewing capacity is maxed out.

Still, the brewery (named for Charles Mingus's stringed instrument) remains low-key, with just six wall mounted taps, a couple of picnic tables, and barrel racks of aging ales to admire as you sip away. Be sure to check out the open steel fermenters behind glass. The five year-round beers are Four (4.5% ABV; light/wheat/lightly sour), Five (5.5% ABV and markedly hoppier), Six (spicy and caramel tinged at 6.7% ABV),

Seven (8% ABV and floral, aromatic), and the delicious, draft-only Engleberg Pils (5.5% ABV). My advice: order a tasting tray and try every one.

PHILOSOPHY

Urban farmhouse—Ganum's beers exhibit the spice and earthiness of styles Portland brewers haven't explored much until now: Belgian *saison*, *bière de garde*, and other, sometimes wild barrel-aged experiments resulting in funky, sour, earthy ales. But rather than just try to mimic Low Country classics, Ganum is also stretching out with experiments that place these beers firmly in Oregon soil.

KEY BEER

Upright's April seasonal is Gose (5.2% ABV), based on a near-extinct German style developed in Leipzig, which incorporates salt and ground coriander seeds. The result is an unfiltered wheat beer with a cloudy yellow color and appealingly tart, dry finish. The beer put Ganum on the podium at the 2010 World Beer Cup in Chicago.

WIDMER GASTHAUS PUB

955 N. Russell • Portland, OR 97227 • (503) 281-3333
widmerbrothers.com • Established: 1984

SCENE & STORY

Kurt and Rob Widmer are the paradigmatic home-brewers-gone-pro, with a handsome *bierstube* (across from the big brewery HQ) and a national brand built by their American-style hefeweizen, a cloudy gold refresher. Their Gasthaus (which in German means "inn" but is really just a brewpub) is a Portland institution. With fifteen taps, you can try all the beers in their catalog, which has taken a turn for the more adventurous lately, keeping pace with Portland's many beer innovators.

Credit goes to the brothers for not forgetting their roots: they've sold enough beer to be playing Baccarat in St. Tropez, but instead, the Widmers still hang out at home brew meetings and keep an eye on their pilot brewery, where Widmer sponsors a project called Collaborator with a local home brewing group ("The Oregon Brew Crew"), started in 1998. About four times a year, a member's recipe gets selected for a run on the big boys' equipment under pilot brewer Ike Manchester's watchful eye. Then beer goes on tap at select area pubs, and can even hit the big time: Snowplow, a 1998 Collaborator beer, was tweaked in 2004, released commercially, and won a gold medal at the Great American Beer Festival.

PHILOSOPHY

"Keep learning," says Manchester, who works closely with the brothers. "You can't know everything there is about brewing. When it comes down to the beer, it's always evolving. It's a living thing." Refreshing words.

KEY BEER

Manchester loves brewing (and drinking) the nutty, limited-production Alt Bier (5% ABV) on tap at the Gasthaus. Because it was the Widmer Brothers' first recipe, and was also a favorite of the late, legendary beer writer Michael Jackson, the beer is a cult classic in Portland.

SCENE & STORY

With the exception of one ill-fated USFL (United States Football League) team, the Portland Breakers, Portland has never had anything approaching professional American football to cheer about (the MLS Timbers, on the other hand, are a different story). So it is incredibly refreshing to walk into Wisconsin native Sarah Pederson's northeast Portland shrine to the Green Bay Packers and beers of every era. Overhead, check out the vintage signage and bottle cap murals as intricate as any ancient Roman mosaic—and settle in for some down-to-earth conversation, or take in a gridiron game on TV. Before you head out, take a little shopping spree through the 250-plus international beers in cool old green vintage coolers. Saraveza—a play on Pederson's name and on the Spanish word *cerveza*, for beer—has nine beers on tap, homemade soups, and those made-from-scratch pasties—try the Nater, a delicious blend of braised beef, potato, carrot, rutabaga, and onion. It doesn't matter if you're not into rushing stats and field goal attempts; you're just here to soak up some good old-fashioned, unironic Midwestern hospitality.

PHILOSOPHY

Pederson has assembled the best bar staff in Portland, helpful and open-minded, a major selling point in the occasionally too-cool-for-school city of "Beervana." Brewers and purists might cringe at the thought, but certain bartenders here (Jonathan Carmean, to name the starting quarterback) are experienced and confident enough to hand you a blend of tap beers of different origins and profiles. Want a little more zing and hops in your malty Belgian tripel? Done.

KEY BEER

The beer list is superb; up-to-the-second, heavily local on draft and Low Countries-focused in the coolers, as good as it gets. Look for complex, handmade beers from Block 15, in Corvallis, Portland's Upright, McMinnville's Heater-Allen, Hood River's Logsdon, and Boneyard in Bend. Or, to go Saraveza native, don't be afraid to order the pride of Milwaukee, Wisconsin, an icy-cold mug of Hamm's (4.7% ABV).

GET FRESH *with your* ALES

Every fall in the Pacific Northwest, America's cradle of hops production (second only to Germany), ripened hops' tall, leafy trellises begin to sag with the weight of millions of flowers. On the best back roads, the air in Oregon's Willamette (say "Will-am-ett" dammit) is redolent with the grapefruity smell of the delicate pinecone-like flowers, which are soon picked, dried, and packaged.

But not all hops make it to the temperature-controlled storehouses where they're monitored to avoid spontaneous combustion (true!). Some are hauled off the lines and added directly into unfermented beers in nearby breweries, creating a fresh—and fleeting—genre of beer, interchangeably referred to as fresh-hopped or wet-hopped. Brewers in the south of England have long called them harvest ales, always an excuse for a roaring party. (Portland's first big fresh hop festival kicked off in 2010.)

How it works: Working with growers, brewers time their arrival to a farm to coincide with a batch of beer nearing the boil stage. Then they race back and plunge the flower cones directly into what's called the whirlpool step. In the best years, this translates into pure brewing magic, with floral aromas that hit your nose within milliseconds of cracking a finished beer open.

The only drawback to fresh hop ales? Now you see them, now you don't. Brewed only in the fall, these beers don't age or travel well. What's more, they tend to drain from kegs faster than Keystone Light at a tailgater. Fresh hop ales are catching on around the country, but Oregon leads the pack, with fifty-seven different commercial fresh hop ales in 2010. Look for them from Laurelwood, Deschutes, and Full Sail on tap (and sometimes bottled, like Deschutes' Hop Trip). Whatever you do, don't miss the freshest beers of the year.

BAILEY'S TAPROOM

213 SW Broadway • Portland, OR 97205 • (503) 295-1004
baileystaproom.com • Established: 2007

SCENE & STORY

Unlike hilly Seattle, Portland's downtown is wonderfully walkable, with airy park blocks leading from the river nearly to the West Hills and Forest Park (a must for city dwellers in need of a quick urban escape). Located within walking distance to the iconic Powell's Books and several of Portland's better boutique hotels, Bailey's Taproom has high glass windows and a streamlined, almost minimalist interior, keeping the focus on craft beer. There are twenty taps and ninety-nine bottled selections (bringing a certain song to mind), all specializing in Oregon's diverse craft beers, with occasional forays outside the borders into California and Washington, and cask tappings on Mondays.

During the week and on sunny afternoons there's a constant crowd of beer lovers, but it's seldom slammed to the point of "no-thanks . . . let's bail." With lots of small festivals throughout the year, it's one of downtown's best beer bar, if a little noisy (thanks to all that glass).

PHILOSOPHY

Efficient. While there's no food, the owner of Bailey's ingeniously struck a deal with Santeria, the excellent Mexican joint across the street adjoining the venerated Mary's Club (Portland's oldest strip joint). Simply call up to order (menus are kept behind the bar), and Santeria will deliver

the goods directly to your table (try the *tinga* with anything).

KEY BEER

Silver Moon Bridge Creek Pilsner, from Bend (4.7% ABV) would make the ideal companion to some spicy Mexican food.

BRIDGEPORT BREWING CO.

1313 NW Marshall • Portland, OR 97209 • (503) 241-3612
bridgeportbrew.com • Established: 1984

SCENE & STORY

Richard and Nancy Ponzi, a local wine-making family, and Karl Ockert, a UC Davis-trained brewmaster, joined forces on the 600-barrel Columbia River Brewery, built in a three-story, century-old former rope factory in what would become a part of Portland's chic Pearl District. Renamed Bridge-Port Brewing Company in 1986, it was among Oregon's very first craft breweries and is now distributed in eighteen states. Now part of the Gambrinus family (the Texas-based importers of Corona and owners of Trumer, Spoetzl, and Shiner Bock), the beer is still good with strong one-offs and seasonals, and the old brewpub pizzeria got a multimillion dollar makeover in 2006, complete with its own bakery.

PHILOSOPHY

British-style beers with Northwest attitude and hoppy character.

KEY BEER

Introduced in 1996, BridgePort IPA (5.5%

ABV) was a game-changer in Portland, with a jaw-tingling array of five different hops. Look for that and the old classic, the softly malty Blue Heron Pale Ale (4.9% ABV), first brewed in 1987 for the Audubon Society and named for Portland's official bird.

HENRY'S 12th STREET TAVERN

10 NW 12th Ave. • Portland, OR 97209 • (503) 227-5320
henrystavern.com • Established: 2004

SCENE & STORY

The bar area of Henry's is built in the former powerhouse section of the historic Blitz-Weinhard Brewery, which stopped making beer in 1999 after the brand was sold off to Miller. The beers are still brewed under Miller's watch in various locations, including by Full Sail Brewing in Hood River, and the renovated building has been transformed into stunning, environmentally-friendly mixed retail and office spaces. As for the bar, Henry's has a multi-level, flat-screen-equipped 100-tap bar, upstairs lounge (former hops storage), and fine dining area (once the brewhouse section), all tastefully appointed in comfortable banquettes, sleek metal stairs, and artful lighting.

PHILOSOPHY

It's too slick and sceney for many Portlanders' tastes—less fleece, more Diesel—but where else are you going to keep your beer cold on an iced rail embedded in the bar, take in the game on a massive overhead screen, and nibble on insanely decadent Gorgonzola fries?

KEY BEER

Oakshire Amber (5.4% ABV) is nutty and slightly sweet, with only the faintest note of citrusy hops.

HIGGINS RESTAURANT & BAR

1239 SW Broadway • Portland, OR 97205 • (503) 222-9070
higginsportland.com • Established: 1994

SCENE & STORY

Located just off the leafy park blocks in downtown Portland, Higgins is a restaurant in two parts; one, a white tablecloth dining room with an open kitchen; two, a warm and inviting beer café/bar with a deep list of Belgian and craft beers and mouthwatering appetizers. How do a fresh saison beer and a warm tart of leeks, oyster mushrooms, and cave-aged Gruyère served with hazelnut and fennel salad sound?

Find a reason, if you need one. James Beard Award–winning chef Greg Higgins and co. will cook your socks off. You could, for example, head there after a concert, or an art opening at the Portland Art Museum, a couple of blocks away. You don't need a reservation to walk into the bar on a random night, and you're likely to meet a local brewmaster refreshing at the bar, talking shop with the knowledgeable—and ultra courteous—staff.

PHILOSOPHY

As ambitious and eco-minded as they come.

Higgins is an ardent champion of local purveyors, and that includes brewers, of course. Long before it was fashionable, Higgins worked with Hair of the Dog brewer Alan Sprints on a beer made with organic kabocha squash (4.5% ABV and called Greg), and promoted a series of elegant beer and brewmaster dinners with the likes of Pike Brewing Company.

KEY BEER

Beer steward Jason Button looks after the 10-tap, 100-bottle list, packed with unusual domestic and European choices. But sometimes an easy local sipper is the way to go. "Come summer, with sweet corn and peppers coming in, we like to steam clams in *Kölsch*," he says. "Double Mountain in Hood River makes a nice one. So: steamed clams, sweet corn, peppers, and a Kölsch for yourself. Always hits the spot."

GOOSE HOLLOW INN

1927 SW Jefferson St. • Portland, OR 97201
(503) 228-7010 • goosehollowinn.com • Established: 1967

SCENE & STORY

Of course, Portland's love for craft beer runs so deep that a light-hearted tavern keeper with a thing for the good stuff got himself elected Mayor from 1984-1992, coinciding with the Rose City's embrace of microbreweries.

Former Portland Mayor Bud Clark did a lot of great things for the city, not the least of which was opening Goose Hollow, a thoroughly unpretentious and cozy little spot in the neighborhood of the same name.

Inside is a timeless tavern with old-timers (and Clark himself, some days) chatting amiably and an excellent pub menu as well, with dishes. The patio outside is one of the best outdoor drinking spots in all of Portland, ideal for a pre-Portland Timbers game warm-up, as it's no more than five minutes by foot from the soccer stadium. Clark brags Anheuser-Busch honored the Goose in the 1970s for serving the most beer per square foot in America, which seems about right.

PHILOSOPHY

Old school, with better beer. Today the tavern still has its old wood beams and bric-a-brac charm, but the beer list has considerably evolved.

KEY BEER

Sip on the latest local brews from Hopworks Urban Brewery, Terminal Gravity, and Deschutes, for starters. With a Reuben sandwich to eat and the sun dappling over your picnic table, you might just miss the first half of the game. Wait, what game?

★　★　★

Astoria

FORT GEORGE BREWERY & PUBLIC HOUSE

1483 Duane St. • Astoria, OR 97103 • (503) 325-7468
fortgeorgebrewery.com • Established: 2007

SCENE & STORY

Astoria, positioned at the mouth of the Columbia River as the Oregon Coast's northernmost town, began as an outgrowth of Fort Clatsop, the settlement established by Lewis and Clark upon reaching the Pacific. For years, Astoria was a roughneck port—in the 1920s it was deemed the most dangerous town in America because so many unsuspecting tavern goers were shanghaied onto fishing vessels never to be seen again. Today, the town is still a bit gritty, a mosaic of nineteenth-century canneries, warehouses, and craftsman homes but with an indie rock appeal. Visitors should check into the eighteen-room Commodore Hotel, which was recently renovated with a Wes Anderson–like attention to detail, plus, it's walking distance to Fort George Brewery.

Brewery founders Jack Harris and Chris Nemlowill, too, have a near-obsessive attention to detail, and took over the derelict Fort George building they'd first toured in late 2005, which was built on the site of the city's old fort and a healthy spring. After opening in 2007 to steady crowds, the duo arranged to buy the whole block with help from a city loan. Today, there's an open-air, multilevel deck, and space for artisan craftsmen (a glassblower, a metal smith), and other community-centered draws. The twelve-tap brewpub is classic Northwest, with heavy exposed beams and big windows looking out to the streets. Order up a fresh beer and some house-made sausages or perfectly ungreasy fish-and-chips, and you'll taste the wisdom of their plans.

PHILOSOPHY

Classic local brewpub, with big ambitions (hence a new canning line added in 2011). And they love their stouts: February is always "stout month" featuring their own stouts on tap and a bunch of guest handles, concluding with a stout-and-oyster pairing dinner.

KEY BEER

Vortex IPA (7.7% ABV), served right out of a mason jar, honors the original brewhouse, which was transported through a tornado en route to Oregon from the Midwest. Now available in sixteen-ounce cans, it's a juicy twister of lemon, grassy hops, and sweet, fruity graininess.

DETOUR ➡

THE GOOD BEER COAST:
THE BEST BEER AND SEAFOOD ON THE NORTHERN OREGON COAST

No trip to the Oregon coast would be complete without a serious seafood and beer fest, and there's no more classically Oregonian place to do it than Jetty Fishery, a ramshackle seafood shack and campground on Nehalem Bay just north of Rockaway Beach on Highway 101 (800-821-7697; crab from $9 a pound). If you've got the time, rent a boat and go out with some crabbing pots to get your own haul ($75 for two hours, up to five people), then have the guys at the pier clean and cook it on the spot while you swig post-expedition brews. Short on time? There's plenty pre-caught grub, too. Grab a sixer of Anchor Steam or Kona Longboard Lager, some hot sauce, and paper napkins from inside the little store, then sidle up to the old yellow picnic tables outside by the water's edge and a fire pit while you wait for fresh-as-fresh-gets grilled oysters, steamed clams, and mussels, or Dungeness crab boiled in Nehalem Bay seawater. Word to the wise: try to go on a midweek afternoon. Weekends get crowded and crazy, especially when the owners fire up their 10,000-watt karaoke system for locals, RVers, and assorted campground yahoos.

After Jetty Fishery, head up to Manzanita, nine miles north on Highway 101, a 564-person town that used to be just a blip on the map. Perhaps because of this anonymity, Manzanita has started to draw in creative types, just as Big Sur, California, did back in its heyday, and its got a peaceful, progressive vibe. Down on the main drag of Laneda Avenue, pop into the relaxed San Dune Pub (503-368-5080; sandunepub.com) and sip a juicy, intense Inversion IPA from Deschutes with an oyster po' boy and warm up by the fireplace.

North of Manzanita, 101 unwinds like a wire, bending around headlands and plunging into cathedrals of Sitka spruce and Douglas fir. Empty beaches emerge unexpectedly, the most striking of which is at Oswald West State Park (503-368-3575). The sandy stretch has become famous for its protected break, and you're likely to see some surfers braving the frigid waters. The short wooded path down to the beach is worth the trouble, without question.

After a day of crabbing, surf scoping and beach walking, you'll be ready for some seaborne comfort food again before long. And if Manzanita is Oregon's Big Sur, then Cannon Beach, ten miles north, is its Carmel, a stretch of Cape Cod–style homes with not a chain store in sight. It's also home to Bill's Tavern & Brewhouse (503-436-2202), a sunny and cheerful spot with bright murals on the walls and a good, pet-friendly patio. Wind up your afternoon with some fresh, flaky beer-battered halibut fish-and-chips and a pint of fresh-brewed beach beer, like the Duck Dive Pale Ale (4.8% ABV). Mission complete.

DESCHUTES BREWERY

1044 NW Bond St. • Bend, OR 97701 • (541) 382-9242
deschutesbrewery.com • Established: 1988

SCENE & STORY

Making their debut in 1988 at Gary Fish's little Bond Street brewpub in Bend, the beers were good—*really good*. There was—and still is—something ideally calibrated about Deschutes's juicy, quaffable Mirror Pond Pale Ale. Is it the prismatic Cascade hops, perfectly applied? Jubelale, a malty and warming winter seasonal, was also an instant smash hit in bottles (the first Deschutes beer packaged in glass). It seemed the brewery would never be big enough for demand. Sure enough, the latest in a series of expansions was announced in 2011.

Today, Deschutes has also opened an upscale brewpub in Portland's swank Pearl District—often packed and playing host to a summer street fair and high-profile cooking events. They're expanding the little old Bond Street pub too. From ski-bum hangout to industry heavyweight the company is (currently ranked around fifth in the land for sales volume), Deschutes has come far.

PHILOSOPHY

Success hasn't come at the expense of quality. The more states that pick up the beer (some twenty at this stage), the more brewers seem freed to experiment on the side with barrel-aged stouts like The Abyss and sours like The Dissident, a Flanders-style *oud bruin* aged in oak barrels with cherries, both of which are excellent.

KEY BEER

Deschutes has pulled off some exceptional Belgian styles here and there, but their area of domination is truly in the British-style ales, IPAs, porters, and stouts. Black Butte Porter deserves a victory lap. It's a little-known fact that Guinness Extra Stout debuted under the brand Extra Superior Porter and remained so for forty-one years, a stronger, darker version of the dark-hued London-born drink. Today the style has taken on many forms of its own around the world, from purist English versions to fiery Baltic variations and American riffs that incorporate peppers and sour notes. In Deschutes's formula, tangy Northwest hops come to the fore with finesse, balancing its cocoa, coffee, and toffee notes from its blend of roasted malts. And, at 5.5% ABV, it's a touch lighter than the old Extra Superior.

AN OREGON BREWER'S MANTRA, ►►►►►►► APPROPRIATED ◄◄◄◄◄◄

"I come from the West where the illimitable mountains lift up their heads . . . where in a civilization founded on the mine and the camp, we believe that the saloon and the theater has as good a right to be open on Sunday as the church and the school . . . where we think that it is the right of every American to go to hell and be damned if he wants to. That is not humor—it is the truth."

—*Oregon writer and soldier
C.E.S. Wood, 1852–1944*

BLOCK 15 BREWERY & RESTAURANT

300 SW Jefferson Ave. • Corvallis, OR 97333
(541) 758-2077 • block15.com • Established: 2008

SCENE & STORY

Housed in the historic corner building that used to be the *Gazette-Times* newspaper office, Block 15's name comes from its address (or block number) from the early days of Corvallis. It's a small brewery, relatively speaking, but it holds a lot of significance locally as a popular watering hole, with fourteen taps (seven rotating), two floors, and room for about 120 imbibers. There's a appealing menu of fare like house-smoked pork shoulder, burgers, and crispy fries. It's also a rallying point for the fermentation science majors at Oregon State University, who get their own dedicated tap to showcase experimental brews. Suddenly, Corvallis has a bigger beer scene. "We're in our own little island," says brewer and co-owner Nick Arsner, "but we've got a great little beer culture growing here in Corvallis."

PHILOSOPHY

Nonconformist. Given that Corvallis is something of a conservative town, with endless acres of corn, hops, and locals in big pickup trucks, Arsner's cutting a different track. "I love the art in barrel aging and mixed fermentations rather than kicking out IPA," he says. There's even a cool ship in the works, which would be among the first in the country.

KEY BEER

Pappy's Dark, brewed with six different Belgian and British malts and aged in nine- and ten-year-old bourbon barrels, is a velvety, deep, and rich beer with flavors of bourbon, caramel, and woody vanilla (10% ABV).

TERMINAL GRAVITY BREWING CO.

803 SE School St. • Enterprise, OR 97828 • (541) 426-0158
terminalgravitybrewing.com • Established: 1998

SCENE & STORY

East of the Cascades, dense Douglas fir forests yield to rolling hills of wheat, with narrow ribbon roads connecting small towns like Enterprise (population: 1,000). After a series of brewing jobs big and small, brothers-in-law Steve Carper and Dean Duquette moved back there to launch their own operation, Terminal Gravity (a brewing term for the end of fermentation). This is pristine Wallowa County mountain country, spitting distance from Kokanee salmon-filled Wallowa Lake, one of America's only true glacial lakes, and the Hells Canyon recreation area, a major adventure-travel hub. And what's a spin through the great outdoors without a beer to cap off the journey?

PHILOSOPHY

Live life to the fullest. Carper and Duquette's

brewery is a treasure, a quaint yellow-painted, Craftsman-style cottage with a few tables and stools inside and three acres of grounds outside where travelers meet to drink beer on the porch, play volleyball, and toss horseshoes—then stand around a roaring bonfire: the definition of summer itself.

KEY BEER

Terminal Gravity IPA, the tangy and ultra bitter bottle-conditioned beer that made this tiny brewpub regionally famous (6.9% ABV).

Eugene

NINKASI BREWING CO.

272 Van Buren St. • Eugene, OR 97402 • (541) 344-2739
ninkasibrewing.com • Established: 2006

SCENE & STORY

Back in 1994 the irrepressible Jamie Floyd was just slinging hobby home brew for University of Oregon parties. After graduation he considered academia but scored a gig manning the kettles at Steelhead Brewery in Eugene instead. Now Floyd has a staff of three dozen, and a 90,000 barrel-capacity brew house, not to mention a rabid fan base. In part by harnessing the power of community involvement through the arts and social networks (the company boasts a massive Facebook presence, and has both an iPhone and iPad app) and guerilla marketing (at night, for example, with the Ninkasi logo "Bat Signal" spotlight), the firm has all but conquered Oregon. Next up, the world?

Ninkasi's new tasting room and outdoor patio features year-round beers, seasonals, and occasional limited specialty releases on tap, and big summer block parties are guaranteed. For edibles, there's a limited menu of large soft brewery-dough pretzels, pasties, and soup.

PHILOSOPHY

"We make beer geek [approved] beer, but we don't make beer for beer geeks," says Floyd. "We encourage everybody [to drink beer], not just the super nerdy 1 percent."

KEY BEER

The intensely bitter and tangy Total Domination IPA (6.7 % ABV) is one of the top-selling twenty-two-ounce beers in the state.

Hood River

DOUBLE MOUNTAIN BREWERY & TAPROOM

8 4th St., No. 204 • Hood River, OR 97031 • (541) 387-0042
doublemountainbrewery.com • Established: 2007

SCENE & STORY

After hiking waterfalls in the Columbia Gorge you're going to have a wicked appetite, so get yourself to Double Mountain to set things right with a fresh pint and tasty pizza. Named for a local viewpoint where you can see both Mt. Hood and Mt. Adams (two of the many impressive Cascade Range peaks), the family-friendly brewpub was founded by Full Sail brewery alumnae Matt Swihart and Charlie Deveraux who met working in production and began a series of tactical brain-storms masquerading as long nights of drinking. Pinned with demand immediately after opening, Double Mountain pub is close to Full Sail and Hood River's main drag, with a cool sage-green interior, living room couches, off-beat local artworks, and the odd live band.

PHILOSOPHY

Hop lovers to the hilt, Deveraux and Swihart (who handles the brewing duties) go for huge additions of whole flower hops and minimal handling of the beer, for a powerful but not overly aggressive character, followed by long conditioning rests and no filtration.

KEY BEER

The 6.5% ABV India Red Ale ("I.R.A."), a scarlet, malty beast with the hop profile of an IPA, is a good match for the piquant pepperoni pizza. Or take a pull off The Vaporizer, a dry, golden-hued pale ale with Pilsner malt and Challenger hops, grown in Washington's Yakima Valley (6% ABV).

FULL SAIL BREWERY & TASTING ROOM & PUB

506 Columbia St. • Hood River, OR 97031 • (541) 386-2247
fullsailbrewing.com • Established: 1987

SCENE & STORY

Early settlers here braved Hood River's wind tunnel conditions, and the fruit orchards they established thrived and made it famous. Fast forward two hundred years: today, the quaint Columbia River-side town of 6,500 located an hour east of Portland still boasts the same majestic views of Mt. Hood and fertile fruit trees. But thanks to that steady wind, it's now regarded as one of the world's top destinations for windsurfing and kite boarding. Since 1987 it's been a beer town, too, home to the once-tiny, now huge Full Sail, where you can drink a beer and watch the speeding sails embroider the waves. (This is preferable to attempting actual windsurfing, which, for most of us, becomes an infinite wipeout.)

PHILOSOPHY

Progressive and green-minded. In 1999 Full Sail became 100 percent employee-owned, and employees work four 10-hour days to save resources (and make the most of powder days up on Mt. Hood and winds on the Columbia, no doubt).

KEY BEER

If you're visiting in the fall (a beautiful season to be in the area), look for the fresh hop ales—there's often two or three on at a time, made with huge quantities of just-picked hop flowers. "To get a comparable extract out of the hop (compared to the dried version), you have to use about five times the amount, and when you add that much more, you get more of a green, chlorophyll, leaf, and vegetative matter flavor," says Full Sail brewmaster John Harris, who has made many in his day. The rest of the year, try Full Sail Amber, the company's flagship and Oregon's first craft beer in bottles, which came out in 1989 and won a gold at GABF the same year. It's 5.5% ABV and on the sweet and malty side, with a light touch of Mt. Hood and Cascade hops.

The Columbia Gorge—a short drive east from Portland on highway I-84 toward Hood River—is braided with postcard cataracts that lure masses. Multnomah Falls, at 620 feet, is the nation's second highest waterfall after Yosemite. Hike eight hundred feet up to stroll past the more serene Weisendanger and Ecola falls, invisible from ground level. Marginally tougher to reach (but far lesser known) is Oneonta Gorge, a gloomy slot canyon lined with neon-bright lichens accessed by fording a logjam (one that, thankfully, turns back Fast Food Nation) merely a quarter of a mile away. (www.oregon.com/hiking)

LOGSDON ORGANIC FARM-HOUSE ALES

785 Booth Hill Rd. • Hood River, OR 97031 • (541) 490-9161
farmhousebeer.com • Established: 2011

SCENE & STORY

Plenty of American brewers these days claim to brew "farmhouse" ales (meaning the refreshing, yeast-driven beer that was traditionally brewed in the Belgian and French countryside for local consumption) but there's just one problem: no farmhouse. Not so for Oregon's Dave Logsdon, who was the founding brewmaster of Full Sail, and went on to found Wyeast Laboratories, a hugely successful wholesale and retail yeast company for the wine and beer industries. With a partner, experienced brewer Charles Porter, Logsdon opened the brewery on his family's beautiful working farm outside of Hood River, complete with a big red barn (where the kettles, tanks, and barrels live), pets, horses, and highland cattle, in 2011.

PHILOSOPHY

Purist, with hometown allegiances. "How do you make a farmhouse beer if you're not in a farmhouse? That's a really important part of the definition for me," says Logsdon, who has imported *schaerbeekse kriek* (cherry) trees from an orchard in East Flanders to use in barrel-aged beers, including a planned Cascadian Red, named for the Pacific Northwest region. The ingredients are all certified organic (as in the homeland). With his wood-aged beers, he's going for a smidge less sourness than some of the more intense Belgian ales: "I try to create a lot of maltiness to carry the acidity but also to keep the acid in check, so it makes it a nice drinking beer—tart and thirst quenching at the same time."

KEY BEER

Seizoen Bretta (8% ABV), a traditional

malty, yeasty saison with an addition of Brettanomyces adding fruity notes, acidity, and woody, earthy, almost leathery notes.

HIGHLAND STILLHOUSE PUB

201 S 2nd St. • Oregon City, OR 97045 • (503) 723-6789
highlandstillhouse.com • Established: 2006

SCENE & STORY

Themed "Hibernian" (Irish), English, and Scottish pubs can be tiresomely phony. Not this one. Though it's hardly old, this bar has all the character and patina one would expect from the real McCoy (i.e. Glasgow's Pot Still bar), with one of the best—if not *the* best—selection of whiskey in the Portland area. Overlooking Willamette Falls, it's a charming two-level warren of rooms built into a 1920s gas station building, all dark wood paneling and few right angles, with an impressive deck outside. Families can gather downstairs; the adults-only upstairs "snug bar" is exactly as it should be: cozy and embracing. When you go, you're likely to meet the owners Tammy and Mick Secor—that is, unless they're off on their twice-annual Scotland distillery touring adventures, especially in Islay.

PHILOSOPHY

Classic Highland pub—friendly, warm, and comfortable. Thanks to its distance from Portland (about 15 miles south), it's a bit of a sleeper.

KEY BEER

It's especially rare to see Scottish brewery Belhaven's Twisted Thistle IPA (5.3% ABV) or the Wee Heavy (6.5% ABV), so do your duty and try them out. There are a total of twenty taps and seventy-five bottles to choose from, with added treats like Full Sail's Bump in the Night Black IPA on cask.

PRODIGAL SON BREWERY & PUB

230 SE Court Ave. • Pendleton, OR 97801 • (541) 276-6090
prodigalsonbrewery.com • Established: 2010

SCENE & STORY

Most of the time there's an inversely proportional relationship between average belt buckle size and the number of craft brews available in any given town. Located in the home of the massive annual Pendleton Round-Up rodeo, Prodigal Son is helping turn those numbers around. Tucked in on a main drag among dive bars, the brewpub is the work of three friends who grew up in Pendleton, left town, and then came back to get serious about brewing (hence the name). The brewpub is a big and open space with tall ceilings, concrete floors, exposed wood beams, exposed air ducts, and a weathered brick wall on one side of the pub that has an old ad painted on the surface. It's also family friendly with a theater room off to the side of the pub with a large screen and theater seating. Head brewer Brian Harder used to brew at Rogue in Newport and was mentored by John Maier, which means he's got the experience he needs to make it as a craft brewer in a cowboy town.

PHILOSOPHY

Conservative, for now. They're making fairly standard ales by Portland or Seattle standards, but that's what the market demands, says Harder. It's only a matter of time before the big belt buckle crowd comes around, growlers in hand.

KEY BEER

The 7.5% ABV Bruce/Lee Porter is as big and roasty and rich as cowboy coffee—but tastes a whole lot better.

Troutdale

McMENAMIN'S EDGEFIELD

2126 SW Halsey St. • Troutdale, OR 97060
(503) 669-8610 • mcmenamins.com • Established: 1991

SCENE & STORY

For those who live in the Northwest, the McMenamin Brothers' quirky empire of fifty-nine (and counting) inns and brewpubs in artistically converted old churches, schools, theaters, utility buildings—even a light-house—are everyday neighbors, seldom spoken of with much passion anymore. It's all too easy to forget that the Dead Head brothers Brian and Mike were right there at the start of things, though, with the Widmers and Ponzis of BridgePort in lobbying the Oregon state legislature to legalize brewpubs.

The fact is that while the beer and food are indeed unremarkable, most—if not all—of their loving, Age of Aquarius–inspired restorations, earnest local history murals, and other psychedelia-tinged whims will stand the test of time. The bars might serve only McMenamins' beer—often uninspiring—but the quirks and design are worth celebrating. Edgefield, a sprawling 74-acre Works Progress Administration compound built in 1911 just outside of Portland—is the jewel in the crown, with a 100-room inn, brewery, distillery, winery, movie theater, multiple bars, concert stage, and rambling grounds complete with gardens and a par-3 golf course. (What else? Oh, yes, a resident glassblower, naturally.) On a warm summer night, you can't do much better than strolling around the grounds with a beer in hand, ducking into the cigar-friendly Little Red Shed, a tiny, candle-lit ten-seat hide-away built in the farm's former incinerator, now covered with creeper vines.

PHILOSOPHY

"Welcome to The Kingdom of Fun."

KEY BEER

On a hot day, the raspberry sweet-tart 4.4% ABV Ruby does the trick, getting plenty of zing from 42 lbs of berries in every small batch.

★ ★ ★

BEST *of the* REST: OREGON

THE 5th QUADRANT and SIDE BAR

3901 N Williams Ave. • Portland, OR 97227 • (503) 288-3996 • newoldlompoc.com

The 5th Quadrant is one of New Old Lompoc Brewing Company's four locations, all of them worth a stop. The late Don Younger (of Horse Brass fame) was an early partner, and at the original NW 23rd Avenue location, now called the New Old Lompoc, the sun deck is an ideal spot for one of their ultra-hoppy, assertive beers like Proletariat Red (6.2% ABV). Meanwhile the newer 5th Quadrant has a bigger brewery system, slicker dining area, and an attached barrel-tasting room.

THE VICTORY BAR

2509 SE 37th Ave. • Portland, OR 97202 • (503) 236-8755 • thevictorybar.com

A diminutive but perfectly thought-out beer bar out in neighborhoody southeast, Victory (established in 2007) has six taps and sixty bottled selections from Oregon and around the world. Food options go the tapas route, from soup to clams, burgers, and some very tasty spaetzle. A recent gem on tap: the funky, bready, and sour Moinette Brune (8.5% ABV) from Belgium.

CALDERA TAP HOUSE

31 Water St., No. 2 • Ashland, OR 97520 • (541) 482-HOPS • calderabrewing.com

Green-minded Caldera, which sold its first beer in 1997, was the first microbrewery on the West Coast to can its beer, starting in 2005, a line of fragrant whole-flower hopped beers best sipped on their huge, sun-dapped deck overlooking a creek right in the middle of Ashland. Head brewer Todd Kemp is going for "a clean, accurate representation of the style, and a true expression of the ingredients used to make it," he says. His Caldera IPA (6.1% ABV) is excellent, deep amber-hued with a thick, eggshell white head of foam.

10 BARREL BREWING CO.

20750 High Desert Ln. • Bend, OR 97701 • (541) 585-1007 • 10barrel.com

In addition to Deschutes, the granddaddy in town, there are six or seven other breweries in Bend. Among the best of those is 10-Barrel, opened in 2006 with innovative beers like S1NIST0R Black Ale (5.4% ABV), made with special dehusked German black malt meant to impart color without astringency. Try this sleek, modern spot with polished cement floors and garage doors opening to patio seating for enjoying a pizza (pesto, chicken, prosciutto) and a couple light-bodied, fragrant summer ales by the fire pit, an idyllic spot on a clear, chilly night in Bend.

THE BIER STEIN BOTTLESHOP & PUB

345 East 11th Ave. • Eugene, OR 97401 • (541) 485-BIER • thebierstein.com

A central meeting place for Eugene beer fanatics since 2005, the Bier Stein has ten taps and over a thousand bottled selections from all over the world and a small menu of salads, sandwiches, and soups. Owners Chip Hardy and his wife, Kristina Measells, cultivate close relationships with breweries and distributors to get specialty bottles and drafts. The only thing you won't find? B.M.C. (meaning Bud, Miller, Coors) and 40 oz'ers.

CHATOE ROGUE

3590 Wigrich Rd. • Independence, OR 97351 • (503) 838-9813 • rogue.com

Independence, Oregon, was once known as the Hop Capital of the World, and the land there is still embroidered with huge stands of trellised hops supplying brewers in Oregon and beyond. Chatoe Rogue is essentially a compound in Independence consisting of forty-two acres of proprietary hops surrounded by cherry and filbert orchards; a 100-year-old, five-bedroom farmhouse available for rent as accommodation; and a small tasting room containing Rogue's Farmstead Nano-Brewery operation.

BREWERS UNION LOCAL 180

48329 East 1st St. • Oakridge, OR 97463 • (541) 782-2024 • brewersunion.com

You don't need a union card to get in to this atmospheric brewpub established in 2008. You just need a thirst for some ultra-traditional British-style cask-conditioned beer, which brewer-owner Ted Sobel spares no effort to create, store, and serve. Out of the best traditional ingredients and gear, such as Maris Otter malts and torrified wheat, the resulting bitters, stouts, and a traditional ginger ale come in around 3% to 5.5% ABV, matching the English-type pub fare.

THREE CREEKS BREWING CO.

721 Desperado Ct. • Sisters, OR 97759 • (541) 549-1963 • threecreeksbrewing.com

If your trip to Bend from Portland takes you through Detroit Lake on the Santiam Highway, aka Highway 20—and it should, as it's an incredibly pretty drive in good weather—you'll pass through the historic town of Sisters (population: 1,700). Just south of Sisters, this big, comfortable log cabin–like brewpub opened in 2008 amid a stand of Ponderosa pines. A combination family restaurant, beer bar, and brewery, it's got ten decent—sometimes good—taps. Try the 5.8% ABV Firestorm Red if Rudolph's Imperial Red (8.6% ABV) isn't on. With good burgers, sandwiches, steaks, and a sunny patio, it's a great stop to make before the long trek back to Portland after a fun weekend in Bend.

Washington

★ ★ ★

SIP ON THIS: WITHOUT WASHINGTON'S CRAFT BEER REVOLUTION,

Starbucks Coffee might never have gotten off the ground (read on to see why). The fact is, Washington's beer history goes all the way back to the 1850s, but it's the last couple of decades that tell the most about this beautiful and diverse state's beer potential and how it's now a part of daily life for many living here. With a gold mine of hops from the Yakima Valley (the country's biggest hop-growing area and second largest in the world, after southern Germany), this was fertile ground for Red Hook, the first microbrewery to make a major impact in the early 1980s. In converting beer drinkers from the classic, if underflavored Northwest beers like Rainier and Hamm's, newcomers like Red Hook, Pike, Hales, and later pathbreakers have carved out quite a legacy. Now Seattle is a genuinely great beer bar town, and all around the state new breweries are popping up. So what if it rains all the time?

ITINERARIES

1-DAY Beveridge Place Pub, Elysian Brewing, Quinns, Naked City Brewing

3-DAY One-day itinerary plus Parkway Tavern, Brouwer's Café, Pike Brewing, Latona Pub

7-DAY One- and three-day itineraries plus Red Hook, Chuckanut, Diamond Knot

BEVERIDGE PLACE PUB

6413 California Ave. SW • Seattle, WA 98136 • (206) 932-9906
beveridgeplacepub.com • Established: 2003

SCENE & STORY

If for nothing else, step inside this West Seattle landmark beer haunt (on the corner of California and SW Beveridge Place, hence the name) to check out the 11-foot-high, 20-foot-wide back bar, a turn-of-the-twentieth-century showpiece salvaged from a defunct Kent, Washington tavern called the Buzz Inn. At first, its three mirrored archways and gorgeous carvings were stained a deep brown (thanks to a century of cigarette smoke), but after three months spent cleaning the patina, a sumptuous cherry-stained tiger maple was revealed. A local metalsmith provided a custom tap tower and today the 25-tap, 100-plus selection of bottles draws a steady crowd of loyal locals.

PHILOSOPHY

Owner Gary Sink was inspired by a trip to the British Isles; the bar exudes community with couches, books, darts, a few (but not too many) TVs, well-maintained pool tables and retro video games—Tron, anyone?

KEY BEER

The list focuses on Washington crafts and international bottles, with casks frequently. Look for the orange-hued Manny's Pale Ale (5.4% ABV) from Georgetown Brewery,

which is slightly sweet and honey-ish, but balanced perfectly with fresh, floral hops.

BIG TIME BREWERY & ALEHOUSE

4133 University Wy. NE • Seattle, WA 98105
(206) 545-4509 • bigtimebrewery.com • Established: 1988

SCENE & STORY

Smack in the middle of "the Ave" in the U District in Seattle (University of Washington), Big Time is more relaxed-but-thirsty grad student than college-frosh-getting-sloshed. With its faded wood walls and shuffleboard, it's a sure bet in the area for good beers and a good bite (try the pizzas). Brewer Bill Jenkins left in 2011, handing the reins to Drew Cluley, former head of Pike's operations—no remedial student of the brewer's arts.

PHILOSOPHY

These guys are big-time hopheads. There are up to four house IPAs on tap at any given time, with dozens of recipes in the brewer's logs.

KEY BEER

Old Sol is beer of the wheat wine style, which is something like an English-style barley wine but made with a majority of wheat, giving the beer some softness on the palate. Released on the summer solstice each year, it's spicy and fulsome at 10% ABV, but disappears all too quickly, like summer in the Pacific Northwest.

BROUWER'S CAFÉ

400 North 35th St. • Seattle, WA 98103 • (206) 267-2437
brouwerscafe.blogspot.com • Established: 2005

SCENE & STORY

Owners Matt Bonney and Matt Van De Berghe have created a beer fortress of sorts, with a dark and somewhat castle-like interior featuring a parlor-level balcony curling around the main bar floor and some heavy chandeliers. The sixty-four taps and 300-plus bottled selections are stored with care and served in beer-specific glassware, but it's the policy of using a new piece of serving tube for every new beer on tap that shows how far Brouwer's goes to present craft beer at its best. The food is hearty, stick-to-your-ribs fare like croquettes, mussels, and a spicy lamb burger with fries (and go for a side of roasted garlic to take your taste buds even deeper).

PHILOSOPHY

You know you're in a Belgian beer shrine when you're greeted by a heraldic metal lion symbolizing Belgium and the Netherlands on the door, while inside there's a replica of the Mannekin Pis, a Brussels sculpture of a boy playfully taking a wiz that has come to symbolize the carefree joie de vivre of Belgian café culture.

KEY BEER

Orchard White, a 5.7% ABV *witbier* (unfiltered wheat-based beer doped with coriander and other spices) from Orange County, California's cult-hit The Bruery, is light on the tongue, with hints of dry apple flavor. It's one of the most interesting and versatile beers to come along for some time, and would make a good start before heading into bigger beers and barley wines, which are a specialty here.

CRUNCH TIME

Local potato chip guru Tim Kennedy introduced Tim's Cascade Style Potato Chips—the ultimate beer snack—in 1986, giving them a signature crunchiness that may be audible from space. With their classic old-timey red-and-white bag, they're easy to spot, too, but even easier to eat in embarrassing quantities. Don't pass them up, especially the sea salt and vinegar or jalapeño flavors, and wasabi for the brave. *timschips.com*

COLLINS PUB

526 2nd Ave. • Seattle, WA 98104 • (206) 623-1016
thecollinspub.com • Established: 2003

SCENE & STORY

Downtown Seattle's Pioneer Square area can sometimes feel like a drab warehouse district, even a bit sketchy at night. Thankfully, the Collins Pub, fourth-generation local Seth Howard's craft beer shrine in the historic five-story brick Collins Building, is a welcome oasis, especially on weekends when the workweek happy hour crowds have dispersed and it's warm enough to take a seat on the enclosed sidewalk patio. There are twenty taps and more than sixty-five bottles, and amid the exposed brick dating to the 1890s, hardwood details, a heavy hanging mirror flanked by hand-blown glass-and-metal sconces, cozy booths, and way-above-average pub fare, it's easy to see an evening or afternoon disappear in a hurry.

Carnivores must try the lamb chops or hand-formed Collins Burger with Oregon Tillamook cheddar cheese while the fresh ling cod fish-and-chips, fried with a Chuckanut Pilsner beer batter, is a strong option, too. For the best service, sit at the bar, and be sure to come long before the 2 a.m. posted closing time; it often closes much, much earlier, around 11 p.m.

PHILOSOPHY
Affordable gastropub meets private beer bar.

KEY BEER
Dogfish Head Palo Santa Marron (12% ABV), a rich stout aged in Paraguayan wood related to frankincense, crude-oil-black and milkshake creamy.

ELYSIAN BREWING CO.

1221 E. Pike St. • Seattle, WA 98122 • (206) 860-1920
elysianbrewing.com • Established: 1996

SCENE & STORY
Which came first, the age or the wisdom? The original Elysian location represents the paradigmatic brewpub—exposed beams, polished cement floors, high industrial ceilings, and walls lined with gleaming brewing tanks in a ninety-year-old converted warehouse. (There are two other newer locations: Elysian Fields, a large brewpub in the Stadium District, and Tangletown, a smaller location in South Greenlake, with at least one more location in planning stages.) Behind it all is founding brewer Dick Cantwell, born in Germany and raised in the United States, who has led the Seattle firm to scores of awards by doing what he has always done best: brew a massive array of styles with sure-handed skill. With sixteen taps including two guest beers, you can try a serious slice of the Cantwell oeuvre here, from the well known to the obscure.

PHILOSOPHY
Collaborative. In 2008 Elysian began an exchange program of sorts ("collabeerations") with New Belgium Brewery resulting in the Trip Series of experimental beers like a Black Belgo IPA and a juniper-infused ale, for which brew houses, knowledge, and manpower are exchanged in order to keep things fresh and innovative.

KEY BEER
Like Boston Lager, the Wise ESB (a reference to the Goddess Athena, and Elysian's first beer) shows a lot of malty backbone, a grain-given sturdiness that's typical for the style. But alas, ESBs also occasionally suffer from a cloying, fruit-like sweetness. Not so with the Wise: Its drier profile makes it far more quaffable in high volumes, which, frankly, has its own intrinsic wisdom. Even better, there's an overlay of mellow spiciness derived from three different kinds of tangy Northwest hops, making it perfect for fall's cool nights (5.9% ABV).

HALE'S ALES

4301 Leary Wy. NW • Seattle, WA 98107 • (206) 706-1544
halesbrewery.com • Established: 1983

SCENE & STORY

Like many Americans, Mike Hale tasted his first old-world craft beer in college while traveling abroad, and studied its curious properties with a deep and abiding conviction. About ten years later, still searching for the flavor and fired up by stories about Jack McAuliffe's efforts down at New Albion in California, he relocated to southern England in 1982, volunteered at Gale's Brewery and Guinness, and within a year of returning home to the Seattle area, he'd founded Hale's Ales.

The new little brewery was immediately hit with demand. After a few expansions in different locations over the years he settled on the current 17,000-square-foot location between Fremont and Ballard (in an old hose manufacturing plant) and opened a brewpub and beer garden to go with his new bigger brew house. It's got a wide-open feel with views directly into the operations area, complete with mirrors angled for views into the open fermenters.

PHILOSOPHY

"The main thing is to keep the main thing the main thing," Hale says, speaking about quality brewing practices. And to keep things running smooth with his accounts across the Pacific Northwest, Hale also restored a beautiful red double-decker bus and outfitted it with a draft bar, hot water,

bathrooms, and plush club seating. Don't be surprised if you see him, Red Baron–style in the cockpit, the engine juddering away and the passengers raising toasts. It's a beautiful sight, but alas, not one he can legally open to members of the public. It must be used for "educational purposes" only. Isn't school great?

KEY BEER

Hale's 5.2% ABV Pale American Ale set a new standard in the Northwest when it was released, but it's the smooth, sessionable Cream Ale; grassy, grainy Kölsch; and recent spate of double IPAs like Supergoose (7.5% ABV) that are the ones to try.

LATONA PUB

6423 Latona Ave. NE • Seattle, WA 98115 • (206) 525-2238
3pubs.com/Latona.html • Established: 1987

SCENE & STORY

With its corner spot and high, wide windows, the Latona looks inviting from the outside, but it's the warm service, approachable clientele, and healthy but hearty pub fare (served on classic Fiesta ware plates) that really set this beer bar apart. The menu reaches for a culinary grace note or two without grasping, and the beers (ten on tap, thirty bottled) are fresh thanks to quick rotations and a steady, curious clientele.

PHILOSOPHY

Reverential. "The beer brewed in our own backyard is created by some of the most talented, creative people in the world," write the owners on the website for the Latona and their two other Seattle pubs, Hopvine and Fiddler's Inn. "At our pubs, we want to present to you the closest thing to what the brewers create. We take care of the beer we pour."

KEY BEER

With its light-bodied notes of coffee and bitter chocolate, Big Time Brewery's Coal Creek Porter (4.5% ABV) would go nicely with the green chile chicken quesadillas.

NAKED CITY BREWERY & TAPHOUSE

8564 Greenwood Ave. North • Seattle, WA 98103
(206) 838-6299 • nakedcitybrewing.com • Established: 2009

SCENE & STORY

Owners Don Webb and Donald Averill were home brewers with a common dream of opening their own breweries when they met and joined forces. Webb is a major film buff, hence the noirish theme running through the signage and art in the place; *Naked City* came out in 1948 based on the iconic book of New York real-life crime photos of the same name by Arthur Fellig, aka Weegee, in 1945 (check out the big framed movie poster for it). In filmmaking terms, Webb and Averill were thinking in big-budget 70mm Technicolor; in the end, budget constraints were more along the lines of an indie production, though hardly Spartan. They installed a 3.5-barrel system (about a hundred gallons) and a 24-tap bar, curated a vegan-friendly menu with sandwiches and

starters like white truffle pâté and land-jäger, a dried German sausage. It's a simple, smart arrangement.

PHILOSOPHY

Respect greatness, in beer or film form. Instead of reality shows and sports, the TVs show iconic old films; the taps are dedicated to craft beers made in small batches.

KEY BEER

Local and regional breweries like Snipes, Chuckanut, and Schooner Exact dominate the list; try Naked City's the Big Lebrewski, a 12% ABV Imperial Stout with blockbuster levels of roasted malt.

THE PIKE PUB & BREWERY

1415 1st Ave. • Seattle, WA 98101 • (206) 622-6044
pikebrewing.com • Established: 1989

SCENE & STORY

Located in the Pike Place Market area, the pub is a multilevel, brightly painted beer lover's warren of three bars chockablock with a truly impressive collection of breweriana. The story this collection tells is the story of Charles and Rose Ann Finkel, who founded Pike after helping launch the American craft beer scene through Merchant Du Vin, a gourmet food, wine, and beer importing company they created in 1978. Through that pathbreaking firm, the Finkels introduced American palates to extraordinary beers never before tasted on these shores, including such iconic brands as Orval and Rochefort of Belgium, Samuel

Smith's of Yorkshire, England, and Ayinger of Bavaria, Germany, all of which are considered classics of European brewing traditions.

Along the way, Finkel emerged as a talented graphic artist, designing beer labels for U.S. markets and eventually several books about beer and design. The Finkels opened Pike, their dream brewery, in 1989, and quickly accrued a trove of brewing industry medals and thirsty accounts. By 1997 they sold the brewery and import company to an unnamed investor, but longed to be back in the beer fold, and bought the brewery back in 2006.

PHILOSOPHY

The warm and charming Finkels are both conservationists and foodies, involved with Salone del Gusto (the biannual Slow Food convention in Turin, Italy), and they're ambitiously ramping up both the beer and food options in their brewpub accordingly.

KEY BEER

While Pike's excellent Pale, IPA, XXXXX Stout, and Kilt Lifter Scotch Ale made the company famous, new releases such as Pike Dry Wit are gaining notice from the likes of legendary Chez Panisse chef, Alice Waters. It's a *wit*, or unfiltered, Belgian-style white beer spiced with Nugget and Cascade hops, dried orange peel, coriander, chamomile, and organic lavender (5% ABV).

QUINN'S

1001 E. Pike St. • Seattle, WA 98122 • (206) 325-7711
quinnspubseattle.com • Established: 2008

SCENE & STORY

There are times when the only question is this: Where to find a great burger? For those moments of doubt, this Capitol Hill eatery a block off of Broadway created the secret answer, only available by request and "never, ever" printed on the menu: the Ultra Burger. A hefty, hand-formed patty of natural, barley fed beef, the Ultra could include—in addition to foie gras and "depending on the chef's mood," says manager Reagan Vaughn of chef-owner Scott Staples—oxtail, braised short rib, or whatever he feels like.

For $30, this beauty comes piled with beef-fat fries topped with fontina fonduta cheese and demi-glace—a highbrow poutine. Pair this with a great fresh beer and life, for a moment, is complete. The cool, 1900s converted-loft feel of the place, with its big windows, only enhances the effect. Beyond the Ultra, there's roasted bone marrow (a specialty), slow-roasted pork ribs, Idaho trout, and beer-battered fish-and-chips, among other seasonally driven dishes. Order the marrow *and* at least one Ultra Burger for the table.

PHILOSOPHY

Life is short—order wisely.

KEY BEER

There are fourteen taps and seventy bottles

featuring the latest Elysian, Maritime Pacific, Odin, and Naked City brews, cask-conditioned ales, a wide selection of Trappist ales, and burger-friendly nectars like Russian River's Pliny the Elder.

Woodinville

RED HOOK BREWERY & FORECASTERS PUBLIC HOUSE

14300 NE 145th St. • Woodinville, WA 98072
(425) 483-3232 • redhook.com • Established: 1981

SCENE & STORY

Red Hook is one of the cornerstones in the church of Pacific Northwest craft brewing, but there was little hope things would go as incredibly well as they have. Founders Paul Shipman and Gordon Bowker started out inauspiciously with a Belgian ale brewed in a converted transmission shop in Seattle's Ballard neighborhood. Locals dubbed it "banana beer" and fewer than 1000 bbl sold in year one. But Blackhook Porter and Ballard Bitter, released in 1983 and 1984, respectively, changed them from laughing-stock to growing concern, and in 1987 the E.S.B. (Extra Special Bitter) became a clarion call to beer drinkers around the region. Bowker went on to found a little coffee shop called Starbucks, and today the brewery is a huge national brand with three plants and national distribution through Anheuser-Busch, an arrangement that irks some craft beer industry watchers and no doubt fills others with envy.

The Woodinville operation is a big draw for Seattleites and area beer lovers for the al fresco movies and concerts, $1 tours of the brewery, and a bite in the brewpub (Warning: hit-or-miss food; slow service). The best way to visit is on bike. Each year the Haul Ash Tour de Brew commemorates the 1980 eruption of Mount St. Helens. It's a round-trip ride from the brewery in Woodinville to Seattle's Fremont neighborhood—where it all began—along the verdant Burke-Gilman Trail.

PHILOSOPHY

Loosely? "Ya sure, ya betcha," as the Ballard Bitter labels once read in homage to the area's Scandinavian roots. These are clean, malt-forward beers taking off on British styles (mostly) with admirable fresh Pacific Northwest hop character.

KEY BEER

Just as good as it was back in '87—if not better today—the 5.5% ABV Redhook E.S.B. is a throwback to the English Extra Special Bitters, redolent of toasted malt with a pleasant sweetness and the tang of four hop additions. In 2009, the beer took a gold at the Great American Beer Festival, proving it's a still a benchmark beer twenty-two years after the first batch.

★ ★ ★

PARKWAY TAVERN

313 N. I St. • Tacoma, WA 98403
(253) 383-8748 • No website • Established: 1936

SCENE & STORY

Sometimes little old bars open since the 1930s with no website translate as: cool spot/bad beer. Not so with the Parkway. Its home of Tacoma (located down I-5 a bit between Seattle and Olympia) has a proud beer history, with no fewer than eight breweries up and running between 1888 and Prohibition. Built upon the restoration of lawful beer drinking in what appears to be a converted old shingled house in a quiet residential neighborhood, the Parkway Tavern is a retro gem with a beer list very much of the moment.

As for the bar itself, I'm sure you've heard those stories that begin "there used to be a beat-up old drop ceiling in here. We pulled it down and found *this* . . ." Which, when you look up, turns out to be acres of gorgeous stained wood. That's the Parkway's thirty-plus tap front room, with mahogany paneling, cherry wood tables, and polished bar. There's also a working fireplace and a game room of sorts in the back where guests play pool, darts, shuffleboard, and pinball (yes!). And don't leave without a visit to the Zebra Room. You'll know it when you see it.

PHILOSOPHY

There's an old bar sign that reads "THE LIVER IS EVIL . . . IT MUST BE PUNISHED," but with the excellent beers on tap here, you're more likely treating yourself with kid gloves. There are multiple festivals and tasting events here year-round for barrel-aged beers, barley wines, and IPAs.

KEY BEER

This would be the perfect place for the roasty but unpunishing Moylan's Dragoons Dry Irish Stout (5% ABV), or perhaps a fresh Russian River tap, as they're frequent.

CHUCKANUT BREWERY & KITCHEN

601 W. Holly St. • Bellingham, WA 98225 • (360) 752-3377
chuckanutbreweryandkitchen.com • Established: 2008

SCENE & STORY

Founder Will Kemper tells the story of walking into the old Rainier brewery (now shuttered) in Seattle to ask the brewmaster how he might get started in the trade. The brewer told him he'd have to have been born into it. Wrong answer. Kemper armed himself with the top degrees in brewing (which would lead to eventual teaching appointments in California and London) before going on to found the influential Thomas Kemper brewery (a venture which was later sold to Pyramid). He became a globetrotting consultant, setting up or running scores of breweries in Mexico, Europe, and in Turkey before making his most recent move, to Bellingham, where he set up this technically advanced brewery with an off-kilter name. Today the little seventy-five-seat Chuckanut brewery (built in a converted waterfront warehouse) is a sunny affair with six rotating taps, buttery walls and a gleaming, fully automated brewhouse. Kemper's latest venture was honored with best brewer and small brewpub of the year in 2009 at the Great American Beer Festival, which just goes to show: You can't keep a good brewer down.

PHILOSOPHY

Clean, controlled, and mostly true to established styles, Kemper's operation is one of a variety executed with a true perfectionist's eye for detail. There's an open kitchen with a wood-burning oven for preparing pizzas and tasty, healthy food to pair with his beers.

KEY BEER

Try the pale golden Kolsch, with a refreshingly light, herbal, hay-like taste and crisp finish (5% ABV).

DETOUR→

THE ULTIMATE ALE SAIL

SCHOONER ZODIAC • 1221 Harris Ave., PNB 2 • Bellingham, WA 98225
(206) 719-7622 • schoonerzodiac.com

Washington's Puget Sound is known for roving pods of killer whales and soaring bald eagles, craggy remote islets with sleepy sea lions, bobbing otters, barking harbor seals, and the occasional humpback. It's also home to a handful of breweries accessible by sea. What better way to tour them than on a majestic 127-foot topsail schooner built in 1924? Three times each summer, Schooner Zodiac sets sail from Bellingham on a four-day, three-night adventure tour with steaming breweries in the looking-glass every day, including but not limited to stops at Snoqualmie Brewery & Taproom, Chuckanut Brewery & Kitchen, and Port Townsend Brewing Company. In between brewery tours, the skilled onboard chef keeps your belly full, fueling afternoon kayak excursions among forested islets and sessions spent learning the ropes, hauling sheets and lines, and generally earning a bit of ale (dispensed freely when the anchor's down). At last, it's time to home brew some "Schooner Rat IPA" under the stars with noted Northwest brewers—if you've got the energy to stay awake. From $775 per person all-inclusive.

Mukilteo

DIAMOND KNOT

621-A Front St. • Mukilteo, WA 98275 • (425) 355-4488
diamondknot.com • Established: 1994

SCENE & STORY

The merchant ship *Diamond Knot* sank in 1947 a quarter mile from Port Angeles in 135 feet of water carrying precious cargo: an estimated 5.7 *million* cans of choice Alaskan canned salmon. Insurers said it was a lost cause, but crewmen and locals jury-rigged a vacuum system to hoover the edibles out of the ocean, and the successful mission came to symbolize local, er, can-do spirit. When home brew buddies and coworkers at Boeing Bob Mophet and the late Brian Sollenburger decided to launch a self-distributing brewing company without quitting their day jobs— they were discouraged, too. But they channeled the fabled can-rescue operation, took over a converted transit building garage that once housed a pub, and started brewing big beers with boatloads of Northwest hops in every batch. Just fifteen years later, the business has grown to include this location, a gloriously funky spot with sawdust on the floors and crowds of locals, a second brewpub, and a third establishment, a beer bar.

PHILOSOPHY

Where there's a will, there's a way.

KEY BEER

The big, burly, and pungent Diamond Knot IPA put these Boeing cabin boys on a down-wind run. Look for dry-hopped versions with Simcoe, and the Shipwreck XXXIPA, an Imperial IPA with a leviathan's bite.

Stevenson

WALKING MAN BREWING CO.

240 SW First St. • Stevenson, WA 98648
(509) 427-5520 • No website • Established: 2000

SCENE & STORY

Just across the river in Washington from the Oregon beer-blessed town of Hood River in the scenic Columbia Gorge this small-town brewpub has a bevy of tanks shoehorned into a back room, twelve taps, lots of wood paneling, and a collection of bottle openers on a vertical wood beam next to the cash register. The pub fare is heavy on pizzas, and the patio is great in the summer, with live music in a grassy little garden area. In homage to the legendary Sasquatch, there's an ambulatory theme to most of the beers (Jaywalker; Old Stumblefoot; Pale Strider). And there's just something to love about a place where the bathrooms are themed "Readers" and "Dreamers."

PHILOSOPHY

Big beers with big feet. Higher-than-usual alcohol and hopping rates define most of the Walking Man beers, which vary in drinkability. The brewery also hosts the Sasquatch Legacy Project, a yearly charity brew by recipients of the Glen Hay Falconer Scholarship named in honor of the late influential Oregon brewer.

KEY BEER

Knuckle Dragger, an American Pale Ale of 6.5% ABV, is a malty, hoppy citrus bomb that would send Big Foot into naptime in no time.

BEST *of the* REST: WASHINGTON

PYRAMID ALEHOUSE

1201 1st Ave. South • Seattle, WA 98134 • (206) 682-3377 • pyramidbrew.com/alehouses/seattle

The original location of Pyramid's minichain of vast beer bars (est. 1994), this Alehouse is located right across from the Seattle Mariners' Safeco Field (and just a block from Qwest Field, where the Seattle Sounders MLS soccer team plays) and features eight taps plus a few bottled releases to tide you over before the big game (or after) in the beer garden patio or spacious interior. The best matchup: pizza and some Uproar Imperial Red (7.3% ABV).

THE STUMBLING MONK

1635 E. Olive Wy. • Seattle, WA 98122 • (206) 860-0916 • No website

This tiny little corner beer bar on Capitol Hill has twelve taps and fifty bottled selections, and better yet, no loud music or TVs. Nor is there a menu of food (unless you count potato chips as food), but you can order in. In classic dive bar fashion, you come here for board games like Scrabble, Connect Four, and Battleship. It gets cramped and sweaty. But this is a dive bar that also happens to boast a great list of beers, from the exotic sours of Portland's Cascade Barrel House to Belgium's iconic pale ale with *Brettanomyces*, Orval (6.2% ABV).

ÜBER TAVERN

7517 Aurora Ave. North • Seattle, WA 98103 • (206) 782-2337 • uberbier.com

There's a reason locals talk of the Über warp—time disappears when you step in the door. Opened in 2006 with 17 taps and 150 bottled brews (heavy on the Belgians and upstart regionals like Black Raven and Beer Valley, of Ontario, Oregon), this idyllic little Green Lake–area beer bar is neither dive nor stuffy beer snob perch, with cool neon signage outside and a rapidly rotated beer list within its cobalt blue walls (and I have to mention the gas-flame fireplace table). Look for Anacortes Brewery's Locomotive Breath, a bold, barrel-black Imperial Stout (8.5% ABV).

BOUNDARY BAY BREWERY & BISTRO

1107 Railroad Ave. • Bellingham, WA 98225 • (360) 647-5593 • bbaybrewery.com

Bellingham, the college-y "City of Subdued Excitement," got quite a bit more buzz in 1995 when this standout brewpub came online. With twelve taps, nine bottles, and two casks at any given time (plus a hearty menu of burgers, beer-barbecued pork, smoked salmon chowder, mac-and-cheese, and fish tacos), this large brick neighborly hangout has scored high marks thanks to beers like Inside Passage Ale (an IPA of 6.4% ABV) and the outdoor patio and grassy beer garden, hosting live music and spontaneous hula-hoop contests.

THE NORTH FORK BREWERY, PIZZERIA, BEER SHRINE & WEDDING CHAPEL

6186 Mt. Baker Hwy. • Deming, WA 98244 • (360) 599-2337 • northforkbrewery.com

True to its name, this quirky destination (est. 1997) along the Mount Baker Highway about thirty minutes from Bellingham has a whole lot of love going on for one place. With just five taps from a tiny little 3.5 bbl system, it may look a little like Navin R. Johnson's family home from *The Jerk*, but that's exactly why you'll want to make the drive. Where else can you hang out in a log house with ninety years' worth of beer bric-a-brac, drink nano-brewed beer (try the 11% ABV Barleywine to steady those nerves), eat pizza pie, and get hitched?

EVERYBODY'S BREWING

151 E. Jewett Blvd. • White Salmon, WA 98672 • (509) 637-2774 • everybodysbrewing.com

Established in 2009 with sixteen taps (up to nine of their own) Everybody's has a 26-foot-long handcrafted bar, wood banquet tables, and idyllic views of Mount Hood across the Columbia Gorge in Oregon. Remember, you're in hop country, so order the Country Boy IPA (6.2% ABV) and head out to the porch.

Idaho
★ ★ ★

Victor

GRAND TETON BREWING CO.

430 Old Jackson Hwy. • Victor, ID 83455 • (208) 787-9000
grandtetonbrewing.com • Established: 1988

SCENE & STORY

Grand Teton Brewing Company was actually founded seventeen miles away from Victor, in Wilson, Wyoming, as Otto Brothers' Brewing in 1988, by Charlie and Ernie Otto. It was the first modern microbrewery in the state, and represented the first malt beverage production permit in Wyoming in thirty-five years. Eventually changing their name and relocating to beautiful Victor in 2000, the brothers have embarked on a few interesting firsts.

One, they claim to have reintroduced the sixty-four-ounce growler into modern use after an offhand comment by their father, who recalled using lidded tin pails in Germany to transport beer. And more recently, they created an all-Idaho beer, using only ingredients grown or sourced from within the state. The uncommon Zeus and Bravo hops were grown in southwest Idaho, the barley was grown and malted in the southeast, and the water came from a spring in the Tetons. If you're anywhere near Victor and the Grand Tetons, you can get a taste of this brew at their quaint little taproom (no edibles) seven days a week.

PHILOSOPHY

Progressive. The brewery has worked with fifty charities in the area, and the beers keep getting more innovative with each batch.

KEY BEER

There are five year-round beers, including the flagship, Bitch Creek Extra Special Brown (6% ABV), which has nutty, cocoa-like flavors mingling with a lightly hoppy finish. But look for the Cellar Reserve brews, like a recent imperial Pilsner, Persephone (8.75% ABV).

BEST *of the* REST: IDAHO

BITTERCREEK ALEHOUSE

246 N. 8th St. • Boise, ID 83702 • (208) 429-6340 • justeatlocal.com/bittercreek

Opened in 1996, this Boise standby is plushed out with dark woods and leather and stocked with thirty-nine taps from Idaho, Oregon, Washington, Montana, Colorado, and California (and a small selection of regional bottled beers). They'll throw a cask on the bar on occasion, and the pub grub ranges from sandwiches and burgers to fish-and-chips, Alaskan salmon, Idaho pork chops, and a BBQ plate. Look for the Terminal Gravity Breakfast Porter (5.7% ABV), especially if you're in the place for your first meal of the day.

LAUGHING DOG BREWING

55 Emerald Industrial Park Rd. • Ponderay, ID 83852 • (208) 263-9222 • laughingdogbrewing.com

A very dog-friendly brewery with very hoppy beers, Laughing Dog is a chilled-out, home-town, family kind of place. Established in 2005, production is up to 4,500 bbls, and the tasting room has twelve taps, with a few goodies stashed away. Look for Dogzilla (6.9% ABV), considered one of the earliest India Black Ales (aka Black IPA), brewed with Simcoe and Cascade hops, pale and Munich malts, and black barley.

Alaska

★ ★ ☆

FOR A CITY THAT CANNOT BE ACCESSED BY ROAD—TO GET TO THE STATE

capital of Alaska, you must fly or arrive by boat—there have been a lot of firsts here. The state's first big gold strike, in 1880, was close by. About a century later, the state struck gold again, in say, drinkable form. In 1986, Geoff and Marci Larson founded Alaskan Brewing Company—Alaska's first brewery since Prohibition—in Juneau.

In all seriousness, consider a midwinter visit, not only to coordinate with the Great Alaska Beer & Barley Wine Festival in Anchorage, held in mid-January, but also to get a sense of the authentic character—and characters—of the place. The millions of cruise ship passengers trundling ashore all summer long to gawk at glaciers and buy a plastic king crab refrigerator magnet have no idea what local dwellers are really made of. It's in the winter you discover that even mild-mannered locals like Donovan Neal—comptroller of Alaskan Brewing Company—moonlight as alpine guides, leading winter climbs (and ski descents!) of Cascade volcanoes. You see the Larsons (of Alaska Brewing Company fame) and their neighbors up near the Eaglecrest ski area on Douglas Island, just across the channel, with huskies and malamutes volunteer training for catastrophic avalanche victim recovery. The sheer 3,576-foot face of Mount Juneau looms immediately behind town, and a 1962 slide took out seventeen houses. *National Geographic* later pronounced it the city with the highest avalanche danger in America.

You won't miss the sun and you sure won't miss the crowds. And you've got incredible powder to ski; a mid-January weekday run to the excellent Eaglecrest ski area (a 20-minute drive) can mean lift lines in the single digits—as in you and a buddy. And most of all, you've got great fresh beer to drink in atmospheric old bars like the Alaskan (since 1913) and the Imperial (1891). Gold rush, indeed.

1-DAY	The Hangar, Alaskan Brewing Co., the Imperial, the Alaskan Hotel, Pel'meni
3-DAY	One-day itinerary plus the Island Pub
7-DAY	Three-day itinerary plus Chair 5

THE ALASKAN BREWING CO.

5429 Shaune Dr. • Juneau, AK 99801 • (907) 780-5866
alaskanbeer.com • Established: 1986

SCENE & STORY

Geoff and Marcy Larson met while bouncing around in various national parks jobs in the late 1970s. "I was hitchhiking across the country during a summer off college and ran out of money in Montana," recalls Geoff, who was previously somewhat more stably based in Maryland. He met Marcy, a Florida native with a photojournalism degree, while both were working in Glacier National Park, where the two embarked on a "summer romance gone really wild," recalls Marcy. Geoff went back to finish his five-year chemical engineering degree in Maryland and started home brewing; Marcy decamped to parts north. "I came up here to work in Glacier Bay, and just fell totally in love with Alaska," she recalls. "It was just so big, so wild, and so untouched." The letters and phone calls began.

By 1981, they were reunited in the Klondike State, Marcy working nights as an auditor in the Department of Revenue, and both dreaming full-time about opening a brewery for the locals, who seemed interested in high-quality imported brews but had no local options. "All the beers people were drinking were really oxidized. Alaska got the remnants," Marcy says. "But fresh beer—it was like, 'Yeah! This is great stuff! We need this up here.'" A big Anchorage-based German brewery built during the pipeline years called Prinz Brau had gone under in the late 1970s; the Larsons felt they could succeed with something more, well, Alaskan.

They decided to go for it themselves. With "no experience and no money of our own, nothing whatsoever" as Marcy recalls, and after thirteen stressful months of raising loans from various friends, family, and locals, the Alaskan Brewing Company became the sixty-seventh operating brewery in the United States and the only one in Alaska. It was 1986. The early days were rocky; Alaska's economy was in the tank, and skeptics said they'd soon go under.

Not so fast. In 1988, Alaskan won the consumer preference poll at the GABF, and sales were rocketing. Today it's the twelfth largest craft brewery out of some 1,700 in the country (and still employee- and local investor-owned), manufacturing over 100,000 bbl per year. The first brew (now the flagship) was their Amber, based on a 1907 purchase order for altbier ingredients a local collector had preserved from a long lost area brewery. Smooth and full of caramel malt goodness, with a compelling if faint noble hop spiciness, the die was cast.

Today the brewery offers five year-round beers, including the Amber and two seasonals (Summer Ale, a superb Kölsch-style brew, and Winter Ale, spiced with spruce tips, after the brewing methods used by Captain Cook to combat scurvy among his crew). A special edition beer, Alaskan Smoked Porter, is an intense, collectible brew that has spawned scores of imitators among domestic brewers. Lastly, there is the Pilot series of experimental and specialty styles like barley wine and Baltic porter, and occasional Rough Draft brews, small batch riffs from Pilot batches for local distribution. All of them are made from water out of Juneau's glacier-fed aquifers. The tasting room is a charming affair, with free tours, nine taps, and cool old photos and memorabilia from the early days, all of it thanks to one hot, dusty, inspiring summer in Montana.

PHILOSOPHY

High quality, eco-friendly, and unpretentious. "You have to make the best beer you possibly can for a whole variety of reasons," says Geoff. The brew house utilizes a number of sustainable practices, such as the country's first CO_2 recovery system (which has become more common these days), a mash filter press (a system common in Belgium which reduces water and grain consumption without compromising beer quality), and a spent-grain dryer to prepare brewery by-products for shipping down to farms to use as feed in the lower 48.

KEY BEER

Alaskan's 6.5% ABV Smoked Porter, introduced in 1988, is a *rauchbier*, or traditional German "smoke" beer, made by smoking brewers' malt over alder wood branches, which is done by hand in small batches in Juneau. True to its name, it's got all the spice and char of a campfire, with appealing cocoa and chocolate notes. Alaskan's is one of the first brewed successfully outside of Germany, and is one of the winningest—if not *the* winningest—beers ever at the GABF.

Who needs a menu? At Pel'meni, a hole-in-the-wall Russian café in the classic old blue Merchants Wharf building down by the water, there are really only two choices—beef or potato (you want both). When you walk in, it's just five little tables, a small counter, and a wall of vinyl records with an old record player spinning tunes (recent cut: Sérgio Mendes and Brasil '66's "Agua de Beber"). What you get for a few dollars is a Styrofoam box of piping hot, tortelloni-like Russian dumplings called *pelmeni*. Once steamed, they're zipped around in a hot pan with butter and served with a dash of vinegar, cumin powder, fresh cilantro, a dollop of sour cream, and Sriracha sauce. There may never be a better late-night snack. And thankfully, it's open after the bars close. (A word to the Juneau authorities: never, ever tear down the Wharf building or close this effortlessly perfect place.)

THE HANGAR ON THE WHARF

2 Marine Wy., No. 106 • Juneau, AK 99801 • (907) 586-5018
hangaronthewharf.com • Established: 1996

SCENE & STORY

With its location convenient to everything in the Merchants Wharf building, the bright, clean, and crisply run Hangar is a beloved local watering hole and tourist favorite during the season. It's got an airplane and seaplane theme thanks to the building's 1940s tenant, Alaska Coastal Airlines, but isn't kitschy or overdone. Overlooking the channel with huge glass windows and outdoor seating, it makes an ideal spot for an afternoon beer and a bite as the seaplanes buzz in and out and the big ships dock (it's just as convivial in the quiet winter, as well). There are some twenty taps and seventy bottled beers, with a surprisingly deep collection, and a solid menu of sandwiches, wraps, and fresh local seafood dishes like King crab legs, oysters, prawns, and salmon. Try the Cajun Caesar wrap with blackened salmon.

PHILOSOPHY

Cheery waterside seafood palace meets craft beer bar.

KEY BEER

Much of the lineup of Alaskan's beers are available, including whatever's freshest and the Rough Draft releases, and there are a number of good Pacific Northwest craft brews as well.

THE ISLAND PUB

1102 2nd St. • Douglas, AK 88824 • (907) 364-1595
theislandpub.com • Established: 2005

SCENE & STORY

Across the Gastineau Channel from Juneau lies Douglas Island, a 77-square-mile tidal isle with a sandy beach made of mine tailings. It's the home of the long disused Treadwell mine, largest in the world in its day, and the vastly underrated Eaglecrest ski area, which has 1,400 feet of vertical (40 percent of it expert) served by four double chairs. But perhaps best of all, it's home to the Island Pub, the ultimate après-ski pizzeria. With open seating, large picture windows, and a sleek square center bar area, it's surprisingly contemporary, but entirely inviting. Built in what was once "Mike's Place," a quaint former dance hall dating to the 1930s, it's updated now, but make sure to stroll around and look at the historic photos of patrons sashaying over the wood floors.

PHILOSOPHY

Quintessentially local. Six of the pizzas on the menu are the handiwork of area residents who competed for the honor of having their own pizzas on the menu for an entire year.

KEY BEER

There are nine taps and twenty-five bottled selections, including the local treats, of course: the Sitka spruce-tip-spiced, 6.4% ABV Winter Ale from Alaskan, in season, makes a great match for meaty, zesty pizza.

HAINES BREWING CO.

Southeast Alaska State Fairgrounds
P.O. Box 911 • Haines, AK 99827 • (907) 766-3823
hainesbrewing.com • Established: 1999

SCENE & STORY

Fans of Paul Wheeler's beer used to traipse through tidal bogs and dense forest to try his beers at his house. Since 1999, the bright-eyed brewer—who sports a beard that would have made Walt Whitman jealous—has been operating a little 3.5 bbl brewery in another out-of-the-way location—inside a quaint Old West general store building on the "Dalton City" set for the movie *White Fang*. It's a short seaplane or ferry trip from Juneau. The ideal visit would be at the end of May, during the Great Alaska Craft Beer and Home Brew Festival, held on the Dalton City site at the Southeast Alaska State Fairgrounds.

PHILOSOPHY

Big, brawny, frontier beer, no apologies. There's even a "no cell phones" sign in the taproom. These beers deserve your undivided attention.

KEY BEER

Wheeler's beers are excellent, especially DMMDI IPA (Devil Made Me Do It IPA; 6.66% ABV), Black Fang Stout (9% ABV), and Captain Cook's Spruce Tip Ale, an homage to Cook's method of brewing without hops—as well as to Wheeler's former job as a forester.

Anchorage

Life in Alaska has never been easy, but beer helps, especially if you don't have to import it. Stoked by home brewers who could make beer affordable by brewing it at home rather than paying for cost-prohibitive beer shipments, the craft beer scene in Alaska is hitting a rolling boil. While Alaska's capital, Juneau, has the state's oldest bar and first craft brewery, Anchorage is pulling its weight in the beer department with a slew of high-quality brewpubs, beer bars, and the annual Great Alaska Beer & Barley Wine Festival, held in the icy depths of mid-January. *But isn't it cold at that time of year?* Yes. It's bleakly, face-numbingly, eye-frostingly cold, though locals walk around in windbreakers and wonder aloud how warm it seems. *But it gets dark so early.* (Yes; all the more reason to make hay while the sun shines and then go drink delicious beer.)

Fact is, the winter weather in Anchorage doesn't stop locals from gathering, much less going mountain biking (with snow tires!) along the water with views of Mount McKinley (elevation: 20,320 feet) or even across a frozen lake, with the soaring Chugach peaks behind town. Nor does the drop in the mercury stop brewers from showing up with their best stuff— high-strength, cellar-worthy barley wines are popular up here—especially during the festival. A midwinter visit to Anchorage is all about the camaraderie of the state's growing brewing scene: for the annual Great Alaska Beer & Barley Wine Festival, some fifty breweries band together, including twenty-plus operating in Alaska—and about two thousand locals a night don their finest going-out-on-the-town clothes, making it fun and unexpected—kind of like mountain biking in January.

ITINERARIES

1-DAY Glacier Brewhouse, Snow Goose Restaurant & Sleeping Lady Brewing Co., Anchorage Brewing Co., Humpy's

3-DAY One-day itinerary plus Café Amsterdam, Midnight Sun Brewing Co.

7-DAY Three-day itinerary plus Haines Brewing Co.

⟫⟫⟫ WINTER WARMER ⟪⟪⟪

The Great Alaskan Beer & Barley Wine Festival, started in 2005, is held every January, traditionally in downtown Anchorage's Egan Convention Center. Brewers compete for medals and bragging rights in the Barley Wine category and mingle with about two thousand fans a night. Do as the locals do and hang out in the Alaska end, where just about every single commercial brewery in Alaska has a booth with fresh beer. There's a Connoisseur Session on the final afternoon, for which the brewers present beers they used to hide under the tables. Highly recommended for tried-and-true craft beer lovers. For info: auroraproductions.net/beer-barley.html

ANCHORAGE BREWING CO.

717 W. 3rd Ave. • Anchorage, AK 99501 • (907) 360-5104
anchoragebrewingcompany.com • Established: 2011

SCENE & STORY

With a projected annual output of just 360 barrels a year, Alaska's newest brewing project is the vision of Gabe Fletcher, formerly the soft-spoken head brewer at Anchorage's Midnight Sun who is credited with improving the brewery's fortunes early on. It's also the most unusual brewing operation to come along in Alaska since that day in 1986 when Geoff and Marcy Larson dared to open Alaskan Brewing Company, now one of the biggest breweries in the country in a state formerly without craft beer.

Fletcher works in tandem with another Anchorage brewer, Sleeping Lady Brewing Company, by brewing his own batches there and then gravity-flowing the wort (unfermented beer) straight down through the floor and into a steel tank of his own for primary fermentation. Later, he racks (transfers, in brewers' parlance) the ales into a collection of French oak barrels for aging, during which time they accrue interesting acidic angles, tannins, and vanillin from the wine-soaked wood. After a period of time, he blends, then bottles the Belgian-style brews before refermenting them in the bottle according to the *méthode champenoise*. It's a simple, immaculately clean operation, one in which he anticipates installing some kind of tasting area. For all those who can't make the trip to Anchorage, Fletcher's beers became only the third brewery on American soil to be distributed by the Shelton Brothers, America's most adventurous importers of specialty, small batch, and farmhouse ales from around the world.

PHILOSOPHY

Flanders on the Klondike. This is innovative, Belgian-style brewing in the heart of wild Alaska—as unexpected as they come.

KEY BEER

Fletcher debuted his Anchorage Brewing Company at the 2011 Great Alaskan Beer & Barley Wine Festival with Anticipation, a superb double IPA (9% ABV), though it was more a test run (not barrel aged in the cellar), and began releasing his main line of six distinct beers in 2011. These included the intriguing Love Buzz Saison, brewed with rose hips, peppercorns, and fresh orange peels, then dry hopped in the pinot noir barrel with Citra hops, and bottled with a cork-and-cage, in the manner of traditional Belgian beers.

DETOUR ➡ MEET ME ON THE BEER FRONTIER

The Great Northern Brewers Club and Brewers Guild of Alaska Annual Meeting

For a small group of Alaskans, there's an eagerly anticipated event that takes place each year at the Snow Goose Brewing Company's early 1960s ballroom. Amid giant tapestries hung from the wood-paneled walls (polar bear, grizzlies, a unicorn), the Great Northern Brewers Club—a statewide organization founded in 1980 that appears to consist partly of fur trappers, Woodstock time-travelers, and Carhartt-clad loggers—calls itself to order, and simultaneously hosts the Brewers Guild of Alaska for its only meeting of the year.

This is a beer thing of course, so it's not exactly solemn. The hundred or so home-brew club members—some of whom were said to have bush-planed in from the interior—bring potluck dishes of chili (and one labeled simply "moose") and coolers with beer, and gather around in circles of folding chairs.

I crashed the 2011 meeting, during which Jim "Dr. Fermento" Roberts (head of the state brewers' guild, a separate entity, and a local beer authority for the *Anchorage Press* and the California-based *Celebrator Beer News*) took the little stage in a plaid shirt, khakis, and a pair of spectacles to read Important Announcements, which he unfurled like a scroll to the floor. It was a warm welcome to just about everyone in the room, including two "Beerdrinkers of the Year" (a contest held each year at Wynkoop Brewing Company in Denver), representatives of most of the Alaska-based breweries, and the keynote speaker, Sierra Nevada's Ken Grossman. Dr. Fermento wound it up five minutes later with the admonition "Drink responsibly; throw up strategically—make it count," which provoked a laugh because Fermento seems about as wild as a ceramics teacher.

The introductions complete, Fermento passed around a Victoria's Secret shopping bag; this was to collect donations for an injured community member. Next was Ken Grossman's absorbing I-was-a-home-brewer-too-talk; you could have heard a pin drop. For the rest of the night, Grossman, Alaskan Brewing Company founder and Guild "Lead Berserker" Geoff Larson, Fermento and others mingled as a few *Big Lebowski*–era John Goodman types in hunting vests and trucker hats discussed delicate brewing experiments gone amok in one breath, and tropical illness and Thailand's phallic shrines the next.

Things were just warming up when the band took the stage. Clad in a Hawaiian shirt, Tom Dalldorf, publisher of the *Celebrator*, gamely led his Rolling Boil Blues Band in a rendition of "Home Brew," to the tune of Clapton's "Hand Jive." As I wandered around and sampled beers of varying ambition—from good IPA to stout and then one Pilsner that tasted, well, a little like cat pee smells—I got the sense that if it weren't for this club, there would be no surging Alaskan brewing industry today (and thus no Guild), and that certain Alaskan citizens might never venture out of their snowbound cabins in the dead of winter, if not for the chance to toast each other's hard work—and share some of that tasty moose.

HUMPY'S GREAT ALASKAN ALEHOUSE

610 West 6th Ave. • Anchorage, AK 99501 • (907) 276-2337
humpys.com • Established: 1994

SCENE & STORY

The twin sister to Humpy's in Hawaii, Humpy's is Alaska's most serious beer bar, but is by no means pretentious. It's named for pink salmon, a species also known as humpback salmon because the spines of the males eventually bend (developing a hump) from the effort of chasing females upstream and back to their birthplace every summer. And it's consistently busy, especially in the summer, when cruise ships bring hordes of tourists in and out of ancient fjords, so

there's really no time for attitude here.

It's a casual place inside, with padded booths and octagonal bar and a back patio for King crab feeds in season. Founder Billy Opinsky is thoughtful and polished, and stands somewhat apart in the land of unironic trucker hats and foot-long beards with his passing resemblance to a young Al Gore. Deeply involved with Alaska's nascent craft beer scene from its early days, he has stocked the bar with fifty-five taps and fifteen bottled selections, with about half of the tap row consisting of beers from the state. The bar is known for good live musical performances from local and touring acoustic acts, and for unusual beer-tasting events during the big festival in January. For a dinner in 2011, Opinsky laid in aged rarities including beers from Cantillon, Gouden Carolus, and a Thomas Hardy Ale from 1996, which gave locals a chance to try beers seldom available anywhere.

PHILOSOPHY

For beer lovers, by beer lovers. This is a classic good beer spot with no extraneous frills.

KEY BEER

Ask what's freshest. A dependable tap is Midnight Sun's coppery Sockeye Red IPA (5.7% ABV), with a powerful, fragrant, and spicy hop character.

BEERS *with* YEARS

An aged-beers dinner might sound like a lark, but it's not only wine and whiskey that can benefit from a bit of cellar time. Good beer is universally drinkable the minute it leaves a brewery, but, like a good dry-aged steak, time can add new layers of complexity to the biggest brews with a higher alcohol content—roughly 2.5 times stronger than your average supermarket lagers. (Which don't improve with time. Hence their "drink by" dates. Chug away.) There's an array of styles that lay down well, including imperial stouts, English-style barley wines, Belgian lambics and other sours, as well as barrel-aged and other strong beers. Alcohol by volume needs to be in the area of 9 to 10 percent to give the beer any chance of improvement, and the cork or cap should be in good shape to avoid oxidation, which gives beer a wet cardboard taste. Ultraviolet light must be avoided to spare a beer from the skunk effect, a more serious problem with green or clear bottles (as opposed to brown ones, which filter UV light).

With the exception of sour-style beers, which ought to have little hop character, the process of aging mellows bitterness and aroma while deepening and accentuating malt characteristics, drying out the last molecules of fermentable sugars and sometimes adding an acidic, vinous note that can pair well with desserts or certain rich poultry and beef dishes. Some ageable beers are aged in the brewery before being released; Sam Adams's Utopias, a rare port-like concoction, contains a blend of barrel-aged beers up to sixteen years old. Aging beers simply requires patience, the proper setting: a cool, dark place, and an open mind.

MIDNIGHT SUN BREWING CO.

8111 Dimond Hook Dr. • Anchorage, AK 99507
(907) 344-1179 • midnightsunbrewing.com • Established: 1995

SCENE & STORY

Under the watch of brewer Gabe Fletcher for twelve years, Midnight Sun emerged as Alaska's most innovative brewery, and built a strong reputation in the Pacific Northwest for big, interesting beers. New brewer Ben Johnson has a tough act to follow, but he's got plenty of training and a huge standing army of dedicated fans. And with a new brew house and "the Loft"—an upstairs area with some fifteen to twenty taps, sleek metal tables and chairs and polished cement floors—MSBC remains a top draw for beer travelers (and locals) every day of the week from 11 a.m. to 8 p.m. (Note: Alaska state law forbids breweries without certain licenses from staying open past 8 p.m. or serving individuals more than thirty-six ounces, but package and growler sales help take care of that wrinkle.) Call for detailed directions or a map, as the brewery can be tricky to find.

PHILOSOPHY

"We make a lot of crazy stuff," says Midnight Sun owner Mark Staples. "We always try to avoid what everybody else is doing; we didn't brew an amber for like ten years because Alaskan Amber dominated this market. Every brewer that works for me started on the bottling line and washing kegs. Not one of them is some fancy brewer from some school. As a result, our beers are a little bit unique. We just brew what we feel like brewing."

KEY BEER

There are ten year-round offerings, including the flagship Sockeye Red IPA (5.7% ABV), four seasonals, five special edition beers, and several other one-offs and collaborations to try. Try the clove-y, creamy, Belgian-style dark Monk's Mistress and Arctic Devil, a nutty, warming, complex barley wine (typically around 13% ABV) that has cleaned up in the medals department at the Great Alaskan beer festival for years.

GLACIER BREWHOUSE

737 West 5th Ave., No. 110 • Anchorage, AK 99501
(907) 274-2739 • glacierbrewhouse.com • Established: 1997

SCENE & STORY

Glacier BrewHouse enjoys a superb location downtown and seems disconcertingly like just another high-end brewpub chain at first glance. But tastes of the beers (especially stronger styles, including eisbocks and barley wines, head brewer Kevin Burton's passion) prove you're in a special place. There's an expansive menu of good food here, and a huge array of beers available, from clean interpretations of classic styles like IPA and stout, to wilder, bigger beers fermented in "the wall of wood," Burton's basement stash of fifty wine, bourbon, and other oak casks from around the world. The yearly highlight is Burton's Twelve Days of Barley Wine, leading right up into the Christmas holiday, with a different pair of aged barley wines on offer in the brew-pub each day.

PHILOSOPHY

Ambition is its own reward. "You're always striving for that perfect one," says Burton, who mentioned Thomas Harvey and J. W. Lees as exemplary barley wines. He was the first to start barrel aging in Alaska.

KEY BEER

Big Woody, an annual vintage-dated barley wine release. Using pricy English floor-malted barley and aged in various oak barrels including Jim Beam and Napa Valley wine barrels for a minimum of a year, it's intensely malty with notes of vanilla, wood, cherry, and toffee, and usually about 11% ABV.

SNOW GOOSE RESTAURANT & SLEEPING LADY BREWING CO.

717 West 3rd Ave. • Anchorage, AK 99501 • (907) 277-7727
alaskabeers.com • Established: 1996

SCENE & STORY

The Goose, as it's known, was one of the early brewpubs to fire up the kettles in Anchorage, and sits atop a former Elks Lodge. In addition to some impressive quilt work by founder Gary Klopfer's wife adorning the walls, it features some casual upscale tables on the lower level with a sizeable pub area upstairs furnished with booths and a central bar area. It's up there that a huge attached deck overlooks Cook Inlet and Mount Susitna, aka the Sleeping Lady, with still one more deck one floor up, solely for the use of drinking beer, which is exactly the thing to be doing here around sunset on a clear evening.

PHILOSOPHY

Beer first, ask questions later. "When I started out, I wasn't planning to do a restaurant; I *only* wanted to make beer," recalls Gary Klopfer, the former home brewer who founded the Goose. "The place was laid out exclusively for brewing," (and by extension, not as much for offering a culinary experience, though the food and service have shown improvement). This is your ideal spot for beers on the deck in the fresh air.

KEY BEER

The brewery offers eight year-round beers on tap and five specialty brews. It also has one cask-conditioned ale at most times, hand pumped directly from a firkin. The flagship is Urban Wilderness Pale Ale (4.9% ABV), a daytime-drinking, English-style session ale with moderate, grainy sweetness and a touch of tangy hops.

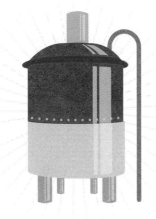

BEST of the REST: ALASKA

THE IMPERIAL BILLIARD & BAR

241 Front St. • Juneau, AK 99801 • (907) 586-1960 • No website

Opened in 1891, the Imperial is Alaska's oldest continuously operating tavern but doesn't go the old-timey route, having been buffed to a shinier condition in recent years. The bar offers ten taps, another eighteen in bottles (mostly macros), and a limited pub menu. Inside, it's low-lit with occasionally loud music and a chilled out local crowd. You're here for the history, the scrappy pool games, the locals drinking Alaskan and Deschutes Mirror Pond Pale Ale.

THE ALASKAN HOTEL BAR

167 S. Franklin • Juneau, AK 99801 • (907) 586-1000 • alaskanhotel.com

Built in 1913, this is the bar where you go to "drink with an Alaskan at the Alaskan." But it's not the tourist trap one might imagine from that old chestnut of a phrase, nor from the spindly Victorian-era balustrade, weathered felt-pattern wallpaper, or corny wrought iron park lantern next to the parlor stairs. Instead, local rabble and well-heeled citizenry alike gather around the old antique bar without going all Wyatt Earp, to name one former carouser in town. They're bobbing heads to an acoustic ballad courtesy of the open mike and drinking the lemony, coriander-kissed Blanche de Chambly, a 5% ABV *witbier* on tap from Quebec. How gunslinger is *that*?

CAFÉ AMSTERDAM

530 E. Benson Blvd., No. 3 • Anchorage, AK 99503 • (907) 274-0074 • cafe-amsterdam.com

Established in 1999 in a little mini mall, this charming European-style beer bar has one of the state's all-time great beer lists, with seventeen taps and a hundred bottled selections, especially strong in Belgians, Alaska-born microbrews, Trappist ales, cask beers, and meads. It's a popular spot for revelers after the Barley Wine Festival as well.

BEAR TOOTH THEATRE PUB & GRILL

1230 W. 27th Ave. • Anchorage, AK 99503 • (907) 276-4200 • beartooththeatre.net

The latest member of the Moose's Tooth Brewing Company (which includes a pizzeria pub; moosestooth.net) and a brewing company headquarters, the Bear Tooth combines a sleek, remodeled concert and film venue (featuring headline acts from the lower 48 and both first run and 3-D movies) and a cool little glass-and-brick enclosed bar and eatery. The brews are standard but far from disappointing; try the hazy orange Fairweather IPA, 6.1% ABV and strongly redolent of graham crackers and grapefruit.

CHAIR 5

171 Linblad Ave. • Girdwood, AK 99587 • (907) 783-2500 • chairfive.com

The Aleyeska Resort, opened in 1954, is a classic expert ski area with a reputation for steep terrain and flinty locals. And Chair 5, established in 1983, is Girdwood's après-ski beer playground, with twenty taps and forty-nine bottles of Alaskan and lower 48 specialty beers from Deschutes to Sierra Nevada, Midnight Sun, and Kona.

DENALI BREWING CO. & TWISTER CREEK RESTAURANT

13605 E. Main St. • Talkeetna, AK 99676 • (907) 733-2536 • denalibrewingcompany.com

The gateway to Denali National Park, little Talkeetna (population: 960) is both a stopover for climbers headed to Mount McKinley and a destination in itself for its excellent fishing and whitewater rafting. Denali Brewing Company's light, silky, black, and roasty Chiuli Stout is fast finding fame in Anchorage beer bars, but there could be no better place to drink it than on the sunny patio of the log cabin–style Twister Creek restaurant.

SILVER GULCH BREWING & BOTTLING CO.

2195 Old Steese Hwy. North • Fairbanks, AK 99712-1023 • (907) 452-2739 • silvergulch.com

Built in the historic mining town of Fox in 1998, Silver Gulch is one of the largest breweries in Alaska and as of 2011 the furthest north. The corrugated metal exterior gives it the look of a farm facility, but the interior is spacious and cleanly furnished with lots of dark-wood tables, chairs, and booths. In addition to the brewpub's own ten taps there are around 100 to 125 international beers available in bottles, including a surprisingly deep collection of rare British, German, and Belgian beers. It's hugely popular with locals so make a reservation ahead of time to secure a spot; try the 5.8% ABV Coldfoot Pilsner, a hybrid of German and Czech styles.

CALIFORNIA *and* HAWAII

California

IT'S GOSPEL AMONG CRAFT BEER FANS THAT MODERN AMERICAN

microbrewing was born in Sonoma County at John "Jack" McAuliffe's New Albion Brewing Company in 1976. That ragtag operation didn't last long, but McAuliffe's English-style ales, some with whole peppers in the bottle, did leave a gigantic impression on locals like Ken Grossman, who was on his way to starting what would become Sierra Nevada. And that was almost ten years after Fritz Maytag, another ambitious beer lover, took over the foundering Anchor (of Steam Beer fame) and began to burnish that old company's shine.

Today, what is happening throughout the state is nothing short of revolutionary: like Napa's wine boom in the 1970s, and Sonoma's in the 1980s, there are now pockets of brewing innovation dotting the entire state. From airy coastal beer gardens in San Diego to chic gastropubs in San Francisco and barn-like wine country hideouts in the North—and even throughout Los Angeles—the entire freewheeling, sun-bleached state has good beer to discover. There are nearly a hundred breweries in California, far too many to take in on a single trip. That shouldn't stop you from trying. Maybe it's the sunshine, or the sea, or the good vibes from the Golden State's surfer days and Beatnik nights, but California has always been an inspiring place to travel and, now more than ever, it's one of the world's finest places to drink delectable craft-brewed beer.

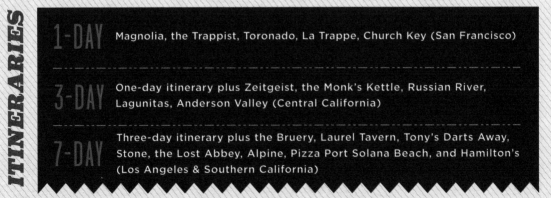

ITINERARIES

1-DAY Magnolia, the Trappist, Toronado, La Trappe, Church Key (San Francisco)

3-DAY One-day itinerary plus Zeitgeist, the Monk's Kettle, Russian River, Lagunitas, Anderson Valley (Central California)

7-DAY Three-day itinerary plus the Bruery, Laurel Tavern, Tony's Darts Away, Stone, the Lost Abbey, Alpine, Pizza Port Solana Beach, and Hamilton's (Los Angeles & Southern California)

MAGNOLIA BREWING CO.

1938 Haight St. • San Francisco, CA 94117 • (415) 864-7468
magnoliapub.com • Established: 1997

SCENE & STORY

Some places just get it right. Magnolia, on the corner of Haight and Masonic, is one of them, and should be your first stop in the Haight, for brunch and a breakfast beer. The carefully aged patina of the place (faded paint, antiquely sconces, padded black leather booths) exudes cool, but the menu is generous. Start with the crispy pork belly served with baked beans, fried shallots, and a poached egg. It makes the ideal base for a beer tasting. Owner and founding brewer David McLean's recipes manage to be inventive, fresh, flavorful, and artfully balanced, qualities that can be elusive in the anything-goes world of today's craft beer scene.

PHILOSOPHY

Quirky and classic. Freshness is paramount, and the servers know how to recommend beers to pair with Magnolia's seasonal, market-driven menu.

KEY BEER

Kalifornia Kolsch (4.8% ABV), Dave McLean's take on the northern German classic style, all bright, golden hues and lip-smacking finish. It's the ultimate breakfast beer, as light and bright on the tongue as a good Mimosa. McLean serves it in the proper glass, called a *stange*, or "rod," a slim

1/5 liter (6.8 ounces) that is only .04 inches thick, akin to the heft of a champagne flute, easy (and soon empty) in the hand.

THE CHURCH KEY

1402 Grant Ave. • San Francisco, CA 94133
(415) 986-3511 • Established: 2009

SCENE & STORY

A sly little space in North Beach with exposed brick, understated décor (retro wallpaper inside; no sign outside except the symbol of an old key), and a quiet loft upstairs, the Church Key draws a cool crowd, and its beer menu is one of the smartest in San Francisco. Beer hunters will find rarities they're after, such as Firestone Walker's Oaktoberfest, a barrel-aged *märzen*-style beer (a clean, coppery German style of lager), and an unusual black India Pale Ale from Stone Brewery in San Diego. The bartenders are knowledgeable, but not obnoxiously so, and the music (by DJ, on vinyl) hits the right notes. Should hunger arrive, as it always does, there's a great pizzeria down the block (Golden Boy Pizza; 542 Green St.; 415-982-9738) and the Church Key owners don't mind if you bring it in and eat right there.

PHILOSOPHY

Call it the David Bowie of beer bars. This is the place to find genre-benders that push the envelope in terms of stylistic interpretation, defying easy categorization. And it's stylishly understated, an elusive quality in beer bars.

KEY BEER

Two dollars gets you a "mystery beer," but this is usually a can of bland American lager. Better with your pizza would be the ultra-rare hybrid-style Belgian IPA called XX Bitter from Brasserie De Ranke (6.2% ABV), which has a melony roundness but finishes dry and bitter, with an herbal afterglow.

TORONADO

547 Haight St. • San Francisco, CA 94117
(415) 863-2276 • toronado.com • Established: 1986

SCENE & STORY

Further down the Haight into the Fillmore, Toronado abides. It's been open for over twenty years, and has the dust and clutter to show for it, but what's more important is behind the bar. Or behind the antlers, tap handles, and other ephemera . . . somewhere. Despite its tiny size, you're not likely to find many better, more well thought-out beer lists (including rarities and aged beers) anywhere in California. It's one of those bars that emit a tractor beam for serious beer lovers, and, one day, they find it. Some never seem to leave, growing long beards and huddling over their barley wine with contented grins. True, certain bartenders seem to ignore you if you ask for the wrong beer, or one they don't have. And the crowds, during special cask nights and tastings, resemble a rugby scrum. But in the end it's worth it. Beer lovers the world over know Toronado, and to visit it is to enter into a kind of covenant with them.

PHILOSOPHY

Drink big or go home. All the great Northern, Central, and Southern Californian beer makers are represented here, with special focus on barley wines and other high-alcohol styles. Order with authority.

KEY BEER

Publication, brewed by Vinnie Cilurzo at Russian River in Sonoma County (with input from Toronado founder David "Big Daddy" Keene, among other noted publicans), is a 8% ABV golden ale finished with brettanomyces, resulting in an earthy, funkified hybrid of traditional Belgian *saison* and strong golden ale.

ANCHOR BREWING CO.

1705 Mariposa St. • San Francisco, CA 94107
(415) 863-8350 • anchorbrewing.com • Established: 1896

SCENE & STORY

Founded as Anchor in 1896, this is a shrine for any self-respecting beer pilgrim for one reason: the brew house. It's a thing of exquisite beauty, all gleaming copper kettles and creamy tile work; to tour the facility and see the brewers working in their white work suits (in the un-hippified fashion of traditional German brewers) is to see a true classic in action. Facing closure after a string of half-interested owners from the end of Prohibition to 1965, this brewery found new life in the hands of a young Stanford graduate named Fritz Maytag (great-great grandson of the man who founded Maytag appliance company), who bought it in 1965 and helped kick-start the American craft beer revolution. Anchor is famous, of course, for Anchor Steam Beer, a kind of ale-lager hybrid also known as California Common. There's no steam used in the brewing process; the word refers to the hissing sound old wooden kegs used to make when aging.

Maytag developed several beers before selling the company in 2010, including Old Foghorn, a viscous, almost brandy-like barley wine; a Christmas ale with a secret yearly-changing recipe; and a light, brightly spiced summer wheat beer, among others. He also added a microdistillery, with house-made gin and rye whisky, and tirelessly publicized America's craft brewing revolution.

One of the best brewery tours in America, it's not to be missed.

PHILOSOPHY

Old-world sophistication with quiet, unpretentious skill. Let us hope the new owners, the entrepreneurs who created Skyy Vodka, will do right by its proud heritage.

KEY BEER

Liberty Ale (6% ABV) was first brewed in 1975 to commemorate the ride of Paul Revere. It has a Champagne-like dryness and aromatic, crisp finish that goes well with local foods like Dungeness crab and sourdough bread.

DETOUR ➡ BRIAN HUNT, MOONLIGHT BREWING COMPANY

Windsor, Sonoma County • www.moonlightbrewing.com (no tours or tasting room at present)

Almost as soon as I'd arrived in the Bay Area I began hearing about a man named Brian Hunt of Sonoma County's Moonlight Brewery in the hushed, reverential tones normally reserved for exiled Tibetan leaders. *He doesn't allow visitors. He's like a mad scientist. He brews the best beer in the whole Bay Area. He's really cranky. No one visits Brian Hunt.*

The last statement is basically true. But because I had some help from my friend Sean Paxton, aka the Homebrew Chef, I had the chance to meet the man behind Death & Taxes, a silky 5% ABV black lager on tap in San Francisco's best beer bars. And while I don't recommend driving up his dirt road outside the hamlet of Windsor unless he's expecting you, he's not the crank some had made him out to be.

No indeed. What I found at Moonlight was sort of everything and nothing I'd been expecting, a crucible of California's future brewing ingenuity and a potent symbol of its roots. His brewery, founded in 1992, is tiny, packed improbably to the ceiling of a former tractor barn. Steel tanks called grundies precariously crowd around the kettles and tables strewn with tools and parts.

And in the middle of it all, Hunt—a graduate of UC Davis's fermentation science master's degree program and a self-described dropout from the industrial brewing world—holds court on his creations with a combination of pride and prejudice (toward those who would classify his beers in rigid styles, mainly). He's Moonlight's only full-time employee, and brews about a thousand barrels per year, available in only about seventy-five locations around the Bay Area, which he personally keeps supplied. In any case, we tried his whole repertoire, retiring to a set of Adirondack chairs near some anemic-looking hop trellises. Lambs baa'd in the distance. This was a farm brewery if there ever was one. Hunt's beers were a revelation: some rock solid classic, others wildly inventive, nearly all delicious.

What Hunt is trying to do, in his own cantankerous way, is shake things up. He bristles at the notion his beers can be classified into set styles, scoffing at what he considers hidebound conventions of acceptable brewing norms. He's the guy who stands up during brewing conferences of industry types and asks the probing questions everyone's thinking but don't quite have the guts to ask.

First came the jet black Death & Taxes, which is as light as an American canned lager like Budweiser but vastly more flavorful, bursting with tangy hops and roasted malts. Then we moved on to a spicy, clean Reality Czech and bready Lunatic Lager, another black lager called Bony Fingers, and an IPA-like offering, Twist of Fate California Style Bitter.

But with the next beers Hunt veered into *terra incognita*. Hunt is doing something few brewers in America would ever consider: making completely *unhopped* beers, to test the possibilities of using other plants to spice and balance flavors. It's a bit like attempting to make gin without juniper, but to the 54-year-old provocateur, such rules mean nothing. We tasted his Artemis, an ale spiced with mugwort, bee balm, and wild bergamot that tasted a bit like pencil wood (in a good way). Working For Tips, an ale spiced with redwood needles, was one of those beers you don't forget—ever—and its garnet color had me mesmerized.

By that point I was beginning to believe what I'd heard in all those San Francisco beer bars. We finished with what Hunt called a "Norwegian farmhouse beer" by the name of Uncle Fudd, named for a song lyric Johnny Cash made famous ("The Tennessee Stud"). It's ale made with rye grain and branches of the Thuja tree, a cousin of Western Red Cedar. The result? At that hour of the day, after tasting about a dozen of Hunt's concoctions, my palate was fairly shot. But there was something intangible in that beer, like the others, something compelling, if radically unfamiliar. Maybe, as Hunt might say, it's just moonlight. Who knows what he'll come up with next? This is brewing as alchemy. Hunt's mystic approach, otherworldly skill, and mischievous persona give Moonlight an inescapable aura. Look for it.

LA TRAPPE CAFÉ

800 Greenwich St. • San Francisco, CA 94133
(415) 440-8727 • latrappecafe.com • Established: 2007

SCENE & STORY

Amid the tacky red sauce joints of North Beach, there's a salve for the soul at the corner of Mason and Greenwich: a broad list of good Belgian ales and an array of classic Belgian dishes, like *moules à la bière* and well-made *waterzooi*, a seafood stew made of manila clams, mussels, and shrimp served over a piece of grilled sea bass. Skip the blah upstairs and immediately head to the subterranean bowels for 19 taps of beer and a 250-plus bottle menu, the best possible antidote to Fisherman's Wharf tourist overload. It's also right on the Powell cable car line, for an escape up into Chinatown or up over the hill toward Market Street and the Ferry Building, and some of San Francisco's best beer bars and breweries.

PHILOSOPHY

La Trappe proclaims a zero-tolerance for the plastic kegs some bars and breweries have been using for convenience, believing them to have adverse effects on beer.

KEY BEER

On draft, North Coast La Merle (7.9% ABV) is a Californian take on the Belgian style of saison. The Fort Bragg brewer's version is wheaty and hazy gold with a lemony, slightly herbal kick.

ZEITGEIST

199 Valencia at Dubose • San Francisco, CA 94103
(415) 255-7505 • zeitgeistsf.com • Established: 1986

SCENE & STORY

Zeitgeist is a biker-style dive bar with decaying, red-shingled walls, razor wire fences, and a vista of a highway overpass. On entering, it is normal for most to feel somewhat apprehensive. Then you scan the beer list of more than forty taps, pick out something inordinately good and cheap, and amble outside on a vast patio with picnic-style tables lined up in the gravel. On warm nights the garden fills up with lanky bike messengers, big-bearded musicians, and energetic beer fanatics taking advantage of the reasonable prices and cheap burgers and dogs off the grill.

PHILOSOPHY

Officially, it's "Warm Beer and Cold Women," but it's not all really so bad. Don't take photos, though, of anyone or anything but your own friends. You can get the boot for that.

KEY BEER

Moonlight Death & Taxes Black Beer—inevitably.

★ ★ ★

21st AMENDMENT

563 2nd St. • San Francisco, CA 94107 • (415) 369-0900
21st-amendment.com • Established: 2000

SCENE & STORY

It would be all too easy to dismiss this brewery on the basis that they make a popular canned beer intentionally laden with chunks of watermelon and contract brew some of their beer (in general, this means using excess capacity in other companies' breweries rather than brew and ship from a single location to save money). But freewheeling founders Nico Freccia and Shaun O'Sullivan—who met in a brewing class at UC Davis—are producing a whole range of great beers in cans, and their huge, loft-like brewpub and beer garden complex in San Francisco's South Park area (south of Market Street, a couple of blocks from the San Francisco Giants Stadium) is the kind of place anyone would feel at home drinking some flavorful, expertly made beers.

PHILOSOPHY

Freedom to brew. Named for the constitutional amendment that abolished Prohibition, 21st Amendment embodies good-natured fun, and the cans (their only packaging) have inspired names and label art.

KEY BEER

21st Amendment Back in Black IPA combines the evergreen pine of ample hops with the dark cocoa and coffee flavors (and onyx hue) of darkly roasted barley. Also known as Cascadian Dark Ale and Black IPA, this style—India Black Ale—is the latest brewing to be recognized by the Association of Brewers, and in 2010, 21st Amendment released the first year-round version available in cans, their chosen packaging. It's got all the vintage attitude of AC/DC's Bon Scott in his prime, but not so much bite you can't have more than one.

THE ALEMBIC BAR

1725 Haight St. • San Francisco, CA 94117
(415) 666-0822 • alembicbar.com • Established: 2007

SCENE & STORY

The Alembic isn't a beer bar per se, but it is the brainchild of Magnolia's David McLean, so it has a considered list and the décor—a warm, dark, enveloping interior and exposed-bulb lighting—to go with it. San Franciscans have come to expect nothing less from the hirsute Deadhead-turned-craft-beer-lover, who has been working on a brewery project in the Dogpatch neighborhood as well (to alleviate shortages of beer and lighten crowds, which may have the opposite effect). The Alembic has ten taps and thirty bottled selections, many hard-to-find-Belgians, and high-end gastropub fare like sweetbreads, duck kebabs, and foie gras.

PHILOSOPHY

Neo-nineteenth-century urban chic meets locavore food and drink.

KEY BEER

Beer cocktails have been around for a long time now, but recently have been getting more attention. Most interesting for beer lovers here is a pair of cocktails using beer: the Vice Grip, a mixture of coffee-flavored rum liqueur and red wine topped with foam made from Marin Brewing Company's Point Reyes Porter, a smooth, rich sipper; or the tart-sweet Pale Horse, made with cachaça, lemon, and caramelized pale ale syrup.

THE MONK'S KETTLE

3141 16th St. • San Francisco, CA 94103 • (415) 865-9523
monkskettle.com • Established: 2007

SCENE & STORY

Monk's has something of the classic beer bar feel—dark woods, low light, sparkling clean glassware—but the menu is tuned in to the "delights and prejudices" of ambitious farm-to-table cooking more than most (to borrow a phrase from the title of one of James Beard's classic books). Expect house-cured ham and hand-ground sausage, braised pork belly and beef cheek, and suggested menu pairings from the 24 tap, 180 bottle list, with a special stash of vintage beers stored in a temperature-controlled cellar ($25 to $60 and up, depending on size and year).

PHILOSOPHY

Seasonality is everything: the small, producer-driven beer list morphs with the calendar, just like the heirloom fruits and vegetables.

KEY BEER

Burning Oak Lager, a German-style black lager of 5.2% ABV from Linden Street Brewery in Oakland, is nearly opaque, with notes of char and smoke mingled with a faint sweetness and light spicy hops.

THE TRAPPIST

460 8th St. • Oakland, CA 94607 • (510) 238-8900
thetrappist.com • Established: 2007

SCENE & STORY

Sometimes the best bars are in the most unlikely places. Just a short hop east across the bay on the BART train delivers you right down the block from The Trappist. Despite the somewhat forlorn downtown Oakland location, it's the kind of bar you'd plan a vacation around. You'll feel it when you walk through the "front bar" door and enter a narrow space with exposed brick, gorgeous dark wood trim, white and black tile floors, and vintage lighting. Then you consider the 28 rotating taps, with another 100 to 130 bottled selections. Once you have a beer in hand, it's time to wander back past barrels on end (ersatz tables), the stained glass doors leading to the bathrooms, and into the warmly lit "back bar," with deep green trim, wainscoted ceiling, and a lovely old bar of its own.

Back in front there's a line of smiling faces at the bar, and perhaps a great California band's song playing—the rootsy anthem "Home" by Edward Sharpe and the Magnetic Zeros on a recent visit—and you realize this is exactly where you want to be.

PHILOSOPHY

Belgian beer, speakeasy style.

KEY BEER

Moonlight's Reality Czeck, a 4.8% ABV Pilsner, which may not be Belgian style but it's very rare and very good, like this bar.

WINE COUNTRY

ANDERSON VALLEY BREWING CO.

17700 Hwy, 253 • Boonville, CA 95415
(707) 895-2337 • avbc.com • Established: 1987

SCENE & STORY

By all means if you get the chance, "jape" on down to the verdant farm-country town of Boonville to enjoy one of America's most distinctive breweries. Jape? Yep. That's the word for "drive" in Boontling, the folk language of this old farming community, said to have been developed by isolated farmers in the area's early sheep and hop fields. Few use the dialect now, but you might be able to find some locals to teach some choice phrases over some *bahl hornin* ("good drinking") at Anderson Valley Brewing. The partially solar-powered brewery itself is a down-to-earth affair, quaint and unpretentious, located on a farm with its own well, livestock, tasting room, and 18-hole Frisbee golf course. But inside the brewery are some of the most beautiful brewing kettles in the United States, polished to a mirror finish, and tours are a popular primer for the twelve-tap tasting room. In 2011 the brewery celebrated the fifteenth annual Legendary Boonville Beer Fest (held at the Mendocino County Fairgrounds), with over fifty California breweries and thousands of thirsty fans.

PHILOSOPHY

Traditional, unpasteurized brewing using well water rich in bicarbonates, pristine practices in the brew house, and a sense of humor everywhere outside it.

KEY BEER

With the soaring ascent of IPAs and Belgian-style beers over the last few years, an uncommon but essential beer style has slipped off the radar: the humble amber. This is too bad. Unpasteurized and never sterile-filtered, AVBC's flagship Amber (5.8% ABV and brewed under the watchful eye of respected industry veteran Fal Allen) has a lively kick and caramel-kissed smoothness, not to mention a glowing garnet color that's as attractive as the copper kettles inside the brewery. And don't miss the mahogany-hued Brother David's Double, a rich and malty Belgian-style ale melding cavalcades of malt flavor with a bracing 9% ABV.

★ ★ ★

DETOUR → THE RUSSIAN (RIVER) REVOLUTION

If there is one brewery that defines the changing American craft beer landscape of late 2011, it is Russian River, led by the affable Vinnie Cilurzo and a lineup stretching the parameters of American tastes for beer.

The son of winemaker parents, Cilurzo could have his own winery by now, a patch of heaven near Temecula, California, where he worked in the cellar during harvests as a boy. "Pretty much all I've done in life is fermentation," he says. But it wasn't winemaking that got him excited during his college years. It was brewing beer.

By 1997 Cilurzo had brewed enough in his free time to score a job running Korbel Champagne Cellars' fledgling beer division, Russian River. But soon Korbel, like so many other Johnny-come-latelies, facing a looming industry-wide downturn, planned to drop the line. Cilurzo decided to buy the division out, firm in the belief that beers like Blind Pig, a 6.5% ABV Double IPA he'd come up with in 1994—the nation's first such concoction—would find its fans. "We didn't do any market research," he claims. "We just believed passion would carry us through." Cilurzo scraped up investors and reopened Russian River in 2004. Good move: Soon the craft beer market had returned to double-digit growth and Cilurzo was dominating prestigious tastings. Today fans of his best-known beer, Pliny the Younger (a resinous double IPA of 11% ABV, brewed once a year) line up—quite literally by the hundreds, for days—to take home a few bottles before it's gone.

Aside from Pliny, most of Cilurzo's beers are fermented in French oak barrels for up to two years. They're fermented using wild yeasts and rogue bacteria (that give the beer funky flavors more commonly found in rare cheeses), then wire- and cork-topped to create an ironclad seal for vigorous natural carbonation in the bottle.

And they're incredibly rich, complex, and drinkable. But his mad scientist approach—he adds volatile bacteria like *Lactobacillus* and *Pediococcus* to certain creations—has its risks. *Brettanomyces*, the wild yeast strain with a leathery, earthy-sour profile used in certain Russian River beers and some of Cilurzo's Belgian inspirations, can run amok, altering fermenters, pumps, and hoses for good, and must be carefully quarantined. "It's like playing with fire," Cilurzo says. "You know how a dog can sniff out a person who's afraid? With *Brett*, bugs, and critters, if you're afraid of it, it's going to bite."

These days Cilurzo is busy overseeing the new Russian River brew house, a $2.5 million showpiece that tripled capacity, but one that, at a maximum capacity of 7,000 barrels a year, keeps Russian River firmly in rebel territory. "I don't think we'll ever be mainstream," he says, "but I never say never."

725 4th St. • Santa Rosa, CA 95404 • (707) 545-2337
russianriverbrewing.com • Established: 1997

SCENE & STORY

The little brewpub in downtown Santa Rosa where Russian River sells its beers directly and a vast menu of Italian-American pub grub isn't long on atmosphere, and you can't tour the brewery (for now at least), but it is still a top stop for beer travelers in wine country. There are fifteen beers on tap, eight bottles to go, occasional live music performances and other beer-related events, and dependable crowds on weekend nights. Lunchtime and Sundays are quieter; order the $15 sampler immediately to taste everything.

PHILOSOPHY

Belgian beers and a laid-back West Coast attitude.

KEY BEER

Sour, fruit-enhanced Belgian-style beers run the gamut from offering a nice, mild, back-of-the-tongue zing to the sort of full-on, face-contorting shock human taste buds seem designed to avoid. Supplication (7% ABV) is complex, woody, tart, and fleetingly sweet, infused with the juice of whole sour cherries while aging in pinot noir barrels. It's one of those beers referred to as a "life-changer."

1280 N. McDowell Blvd. • Petaluma, CA 94954
(707) 769-4495 • lagunitas.com • Established: 1993

SCENE & STORY

Suddenly, Lagunitas is everywhere. In 2011, the makers of some of America's cleanest-tasting and most distinctive Pilsner and IPA announced $9.5 million plans to *quadruple* capacity to around 600,000 bbl/yr, putting them in the league of Boston Beer Company (Sam Adams), Sierra Nevada, and Goose Island. In the meantime, for the last two years their headquarters on the outskirts of sleepy Petaluma has turned into a circus—literally.

For the "Beer Circus," a series of raucous parties held in the spacious new beer garden outside the brewery, the fun-loving owners have gone more Burning Man than Bozo, with crazed looking stilt-walkers, burlesque, the "R-Rated Marching Band," and a bondage demonstration for good measure (all fairly tame, actually, and the beer garden is understated and quite stylish). Should you miss the big top (the parties always sell out in advance), visit for a brewery tour and then beers on a warm night under the stars with live music (roots, rock, and reggae, of course, offered about five nights a week during the warmer months). And with the Bay Area, redwood forests, and the Point Reyes National Sea Shore within easy reach, Lagunitas makes a great place to cap off an idyllic Golden State adventure. Brewery walking tours are free Wednesday through Friday at 3 and 5 p.m.

PHILOSOPHY

Hippietarian with a great sense of humor. Amid the Great Recession of 2010 and 2011 their contribution to gross national happiness was a protest beer called Wilco Tango Foxtrot, or WTF for short, "a malty, robust, jobless recovery ale." Back in 2005, founder Tony Magee (a sometime reggae band member) was hit with a potentially ruinous one-year license suspension for an employee caught smoking some of California's largest cash crop on-site during a sponsored "420" party (the cops were undercover for weeks). On appeal, the sentence was cut to three weeks, and Lagunitas used the ban time to install a massive new bottling line.

Their dues to society paid, they later dared the regulators to approve a new beer called Undercover Investigation Shut-Down Ale, printed with some choice anti-establishment Benjamin Franklin verbiage and pointed mockery of the agents who had been unable to get anyone to sell them any pot—it was, naturally, always offered for free.

KEY BEER

Lagunitas Pils Czech Style Pilsner (6.2% ABV) is on the verge of becoming a new standard, a go-to beer suited for all occasions. And it may have a goofy name, but their Sonoma Farmhouse Hop Stoopid Ale (8% ABV) is a serious beer in the Double IPA style (aka Imperial IPA), with cavalcades of tangy West Coast hops "for those mornings when you have to cut right to the chase."

Chico

SIERRA NEVADA BREWING CO.

1075 E. 20th St. • Chico, CA 95928 • (530) 893-3520
sierranevada.com • Established: 1980

SCENE & STORY

These days Sierra Nevada's beers are easy to find, but not long ago, out in the fertile farm country of the northeastern Sacramento Valley in Chico, home brewer Ken Grossman—on an obsessive quest for the perfect pale ale—was the only one drinking them. While roasting his grains at home, jury-rigging brewing equipment out of fish tanks and washer-dryers (for an ill-fated experimental malting operation), and squeaking out rent as a bike shop repairman, he dreamt of bigger things: real brewing kettles, the copper kind. He had a long way to go and little money. In 1976 he opened a home-brew store "to feed my hobby, really," Grossman recalls.

Grossman doggedly kept home brewing, keeping meticulous notes, dreaming big. Inspired by Anchor and New Albion, he wrote a business plan with a partner in 1978, then hit up the banks, who weren't the least bit interested. To get started, "I spent all my savings, all my business partner's savings, and the savings bonds my grandfather had given me for school," Grossman recalls. Finally, with the help of family and friends, Sierra Nevada (named after the mountain range), brewed its first batch, a stout; the first pale came a few days later. (A dozen batches went down the drain until he arrived at a brew he was happy with.) And with his young daughter in the passenger seat, Grossman delivered the first pallet of Sierra Nevada beer from the back of a beat-up one-ton '57 Chevy pickup.

The pale ale he labored so long to get right struck a chord, and today, the piney, balanced brew is widely imitated, and one of the two best-selling craft beers in the United States, next to Samuel Adams Boston Lager. Grossman, who was fifty-seven in the end of 2011, got those gleaming copper kettles, to say the least. Production stands around 765,000 bbl (just under 24 million gallons) a year for a variety of styles, all of them excellent, and the awards wall is running out of space.

Tours take in lovely *trompe l'oeil* murals in the brew house from a glassy elevated platform and other marvels no other American brewery can boast, like one of the largest private solar arrays in the country, utilizing heliotropic cells. There is nothing unconsidered, dusty, or out of place; the scope is awe inspiring, and the rows of 25,000 gallon conditioning tanks lined up in majestic symmetry are a sight to behold.

Today, the operations take up fifty acres, with estate-grown hops and a 35-acre barley field. The taproom and restaurant has its own organic herb and vegetable garden the size of a Walmart. The brewery's own cows are fed partly on healthful spent grain from the brewing process, and the restaurant and taproom cook over almond wood fires. The bright and comfortable eatery is full of art nouveau stylings, stained glass, and brilliant copper trim work. And no matter what beer you try, from the lightest Summerfest lager to the Estate line (using all ingredients from the property) and high-octane barley wines and collaboration beers, the beers are all superbly crafted (try the too-often overlooked Porter, for example). After a bite, visitors can catch concerts in the state-of-the-art concert venue, or catch a ride on a kooky (but highly enjoyable) pedal-powered, stereo-equipped rolling tap-mobile. It's a brewmaster's dream come true.

Of a company that does all this for its fans without spending a dime on shameless TV advertising, there's little left to say but "Thanks. What are you brewing next?"

PHILOSOPHY

Pioneering, eco-conscious, and consistently delicious, Sierra Nevada's beers are made with fanatical attention to detail and a generous, family-driven spirit.

KEY BEER

The beer that changed everything is Sierra Nevada Pale Ale. It's still brewed with whole Magnum, Perle, and pungent Cascade hop flowers, giving it a satisfying bite and grassy, floral nose. It's easy to forget that it's bottle conditioned, meaning each individual bottle is carbonated by means of tiny additions of yeast and brewer's sugar—an insanely difficult thing to pull off on such a large scale.

★ ★ ★

FIRESTONE WALKER BREWERY

1400 Ramada Dr. • Paso Robles, CA 93446 B (805) 238-2556
firestonebeer.com • Established: 1996

SCENE & STORY

Run by former Marine Corps captain Adam Firestone and his brother-in-law, British expat David Walker (a former high-tech entrepreneur), Firestone is located in somewhat of a flavorless industrial area just outside town. There is a good-sized tasting room and gift shop with dark wooden tables, but the most interesting action is amid the fifty-barrel brew house and its extensive barrel program; you'll want a tour. There's also a restaurant in Buellton (near Santa Barbara) with high-end fare and fresh Firestone beers.

PHILOSOPHY

Experimental yet restrained. The brewery uses a variation on something called the Burton Union System, a Rube Goldbergian contraption developed by the British that links oak barrels with a yeast-collecting network of troughs, resulting in extraordinarily soft, smooth beer. Marston's, in England's Burton-on-Trent, is the classic example of a brewery making beer in this fashion, and explains it all by means of a three-hour tour. You won't need quite that much time at Firestone Walker, and the beer at the end is more interesting across the board.

KEY BEER

The pale ale has been around so long it's almost retro. But don't pass it up. Building on the tradition of great California pale ales started by Sierra Nevada, Firestone Walker's Pale 31 has racked up scores of accolades. It combines the subtlety of a great British ale with the fragrant bite of American hops craft beer lovers have come to expect.

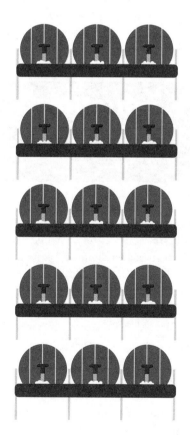

Until recently L.A. (like New York), was a craft beer Mojave Desert. But thanks to the arrival of several craft breweries plus some beer-savvy chefs, a nascent beer culture is changing the entire timbre of the L.A. food-and-drink scene. Angelenos (like Portlanders, Denverites, and even New Yorkers before them) have embraced craft beers, all the better when made with locally foraged ingredients like so many snap peas, heirloom pork bellies, or pinot noirs. Instead of the coolly manufactured glam of, say, Spago, a more communal, unshaven, nose-to-tail chic is all the rage now.

Food carts are going upscale; local coffee roasters and farmer's markets are multiplying. And yet, there are only a few local breweries—so far. In a city with 9.8 million people (compared to, say, Portland, Oregon, which has 583,000 people and around 35 breweries), it's only a matter of time before Tinseltown gets the beer bug in a bigger way.

BOUCHON

235 N. Canyon Dr. • Beverly Hills, CA 90210
(310) 271-9910 • bouchonbistro.com • Established: 2009

SCENE & STORY

Order *beer* in a chic Thomas Keller Beverly Hills bistro? Absolutely. "A beer mood is different than a wine mood," explains Head Sommelier Alex Weil, adding that recently the restaurant added two proprietary beers, Blue Apron and White Apron, from New York's Brooklyn Brewery and Santa Rosa's Russian River, respectively. "A lot of bistro food is based in a beer culture," says Weil, a novice home brewer himself. "We have dishes like the classic *moules frites* or fried green tomatoes with shrimp and corn relish and a tomato salsa verde. We cook with beer all the time here," he adds. What's more, customers are also starting to order beers from the three-tap, ten-bottle list based on

the reputation of brewers, rather than saying they'd like something, say, light or not too hoppy. "People are gravitating toward the producers," Weil explains.

PHILOSOPHY

Visionary. Says Weil, "We still have the question, 'don't you have anything normal?' But we're not wanting to serve 'regular' beer. We want to push the envelope. We're going to lightly force change through the absence of choice."

KEY BEER

To start a meal, try White Apron, a dry, herbal, aromatic pilsner style made by Russian River (5.5% ABV). When it's time for rich meats or cheeses, select the 7.2% ABV Blue Apron, Brooklyn Brewery's offering, formerly only available at Per Se in New York and redolent of dark fruits (dates, figs), orange peel, and spices.

PROFILE: MARK JILG
CRAFTSMAN
BREWING COMPANY
1260 Lincoln Ave., No. 800 • Pasadena, CA 91105 • www.craftsmanbrewing.com

Pasadena's Mark Jilg is as likely to expound on the paradox of being an artisan brewer in the middle of Tinseltown as he is to offer an impromptu lecture on the tendency of hops to spontaneously combust (true story). About fifteen years ago, Jilg left his job as an analyst for NASA's Jet Propulsion Laboratory to make beer instead, founding Craftsman in 1995. Today, his tiny brewery, in an unassuming industrial park about 40 miles from Disneyland, produces beers that are defiantly pushing the outer limits, too, with Valencia orange rind, Cabernet grapes, white sage, and *Brettanomyces*. "There are a lot of people that are focused on food culture here, savoring wine and so on. But they haven't considered beer, so when they taste something like mine, it blows their mind," he told me.

His best-selling beer reflects craft brewing's return to America's pre-Prohibition beer landscape: 1903 is a 5.9% ABV lager using a proportion of corn in the mash (as lagers of that era did, adding body and a certain corn flakes–like flavor profile), bittered with Nugget hops and finished with late additions of Mt. Hood to add a nice delicate hop presentation and aroma.

Jilg doesn't have a taproom or take visitors—it's basically a one-man show in a 2,500-square-foot space—so look for the beer on tap at good L.A. beer bars like Laurel Tavern and Lucky Baldwin's in Pasadena. Jilg hasn't started bottling, but if he does, the whole operation ought to blast off. His delivery van may be a green 1946 M-15 Studebaker, but the beer is next generation.

LAUREL TAVERN

11938 Ventura Blvd. • Studio City, CA 91614
(818) 506-0777 • laureltavern.net • Established: 2008

SCENE & STORY

With its simple black façade, hardwood floors, exposed brick walls, pressed tin details, and L-shaped bar, this San Fernando Valley bar looks almost too perfect—like a movie set instead of a real, live, breathing beer bar. But it's definitely the real deal. With sky blue metal stools along the bar, Edison lighting, and an artful food menu, there's little not to like. The short but sweet menu is based around beer-friendly foods like prosciutto and burrata, chorizo fondue, roast marrowbones, a bratwurst plate, and a famed burger with white cheddar, arugula, and caramelized onions. As for the beers (sixteen on tap, no bottles), most are California taps, with a pair or three for East Coast treats like Allagash and Dogfish Head. Word to the wise: avoid weekend nights, or come in very early to get in position for the best people-watching.

PHILOSOPHY

Craft beer gets its SAG card.

KEY BEER

Craftsman Heavenly Hefeweizen for starters (4.7 % ABV), which has the lively spice and ample heft of authentic German hefeweizen. "I think it's completely misunderstood in America," says Craftsman brewer Mark Jilg, citing Widmer and Pyramid brewing companies by example, whose hefeweizens are markedly less spicy. "We're going for a dry, crisp beer, with a clovey, banana-like estery palate. And we encourage people to lose the lemon slice."

TONY'S DARTS AWAY

1710 W. Magnolia Blvd. • Burbank, CA 91506
(818) 253-1710 • tonysda.com • Established: 2010

SCENE & STORY

This dive bar reborn as an eco-friendly, full-on craft beer palace has forty taps of hard-to-find beers and a no-bottle, no-can policy—the conservation ethic runs deep. The main menu item is gourmet sausages (with vegan options, too); beers are organized into IPA and "Not IPA." Both categories are filled with exceptional beers from the likes of Stone, Alpine, AleSmith, Bear Republic, and Russian River. In 2011, founder and owner Tony Yanow organized the "colLAboration" series of pop-up beer gardens around L.A. with Verdugo and the Surly Goat's Ryan Sweeney, among others, bringing craft beer to the streets of Los Angeles. A new classic bar—and likely, a new tradition—was born.

PHILOSOPHY

"All Craft, All Draught, All California."

KEY BEER

Stone's Smoked Chipotle Porter (6% ABV), which is sable black and laced with spicy, rich notes of pepper and smoke.

THE SURLY GOAT

7929 Santa Monica Blvd. • West Hollywood, CA 90046
(323) 650-4628 • surlygoat.com • Established: 2010

SCENE & STORY

When you tire of dodging the beautiful people who cram the streets of Hollywood, sipping beer under the mounted head of a mountain goat named Gus starts to sounds a whole heck of a lot better. Luckily, this nearly unmarked beer bar has a sweet rotating list, solicitous bartenders, leather seating, and a couple of old arcade games and a foosball table to keep things on the lighter side. There are even a few screens with a rotation of retro movies (*Star Wars, Ferris Bueller's Day Off*); if you get hungry, you can bring in food from the BBQ place next door, to name one option. There are twenty-seven taps and a cask beer, with genuinely rare bottles to choose from as well (ask for the leather-bound list). This is a spin-off of local beer maven Ryan Sweeney, who opened Verdugo Bar and helped propel Los Angeles's interest in craft beer into what it is today: a genuine movement.

PHILOSOPHY

Not particularly surly, really. Just remember the usual Friday and Saturday night caveat—you might have to wait to get in.

KEY BEER

Sour beers are showing up all over the place, taking beer drinkers on mouth-puckering rides of various intensity. Marrón Acidifié is the result of a rare collaboration between Florida's Cigar City and the Bruery in Orange County, and the Surly Goat has put it on draft. Dark with whiffs of roasted malt, woody vanilla, balsamic, and cranberry, it's tart—but not eye-wateringly so.

VERDUGO BAR

3408 Verdugo Rd. • Los Angeles, CA 90065
(323) 257-3408 • verdugobar.com • Established: 2008

SCENE & STORY

A complete renovation of a 1930s bar known for being quite sketchy—in a neighborhood that still is, so heads up—the Verdugo Bar has no windows and just a simple old glass, black lettered sign-light reading "cocktails." It's not much to look at, but then you walk inside to its serpentine, dimly lit bar, low couches, DJ in a booth, and epic beer list. There's a California-centric twenty-two-tap row, eighty-five bottles, and one cask to choose from, all served at the proper temperature and in the right glass, never sloshed on the bar. Thanks to L.A. craft beer scene maker Ryan Sweeney, a Certified Cicerone (one step down from beer's equivalent to Master of Wine), things are looking even better already.

Once you've got your beer, step outside to the patio and picnic table area. On the best weekend afternoons at 3 p.m., you'll find a "patio session" in progress: as the DJ spins, a chilled-out crowd lounges in the sun enjoying some of the city's best gourmet food carts like the famous Grill 'Em All (burgers) and Danky's Döners (kebabs and sandwiches).

PHILOSOPHY

Beer, booze, and beats.

KEY BEER

Stone Cali-Belgique IPA (6.9% ABV). This San Diego-brewed, Belgian-accented ale has the best of both worlds, with a peach-like graininess and citrus-y tang of three varieties of West Coast hops plus the peppery earthiness of Belgian yeast.

BLUE PALMS BREWHOUSE

6124 Hollywood Blvd. • Los Angeles, CA 90028 • (323) 464-2337
bluepalmsbrewhouse.com • Established: 2008

SCENE & STORY

While Hollywood these days is full of reality show losers, tourists, and plastic surgeons, it's not *all* bad. Eight blocks from the Walk of Fame and adjacent to the historic Henry Fonda Theater is one of the city's best beer bars, with a strong, constantly rotating, and California-focused tap list of twenty-four (plus ninety bottles and a cask), a tradition for brewmaster appearances and beer dinners, and a good and none-too-pricey food menu. It's got Prohibition-era terrazzo floors, high ceilings in ruddy red, wide wooden beams, oversize mirrors, and some living palms, giving it a nice touch of Old Hollywood ambiance.

PHILOSOPHY

Retro look, today's beer.

KEY BEER

Sudwerk Lager, a German *helles*-style beer from Davis, California, is a classic choice—light, grassy, grainy, and bright on the tongue but not without a malty backbone (4.9% ABV).

EAGLE ROCK BREWERY

3065 Roswell St. • Los Angeles, CA 90065 • (323) 257-7866
eaglerockbrewery.com • Established: 2009

SCENE & STORY

Jeremy Raub, a former film music editor, and his father, Steve, an ex-Navy man and dedicated home brewer who taught his son to brew, overcame a mountain of red tape delays in order to get their 15 bbl brew house open in 2009, making it the first brewery in Los Angeles proper in some sixty years. Its ultra-clean, organized taproom has been busy ever since, giving tours (Sundays only, 12 to 6 p.m.). As at Verdugo, food trucks are often on hand to provide the sustenance.

PHILOSOPHY

"Beer for the People" is the slogan, and the Raubs play with a neo-revolutionary theme in beer names like Manifesto and Solidarity. The beers are technically vegan (in avoiding fining, or clarifying, agents from animal products), and run the gamut of styles, from English mild to American wild, with some experimental ingredients (rose petals).

KEY BEER

Solidarity Dark Mild (3.8% ABV) is a light, chocolaty, grainy-tasting British session beer, meaning it's low in alcohol and meant for sustained periods of beer drinking without intoxication.

THE BRUERY

715 Dunn Way • Placentia, CA 92870 • (714) 996-6258
bruery.com • Established: 2008

THE BRUERY PROVISIONS

143 N. Glassell • Orange, CA 92866 • (714) 997-2337
brueryprovisions.com • Established: 2010

SCENE & STORY

A few years ago, Patrick Rue was reluctantly headed for a law career, but the trouble was, beer brewing was the only thing that held his attention. With his nose buried in a home brewing book his wife bought from a 99-cent bookstore, Rue was soon blowing off homework to craft dozens, even hundreds of batches. "I'd brew almost every weekend and during the week when I was 'studying,'" Rue recalls. In other words, he was preparing for a different kind of bar.

After taking a massive leap of faith with family and personal investments, one of the more successful American breweries of the last decade was born. Rue and head brewer Tyler King hew mainly to Belgian brewing traditions, which, generally speaking, tend to produce beers that are spicier, more intensely flavored, and higher in alcohol content than their American counterparts, and often bear the tannins and acids from wood barrels and wild yeasts. They're wild, but often delicious and food friendly. The hype surrounding the beers has been surprisingly loud, cranking up even higher after a dominant showing in the 2010 World Beer Cup in two hotly contested categories with sixty-eight runners up in all.

Visitors to the brewery in Placentia encounter a bland exterior (with a taco truck if you're lucky), but inside, there's a brighter space, with yellow and sage walls and a small tasting bar area next to fermenters and stacks of oak barrels. This is also the site of beer release parties, like one in October 2009 he might prefer to forget. The plan was to release 2,400 bottles of an onyx-black, 19.5% ABV, bourbon-barrel-aged stout called Black Tuesday, and seven hundred people showed up to buy it, causing a minor melee when supplies ran out, which left about seventy-five people empty handed. "It was insane," Rue recalls. "We heard some people flew in to get it. It's almost embarrassing." The 2010 event was a somewhat smoother affair, only crashing the website.

The Bruery Provisions in Orange is a bottle shop with thirty taps and around five hundred bottled selections to choose from, along with $3 tasting flights—a great deal. There's a large tasting area, and busy calendar of events (talks, tastings, classes, etc.), but beer isn't the only draw: There's also a dizzying array of cheese, charcuterie, chocolates, coffees, olive oils, marmalades, and other edibles.

PHILOSOPHY

Unorthodox. Since its inception, The Bruery has released around eighty-five beers conjured out of such ingredients as Thai basil, pasilla chiles, and purple mangosteen, some of the concoctions only dimly recognizable as beers to the layperson. To make his award-winning Autumn Maple, Rue roasts yams on a barbecue until they are soft and sugary, then smashes them up and adds them to a mash tun, the brewer's tank used to extract fermentable sugars that normally come entirely from grain.

KEY BEER

Orchard White and Black Tuesday have made the biggest splashes, but try the Humulus Lager to really shock your expectations. It's a superstrong lager (in the bock territory, at 7.2% ABV), aromatically hopped like an IPA.

Southern California & San Diego County

That an area often associated with surfing and skateboarding should turn out to be one of the country's top craft beer destinations comes as a surprise to many. But it's absolutely true: There are more than thirty top-tier brewing companies in the entire Southern California region now, and dozens of excellent beer bars. From crisp, refreshing lagers to pungent IPAs, Belgian ales, and even porters and stouts smoked with chipotle and other peppers, the brewers' bold creativity stems from the area's lack of brewing history. There are no expectations to live up to and no pressure to follow rules.

GREEN FLASH BREWING CO.

6550 Mira Mesa Blvd • San Diego, CA 92121
(858) 622-0085 • greenflashbrew.com • Established: 2002

SCENE & STORY

In the tradition of other San Diego County breweries, Green Flash could not be in a more flavorless location, an industrial warehouse space. No matter—even if the walls are adorned with little more than dry-erase boards, the beers are anything but bland, and it's busy every weekend starting at 4 p.m., when space is made available on the bottling floor (Fridays 4 to 8 p.m; Saturdays 12 to 5 p.m; Sundays 12 to 4 p.m.). Standing around tasting amid the tanks and malt mill and bottling line, it's easy to chat and mingle with other beer lovers who have made the trek.

PHILOSOPHY

Hoptopian. The best-known beers of Green Flash are by turns pungent, dank, grassy, piney, and bitter. If that's your thing, this is your place. Lately though, the brewery has been doing a number of Belgian-style beers, including Bière De L'Amitié, a 9.5% ABV collaboration strong pale ale with Brasserie St. Feuillien in southwestern Belgium.

KEY BEER

West Coast IPA gets most of the love, but the fiery Hop Head Red (6% ABV), a copper-hued amber dry hopped with Amarillo, is a fun beer to drink and would go well with pepperoni pizza.

PORT BREWING CO./THE LOST ABBEY

155 Mata Way, No. 104 • San Marcos, CA 92069
(800) 918-6816 • lostabbey.com • Established: 2006

SCENE & STORY

Port Brewing Company and its Belgian-beer-influenced Lost Abbey line of beers are produced under the watchful eye of award-winning brewer Tomme Arthur, founding brewer of Pizza Port, and one of the first American craft brewers to employ barrel aging. The operation is based in an industrial space on the northern perimeter of San Diego County (one that used to house Stone, which outgrew the space and moved a few miles down the road).

One of San Diego county's biggest beer traveler draws, Lost Abbey (as most refer to it now) has a spacious tasting room stacked high with oak barrels and kegs on end with grain or brewers' sugar sacks for cushions at the 42-foot bar. In just six years, it's won over a hundred medals and awards in the competitive craft brewing world and become a real draw for travelers who come to taste, trade stories, and leave with rare bottles in tow. On the weekend there are free informal guided tours, but the main thing to do is sample. There are twenty taps at all times with at least sixteen different beers available to take out in bottles. The scene has real energy and buzz. "It's like Sonoma County in the late 1970s," says tasting room manager Sage Osterfeld, who grew up in a winemaking family. He walked into Tomme Arthur's brewhouse one day and decided to stay for good.

PHILOSOPHY

Belgian-style beers with cork-and-wire cage and a medieval theme running through the label art and brew names.

KEY BEER

Ask for Duck Duck Gooze, a wild yeast beer of 5.5% ABV made of a blend from young and older barrel-aged ales. But it's extremely rare, so you might have better luck with Bourbon Barrel Aged Angel's Share, a beer on the other, less acidic, but no less interesting end of the flavor spectrum (12% ABV). In distillers' parlance, the "angel's share" is the proportion of precious spirit lost to evaporation in the barrel. This barrel-aged brew marries the woody, vanilla-laced smokiness of a classic sipping bourbon to a rich, port-like beer.

PIZZA PORT SOLANA BEACH

135 N. Highway 101 • Solana Beach, CA 92075
(858) 481-7332 • pizzaport.com • Established: 1987

SCENE & STORY

There are now three other Pizza Port locations (San Clemente, Carlsbad, and Ocean Beach), but this one—founded by siblings Vince "Vinny" and Gina Marsaglia, who sold its first beer in 1992—is the original, smallest, and to many, the best. Located in an unassuming stretch of the Pacific Coast Highway with the beach close enough to smell but not see, Pizza Port combines two very elemental things: great pizza and great beer. The inside is cozy and cheerful, and if you sit to the right of the tap row, you can look down into the sunken brewing area to watch the action unfold.

PHILOSOPHY

Pizza and beer, good times are near.

KEY BEER

The rich, dark, and coppery Sharkbite Red (6% ABV) is the big seller here—it goes well with spicy pizza dishes—but try the seasonal as well.

STONE BREWING CO. & WORLD BISTRO

1999 Citracado Pkwy. • Escondido, CA 92029 • (760) 471-4999
stonebrew.com • stoneworldbistro.com • Established: 1996

SCENE & STORY

Founded in San Marcos, Stone moved to its present location in 2006, and it's more or less a Disneyland for beer lovers. First they built a sprawling eco-friendly compound, complete with a natural-boulder-tunnel-like entrance, an acre of gardens, and a huge roof solar array, cutting the power usage considerably. Then there's a chic, glassy, 12,000-square-foot restaurant looking out on the gardens and a patio of reclaimed bricks (with side and outdoor bars, for overflow).

The eatery has a central U-shaped bar area with 32 drafts and 120 bottles from Stone and other excellent domestic and international craft breweries. It's all laid out around an island of boulders and bamboo growing from a bed of river rocks in the center of the room, which has nice old weathered wood tables for a counterpoint. The menu is long, using only local and organic vegetables and breads, hormone-free and natural meats. The spicy duck tacos, made with chile de árbol and the brewery's Levitation Ale-infused barbecue sauce, will require quantities of cold beer close at hand—they're fiery.

PHILOSOPHY

Righteous. Brewing-wise the beers are always well put together, if on the intense side (with notable exceptions). For the most part, Stone Brewing's "extreme" beers are like standard ales in overdrive, with a side dish of attitude. (These are the guys who brought the beer-drinking public "Arrogant Bastard" ale, after all.) Steve Wagner, Stone's brewmaster, has spent years creating radical riffs on traditional styles: aggressively hopped ales fermented to a high alcohol percentage, usually around 7% ABV and sometimes nearly double that. But getting customers soused isn't the point; the point is creating complex layers of flavor through long, robust fermentations with a rich mix of grains and huge amounts of resiny, fresh, green hops.

KEY BEER

Until Levitation Ale came along, the unspoken rule on Stone brews was this: don't drink them before dusk unless you have time for a nap. These beers are tasty; they're also tranquilizing. Like any beer from Stone, Levitation is loaded with grainy, fruity malt flavors and topped off with a sturdy dose of fragrant hops. At 4.4% ABV, though, this is a beer you can have a few of over the course of a Saturday afternoon without a lawyer present.

THE TAP ROOM

1269 Garnet Ave. • Pacific Beach, CA 92109
(858) 274-1010 • sdtaproom.com • Established: 2007

ALESMITH BREWING CO.

9368 Cabot Dr. • San Diego, CA 92126 • (858) 549-9888
alesmith.com • Established: 1995

SCENE & STORY

It's refreshing when a neighborhoody, sports barrish, Fridays-full-of-drunk-people-half-your-age-and-a-DJ bar also happens to have a genuine connoisseur's list. Is the food great? No. But with an impressive, local-heavy tap row of thirty-two handles, this Pacific Beach (PB) taproom is the best in San Diego for local beers, and would make a good stop after hiking Torrey Pines or hitting the waves. You can check the website's "live list" which shows exactly which beers are on on any given day, what percentage of beer is left, and what's on deck.

PHILOSOPHY

Localista, but friendly. Lately the bar has been sponsoring "L.A.B. nights" (Local Art & Beer), bringing together hip young artists and area craft brewers.

KEY BEER

Ballast Point Sculpin IPA, at 7% ABV, is becoming a local standby, with pungent layers of grapefruit and pine needle flavors atop a base of pale, Pilsner-like malt.

★ ★ ★

SCENE & STORY

AleSmith, one of San Diego's early breakout successes—four hundred medals and counting!—has stayed small as others in the area (i.e., Stone) have grown at an incredible rate. But founder Peter Zien is content to keep production where it is (around 1,000 bbl per year), so the little brewery and taproom remain almost a homespun affair, little more than a rectangular room in an industrial park with a walk-in cooler and the brewing tanks off to the side. This is a good thing; beer is the sole focus, and it's no less of a draw for beer travelers (Saturdays get busy). No matter when you seek it out, though, you're likely to meet fellow beer lovers there, who, having trekked from across the country, or even from abroad, are eager try every last beer on offer. There are free tours on the last Saturday of each month; call ahead.

PHILOSOPHY

"Hand Forged" is the MO officially, and it fits nicely with AleSmith, a small, solid operation with consistently high quality in American interpretations of British and Belgian styles, primarily.

KEY BEER

Speedway Stout, at 12% ABV, is already a huge beer, carbon black and dense with coffee, chocolate, and roasted malt flavors. The barrel-aged version takes it to 11, with even deeper notes of vanilla, oak, espresso, and caramel, having lived in wood for a full year.

5401 Linda Vista Rd., Ste. 406 • San Diego, CA 92110
(619) 295-2337 • ballastpoint.com • Established: 1996

SCENE & STORY

Ballast Point Brewing Company, ranked as the top small brewery in the country in 2010, started with a home brewer's dream. Jack White opened his little home brew shop in 1992, and soon a community of home brewers eager to try his beers helped him think even bigger. By 1996, White was ready to install a 15 bbl brew house, and Ballast Point was born. Today there's a newer, larger Ballast Point location, but Homebrew Mart retains the charm (and the original brewing equipment, still in use) of the early days in San Diego's beer revolution.

Brewmaster Colby Chandler is playing around with barrel aging, Belgian-style sour beers, and wild yeasts. These vinous ales overlaid with hints of oak and brandy are blended on site, with production so small-scale that most of these beers are rarely seen outside of San Diego County. Try the full Ballast Point line in the back of the store at the little tasting bar, with the barrel projects available on occasion. It's the best-kept secret for finding—and sharing—beer knowledge in San Diego.

PHILOSOPHY

Beer creates community.

KEY BEER

Ask about the barrel aging projects. And the flowery, tangerine-y Double Dry Hopped Sculpin IPA (7% ABV) offers an aromatic blast of citrus and flowers.

1521 30th St. • San Diego, CA 92192 • (619) 238-5460
hamiltonstavern.com • Established: 2006

SCENE & STORY

Almost end to end, San Diego's 30th Street has turned into a craft beer lover's avenue in recent years, with Hamilton's anchoring the quiet, residential southern reaches near the southeast corner of Balboa Park. Formerly a dive bar known as Sparky's, and site of the oldest liquor license in San Diego (first listed around seventy-five years ago), Hamilton's is the brainchild of owner Scot Blair, who cleaned it out, hung the ceiling with a wild collection of tap handles, and added a sandwich and burger café next door.

There are 28 taps, 150 bottled options, and 2 cask on all times, with a strong focus on California specialties like Russian River, AleSmith, and Firestone Walker, and a few especially interesting choices from small European brewers.

PHILOSOPHY

Come on in. Hamilton's is a friendly neighborhood bar with a superb beer list and great food next door. Herman Hamilton, a teetotaling elderly U.S. Marine who lives in the neighborhood and for whom the bar was named, despite having no taste for drink, is said to have spent a fair amount of time visiting and telling stories with the bearded Blair and his friends, who keep the bar hopping—but seldom slammed to the point of annoyance.

KEY BEER

Brasserie Ellezelloise's Quintine Blonde, an 8% ABV Belgian strong pale ale on the sweet side, with honey, bread, and herbal notes.

ALPINE BEER CO.

2351 Alpine Blvd. • Alpine, CA 91901
(619) 445-2337 • alpinebeerco.com • Established: 1999

SCENE & STORY

From downtown San Diego, it's about a forty-minute drive into the Coast Range foothills on Interstate 8 toward Yuma, Arizona, to get to Alpine Brewing Company, where Pat McIlhenney, a former full-time fire captain, and his son Shawn built their own little corner of heaven: a small-production brewery and BBQ café in an old TV- repair shop, with copper-sided kettles running a few times a week. Or at least, that's how it was supposed to be. Now, thanks to the fast-spreading fame of their IPAs in particular, they're brewing and bottling practically dawn till dusk, adding fermentation tanks and a cold storage room and a BBQ café next door to boot. All of it was built by hand.

It seems to be working. "I cannot make beer fast enough," says the elder McIlhenney. His twelve tap and eight bottled brews enjoy cult status, heightened by their rarity—and a slew of laurels, like a gold in 2010 in American-style strong pale ales for O'Brien's IPA, beating fifty-eight other contenders. Simply put, you have to drive up to Alpine or—at the very least—find a great beer bar in San Diego County to drink the good stuff.

PHILOSOPHY

The McIlhenneys keep it simple: "Drink Alpine Beer or Go to Bed!"

KEY BEER

Duet IPA (7% ABV), full of the fresh, floral flavors of Simcoe and Amarillo hops, two rare varieties.

THE LINKERY

3794 30th St. • San Diego, CA 92104 • (619) 255-8778
thelinkery.com • Established: 2005

SCENE & STORY

You know you're in a good spot when you can not only eat house-cured bacon as part of your meal, but take some home with you after dinner as well, since it is sold separately to take home by request. The bacon in question is Berkshire pork from Eden Farms, a nearby co-op of independent farmers raising hogs with pedigree, and it's the source of the kitchen's ham, sausage, and charcuterie. The handmade, organic approach applies to everything else as well, from wine (forty by the glass, many biodynamic small producers) to garden vegetables to house-baked bread, mustard, sauerkraut, and ice cream. If the place had room for a brewery they might make beer, too, but with San Diego's embarrassment of riches in the craft brew department, no need.

What is needed is time, and a sunny day: with the big garage-style doors open and breezes blowing in, you've got the ideal atmosphere for tasting some meticulously thought-out food and a slew of fresh, well-kept beers from five taps, a cask or two, and about thirty bottles, all of them excellent. You can get four 5-ounce pours of anything on draft for $14, a great way to find your keeper.

PHILOSOPHY

Idealistic. In addition to all the food-sourcing policies, the bar made headlines in 2008 when the *New York Times* addressed its no-tipping policy (although 18 percent is added to every check and distributed evenly among staff), which is meant to encourage better overall service and less distracting competition among servers.

KEY BEER

There are a lot of good beers on the list, and a fast rotating draft selection of mostly locals. But it's not everyday you find Russian River Consecration, a dark Belgian-style ale fermented with wild yeasts and aged with currants in cabernet barrels (10% ABV). Don't miss the chance to try it.

★ ★ ★

THE BLIND LADY ALEHOUSE/ AUTOMATIC BREWING CO.

3416 Adams Ave. • San Diego, CA 92116 • (619) 555-1234
blindladyalehouse.com • Established: 2009

SCENE & STORY

Trained master brewer Lee Chase helped launch Stone Brewing Company into orbit before freeing himself up to consult and help create San Diego's cavernous Blind Lady, a gourmet pizzeria and beer bar with communal seating, its own little nanobrewery setup, and reruns of Michael Jackson's much-loved television series, *The Beer Hunter*. Just like at the Linkery, they go to great lengths to use local, certified-organic *everything*, whether it's peaches from San Diego's Adams Avenue Farmer's Market or sausage and charcuterie from San Diego Meat Company (cheese, with the exception of the mozzarella, comes from Italy). The thin crust pizzas are the main attraction but mussels and fries with seasonal dipping sauces (like a recent trio: Meyer lemon-horseradish aioli; tuna aioli; curry ketchup) get high marks for inventiveness and taste.

PHILOSOPHY

Fair and square. As for the beer, you can be certain that what you order is in good shape, thanks to Chase's attention to proper beer service, a borderline obsession one wishes would catch on far more widely. What it means: kegs are underneath the clean, carefully maintained taps, without long lines to a cellar in which beer would sit for days. Then the servers use clean, rinsed, never-chilled glassware every time (rinsed to rid the glass of Health Department-mandated sanitizer in solution, which inevitably has dried in the glass; never chilled because a freezing pint kills head and aroma). Last key factor: the fair pour. You'll always get one here, and with a head on the beer when appropriate. Sad fact: Carry around a measuring cup and you'd likely find a troubling number of bars using "cheater pints" with thick glass bottoms or merely smaller volumes.

KEY BEER

Chase has brewed up four beers on his system so far: Automatic (a coriander-spiked, 5.6% ABV Belgian pale ale), Chocolate Rain Oatmeal Stout, Sex Panther Strong Pale Ale, and Imperial Coffee Brown. Why not try them all?

TORONADO

4026 30th St. • San Diego, CA 92104 • (619) 282-0456
toronadosd.com • Established: 2008

SCENE & STORY

Cleaner and less cluttered than its parent bar in San Francisco, Toronado San Diego is about one thing, and one thing only: craft beer. A small, narrowish bar in North Park, it has a world-class selection of taps emanating from a metal-plated wall in the corner. The beer list skews toward SoCal brewers like AleSmith, Lost Abbey, Pizza Port, Alpine, and Green Flash, with some Belgian left fielders like De Landtsheer for good measure. The goods are routinely fresh and served in the right glass by someone who knows what they're talking about, and there's a nice little patio out back should crowds get to be a bit much for the stools and small high tables. No matter what, it's worth a trip for anyone looking for a great selection in a relaxed atmosphere.

PHILOSOPHY

Unpretentious excellence. While it can surely happen, attitude is not generally served up at Toronado. It's just a great place to have a beer, try something new, and meet or make friends.

KEY BEER

Alpine's California Uncommon (5.7% ABV), Pat McIlhenney's version of "steam" beer, the sort of lager beer fermented at warmer temperatures that Anchor made famous. It's got a wallop of hop character and a soft, caramel malt base for harmony.

BEST *of the* REST: CALIFORNIA

CITY BEER STORE

1168 Folsom St., No. 101 • San Francisco, CA 94103 • (415) 503-1033 • citybeerstore.com

In this little hole-in-the-wall SOMA bottle and draft emporium (inspired by wine shops and organized by style rather than brand) visitors sip fresh, ultra-rare domestic and imported craft beers and snack on artisan cheese plates and freshly baked breads. There are six taps for growlers and more than three hundred bottled beers to mix and match. Opened in 2006, it has become a key gathering place for San Francisco craft beer fanatics.

BEER REVOLUTION

464 3rd St. • Oakland, CA 94607 • (510) 452-2337 • beer-revolution.com

This combination bottle shop and craft beer bar opened in 2010 has quickly become an anchor of east Bay Area drinking culture, despite its humble location and pallid fluorescent lighting. All five hundred selections are available to take home—or pop open right here for a mere dollar (compare this to the average wine corkage fee of $15 to $25). Then there are forty-seven drafts to choose from and a sunny patio for al fresco tastings. Add in correct glassware for every beer, appearances by notable brewers, and afternoon barbecues, and you have all the makings of the ultimate craft beer party. Look for Marin Brewing Company's San Quentin Breakout Stout (7 % ABV) with creamy flavors of dark chocolate, vanilla, espresso, and bourbon.

ALBATROSS PUB

1822 San Pablo Ave. • Berkeley, CA 94702 • (510) 843-2473 • albatrosspub.com

Being the oldest pub in town all too often means having a selection that could use some dusting off, too. And while the Albatross is Berkeley's oldest pub—it was founded 1964—it's hardly old-fashioned in the beer department. In between contests of skill in the wood-framed dart alleys or a game of dominoes, sip such treats as North Coast Brewing Company's silky, espresso-like Rasputin Russian Imperial Stout (9% ABV), a craft beer classic.

TRIPLE ROCK BREWERY & ALEHOUSE

1920 Shattuck Ave. • Berkeley, CA 94704 • (510) 843-4677 • triplerock.com

A pilgrimage to Triple Rock is a trip into American craft brewing's earliest days: When it opened in 1986 after a lengthy battle with town officials (who feared a factory), it became just the fifth brewpub in the United States. (Today it's the last remaining of those five still owned by the founders.) The interior has all the warmth and wear of a much older establishment, in fact, with wood paneling, ochre walls, framed brewery posters, and a beautiful, wide old bar. Behind all the nostalgic décor, though, is some of the most sophisticated brew-pub equipment anyone had seen in the United States back when the company was founded. It is still a winning setup, and today the Triple Rock is just as welcoming as ever, though with far better beer and a full menu. Try the Dragon's Milk Brown Ale (6.5% ABV) with toffee, smoke, and floral notes that work well together.

HOPMONK TAVERN

230 Petaluma Ave. • Sebastopol, CA 95472 • (707) 829-7300 • hopmonk.com

Built in a gorgeous old stone barn–like structure and lined with hundred-year-old salvaged Douglas fir floors, this spacious brewpub (est. 2008) features house ales among the sixteen taps and a hundred bottled selections including a swath of Russian River, Sierra Nevada, and Anderson Valley beers. The menu features beer-focused cuisine, such as charcuterie plates, cider-braised salmon, and hot beer sausage. If you haven't found it yet, this is the place to try Russian River's superb Temptation, a 7.25% ABV blonde ale aged in Chardonnay barrels with a touch of *Brettanomyces* yeast.

BEAR REPUBLIC

345 Healdsburg Ave. • Healdsburg, CA 95448 • (707) 433-2337 • bearrepublic.com

Racer 5 is an American-style IPA of 7% ABV that, over the past few years, has zoomed into the best beer bars in America based on its incredibly floral aroma alone. It's a reliably deli-cious beer, top in its class at the 2009 GABF, and now produced in a much bigger brewery nearby that isn't open to the public. But the family-owned brewpub where it was born—dec-orated with memorabilia of auto racing—shows off what founder and head brewer Richard Norgrove has in the engine next, including one-offs in the original brew house.

WURSTKÜCHE

800 E. 3rd St. • Los Angeles, CA 90013 • (213) 687-4444 • wurstkucherestaurant.com

Located in downtown L.A.'s arts district, Wurstküche (est. 2008) peddles grilled sausages made with ingredients such as *chile de árbol*, rubbed sage, rattlesnake, chipotle, and cinna-mon; and Belgian fries with toppings (truffle oil, tzatziki, bleu cheese with walnuts and bacon). The refreshment: twenty-four import and craft beers including caramelly *Sticke* ("secret") beer from Zum Uerige brewery in Dusseldorf, brewed only on the third Tuesday of January and October.

FATHER'S OFFICE

1018 Montana Ave. • Santa Monica, CA 90403 • (310) 393-2337 • fathersoffice.com

Even without table service and a strict no-substitutions policy, Father's Office has been Santa Monica's best-known beer 'n' burger destination since it opened in 2000, making it hard to get in at times. (Note: There's a second, larger location in Culver City.) The culprits:

thirty-six top-shelf taps and a sweet bottle list; chef-founder Sang Yoon's Office Burger, consisting of juicy dry-aged strip steak, Maytag blue cheese, Gruyère, arugula, and apple-wood bacon; and a steady stream of beer-loving celebrities like Brooke Shields.

NEIGHBORHOOD

777 G St. • San Diego, CA 92101 • (619) 446-0002 • neighborhoodsd.com

Conceived as a hybrid of the traditional Japanese *izakaya* and a London gastropub, the small, contemporary Neighborhood (est. 2007) makes the otherwise touristy Gaslamp Quarter worth a trip. The beer list (twenty-seven taps and forty bottles) is excellent, with sought-after double IPAs like Port's Mongo. Stave off hunger with eclectic choices like pink-salted deviled eggs, steak tartare, steamed pork buns, and ribs braised in Stone Smoked Porter.

SMALL BAR

4628 Park Blvd. • San Diego, CA 92116 • (619) 795-7998 • smallbarsd.com

Opened in 2009 by Scot Blair of Hamilton's, this local lives up to its name in size, but not stature, with forty-two up-to-the-minute taps and a "handful" of bottled options (mostly local and Californian, with some European delicacies for good measure), served in a dimly lit bar painted floor to ceiling in red and black. Sustenance arrives in the form of chile verde, Wagyu beef sliders, and buttermilk fried chicken.

O'BRIEN'S PUB

4646 Convoy St. • San Diego, CA 92111-2315 • (858) 715-1745 • obrienspub.net

An unassuming soccer bar located in an anonymous strip mall next to a cluster of car deal-erships, O'Brien's has white plastic patio chairs, drop-panel ceilings, and a bar decorated with unfinished wood shingles. But as the self-proclaimed "hoppiest place on earth" it also boasts serious craft beer cred: twenty hard-to-get taps, eighty obscure and collectible bot-tles, regular casks, beer release parties for the likes of Lost Abbey, and the bragging rights to O'Brien's IPA, a world-class example of the style originally brewed for the bar by Alpine.

Hawaii

★ ★ ★

BACK IN THE LATE-1960S "TINY BUBBLES" ERA OF DON HO—AND THE

last days of surfing pioneer Duke Kahanamoku—the Hawaiian Islands' beloved beer was an inexpensive industrial lager called Primo, which lacked much flavor but dated all the way back to 1898. The nostalgic brand withered away over the next couple of decades as corporate owners (Schlitz, then Stroh, then Pabst) moved production to the mainland and scrimped on glass and ingredients, none of which have ever spurred much of a luau.

These days, craft beer is surfing its own wave in the islands, brewing the freshest beer they can for the breezy beaches of the fiftieth state. It's not at all easy to brew in paradise—there are no malt houses or large hop suppliers, for starters—but that's not keeping craft beer from finding a home, their taprooms full, and their kegs running dry.

Maui

MAUI BREWING CO.

910 Honoapiilani Hwy., No. 55 • Lahaina, HI 96761
(877) MAU-IBRE • mauibrewingco.com • Established: 2005

MAUI BREWING CO.

Kahana Gateway Center • 4405 Honoapiilani Hwy., No. 217
Lahaina, HI 96761 • Established: 2009

SCENE & STORY

What's paradise without incredible beer? Exactly. When you tire of nearby Kaanapali Beach (if such a thing is possible), skip the tiki drinks and head for a taste of the best beer in the islands. Known by its unmistakable cans (especially the retro hula girl on Bikini Blonde Lager), Maui Brewing is the only microbrewery on Maui; in many ways it could be the natural heir to Primo, only with a far better beer, but the focus is more on quality than quantity. Founded by the outgoing Garrett Marrero and Melanie Oxley, Maui Brewing Company is nevertheless finding a bigger audience with each batch, having made four hundred barrels by the end of year one . . . and eleven thousand a year later in 2010, with double that planned for 2011 and 2012, putting their capacity on par with or ahead of Kona Brewing Company, part of the Anheuser-Busch-distributed Craft Brewers Alliance (which also includes Redhook, Widmer, and Goose Island).

There's a tasting room at the brewery location, but the newer brewpub—a sleek, modern space with high ceilings and large U-shaped bar island—is a little more accommodating, open every day of the week from 11 a.m. to midnight. The pub serves Maui's three year-round beers, all of them good: Bikini Blonde, Big Swell IPA, and the award-winning CoCoNut Porter—a far better beer than it sounds. Then there are ten more taps of brewpub-only and experimental offerings, a small number of which make their way to the Left Coast on occasion. Marrero, from San Diego originally, features guest taps like Stone alongside his own brews. Recently, Marrero's experiments included a collaboration brew with Pizza Port and brown ale made with a famous local ingredient: the sweet Maui onion.

He sees it as part and parcel of a holistic, back-to-the-land lifestyle. "In these days of mass production of sub par, unnatural products, we need to get some attention back on knowing where your food and drink comes from," says Marrero. "It is sad to see local farms across the country closing at an alarming rate when they really are the backbone of fresh, local, organic, and natural food products. It's also fun to see people's faces when you say 'Hey, try my Maui Onion Beer,' and they look at you almost cross-eyed: *'Onion in beer?* Weird . . . I have to try that!'"

PHILOSOPHY

Marrero preaches a mantra of environmental responsibility and stewardship, supplying local farmers with spent grain, growing hops at a local farm and in Lahaina (which will help reduce the impact of shipping hops from the mainland), making bio-diesel from kitchen by-products in the pub, and using photovoltaic panels to capture solar energy. "Hawaii is generally associated with tropical fruits, nuts, and flowers, and we try to draw from what the *'aina* ("land") provides to make innovative and fun beers," says Garrero. "We take traditional, sometime old-world styles, and give them new life or dimension by adding these agricultural products to the brew."

KEY BEER

While it sounds like it might taste like a mouthful of Coppertone, Maui's CoCoNut Porter, at 5.7% ABV, is actually a silky, slightly sweet delight, a blend of coffee and cocoa flavors mingled with hand-toasted coconut and a dash of spicy hops to balance it all out. Drink it in a sunny place—preferably Maui.

★ ★ ★

KONA PUB & BREWERY

75-5629 Kuakini Hwy. • Kona, HI 96740
(808) 334-2739 • konabrewingco.com • Established: 1994

KOKO MARINA PUB

7192 Kalaniana'ole Hwy. • Honolulu, HI 96825
(808) 394-5662 • konabrewingco.com • Established: 2003

SCENE & STORY

Established in 1994 by father-and-son team Cameron Healy and Spoon Khalsa, Kona Brewing Company is now the thirteenth largest craft brewery in the United States and owned by the Craft Brewers Alliance. Kona's head brewer moved on as of summer 2011; most of the company's beers sold on the U.S. mainland are contract brewed in New Hampshire and Portland, Oregon and distributed by Anheuser-Busch. The brewpub in Kona, built on-site a few years later, brews 2,000 bbl a year for locals; the Honolulu location is a bar and eatery. Beer travelers can count on a fresh and relaxing beer in the Kona location with its verdant patio and menu of hand-tossed pizzas, sandwiches, salads and *pupu* plates (appetizers). Free tours are also offered, and there's a cool little growler station for beer to go. The larger Koko Marina spot in Honolulu overlooks a placid bay of boats tied up to the piers and has a spacious indoor taproom.

PHILOSOPHY

Easy in the islands. They're obviously not too worried about being a contract brewing company, despite the stigma it creates in the eyes of diehard craft consumers. As long as the local beers stay high quality and hopefully even innovative, they'll draw beer lovers of all stripes.

KEY BEER

Da Grind Buzz Kona Coffee Imperial Stout (8.5% ABV) is a winter seasonal brewed in Kona that's made with coffee beans grown, harvested, and roasted in nearby Holualoa. It's as aromatic as a freshly iced espresso but creamier on the tongue and black as ancient lava.

Best of the Rest: Hawaii

HUMPY'S BIG ISLAND ALEHOUSE

75-5815 Ali'i Drive • Kailua-Kona, HI 96740
(808) 324-2337 • humpys.com

Sister bar to craft beer maven Billy Opinksy's famous Humpy's Great Alaskan Alehouse in Anchorage, Alaska, Humpy's opened in 1994 right across the street from the water, overlooking a couple of slender palms and the Pacific. There's ample outdoor seating (though it can get a little windy), a sports-bar-like interior (read: plasma screens), and a vast menu of options, from ten-ounce burgers, local grilled and fried fish, and Hawaiian pork platters, to a full list of pizzas. And the beer? It's only the best beer selection on the Big Island (twenty taps and around twenty in bottles). Order a local Hawaiian variety, naturally, whatever's on and especially fresh.

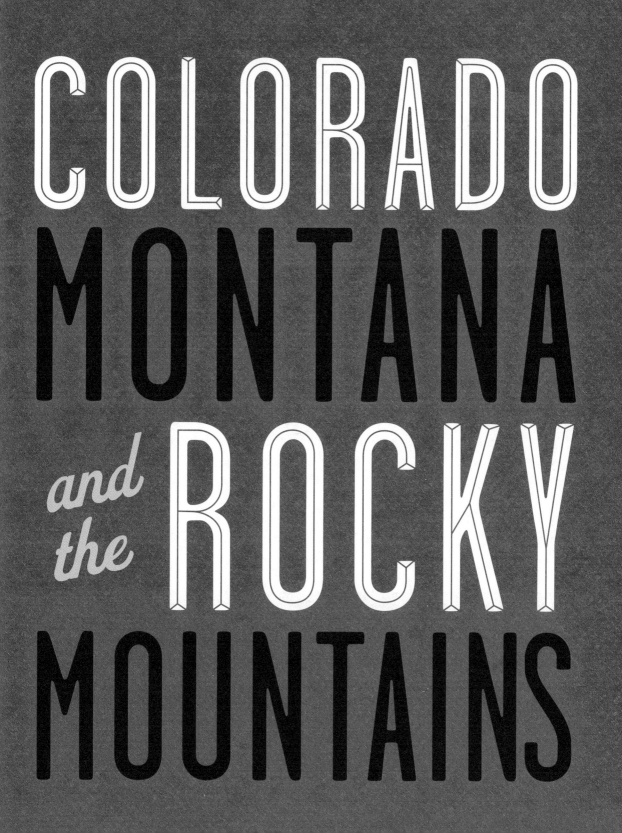

COLORADO MONTANA and the ROCKY MOUNTAINS

Colorado

★ ★ ★

ASK ANY BEER LOVER TO NAME THE BEST BEER STATE IN AMERICA,

and, depending on their zip code, you'll soon be besieged with per-capita statistics and other "inside baseball" minutiae, a puffed chest conversation brewers and industry watchers refer to as "the arms race." The fact is, there's room for more than one Super Power on Craft Beer Planet.

From the leafy streets and sunny taprooms of Fort Collins to the cavernous barrel-aging rooms in Boulder, sleek gastropubs in downtown Denver, and woodstove-warmed, log cabin–like Rocky Mountain brewpubs, there are scores of beer-friendly spots and some of the country's most scenic drives between them. Denver alone merits a stop in this state: the mile-high city is home to the Denver Beer Fest, a ten-day annual craft beer festival culminating in the Great American Beer Festival (GABF), the world's largest mass beer tasting (for number of beers on offer—more than 2,000) and America's largest beer festival of any kind. Denver is also the only major U.S. city since Colonial times to be governed by a brewmaster in chief, John Hickenlooper. No beer lover should miss making a good long visit, especially during the Denver Beer Fest and GABF, to see—and taste— what all the fuss is about. After visiting Denver, Boulder, and Fort Collins, head West into the Rockies and then South to Durango, a 450-mile epic of 11,000 passes, atmospheric taprooms, and thirst-stoking outdoor options.

ITINERARIES

1-DAY Great Divide, Wynkoop Brewing Co., Breckenridge Brewery & Bar-B-Que, Falling Rock Taphouse

3-DAY Denver to Boulder County for Upslope, Oskar Blues, Left Hand, Mountain Sun, Wild Mountain Smokehouse, and the West End Tavern

7-DAY Denver to Boulder/Longmont; Aspen for Aspen Brewing Co., Woody Creek Tavern and the J-Bar; continue on through Ouray to Durango

Fort Collins

NEW BELGIUM BREWING CO.

500 Linden Street • Fort Collins, CO 80524
(970) 221-0524 • newbelgium.com • Established: 1991

SCENE & STORY

Maker of the craft brew smash Fat Tire Ale, New Belgium is the largest craft brewery in Fort Collins and the third largest in the United States. As the story goes, Jeff Lebesch started the brewery with his then-wife (and current company CEO), Kim Jordan, after discovering the incredible array of beers lovingly and idiosyncratically produced in Belgium while touring that country on his mountain bike in 1989. No visit to Colorado's breweries would be complete without a tour here (it's popular, so plan to reserve two to three weeks ahead), followed by beers in the airy, sleek taproom, the "Liquid Center."

While the nave-like brewing hall feels like a cathedral, with creamy, colorful tile work around the bases of the kettles, the beating heart of this operation is in an unassuming corner of a storage warehouse behind the taproom, where sixteen massive *fouders*—French oak fermenters—stand in a tower of amber-hued wood and iron bands. There, New Belgium ages ales into vinous liquids for later blending, some exuding aromas that are the products of alcoholic compounds called esters. Though fruit is not always present, the beers aged in this way can exhibit aromas of pineapple and tangerine, as well as chewy red wine–like tannins, and a flavor like sour cherries.

New Belgium has been a pioneer in introducing Americans to the Belgian styles called Flanders Red and Oud Bruin ("Old Brown") of which the crowning example is generally thought to be Belgium's Rodenbach Grand Cru, reddish ale aged in huge oak vats and later blended with younger beer to round out the acidic flavors created by prolonged exposure to wood. New Belgium's Belgian head brewer, Peter Bouckaert, worked for Rodenbach for years, and he's considered a true master of barrel aging. This is not how all New Belgium beer is brewed, but it's how the best and most interesting ones are matured, sometimes with additional fruits in the tanks.

PHILOSOPHY

Outside magazine has named the employee-owned company one of the "Best Places to Work" in the United States, and it's easy to see why. There's a sense of institutionally mandated fun here: the Tour de Fat is an annual bike festival celebrating zero-emissions commuting, with a concert on a solar-powered stage and beer served in compostable cups. There's a company climbing wall and foosball table, a slide from the second to first floors, and even an on-site dirt bike track. All employees earn a new cruiser bike after one year at the company; after four more they're taken to Belgium to follow in the founder's footsteps.

KEY BEER

Fat Tire Amber Ale, a biscuity tasting brew of light to medium body, made New Belgium a national player, but the company's more adventurous, smaller release concoctions, such as La Folie, New Belgium's version of Rodenbach, are the ones to seek out. Now marketed through the brewery's Lips of Faith line, La Folie is a landmark, polarizing beer—it's uncompromisingly tart, with a bracing flavor profile that can sucker-punch the unprepared. But to the initiated, it's nothing short of nectar.

COOPERSMITH'S

5 Old Town Square • Fort Collins, CO 80524
(970) 498-0483 • coopersmithpub.com • Established: 1989

SCENE & STORY

Next to posters from the Denver Beer Festival going back to 1990, the décor at the easygoing CooperSmith's, located in downtown Fort Collins, includes a photo of a pub regular posing on Mount Everest's summit—sure evidence you've arrived at a sturdy corner of the universe. The exposed brick walls, wooden booths, and a historic, dark, polished bar only reinforce that sense of solidity. Menu options are no less impressive: the High Plains Barbecue Brisket Sandwich is delicious, with zingy spice. There's also a pool bar across the walkway from the original pub, with twelve tournament-size billiards tables and other games.

PHILOSOPHY

Early brews mimicked traditional English ales, but over time CooperSmith's has incorporated elements of German and Belgian brewing. "At this point," says head brewer Dwight Hall, "we're brewing distinctly American beers, but we do not brew to style. We try and create harmony in the glass." And CooperSmith's isn't just about beer; the bar carries one of the largest single-malt Scotch selections in all of northern Colorado, in addition to a good selection of blended Scotches and bourbons.

KEY BEER

There have been about seventy-five beers in the CooperSmith's repertoire, with fourteen at a time on tap. Try the 6.8% ABV Punjabi Pale Ale, a slightly pungent APA (American Pale Ale), bittered with grapefruity Cascade hops. "It's our best-selling beer," says Hall. "It was originally inspired by the English IPAs, but it has evolved over the years and has its own distinct character."

A tour of Anheuser Busch's plant in Fort Collins is a stop I unironically recommend for all craft beer lovers. *Blasphemy*, you say? Not at all. In fact, this is a stop worth making for one simple reason: perspective. Touring this maze of robots churning out millions upon millions of identical beers is a look at beer making's outer technological frontier. Take the "Beermaster" tour ($25) and you'll see massive brewing kettles that look like something out of the movie *Independence Day*. You'll gape at a canning line churning out Bud Light at a rate of *33 cans per second*. Brewers are technical people by nature, and there are many who speak of factories like this with a begrudging reverence. They might not want to make beer the same way, but the sheer mechanical ingenuity is something to behold, even if the end result is akin to "wet air" as the famous 1987 *Atlantic* article, "A Glass of Handmade," by William Least Heat-Moon attested so memorably.

And yet wandering through the futuristic forest of stainless tanks, myriad pipes, conveyor belts, and grated stairways you'll taste something quite remarkable: unfiltered Bud Light. Yes, it's made of 40 percent rice. Hop character: nada. But after the so-called beechwood aging (it's real wood, I can at least tell you that much), and before filtration and pasteurization has rent the last of any remaining flaws asunder, Bud Light has an appealing flavor, surprisingly full bodied and slightly sweet. It's a treat to try beer at this stage of the process. Germans and Czechs have been releasing beers in this state for eons, calling them by various names including *kellerbier, zwickelbier*, and, in the case of the fabled Mahr's brewery of Bamberg, Germany, *ungespundet hefetrub*. For the record, I suggested that the manager pitch a commercial version of unfiltered Bud to her superiors. (I can see the commercials now.) But I'm not holding my breath. We don't really need another ersatz-craft beer from corporate bean counters. But with Bud Light Golden Wheat suddenly a national brand, maybe Bud "Kellerbier" doesn't sound so crazy, after all.

ODELL BREWING COMPANY

800 East Lincoln Ave. • Fort Collins, CO 80524
(970) 498-9070 • odells.com • Established: 1989

SCENE & STORY

Odell was the second craft brewery to open in Colorado (after Boulder Brewing Company), starting with a little five-barrel brewery in a 1915 grain elevator. Early on, founders Doug Odell, Wynne, and Corkie Odell maintained a draught-only focus while struggling to keep up with demand. So they added a bottling line in 1996, which effectively supercharged the marketplace for their beer. Flash forward to 2011, and the brewery is currently making about 45,000 brewers' barrels (or bbl.; one barrel equals 31 US gallons) of beer, sold throughout the middle of the country in nine states.

With live music every Wednesday, the sunny taproom (and outdoor patio) is one of the most popular destinations for beer lovers in Fort Collins. Best of all, success hasn't spoiled the makers of the popular Scottish ale called 90 Shilling. There's a warm, family-friendly feel to the place, which makes more sense when one learns that in all, there are five married couples (some of whom met here) who work together at the brewery. Which is a sizable chunk of the staff. It might be the happiest place in America.

PHILOSOPHY

Fortunately, the original five-barrel system remains in use for special one-offs, in which the beers depart from standard English ales and head into parts unknown, but not unappreciated. One such recent brew was Angry Robin, an English strong ale aged in merlot barrels and spiked with a dash of *brettanomyces* bacteria, giving it a barnyardy kick.

KEY BEER

Every fall, Odell releases a one-off beer aged in American oak barrels, echoing the old-world techniques over at New Belgium, though on a much smaller scale. Woodcut Nos. 1, 2, and 3 were all variations on the theme of strong ale aged in oak, which adds layers of vanilla-like woodiness to the brews. No. 4 was a strong amber lager. These beers are beautifully labeled and corked in 750-milliliter bottles, and may be available in limited quantities at the tap room. Otherwise, try any other barrel-aged "pilot system" beers, such as the earthy, acidic—and interesting—Brett Porter. These are brewed on the original 5 bbl (about 350 gallons) system that started it all.

Longmont

LEFT HAND BREWING CO.

1265 Boston Ave. • Longmont, CO 80025 • (303) 772-0258
lefthandbrewing.com • @lefthandbrewing • Est: 1993

SCENE & STORY

Housed in an old meatpacking plant in an industrial area of Longmont, Left Hand has slowly grown from a raggedy upstart into a world-class small brewery. It all began when head brewer Eric Wallace, who had traveled around the world tasting beers while in the air force, joined up with his college friend Dick Doore, who was a home brewer. In the first year, the guys took home a gold medal at the Great American Beer Festival. They grew in a sustainable fashion, and eventually morphed into what is now a very laid back—but not lazy—brewing company. "It's kind of an after-work place," says Wallace. "We get engineers from all these tech companies and biotechs around here, bicyclists, arborists, and painters."

Originally called Indian Peaks Brewery, for a nearby mountain range, Wallace and Doore's brewery was forced to change names after a branding dispute with another company. They settled on Left Hand, after an Arapahoe word ("Niwot"), which was the name of a chief who spent winters nearby on the banks of the St. Vrain River. And then there's a more, shall we say, colorful connection: Curtis Green, the early sausage maker tenant of the building, lost his right arm in the grinder one day.

PHILOSOPHY

Left Hand isn't trying to outgun other companies in the IPA arms race—they're not heavy-handed with the hops. "Our brewing approach is all about balance," says Wallace. "When we started, we were brewing beers that we wanted, that we weren't really finding out there in the marketplace. We're still out there exploring flavors and styles that we like. Overwhelmingly, we'll always fall back to balance. In the end, is it drinkable? Does it have complexity, depth? And that balance? It's all about the flavor."

KEY BEER

Left Hand Polestar Pils. In the push to brew ever stronger, stranger beers, the subtle pilsner often gets neglected. That's too bad, because a great pilsner is a thing of beauty—an alcoholic beverage that is somehow more refreshing than a glass of ice water on a Death Valley afternoon. Like the best American micros, Polestar also stands out for its perfect use of hops; it's brewed with three varieties, which together lend a powdery floral aroma. While it's only occasionally available, Left Hand Smokejumper Imperial Porter is also worth seeking out. Next to your dog, a smoked beer (made with wood- or peat-fire smoked malt) may be the ultimate fireside companion. Left Hand's is a briny, coffee-black 9.2% ABV beast of a beer that calls to mind bacon. Even better, Wallace and Co. donate proceeds from this rare, hand-smoked seasonal to a scholarship fund for the children of smoke jumpers killed in action.

★ ★ ★

Return OF THE Can

There was a time when only cheap beer came in cans. . . . Even so, the aluminum can, introduced to this country's beer drinking public in 1935, became iconic—even if the beer it contained was often unremarkable. Quality notwithstanding, the *cssffft* sound that issued forth upon opening each new can was a harbinger of good things, especially on a hot summer day.

But today the humble can is new and improved and experiencing a renaissance: since the release of Dale's Pale Ale in a can in 2002, dozens of American microbrewers have started packaging their finest stuff in aluminum. Thanks to special linings, there's no interaction whatsoever between the metal and liquid. More importantly, there's less "head space" between the top of the can and the brew, meaning less beer-spoiling oxygen remains in contact with the beer. What's more, cans offer benefits that bottles don't: harmful UV light rays are blocked, sparing the beer from the dreaded "skunk" effect (avoid green and clear beer bottles when you can; brown glass blocks more UV rays). Today, well over a hundred American craft brewers have adopted cans. They're easier to carry (especially on camping trips), less likely to break and cut someone, and more quickly cooled. Crack one open as soon as you can.

OSKAR BLUES HOMEMADE LIQUIDS & SOLIDS

1555 S. Hover Rd. • Longmont, CO 80501
(303) 485-9400 • oskarblues.com • Established: 2009

SCENE & STORY

Think: bayou-on-the-Front-Range. Equal parts shiny taproom, soul food smorgasbord, and juke joint blues bar, this excellent spot is a must for anyone on the Colorado ale trail. The smell of apple-wood smoke greets you before you reach the door; that's thanks to the "Midnight Toker," an in-house smoker used for slow smoked North Carolina–style BBQ pork, spare ribs, beer-can chicken, salmon, and turkey. Inside, there's a mouthwatering display of shrimp and other shellfish, scores of interesting pieces of folk art from the Deep South, and the sounds of good music, including live blues, alt country, rockabilly, and bluegrass five nights a week. "We made a commitment early on that we were going to do good music," says founder Dale Katechis of the atmosphere. "We weren't just going to book $200 'Mustang Sally' bands." There's even a line of Oskar Blues hot sauces, based on five different beers. Try the Ten FIDY Imperial Stout version, made with the world's hottest pepper, Bhut Jolokia, or "ghost chile," if you dare.

PHILOSOPHY

A rising tide lifts all ships. This Oskar Blues location features scores of guest taps from other Colorado and American brewers, making the forty-three-tap pub a great place for an all-Colorado beer tasting.

KEY BEER

The clean and crisp Mama's Little Yella Pils, at 5.3% ABV, makes a great quencher for spicy ribs and other dishes they do so well here. But don't miss other OB rarities like Smoke on the Water, a lightly smoked, 7% ABV winter warmer.

OSKAR BLUES TASTY WEASEL TAPROOM

1800 Pike Rd., Unit B • Longmont, CO 80501
(303) 776-1914 • oskarblues.com • Established: 2009

SCENE & STORY

The Tasty Weasel is a cozy little taproom within the massive new Oskar Blues brewing facility, a behemoth headed toward a 70,000bbl annual capacity. Expect an industrial yet intimate setting (corrugated metal walls, folk art) popular with beer fanatics and locals, an up-close view of massive, beer-filled fermenters, cool music on the hifi, British-style casks called firkins, and oak-aged beer tappings on Tuesday and Friday nights.

PHILOSOPHY

No risk, no reward. "I grew up in the restaurant business and I always had a dream of opening my own restaurant, and Lyons seemed to be about the riskiest place to do it," recalls founder Dale Katechis. "When I moved there it was Mayberry in the mountains." That roll-the-dice business model has proved a savvy strategy, but the results have presented challenges of their own. "It's just 100 percent growth year after year," he says of the entire operation. "The job now is holding on to the culture and the soul and why we started doing it, and in business sometimes that's hard." The Tasty Weasel—and for Katechis, commuting between parts of the factory on a BMX bike—is part of that quest to maintain that fun-loving culture at the heart of Oskar Blues.

KEY BEER

This would be the place to sample the successful 10.5% ABV Ten FIDY, a roasty, fulsome Russian Imperial Stout, or better yet, the *oak barrel-aged* Ten Fidy, which is quite rare. The wood imparts rich notes of vanilla and caramel.

Lyons

OSKAR BLUES GRILL & BREW

303 Main St. Lyons, CO 80540 • (303) 823-6685
oskarblues.com • Established: 1997

SCENE & STORY

The old mining town of Lyons, (population: 1,500), sits at the confluence of the St. Vrain North and St. Vrain South Creeks, just about twenty miles from Rocky Mountain National Park. Surrounded by reddish sandstone peaks, it's an outdoor lover's paradise, and it's also known for an amazing music scene, with the annual Rockygrass Bluegrass Festival held every summer and regularly drawing such luminaries as David Grisman and Tony Rice. The Grill & Brew is the town's social hub, with its Southern-themed, forty-five-tap bar, dining room,

and outdoor patio overlooking the little brew house building and a barn that has been converted for special events and parties. On a good summery night the patio is the place to be, sipping some fresh craft beer in the breeze.

PHILOSOPHY

"We're all hop heads," says Eric Huber, head brewer at the Lyons location. "We do love classical styles, we do love a lot of what the other guys are doing, but it's about what we want to drink ourselves. We've got a clientele who loves what we've been doing, and we've been training them to drink the hoppy beers we've been drinking for years. The best way to find out if it's a great batch is put it on and see what the local boys think."

KEY BEER

Dale's Pale Ale, 6.5 % ABV. Initially laughed off, Katechis's delicate craft beer packaged in aluminum cans was an unlikely success. For one, Katechis didn't live in Portland or Seattle, where craft is king. He lived in the Deep South. "In 1989 or 1990, there were not too many home brewers in Auburn, Alabama," he says. "Actually, I knew of one—and that was me." He had developed a recipe for Dale's Pale Ale, an extremely hoppy, astringent beer, almost IPA-like, outside of the style guideline of a pale ale, which evolved with his first hired brewers. And the rest, as they say, is history.

UPSLOPE BREWING CO.

1501 Lee Hill Rd., No. 20 • Boulder, CO 80304
(720) 379-7528 • upslopebrewing.com • Established: 2008

SCENE & STORY

In a generic North Boulder strip mall, some enterprising, beer loving, home brewing friends have built a booming little business. The tiny taproom is decorated with photos of the brewery's fans drinking Upslope brews in the wilds of Colorado and beyond. The founders themselves, a garrulous bunch, are quick to recount close scrapes from the early days, coping with limited space, little money, harsh winter temperatures, and other setbacks. But like the Flatiron Mountain images that decorate their cans, things are looking up for Upslope.

PHILOSOPHY

Upslope's MO is simple. Great craft brews should be canned and ready to rock at a moment's notice. "We're all about drinking our beer, not just in a pub, but on the side of a mountain," says assistant brewer Alex Violette. "It's a completely different experience. Take it rafting with you. Get out there and have fun with it, you know?" Better yet, it's easier to leave no trace with canned beer: crush up the cans and pack them out. The approach also makes sense from a business standpoint. The same amount of beer weighs about 40 percent less in the can than in a bottle, and stacks more efficiently in a truck, making it a more energy-efficient product going out of the brewery, as well.

KEY BEER

Upslope's beers are firmly in the middle of the typical Colorado beer lover's palate, with big, malty, hop-accented beers that finish clean. Their marquee beer is Upslope Pale Ale (5.8% ABV). "It's brewed in the tradition of American-style pale ale except for one different aspect: we use Patagonian hops," says Violette. "They add a little bit more of an earthy-spicy flavor to our pale ale. It's also a very approachable beer, not over-the-top hopped. It's something that's really easy to drink on a warm summer day."

ASHER BREWING COMPANY

4699 Nautilus Ct., No. 104 • Boulder, CO 80301
(303) 530-1381 • asherbrewing.com • Established: 2009

SCENE & STORY

One might be forgiven for driving straight through the Gunbarrel area northeast of Boulder, packed as it seems with featureless business parks and endless cul-de-sacs. But it's inside one of those sleepy turnabouts where business partners Steve Turner and Chris Asher have created Colorado's first all-organic brewery, turning out supremely fresh, delicious brews for a small but rapidly growing clientele. It's easy to miss, hidden behind hedges, and a no-frills affair, but worth the effort to find.

PHILOSOPHY

"Boulder is an organic Mecca for everything else," says brewer Chris Asher, "but no one was doing [organic] beer." The Massachusetts native had taught himself to brew during college at Wesleyan, even leading classes on campus for home brewing, then completed stints at Golden City Brewing in Golden and an MBA in his spare time before teaming up with Steve Turner, who had a decade of brewing and sales experience in the busy Colorado brewing scene. Though they knew Boulder, with its multiple craft breweries, would be a crowded market, they also correctly sensed an opportunity, and invested in a fifteen-barrel brewery. Smart move: within seven months of opening in late 2009, Asher Brewing was ready to expand, welcoming a growing stream of visitors, landing their beer in area accounts in neighboring towns, and drawing up plans for both canning and bottling.

KEY BEER

While Asher occasionally offers up rarities like a recent 7.4% ABV Fun Barrel Kriek, a dark ale aged with sweet and tart local cherries in wood barrels, the standard is Tree Hugger Organic Amber, a cleanly made, full-bodied 6.0% ABV sipper that showcases Asher's balanced use of American and New Zealand hops. It's a nice twist on an amber style, which has always been very, very popular in Colorado, at least since the ascent of New Belgium's Fat Tire Amber Ale on the national beer scene.

AVERY BREWING CO.

5763 Arapahoe Ave., Unit E • Boulder, CO 80303
(303) 440-4324 • averybrewing.com • Established: 1993

SCENE & STORY

Like many brewing companies in Colorado and beyond, Avery is built in a rather bland industrial park. But once inside, you find a beautiful seventeen-spigot taproom manned by a chipper, beer-savvy staff. Adam Avery, who started the brewery with his chemist father, is among the best known of Colorado brewers; his beers have always been big in malt and hops. A great many visitors have passed through, but no one can top the Beer Lover in Chief, President Barack Obama, who once visited the taproom. Perhaps he wanted a taste of the 8.75% ABV Ale to the Chief, a special 2008 election season double IPA (it's long been retired, alas). Elected to office or not, the most discerning beer geek couldn't fail to be impressed by the barrel room, so take a tour if one is available.

PHILOSOPHY

Avery's public pledge is to make "big, artful beers" and brew with "utter disregard for what the market demands," while searching out fans with "equally eccentric palates." Judging from their jump from small-time roots to national distribution, it seems to be a useful set of guiding principles.

KEY BEER

Keeping pace with the popularity and possibilities of barrel aging, there are several high-acid beers, too, aged in oak, which are sporadically released in miniscule quantities. Easier to find and diabolically strong at 15.1% ABV, Mephistopheles offers a taste of the awesome power that a beer can unleash—but be careful, you may not be able to feel your taste buds for an hour. This cinder black brew is rich and roasty with flavors of coffee and rum-soaked black cherries, with a velvety smoothness that lures you back sip after sip. It's hell to brew no doubt, but heaven to drink.

BOULDER BEER COMPANY

2880 Wilderness Pl. • Boulder, CO 80301 • (303) 444-8448
boulderbeer.com • @boulderbeer • Established: 1979

SCENE & STORY

Opened with a homemade, one-barrel system (thirty-one gallons) by two University of Colorado physics professors, David Hummer and Randolph "Stick" Ware, in a goatshed outside of town, BBC became the first microbrewery in Colorado and was among the first to open nationally—they were granted the forty-third license to brew beer in the United States. The two friends even consulted the Coors family, who, according to Ware, called them "crazy," but early supporters included famed beer writers Michael Jackson and Fred Eckhardt, joining a nascent groundswell of beer drinkers ready for sweeping change in the beer aisle. While Hummer and Ware ceded financial

control of the brewery to the Rock Bottom chain in 1990, the Boulder beer scene had been well launched, and their brewpub became an institution.

With the Flatiron Mountains rising behind Wilderness Square, the brewpub taproom is a popular spot, with free tours of the brewery offered daily. Should they be full, you can settle for the view of the bottling line from the taproom.

PHILOSOPHY

While the policy of offering a generous sample of beer with a tour of the brewery speaks to the overall relaxed feel of BBC, the company works ceaselessly to keep up with the ever evolving tastes of the American beer lover.

KEY BEER

The easy-sipping, 4.9% ABV Singletrack Copper Ale, an APA launched in 1990, helped establish BBC as a major regional brewery. Today, its piney, copper-hued Hazed & Infused APA (4.85% ABV) is leading the company's charge throughout some twenty states.

THE KITCHEN & THE KITCHEN UPSTAIRS

1039 Pearl St. • Boulder, CO 80302 • (303) 544-5973
thekitchencafe.com • Established: 2005

SCENE & STORY

A farm-to-table restaurant catering to Boulder's most discerning foodies, there's always something cooking at the Kitchen seven days a week, from classes to winemaker and brewer dinners, "community hours" that offer discounted dining, and other charming gastro pursuits.

Chef-owner Hugo Matheson expanded his busy restaurant in 2005 to include the "Upstairs," a candlelit and fireplace-warmed wine bar area above the restaurant with a deep wine cellar. Soon after, bar manager Ray Decker overhauled the beer list, giving it star treatment and including a number of vintage and rare beers. Beer is served with care here and food pairings are readily suggested. It's one of Boulder's most assured restaurants, with knowledgeable, attentive service. It also commands higher prices than some craft beer lovers will be accustomed to paying. But with award-winning chefs at the stove, it's a refreshing change from the usual pub grub, and perhaps the ultimate way to cap off a trip to GABF in Denver.

PHILOSOPHY

Sunset magazine named it "The West's Greenest Restaurant" in 2008, praising Chef Hugo Matheson's fare and eco-friendly approach. And beer steward Ray Decker has assembled a superb, international beer list to complement the cuisine, with special attention to Belgian ales and American pathbreakers like Michigan's Jolly Pumpkin.

KEY BEER

Ask Decker or a server to recommend beers with your meal, as all the menus and lists change constantly. A reddish, Belgian-style farmhouse ale like Jolly Pumpkin's La Roja (recently sampled here) or a barrel-aged beer from Norway's HaandBryggeriet or Belgium's Drie Fonteinen would complement many of the Kitchen's richer dishes.

WEST END TAVERN

926 Pearl St. • Boulder, CO 80302 • (303) 444-3535
thewestendtavern.com • Established: 1987

SCENE & STORY

Boulder has become a craft brew capital with Avery, Oskar Blues, and Upslope breweries, just to name a few. But there's a deep craft brew passion in select bars as well. At the multilevel West End Tavern, New York-born chef-proprietor Chris Blackwood brings a touch of down-home Southern soul to upscale Boulder, with a vast tap list heavy on local brews and a great bourbon list to boot. The upstairs taproom is airy and modern, with metal tables and chairs and sight lines out to the sky, but it's the rotating tap list filled with craft rarities and two outdoor decks that really draw in the locals, especially the brewers themselves, like Upslope's cofounder Matt Cutter.

PHILOSOPHY

There's no telling what will be on tap at the West End, because the list is constantly changing, but expect to see local and West Coast beers heavily represented.

KEY BEER

Look for regional specialties like Avery's Dugana IIPA (8.5% ABV), a big, floral, resinous brew. Other recent taps featured Colorado brews including Odell Double Pilsner and Great Divide Belgica, in addition to West Coast cult beers from Russian River, Lagunitas, Stone, and Port.

THE MOUNTAIN SUN & THE SOUTHERN SUN

1535 Pearl St. • Boulder, CO 80302 • (303) 546-0886
mountainsunpub.com • Established: 1993

Southern Sun: 627 S. Broadway • Boulder, CO 80305
(303) 543-0886 • mountainsunpub.com

SCENE & STORY

A relaxing Boulder standby, the Mountain Sun expanded by popular demand with a second brewpub, the Southern Sun, in 2002. (There's also a related pub in Denver, the Vine Street Pub.) None other than GABF founder Charlie Papazian is a fan of the trio, especially the Southern Sun location, which has Flatiron mountain views. "It's a cool beer scene," he says. "It's all about the beer and a place to meet friends—smaller and more intimate [than the Mountain Sun]. It gets crowded so get there early."

PHILOSOPHY

"There will never be televisions at our pubs because we want our guests to meet and discuss the world in which we live or simply to play Scrabble," reads the company's website. There you have it.

KEY BEER

Try the hop bomb of an India Pale Ale known as F.Y.I.P.A. (about 7.5% ABV)e.

Denver

THE GREAT AMERICAN BEER FESTIVAL

Sep. 29–Oct. 1 (for 2011; future dates vary)
Colorado Convention Center
700 14th St. (near intersection of Colfax and Speer Blvds.)
Denver, CO 80202
Tickets from $20 (for designated drivers) to $55 per session
(303) 447-0816; greatamericanbeerfestival.com

SCENE & STORY

What do you get when you take 50,000 beer lovers, 500 breweries, over 2,000 of their latest creations, and mash them all together for three sunny fall days in Denver? The Great American Beer Festival is what you get, and this bacchanal has reached its 30th year as of September 2011. What started with just a few friends from small breweries and about forty on the list is today the mother of all beer festivals.

It's also a significant event for the brewers that submit beers for judging, culminating in the all-important Saturday afternoon medal announcements that generate roars of approval and surprise. The atmosphere is nothing if not raucous at times—crowds can get boisterous, loud, and drunk, but it's unforgettable to weave through the seemingly endless aisles of smiling brewers, servers, and beer fanatics celebrating the mighty abundance of it all. Wacky costumes? Yep. Silent disco? Definitely a hot spot. It can be a bit dizzying at first, but after a few tastes, the entire thing seems like the smartest festival ever created, as long as you pace yourself.

"If you've never been to the beer festival before," says GABF founder Charlie Papazian, "it's very important to remember that it's not a sprint, it's not a marathon—it's a 100-mile run. Or, actually, a 2,200-beer run." The savvy taster arrives early for each session and comes with a plan, having studied the layout of the exhibitor hall, which is organized geographically beneath a massive banner of the late British beer writer Michael Jackson, aka The Beer Hunter, whose thoughtful gaze should inspire considered sampling. And yet, without fail, a few minutes into any of the sessions (ticket holders should carefully study the hours, which are posted online and supplied at sign-in), all plans for quiet discovery seem to go out the window as the biggest assemblage of beer in the world works its magic on the crowd.

Still, many brewers are on hand to dispense beer from behind the taps, and it's amazing to see how many innovators have come in person to share their favorite creations. The key strategy, beyond that of all-important moderation, is to coordinate meals and hydration throughout the festival to avoid overdoing it, and to pick a hotel that's close to the convention center so you can recharge your batteries easily for sideshows like the Silent Disco or the after-session pub crawls to Wynkoop, the Falling Rock Taphouse, Euclid Hall, and others, where many of the brewers themselves gather to catch up.

PHILOSOPHY

From end-to-end, GABF is a celebration of everything that craft beer has achieved in the United States—the vibrancy, the variety, the quality, the fun, and ambition behind it all. What's missing is adequate space for food vendors whose ambitions equal that of the brewers. One solution would be to dedicate an entire row to food carts, the gourmet type that pack in customers in New York City and Portland, Oregon. But no matter what, it's impossible not to come away awed at what America's small breweries have achieved, and with a broad smile on your face.

KEY BEER

They're all key. The question is, which one will you try next?

★ ★ ★

HIGHWAY *to* ALE

Mercator has his world map, but true beer lovers will fall in love with the ultimate map of Colorado's beer scene, the Beer Drinker's Guide to Colorado. The 27 x 40-inch topo chart can be ordered flat and folded, laminated, or rolled, and includes over 120 destinations, with a table for computing driving distances and $150 worth of coupons for beer and free glassware. From $12.95 plus shipping; beerdrinkersguidetocolorado.com; (719) 636-3565.

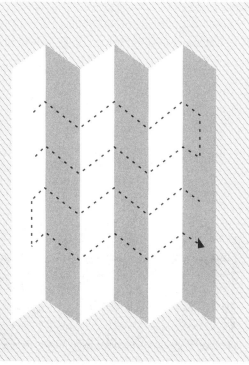

WYNKOOP BREWING CO.

1634 18th St. • Denver, CO 80202
(303) 297-2700 • wynkoop.com • Established: 1988

SCENE & STORY

The Wynkoop as it's sometimes known is a vast, three-story bar with acres of pool tables on the second floor and an inviting downstairs area. The place holds a special place in Colorado beer history: Colorado Governor (and former Denver Mayor) John Hickenlooper was part of the vanguard that made it Colorado's first brewpub. (The company recently returned the favor by brewing him an "InagurAle" for his January 2011 swearing-in.)

Housed in a massive brick fortress known as the J. S. Brown Mercantile Building (built in 1899), Wynkoop has preserved many vestiges of an earlier time without devolving into a kitschy tourist trap, which easily could have happened. It's the home of monthly poetry and science enthusiast meetups (known as "Café Scientifique"), comedy and burlesque shows, beer dinners, and the Beer Drinker of the Year contest, which is a bit more serious than it sounds. This is a very nice place to meet some local beer lovers, or simply enjoy a beer and catch a game.

PHILOSOPHY

Wynkoop feels traditional, local, and a bit roadhouse-esque inside, utterly Western. The owners have long taken great pains to reduce their carbon footprint. It's a no-frills, friendly operation, with malt-forward beers that are generally well made and quite sessionable.

KEY BEER

Railyard Ale, at 5.2% ABV, is a straightforward, copper-hued session beer somewhat similar in flavor to an Oktoberfest or Märzen-style beer, but with a more fruity finish that takes it in another direction. Like many Rocky Mountain brews, it's more on the slightly sweet, malty side, good for extended pool games. Hop heads will want to try Mile Hi-P.A., an American IPA, and Mister Fister, a Double IPA (also known as IIPA), both of which are well-made, big, brassy beers with ample but not too much bitterness.

Not many brewers are asked for their autograph. But not many brewers have résumés like Charlie Papazian's: The University of Virginia-trained, former nuclear engineer heads up the Brewers Association (an industry group representing some 1,000 of America's craft breweries), launched the Great American Beer Festival (GABF) in 1981 and *Zymurgy* magazine, and authored the home brewers' bible, *The Complete Joy of Home Brewing,* in 1984 (now sailing beyond 25 reprintings, 3 editions, 1.2 million copies). He's been permanently elevated to beer demigod, a signer of autographs, a coveted snapshot.

Papazian, for all the hype going on in and around what he's helped create, has a quiet, humble, and considerate air. As he speaks about the Colorado scene, he's struck with what seems like genuine wonderment, a wide smile always on his face. He wouldn't look out of place in a cassock, but he's wearing a simple cotton dress shirt. "When I first came here in 1972, there was no beer scene other than the Coors brewery," he recalls. "Now we have 100 breweries in the state, and I hear there are 20 more on the way. We could have 140 before long. But it all started back in 1978 with the Boulder Beer Company. They were one of the first ten microbreweries in the United States, the first in Colorado."

It didn't exactly take off like wildfire. "Things were slow to start," says Papazian. "But then a guy named John Hickenlooper, then mayor of Denver, changed a law to permit brewpubs in Colorado. After that law changed, [Hickenlooper] started the Wynkoop brewery down here in Denver, and the success of that place really opened up peoples' eyes to what beer could be, what beer culture could be, and what the beer community could be. At the time the whole concept of beer other than light lager was a long conversation with every beer drinker. And not every beer drinker was willing to try something new."

Today Denver's beer scene is indeed enviable. "The community is tight, they help each other out," says Papazian. "And I would guess that half of the 3,400 volunteers at the GABF are avid home brewers. It's that homebrew community. We started back in the 1970s, one batch at a time, making friends. That's what got things going. And we're still on a roll. And if you're involved, the next friend you make here could be a brewer, too, and the start of another community. There could be double the number of breweries here than we have already."

Looking back on all the good he's done for Colorado beer, Papazian remains humble—and deeply honored. "A lot of people come up to me at the festival and say they wouldn't be here if they hadn't read my book five years ago, or twenty years ago, and it's cool to meet people that are so satisfied with their jobs. It makes me feel like I've made a difference in peoples' lives. I've been blessed with many things, and that's one of them. They're thankful for something I shared with them, and they're trying to share it back with handshakes and a smile—and a beer!"

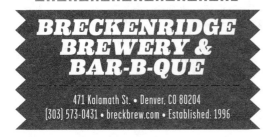

BRECKENRIDGE BREWERY & BAR-B-QUE

471 Kalamath St. • Denver, CO 80204
(303) 573-0431 • breckbrew.com • Established: 1996

SCENE & STORY

Ski bum Richard Squire started Breckenridge Brewery in the ski area of the same name in 1990, and his timing couldn't have been better. Coloradoans were going gaga for craft ales, and by 1992 business was booming enough to expand into Denver, where he added a second and then a third outlet for his Avalanche Amber and other brews. (There's another pub in Grand Junction as well, which opened in 2004.)

The Denver Brew and BBQ outpost is located a short drive from the downtown center in an arty, civic-minded area known as the Golden Triangle, which gentrified during the first Colorado craft beer boom years from 1994 to 1996, when growth rates topped 50 percent. It's home to the production facility for Breckenridge Brewery's bottles and kegs. The airy taproom adjoining the production side serves up a soul food menu with items like hickory smoked pork ribs and pulled pork that earn good, sometimes even rave reviews.

PHILOSOPHY

Breckenridge beers, like many in Colorado, tend to be malt-forward and down the middle in terms of hop bitterness. But that's why they work well with this kind of food.

What's more, the hickory used on the meats is presoaked in the brewery's oatmeal stout, a nice touch.

KEY BEER

Avalanche Amber, at 5.41% ABV, is on the mild side for Colorado craft beers these days, what with all the imperial IPAs and other strong beers afoot. Still, made with a blend of pale and caramel malts, it's a workable foil for the tangy flavors of barbecue. The seasonals and "small batch" series, such as the 471 IPA, are also worth seeking out.

THE FALLING ROCK TAPHOUSE

1919 Blake St. • Denver, CO 80202
(303) 293-8338 • frth.com • Established: 1997

SCENE & STORY

The designated after-GABF victory hall for hordes of visiting brewers and their fans, "The Falling Rock" as most simply call it, is among the most respected (and most visited) beer bars anywhere. Walking distance from Coors Field and the convention center, it's ideally located in LoDo (Lower Denver). From the spacious outdoor patio to massive tap row of hard-to-find crafts from the United States and abroad (75 handles, give or take), deep bottle list of rarities (130-plus), and pool-table-equipped, college-party-time basement, it can be a lot to take in at once. Service has been—predictably for such a shrine—a bit of a crapshoot, but let's face it: You're here for the beer. Locals sometimes line the bar and get first dibs, but once you make yourself at home, the experience can measure up to a slice of craft beer heaven. There are over 2,000 empty bottles decorating the walls, some comfy leather couches, one or two giant screens, forests of tap handles arrayed in endless rows, gloriously dilapidated bathrooms, and a pervasive sense that the world would be a much better place if we all could simply set aside our differences and try an amazing brew from some far away corner of the world.

PHILOSOPHY

As officially stated, it's "No Crap on Tap," and the list generally feels well curated, with a wide geographical and stylistic selection on offer, from mellow session beers to the most cultish, extreme, sour, smoked, and otherwise funked-out brews in the world.

KEY BEER

Certain imported beers seem to show better in the bottle than on tap, so, agitated crowds not withstanding, ask for a few samples before you take the plunge, or at the least, what's freshest. Staffers sometimes announce a "Blue Light Special" style, which means that something rare and tasty is about to start pouring, so listen up.

A recent winning choice: Boulevard Tank 7 Saison, out of Kansas City. The exceedingly clean and crisp tasting Trumer Pils from Berkeley, California seems to be a semi-permanent tap.

DETOUR → CHRIS BLACK, Proprietor, FALLING ROCK TAPHOUSE

When it comes to craft beer in Denver, Falling Rock owner Chris Black is both king and court jester. The taphouse is a monument, he says, to his friends who love beer as much as he does. He seems to feel like he was born for the job. "When I was in high school I went away to Europe for five weeks and found out what beer was supposed to taste like, at least for that time," he says. "And when I was in college, at University of Texas in Austin, there was a very early beer bar there called Maggie May's. I ended up hanging out there so much they gave me a job," he recalls. After a post-college stint for an importer and several more years of tending bar, working in breweries, beer bars, and for distributors large and small, he borrowed money from his father to open The Falling Rock, starting the work in 1996.

"My goal was to make this one of the top beer bars in the United States within five years, and the best way to do that was to tell all the beer journalists who come here from all over the world every year for the beer festival who have no place to go. So that's what we did. We built a place for everybody. I built my own favorite place to hang out." It wasn't an overnight success. "We were very cash poor, but we did everything ourselves and it didn't really matter. As this area has grown, and we got a baseball team that started winning, the business has really grown, and the Great American Beer Festival has been a huge part of it. Here we are thirteen years later. I'm seeing all my friends every year, welcoming them into my place to have a good time," he says. "The highest compliment is when someone brings their mom in. If it's cool enough for your mom, and you like hanging out here too, I think it's kind of an okay place, right?"

The endeavor has been fruitful, to be sure, but its success, Black says, comes at a price: "The hardest thing about this job is this week," he says of the Great American Beer Festival every fall, when Falling Rock bursts at the seams every day. "Physically and mentally, it's completely exhausting. I average five hours of sleep for over two weeks. It's a double-edged sword." Black, who wears a goatee and a contented grin, indulges in the odd cigar, and takes great pleasure in a good bottle of red wine when the workday is done, brief though the respite may be.

EUCLID HALL BAR & KITCHEN

1317 14th St. • Denver, CO 80202 • (303) 595-4255
euclidhall.com • Established: 2010

SCENE & STORY

In bringing her new restaurant Euclid Hall to Denver's tourist and foodie district, Larimer Square, noted Denver chef Jennifer Jasinski has also brought craft beer directly into the heart of the city's food scene. Craft beer lovers laud this development: surely other restaurants in the area will need to step up their approach, which ought to have a ripple effect. Once home to a Masonic lodge, the Colorado Women's Relief Corps, and a high-end brothel (among other organizations, some more dubious than others) the centrally located, two-story brick building is both a bit dramatic and immediately welcoming. On entry one is greeted with a massive chalkboard overflowing with edible ideas. There, Jasinski's open kitchen feeds the cozy downstairs area while a wide staircase leads upstairs to more gastropub tavern tables.

Upstairs or down, the hand-cranked sausages, poutines, and schnitzels shine, and the pickle assortment is a must-order: one pickle is infused with hops. Mustards are also hand-ground and house cured; you can't throw a napkin without hitting some sort of high-low riff like the gourmet corndog and chicken-and-waffle plate. For the beer-obsessed, there's PEI mussels steamed in New Belgium Tripel, beer-battered cod, and an ice cream dessert made with Guinness. It's a fun menu and environment, both resolutely urban and yet down to earth (a credit to the unpretentious staff), and it's often very, very busy. One of the axioms of Euclidean geometry is that the whole is greater than the sum of its parts, which is a fitting assessment of Euclid Hall itself. Its food menu or beer list are both excellent on their own, but taken together, you have something approaching ideal.

PHILOSOPHY

The motto is "Crafted. Not Cranked Out." The canned and bottled beer list is divided into somewhat kooky categories (arithmetic, algebra, geometry, trigonometry, calculus, quantum mechanics) meant to relate to complexity of flavor, but there's no extra credit for only drinking from the complicated end of the spectrum.

KEY BEER

Make sure you eyeball the "Very Special Brews" list, though be prepared for some sticker shock. On a recent visit, Port Brewing Company's Older Viscosity, an American Strong Ale, was going for $36.95 for a 375-milliliter bottle. On the standard can and bottle list, Del Norte's Mañana Amber Lager is a solid, food-friendly choice (way up in the "easy" arithmetic section, a bit unkindly, as it happens—it's not easy to make). And Durango's Steamworks makes the smooth, tasty house beer on draught, Euclidean Pale Ale (5.5% ABV).

★ ★ ★

WILD MOUNTAIN SMOKEHOUSE & BREWERY

70 E. First St. • Nederland, CO 80466
(303) 258-9453 • wildmountainsb.com • Established: 2007

SCENE & STORY

About seventeen miles west and 3,000 feet higher in elevation than Boulder, tiny Nederland—an old Ute Indian trading post turned silver mining town (population: 1,700)— is home to a lot of hippies, mountain bikers, and "the Frozen Dead Guy," aka Bredo Morstoel, a Norwegian whose body has been kept at -60°F by the townspeople for more than twenty years (long story), making him something like the town father. It's also home to a reasonably priced little beer and barbecue getaway very much worth a drive out of Boulder.

With well-made beers, a mountain view from the back patio, and high marks for its soul food (especially the hardwood-smoked ribs and wings, and the sweet potato fries), Nederland's little brewery would be worth visiting on its own accord, but there's still another reason people flock there, in late summer: NedFest, a three-day roots music festival that has welcomed such iconic artists as the mandolinist David Grisman, Cajun jammer Dr. John, and "newgrass" aces Yonder Mountain String Band. And because the town legalized marijuana for those over twenty-one (the first Colorado town to do so), there's a lot of people with the munchies about.

PHILOSOPHY

Beer and barbecue go together like peanut butter and jelly, right? This is a restaurant dedicated to the relatively simple mission of making great beer for great barbecue and vice versa.

KEY BEER

There are always four house brews on tap; try the Brewski Sampler (samples of four draughts and a guest tap for $5.95) to see what's freshest. The house brew Otis Pale Ale has been a standby, and the bottle list has included selections from Russian River, Lost Abbey, Stone, and Left Hand.

THE GOLD PAN SALOON

103 N. Main St. • Breckenridge, CO 80424 • (970) 453-5499
thegoldpansaloon.com • Established: 1879

SCENE & STORY

This swinging door saloon has the enviable distinction of having the longest continuously operating liquor license west of the Mississippi. It also has a wide, old classic bar, a bunch of taxidermy elk heads, foosball, flat screens, some decent pool tables, and the addictive ring game, an iron loop on a string one tries (and tries and tries) to land on a hook, with limited but eternal-glory-giving success.

PHILOSOPHY

While Breckenridge—or "Breck," as it's often called—has a lot of good, even excellent restaurants, this has not traditionally

been one of them. Until recently, it wasn't the place to find much in the way of craft beer, either—Coors Light was the brew of choice. These days, there are five taps, and you can at least get 1554, an excellent schwarzbier from New Belgium. And there are still further signs that the old Gold has picked up the scent of craft beers for good: Last year the pub convened its second annual Beer Fest, with about thirty beers on offer, including the superb Trumer Pils from Berkeley, California, and Alaskan Brewing Co.'s Winter Ale.

KEY BEER

Many a local will still order that light lager, whatever it is, but ask the bartender what's freshest. In a bar like this, it can be the safest bet to stick with something that's very cold and very light unless you can get a sample first to make sure the beer is in good shape.

BRECKENRIDGE BREWERY & PUB

600 South Main St. • Breckenridge, CO 80424
(970) 453-1550 • breckbrew.com • Established: 1997

SCENE & STORY

Breck was fortuitously founded beneath a soaring peak which would later become one of the top ski areas in North America, with steep, exposed, and sought-after black diamond runs like the Lake Chutes. Runs like those wild steeps were the first love of local Richard Squire, who, when not skiing, was home brewing, and doing it very well, as it turned out. As the state's craft beer industry fired up, Squire saw his chance and took it; today Breckenridge beers are available in more than twenty-five states. The original location of the Breckenridge family of brewpubs (an aggressive expansion strategy was scaled back in the late 1990s), this spacious spot has mustard yellow and deep red walls, with metal railings and plenty of space, giving it a somewhat modern feel. The hearty fare, if nothing really adventurous, is just right for après-ski. Score an outside table with a view of the peak (and those Lake Chutes), and the picture is nearly complete.

PHILOSOPHY

Squire had a dream: ski all day and drink great beer every night. That about covers it, doesn't it? Still, there are more wines than beers on the menu, which, for a Colorado craft beer pioneer, is inexcusable. It will take more innovation from this company to keep pace with the fast-evolving craft beer drinker who spends his or her days shredding the fine local powder and looks for sublimity in the glass, too.

KEY BEER

Trademark Pale Ale (5.7%ABV) is a clean, floral APA (American Pale Ale) with a faintly sweet body and easy, grassy hop bitterness, making it a great match for the upscale pub grub on offer. The 7.85% ABV 471 Extra E.S.B., part of the small batch series, deftly blends a roasted and slightly sweet caramel character with astringent hops.

★ ★ ★

304 E. Hopkins Ave. • Aspen, CO 81611
(970) 920-2739 • aspenbrewing.com • Established: 2008

SCENE & STORY

Two friends not too far out of college to be irrationally optimistic about starting a brewery opened Aspen Brewing Co. in a cluttered old architect's studio, decorating the place with hand-carved tap handles, Tibetan prayer flags, maps, and other brick-a-brack. Former Keystone Light drinkers, the roommates had discovered the incredible spectrum of flavors in craft brews on tap while going to school in Boulder. They started home brewing, and, dreamed they could bring the movement back to Aspen, local craft brewing pioneer Flying Dog having long departed. The optimism was well founded: their first batches blew out in a matter of days, a scenario they clearly still regard in awe.

The duo moved quickly to auger into Aspen's social fabric, contributing to charities, bringing in a new brewer and partner, and scouting property for the next level—they were already thinking bigger. "We're not just punks out of college," says Duncan Clauss, one half of the founding team. Today, the crew has graduated to a shiny taproom closer to Main Street and the Hotel Jerome, and to the well-heeled tourists that flock to Aspen practically year-round.

PHILOSOPHY

"We weren't interested in trying to wow people or reinvent the wheel," says head brewer Rory Douthit, a New Englander who took over the brewing duties in the spring of 2010. "We want to make great versions of styles that people will drink and drink often."

KEY BEER

The big, juicy, American-style India pale ale known as Independence Pass (7.5% ABV) is a grassy, floral blast of Cascade, Palisade, Columbus, and Simcoe hops, with a foundation of sturdy malt.

DETOUR → CRAFT BEER, GONZO STYLE

THE WOODY CREEK TAVERN

2858 Upper River Rd.• Woody Creek, CO 81656 • (970) 923-4585

The saying "Good people drink good beer" is not one of the best-known lines from the writer Hunter S. Thompson, whose seminal work, *Fear and Loathing in Las Vegas* scorched the pants off the literary world in 1972, but it is—obviously—one of his best. And, although traveling in the usual manner of Dr. Gonzo is not even remotely recommended it *is* a good idea to visit his two most famous old haunts, one in glitzy Aspen, and one right outside it in a dustier spot.

Start at J-Bar, a Victorian gem with a marble floor and tin ceiling in the lobby of the Hotel Jerome in Aspen proper. This watering hole started hydrating silver miners in 1889 and later became the preferred liquid-rations stop for 10th Mountain Division soldiers-in-training during World War II. Thompson used the place as his headquarters for his campaign for sheriff in 1970, running on his "freak power ticket" with a pledge to regulate illicit drug sales, replace the city streets with dirt, and, more than anything else, as he would later write, prevent "greedheads, land-rapers and other human jackals from capitalizing on the name Aspen." (He lost by only four hundred votes.) For years after, Thompson was a regular here, stopping by after the post office to eat, drink, and read his mail, generally making less of a scene than on the drunken night when he duct-taped fellow partier Bill Murray to a chair and pushed him into the hotel pool, nearly drowning him. The first of Thompson's two memorials was held here after his death in 2005; behind the bar today, there's a print of the poster Thompson and artist Tom Benton created for the sheriff's campaign with its iconic double-thumbed fist clenching a peyote button. On tap, look for locally brewed Aspen Brewing Co; for dinner, there's a good half-pound burger. Good enough for government work, as they say, even if you're not running for sheriff with a head full of high-grade smoke.

Thompson loved the area outside of town, too, which he first visited in 1961. While Aspen itself was (and still is) full of private jets and Hollywood types, Thompson's chosen corner of the woods, Woody Creek, was and is a lot grittier. "He could walk naked on the porch of his mountain house, take a leak off the porch into a blue toilet bowl with a palm tree growing out of it, and squeeze off a few .44 slugs at some gongs mounted on the hillside. He could chew mescaline and turn the stereo up to 100 decibels without pissing off the neighbors," writes Paul Perry in his book, *Fear and Loathing: The Strange and Terrible Saga of Hunter S. Thompson.* Fans of the writer (who coined another personal favorite, "When the going gets weird, the weird turn pro") will deeply enjoy making this pilgrimage, deeper into Gonzo territory.

The Woody Creek Tavern, founded in 1980 by theoretical physicist, spark-plug fortune heir, and longtime HST neighbor George Stranahan, resides up a curling canyon road about eight miles outside the town of Woody Creek. There's not much to see besides; as a local bumper sticker puts it, Woody Creek consists of "a bump, two dips, and a rumble strip." No matter; not only is this glorious dive Thompson's most celebrated watering hole (and a shrine with innumerable photos and tributes adorning its walls), it's also a business intertwined with Colorado craft beer history and even a thread of statewide politics.

Stranahan, a tireless entrepreneur, opened Aspen's first new brewery in a century in 1991, naming it the Flying Dog after a piece of folk art he'd seen on a wild-haired trek to the Baltoro Glacier in Pakistan. By 1994, the business was booming, so he moved operations to Denver and installed a 50 bbl brewing system (a.k.a. brewhouse), collaborating on a bottling plant with John Hickenlooper (Hickenlooper, creator of Wynkoop's Railyard Ale, would go on to become mayor of Denver, and then governor of Colorado in early 2011).

Flying Dog is now based in Maryland, but the Woody Creek Tavern, festooned with American flags, prized by the locals (the "Woody Creatures"), and flanked by a trailer park, isn't going anywhere. With its walls shimmering with thousands of Polaroids and margaritas as strong as mescaline, nor will you.

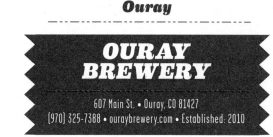

OURAY BREWERY

607 Main St. • Ouray, CO 81427
(970) 325-7388 • ouraybrewery.com • Established: 2010

SCENE & STORY

In a town built at elevation of 7,800 feet and ringed by peaks so high its long been touted as the Switzerland of America (population: 900), it's fitting that the Ouray Brewery feels like a vertical affair, with a ground floor taproom leading up to a brewery and dining room mezzanine, and finally a stunning rooftop deck from which to view a cathedral of soaring 14ers (14,000-foot peaks) including Hayden and Whitehouse Peaks. The taproom has a modernized mountain house feel, with exposed beams, track lighting, and a row of heavyweight bar swings hanging from the ceiling. Once a trinket shop and home of a local newspaper, *The Ouray Plaindealer*, 607 Main is now one of the most bustling watering holes in Ouray.

But it's not just beer: founder Erin Eddy also organizes the annual Ouray Ice Festival, a world-famous ice climbing weekend held every January in the Ouray Ice Park, a daredevil's playground formed each winter when the city runs gushers of water into Uncompahgre Gorge that promptly freeze in place. More than 3,000 alpinists, gear heads, and assorted outdoor mavens pile into town to watch and compete in climbing competitions. After climbing hundred-foot spires of ice or tightrope walking the gorge on a nylon slack line, you can imagine one might develop a bit of thirst; so it's a good thing there's plenty of local beer.

PHILOSOPHY

Eddy's m.o. is straightforward. "Consistency is the philosophy I'm trying to follow. Same four beers on tap at all times. Never run out of beer. Never run out of food. Never give bad service. Hire the best people, and make sure they follow the vision I have."

KEY BEER

San Juan IPA, with a ruddy copper hue, ample, citrusy hop bite, and medium body is the local favorite.

DETOUR ➡ OURAYLE HOUSE BREWERY

215 7th Ave. • Ouray, CO 81427

(970) 903-1824 • ourAylehouse.com • Established: 2005

Getting to the tiny mountain town of Ouray takes some doing. Wedged beneath a scrum of jagged San Juan Mountain passes, it's a solid two-hour drive from Aspen or Durango. But for the love of beer, you should go.

I did, en route to Durango from Aspen, but almost made the mistake of merely passing through. In fact, I'd been hearing about this town for ages—there's a world-famous ice climbing festival every winter, and in summer, tourists flock to ride the Durango-to-Silverton Narrow Gauge Railroad Train as it chugs up and down the 10,000-foot passes. At the time of my travels, though, I wasn't even aware there were breweries in Ouray, having made my plans at the last minute. But its main street, lined with historic, wind-whipped façades, was too pretty to pass up. Sure enough, you can walk right into a saloon that opened in 1891, at the Old Western Hotel, and salute the portrait of "Juanita" on the floor, painted by an itinerant artist for the princely sum of a few beers.

Ask around where to get a good, locally brewed beer, as I did, and eventually some Good Samaritan will point you to the Ourayle House, across the street from the 1891 Historic Western Hotel and tucked into an old garage building. There, with a mangled whitewater kayak hanging on a makeshift fence, stands the brewery, a "one man, one dog" operation, as the owner himself has dubbed it.

Reaching the front door, a hand-lettered chalk sign welcomes with: IT'S NOT THAT WE DON'T LIKE KIDS, BUT WE DON'T DRINK BEER AT YOUR CHILD'S DAY CARE EITHER. Below that: AMAZINGLY, WE ARE OPEN. And, SORRY, WE DON'T TAKE CREDIT CARDS. IT'S NOT YOU, IT'S US. And, hilariously, right below that: WELL, MAYBE IT'S A LITTLE YOU.

Steel your confidence and walk into the company also known as (literally) Mr. Grumpy Pants Brewing Co. (WELCOME! "WELCOME" BEING A RELATIVE TERM, says another sign) and grab a stool as locals turn to see what the cat dragged in. Discarded ice axes, crampons, and carabiners hang willy-nilly on the split and varnished salvage timber walls. A woodstove crackles in one end of the room. Signs, all hand scrawled in chalk, peek out from every corner. There are no TV screens, no gleaming copper brewing tanks, no chef walking around in a toque and whites. Ramshackle rocking chairs and tattered decks of cards are more the style here. To a certain kind of beer drinker—present company included—it practically doesn't even matter what's on tap, because the place just feels like a little corner of heaven.

On one evening I found the owner, James "Hutch" Hutchison, sliding side to side behind the bar on a kind of zip-line barstool with an impish grin. After studying land-use planning and the somewhat vague-sounding major of environmental economics, he began building the brewpub. It's a Reinhold Messnerian hideaway, cranky and cabin-like, sure, but also idealistic, big-hearted, and honest about what matters. IF A KAYAK IS MISSING, reads one totem, THE RIVER IS UP AND NO ONE'S HERE. WE'RE IN A MEETING. And, on another one, DUE TO FACTORS BEYOND OUR CONTROL, MAJOR POWDER DAYS MAY RESULT IN BREWERY CLOSING AT ANY TIME. I imagine Hutch chuckling as he locks up the brew house after a dump of snow to head out backcountry skiing. What's best about Ourayle is how merrily unconcerned Hutch is about it all. "You move down here for the lifestyle, not for the job," he explains. "I love that we have seven months of winter, three months of company. You're just nestled into the Rocky Mountains. People have said it looks so claustrophobic, like Mother Nature is giving you a big hug."

Call it a bear hug. It's the sort of town and place I felt I could disappear in for a while, though I know I would be all too conspicuously visible at the Ourayle House, drinking beer with Hutch and throwing a few darts over pints of ale. "This is where the misfits kind of fit in," says Hutch. "It's real casual—you can bring your own food, you can cook here, every restaurant in town will deliver here," he says with a cheeky grin, "with the exception of the girl across the street. She has a lot of young European waitresses working for her, and apparently they never make it back."

The fact is that this is what matters in a small town: fresh beer, and no Big Country attitude. And while Ourayle House might not have cultivated the time-consuming brewing techniques of, say, Avery, or the polish and feel-good politics of New Belgium, there was something about it that night that made me feel I might well have found the best brewpub in the world. Hutch was sliding side to side on his bar swing, clutching a giant *bierstein* from Munich's Hoffbräu Haus, a couple of regulars hooting and egging him on. "I didn't move here to see how much money I could make, or to see how much beer I could make," he said. "And I didn't come to Ourayle looking for a nice place to live—I was looking for a nice place to *die*. I get to kayak, I get to ski, snowboard, mountain climb; there's unbelievable cycling out here. You know, I brew beer when I just have to come up with money for a new toy, basically, to support what I really want to do. It's rewarding—I've done a lot of brewing, too, and I really love it."

I loved it, too, and paused for a few more minutes to hang out with Hutch and have a few sips of his Biscuit Amber, a malty, copper-hued brew that really needs to be consumed whilst seated in a rocking chair by the woodstove. This was one of the places I was looking for, long before I knew I was looking for it. But for me it was also time to make the white-knuckle drive to Durango over Red Mountain (see "The Million Dollar Highway,"). On the way out, I told Hutch I'd be back and paused to contemplate one last sign. It read, YOU HAVE THE FREE WILL TO FOLLOW YOUR DESTINY HOWEVER YOU CHOOSE. If the good-beer life be a choice, as it was for Hutch, then I'm in.

The MILLION DOLLAR HIGHWAY

US Route 550 snakes between Montrose and Durango, Colorado; up, through, and over Ute Indian country, the Uncompahgre Gorge, several historic towns, and a spate of precipitous passes. The Million Dollar Highway is the route's most famous section; Russian immigrant engineer Otto Mears somehow managed to build this 23-mile stretch between Ouray and Silverton, a tortuous curlicue of switchbacks following old stagecoach routes and mining roads (and lacking almost any guardrails above the plunging ravines).

It's a wonder he ever finished. Soaring skyward through a series of tight turns overlooking void-like chasms, the road tops 11,018-foot Red Mountain before easing—mercifully—down into Silverton. No one's sure if the Million Dollar nickname comes from the richness of those mines, now quiet, or the quality of the views. And while this particular road is the only direct route between Ouray's excellent breweries and Silverton and Durango beyond, it's not a drive to be taken at night, or in a gutless car, or with even the slightest buzz from one of Ouray's excellent local watering holes. On a good day, it's a white-knuckler; in darkness and driving sleet (as I drove it) it's a roll of the dice.

Durango

DURANGO BREWING CO.

3000 Main Ave. • Durango, CO 81301
(970) 247-3396 • durangobrewing.com • Established: 1990

SCENE & STORY

Just the third brewery established in the state of Colorado, Durango Brewing Company's taproom is located perfectly for the local après-skiers headed back to town from Durango Mountain Resort, aka DMR, who huddle around its U-shaped bar. It's worth noting that the resort was founded under the name Purgatory, after a group of Spanish soldiers who got lost and perished exploring the area, and for a flat area near the base of the mountain where later miners without money for a toll road would find themselves stuck. It's also famed for ample snowfall (260 inches per year), so locals ski religiously, and drink with gusto. The taproom was recently (and tastefully) remodeled after a freight train car, channeling Durango's narrow gauge railway history, but despite all the lore it doesn't feel cheesy. There's a consistent local crowd, especially on Bluegrass Wednesdays, and tourist season brings more thirsty travelers.

PHILOSOPHY

With the exception of a big, Belgian-style ale brewed for the company's twentieth anniversary with pilsner malt, Saaz hops, local honey, orange peel, and coriander (ask if they have any bottles left), the beer menu is made up of familiar styles (wheat, amber, winter). Beer geek culture isn't the same up in the mountains; many higher altitude locals seem content with a 1980s-style lineup of brews, and beer snobbery of any kind is likely a form of cool-guy Kryptonite. But one guesses they could fire up the slightly soporific atmosphere with some more risk-taking beers, and likely will. If you brew it, they will come.

KEY BEER

Derail Ale, DBC's 8.5% to 8.7% ABV ale, has varied over the years but hit high points in 2007 and 2008 with category wins at the Great American Beer Festival. It's low in hop character for an American–style IPA, but high in alcohol for a standard English–style IPA. As such, it's a bit of a hybrid with ample grain-given fruitiness.

CARVER BREWING CO.

1022 Main St. • Durango, CO 81301
(970) 259-2545 • carverbrewing.com • Established: 1988

SCENE & STORY

The second oldest brewpub in the state (Wynkoop of Denver opened just slightly earlier), Carver Brewing opened up along Durango's main drag downtown in the waning months of 1988, expanding a bakery operation that had begun as a small family business in Winter Park. The original brewing equipment has an unusual story: it came from a brewery in Milwaukee that had just burned down. "There was a paint store next door to this brewery called Century Hall, and the gentleman who owned the paint store was losing his shirt and decided to set the whole thing on fire," says head brewer Erik Maxson. "It jumped the building, burned down Century Hall, and for whatever reason those folks decided not to rebuild or not to reopen." The Carvers had found their gear, and brought it home to Colorado.

The brewpub became the first new brewery in the Four Corners region since Prohibition, and soon a treasured part of the downtown scene, unassuming and family friendly. Weather permitting, the patio out back is a great place to sip a brew. "This is the 'Cheers' of Durango," Maxson told a reporter from the *Durango Herald*.

PHILOSOPHY

Named Durango's "Green Business of the Year" in 2010, the company uses solar panels to help heat brewing water and the restaurant. Despite the advancements, there's a certain humility about Carver's that is refreshing. "We're just [serving] good honest food made from scratch, and good honest beer without an overabundance of processing, and hopefully a comfortable place for people to hang out," says Maxson. As for the beers, Carver's approach is straightforward: "My philosophy is to utilize the four ingredients that make up beer, and have fun, and try not to get so twisted around things that aren't our concern," says Maxson.

KEY BEER

The Iron Horse Oatmeal Stout, an opaque, roasty sipper, is dependably good. Carver's beers have gotten more adventurous over the years, incorporating cask conditioning and lesser-known styles (such as Baltic porter and braggot, a beer made with honey) so be sure to ask what's on and try whatever's freshest.

STEAMWORKS BREWING CO.

801 E. 2nd Ave. • Durango, CO 81301 • (970) 259-9200
steamworksbrewing.com • Established: 1996

SCENE & STORY

Originally built in the 1920s, the home of Steamworks Brewing Company—Durango's fourth brewery—had long been used as an auto dealership. There were cement floors, a large showroom, and a large, half-shell-like ceiling structure overhead. "There were literally GMCs and Cadillacs and Jeeps parked here," says cofounder Chris Oyler of the space, which now sports rows of taps, tables, stools, and brewing tanks instead of cars. Oyler—and a cadre of some forty-seven initial investors—felt the building's industrial look was a good one for craft beer. "Having those cars parked here, I knew that the floors could hold some weight. I knew it was a solid building," he recalls. At the time, though, the exposed wooden truss beams supporting the roof were hidden above old dusty ceiling tiles. "We started pulling them down and looking up at the rafters, and we were like 'Wow, this is gorgeous.'" It is indeed.

PHILOSOPHY

Durango's soft water—low in magnesium, calcium, and other minerals—is ideal for brewing, requiring little or no adjustment during the brewing process (a luxury not all brewing towns enjoy). The company specializes in lagers, and despite the difficulty of brewing those well, there's an ease about the place. "These are beers you can sit down and have more than one or two of," he adds, mentioning the company's Colorado Kölsch by way of illustration. That approach has worked, at least in terms of growth; today, Steamworks has a busy canning program, widening distribution.

KEY BEER

Steam Engine Lager (5.65% ABV) is technically a California Common, the beer style made famous by Anchor Steam. And like that classic brew from San Francisco, it's technically a lager brewed at warmer temperatures, with a slightly more fruity profile than standard, cold-fermented lagers. Also worth trying, particularly on a hot summer day, is the 4.85% ABV Colorado Kölsch—a lightly bittered golden ale with a touch of biscuit-like sweetness in the body and a crisp, dry finish.

★　★　★

SKA BREWING CO.

1022 Main St. • Durango, CO 81301
(970) 259-2545 • carverbrewing.com • Established: 1988

SCENE & STORY

With a brand-spanking-new, $4.8 million, ultra eco-friendly facility just south of Durango and an everybody-into-the-mosh-pit image—a breath of fresh air, what with all manner of fusty, dusty *Da Vinci Code* self-seriousness running rampant through craft brewing—Ska is a fun brewery to visit, because when it comes to brewing, they're not goofing around. A visit to the sunny taproom (and the gleaming silver Airstream trailer taco truck outside, Zia Taqueria, which sources beef from local ranchers; 970-247-5792) may be the highlight of any beer lover's visit to Durango.

PHILOSOPHY

The well-meaning hell-raisers behind this company, a group of Colorado locals who, one fateful day, decided to home brew because they weren't of legal age, have recently graduated to regional microbrewery status, a fact that still seems to give them a case of the giggles. They're known for pranks on other brewers (like producing a twenty-minute spoof of the Discovery Channel's *Brew Masters* show, starring their friend, Dogfish Head brewery founder Sam Calagione), and make the festival rounds with a posse in tow.

KEY BEER

Ten Pin Porter shows off Ska's more serious side: it's a fulsome, roasty black brew of 5.5% ABV with flavors of cocoa, coffee, and molasses in admirable balance.

>>>>> MAGIC BUS <<<<<

Why drive? It's far safer and more fun to leave it to the professionals. Tour de Brews is a new tour service offering guided, four-hour tours of Durango's four area breweries in a classic blue 1979 VW passenger bus nicknamed "The Dude." At $85 per person, the reservation-only service includes a commemorative pint glass, four 4-ounce tasters in each location, bartender gratuities, a snack at one brewery, a brewery passport to keep, and a knowledgeable, non-drinking tour guide/driver. Dude! Tour de Brews; 970.426.1441; tourdebrews.com

PAGOSA SPRINGS BREWING CO.

118 N. Pagosa Blvd. • Pagosa Springs, CO 81147
(970) 731-2739 • pagosabrewing.com • Established: 2006

SCENE & STORY

Heading east out of Durango toward New Mexico via Pagosa Springs, Colorado, on US 160 to US 84E affords one of the greatest drives in the United States—make it in daylight after leaving Ska and Zia Taqueria so you can see what's around you. On arrival to Pagosa Springs Brewing Co., it's easy to see why this small seasonal resort town is such a haven for vacation-home owners and skiers. Soaring peaks ring the town; Wolf Creek, just a short drive away, is a world-class powder skiing destination. And Tony Simmons's brewpub and beer garden is ideally located right off the highway coming into town. Since the day it opened, it's changed the drinking scene in this very beautiful place, and beyond.

"I don't think we realized how successful we were going to be at the time," says Simmons, who is the owner and head brewer. "We started off really as a beer bar with very limited food, and as we've bootstrapped our way through this it's evolved into a full-service, made-from-scratch menu, and that's really helped tremendously as our business has grown." "Evolved" is putting in mildly: in just five years, Pagosa Brewing Company has garnered an incredible twenty-four medals at the GABF and other competitions, a testament to Simmons' in-depth training at the Siebel Institute in Chicago and Munich.

The HQ is a rustic affair. "Our building was actually a garage," he recalls. "It stored a couple of cars and it had a wood shop, but it really had no significant power, and there was no water or plumbing. That was a big investment to get it ready for a brewery." Today it maintains a down-to-earth feel, with a lazy, expansive beer garden (10,000 square feet, with some fifty tables, heat lamps, and fire pits) and a folksy kitchen-in-a-trailer set up. The trailer kitchen is cranking out interesting, well-made food, from wild-caught Alaskan salmon and local grass-fed Angus beef burgers to pizzas and even soups spiced with hops.

PHILOSOPHY

"We're really proud of the fact that we don't filter any of our beers. It's all natural and I think it shows." Simmons is an energetic presence in the Colorado beer scene and eager experimenter; to date he's released some forty different brews. A contest sponsored by the Benjamin Franklin Tercentenary (a consortium of academic historians and museum curators) in 2006 inspired him to brew a batch of "Poor Richard's Ale," a coppery, low-hopped, Colonial American brown ale utilizing corn and molasses which was meant to approximate what Franklin would have enjoyed in the pubs of the day. A prestigious panel of brewing industry judges (including descendants of Franklin himself, "The First American") picked Simmons's recipe, which was served at the gala event in Philadelphia and was later brewed by more than a hundred commercial brewing companies in thirty-five states and some three thousand home brewers around the country.

KEY BEER

Every visitor should try the Poor Richard's and Kayaker Cream Ale, the brewery's top selling and most sessionable beer. It's a crisp, light-bodied Helles lager tailor-made for hot summer afternoons. When the sun drops and the air cools off, try one of Simmons's heavier-bodied brews, such as the Coconut Porter. "That was a real honor," says Simmons. "Other breweries have tried to [brew the style], but we've been really fortunate in being able to dial it in. People go crazy for it."

BIG BEERS, BELGIANS & BARLEY WINES

Vail Cascade Resort & Spa • 1300 Westhaven Dr.
Vail, CO 81657 • High Point Brewing (organizer)
(970) 524-1092 • bigbeersfestival.com • Established: 2000

SCENE & STORY

Every great day of skiing is best capped off with a good beer. So why not a hundred? For the last eleven years, a brother-and-sister team of beer lovers have put on this weekend of tasting, beer dinners, a home brew competition, informational brewmaster seminars, and, for those who can peel away from the action inside, skiing the world-class terrain of Vail. The eleventh annual Big Beers, Belgians & Barley Wines festival, held in 2011, featured a hundred top brewing companies (mostly from the United States, and a handful from Europe), most of which sent their founders and head brewers along. Which means for the festival attendee, it's a chance to meet some of the most well known brewers in the land over a beer in an intimate but not too crowded environment. Chris Bauweraerts of Belgium's Brasserie La Chouffe, Avery's Adam Avery, Dogfish Head's Sam Calagione, Boulevard's Steven Pauwels, Allagash's Rob Tod, and New Belgium's Peter Bouckaert (among other luminaries) all held court in 2011.

BEST *of the* REST: COLORADO

FUNKWERKS

1900 E. Lincoln Ave.• Fort Collins, CO 80524 • (970) 482-3865 • funkwerks.com

In 2010, award-winning Colorado home brewer Gordon Schuck and his beer-obsessed accountant friend Brad Lincoln opened this small, all-organic brewery in Fort Collins after meeting at Chicago's Siebel Institute to make saison beers, also known as farmhouse ales, starting with a tiny system and quickly ramping up production. Try the Funkwerks Saison (6.8% ABV), a tawny, grassy sipper with a clean, dry finish.

THE YAK & YETI

7803 Ralston Rd. • Arvada, CO 80002 • (303) 426-1976 • theyakandyeti.com

Nepalese chef Dol Bhattarai specializes in "mountain food for mountain people," and the house beers are made to go with his amply spiced cuisine. Try the Chai Stout, which tastes of cardamom, cocoa, and ginger.

THE TWISTED PINE

3201 Walnut St. • Boulder, CO 80301 • (303) 786-9270 • twistedpinebrewing.com

While only distributed in four states, Twisted Pine, established in 1995, casts a tall shadow thanks to a series of big wins at the Great American Beer Festival and a slew of well-regarded beers and experiments including Ghost Face Killah, a pepper beer made with Bhut Jolokia, a pepper that is also known as "Ghost Chili" and is six times hotter than a habañero. An excellent representative brew is the fifteenth anniversary Hoppy Knight India Black Ale (7% ABV), a fulsome, piney sipper.

FRESHCRAFT

1530 Blake St., Ste. A • Denver, CO 80202 • (303) 758-9608 • freshcraft.com

Iowa born and bred brothers Jason and Lucas Forgy present a super eclectic menu (from tacos to barbecue to French) and a vast beer selection with twenty rotating taps and over a hundred bottles; go during the "Beer Session" happy hours (3 to 7 p.m. daily) for discounts on sandwiches and 5.5% ABV-and-below draft beer pairings.

DRYDOCK BREWING CO.

15120 E. Hampden Ave. • Aurora, CO 80014 • (303) 400-5606 • drydockbrewing.com

Established in 2005 and connected to the Brew Hut, a home brew shop, Dry Dock anchors an otherwise flavorless suburban strip mall. The nautically themed Dry Dock has hauled up a treasure chest of top brewing awards and widespread praise. A boost from Obama stimulus money (allowing an expansion, which was later followed by another), helped to propel it to national prominence in a short time, even ranking as "Small Brewing Company of the Year" at the 2009 GABF. For kicks, they've been known on occasion to serve beer from tap-enhanced hollow watermelons and a 208-pound pumpkin. Good brews include U-Boat Hefeweizen, a sessionable 4.3% ABV traditional German-style wheat beer with a spicy, aromatic nose and overtones of vanilla, and Alexander Nevesky Russian Imperial Stout, a 9.5% ABV feast of huge roasted chocolate and coffee flavors.

COLORADO BOY PUB & BREWERY

602 Clinton St. • Ridgway, CO 81432 • (970) 626-5333 • coloradoboy.com

Brewing industry veteran Tom Hennessy's 25-seat brewpub in a converted 1915 drugstore in tiny Ridgway—the northern entrance of the San Juan Skyway Drive—is cozy but updated with pastel orange and green walls, craftsman light fixtures, an antique bar, and art on the wall.

The inspiration for it all came from travels abroad. "My wife and I were hiking in Scotland," he recalls, "and I fell in love with the small breweries up there. This is my sixth brewery and smallest by far. Probably my most fun one also." In terms of styles, he's determined to run against the big malt/big hop Colorado current: "I want to go the opposite way most others are going. My passion is to brew session beers true to style. Our pub is about conversation, not how much hops are in the beer."

GRIMM BROTHERS BREWHOUSE

547 N. Denver Ave. • Loveland, CO 80538 • (970) 593-2636 • grimmbrosbrewhouse.com

Grimm Brothers, one of the latest additions to Colorado's incredible craft beer scene, draws on Teutonic aesthetics and the wicked fun of Grimm's fairy tales.

Little Red Cap is a fine version of *altbier* (a German style of ale conditioned at cooler temperatures, made famous in Düsseldorf). Snowdrop American Pale Wheat Ale is a brew style predating the *Reinheitsgebot*, or German Beer Purity Law of 1516, and contains wheat, oats, honey, and molasses.

Montana

★ ★ ★

THE BEST WAY TO DISCOVER MONTANA'S BURGEONING BEER CULTURE

is to follow all or part of the Montana Beer Trail, dotted with twenty-three (and counting) breweries along some seven-hundred miles of the state's most scenic rural and wilderness areas including Yellowstone and Glacier National Parks, the Bitterroot Valley historic mining rail, and ghost towns, not to mention trout-filled rivers like the Yellowstone and Gallatin.

When you do go, one of the first things to know about Montana, an idyllic state with pure water, some of the finest barley in the nation, and a per-capita brewery density among the highest in the United States, is that for some reason, it has maddeningly confusing alcohol laws that conspire against craft brewers. Brewpubs are technically disallowed, as is production of more than 10,000 barrels (a beer barrel contains thirty-one gallons), unless they close their taprooms. At the same time, microbreweries may not sell more than forty-eight ounces of beer per consumer per day, and then only until 8 p.m. If they want to serve food and house beer from the same location, they must establish separate businesses at the same physical location that then must buy beer from said brewery. And so on, ever crazier with each new rule and exception.

The main reason for all this confusion is that the tavern lobby opposes craft brewers on the grounds that they believe craft brewery taprooms siphon off customers from their own establishments (despite the glaring differences in appeal). It all spells frustration for the small breweries, who are quite obviously offering something different. Drinking good, local, honestly made beer is an inalienable right in this country, as is the right to run or patronize a dive bar. Both can and should exist. Ultimately, craft beer is bringing better beer, jobs, and tourism to Montana and other states that are hurting financially, and it's fun to drink, explore, and manufacture. Time to wake up and smell the hops.

The good news is that Montana's craft beer scene is vibrant indeed. There are, at the time of this writing, twenty-three breweries and several more on the way. "It's growing. In Montana there's really this mentality to buy local," says Chuck Sowell, an assistant at Carter's Brewery in Billings. "So many of the small towns have their own breweries, and you don't have to be a beer connoisseur to come in and drink the local beer."

Change has come slowly, but come it has, and now you can pull into a formerly forlorn city like Billings and find no less than four craft breweries making interesting styles, barrel-aging beers, and educating consumers on life after the fizzy yellow stuff. "We're breeding a culture here where we have more home brewers, and more people that really appreciate the good craft beer, and so more breweries are now branching out beyond the basic wheat, stout, IPA, and ambers," says Sowell. "More breweries are doing barley wines and Belgian styles, and so there's an appreciation for that, too. It's really cool that there's a beer culture in Montana now."

Tony Herbert, executive of the Montana Brewer's Guild, says it's all part of the state's character. "Montanans have long had a history of liking their beer, so it's fertile ground, first of all. And a lot of the beers are coming right out of these Montana fields," he says, referring to the state's own amber waves of grain. "The water is fantastic, too. What I've seen is that people really appreciate the newness of these breweries and the beers that they make. We've been experiencing the same kind of growth that craft beer has recently. We [the Montana brewing industry] grew eight percent in 2009, and I think people have just changed. There's been a palate shift." Time to shift into gear and get to Montana yourself.

ITINERARIES

1-DAY Fly into Billings and hit all four downtown breweries, all within walking distance, experiencing the gamut of Montana beer culture.

3-DAY Combine Billings with Red Lodge and the incredible drive to Bozeman near the Beartooth Highway.

7-DAY Fly into Bozeman or Missoula and drive north to Whitefish along Flathead Lake.

MONTANA BREWING CO.

113 N. 28th St. • Billings, MT 59101 • (406) 252-9200
www.montanabrewingcompany.com • Established: 1994

SCENE & STORY

Situated downtown in the historic headquarters of what was once the Montana Power Company, MBC is a popular dining and sipping spot for locals and out-of-towners alike. Thanks to the ongoing refurbishment of the Babcock Theater, this part of town is becoming the arts core of the city. With a reputation for good burgers, nachos, and pizza, the portions are huge—as they are throughout Montana—but within reason. The interior is traditional brewpub, and a bit dim beneath craftsman glass fixtures. But it's comfortable, with wooden booths and a large central bar area and tables in back that offer of view of a tidy brew house behind glass. It's quiet; the sports bar Hooligan's next door seems to siphon off the loudest cheering sections, but there's a large flat-screen in the front area for the truly devoted.

PHILOSOPHY

The whole place is festooned with banners and descriptions of the company's many GABF and World Beer Cup (held in even years) medals earned over the years, most recently in 2010 (the sole winner for the state, for Sandbagger's Gold), attesting to the effort that goes into the beer. The brewery claims it was the first in the state to do any barrel aging, a costly and time-consuming experiment for any brewery.

KEY BEER

The lineup is fairly standard-issue brewpub fare—they've got a well-made but familiar classic range from pale and golden ale to stout—but MBC's Whitetail Wheat, a GABF winner for American wheat beers, is above par, with a clean-tasting, full-but-not-too-sweet body and a faintly spicy finish. The Sandbagger Gold and the Sharptail Pale Ale are two other beers on the lighter end of the spectrum, but seasonals (such as a recent fall release, Drunkin' Pumpkin), a pleasingly spicy but light at 4.6% ABV amber and slightly tannic coffee stout round out the offerings nicely, too.

ANGRY HANK'S

2405 1st Ave. North • Billings, MT 59101
(406) 252-3370 • Established: 2006

SCENE & STORY

Angry Hank, the story goes, was a cantankerous local that brewer Tim Mohr knew as a kid growing up. But there are no bad vibes here in Mohr's small converted repair shop, with retractable, glass-filled garage doors and a cozy patio. The crowd is lively and eclectic; you're as likely to see a bearded hippy as a U.S. Marine sipping one of the adventurously named beers that give this place some of its ample personality (Head Trauma IPA; Dog Slobber Brown; Street Fight Imperial Red). The high stools, small wood tables, corrugated metal accents, and gray bricks give it a smart, slightly urban feel. On most if not all afternoons, it's well packed (capacity is a scant sixty-four), and there's no kitchen—unless you count the popcorn popper parked along one wall. The staff and clientele are clearly outdoorsy, and the walls display pictures of climbs and rides that don't look the least bit angry.

PHILOSOPHY

Mohr makes use of locally grown hops—a novelty in Montana—when he can, and pushes stylistic limits beyond the norm, resulting in some excellent beers like those mentioned above, and his seasonals, such as a recent Oktoberfest, reveal serious brewing chops. You can tell he's watching the brewing world develop and eager to keep his drinkers enthused and curious about what's coming next. This will be the key to survival for many new breweries across the West: innovate and improve without kowtowing to trends—yet without blindly ignoring them, as the beer world embraces newness with more and more vigor—all while building a base of returning, happy drinkers. Easier said than done.

KEY BEER

The 4% ABV Anger Management Blonde Wheat is a tasty start, with its accents of coriander and orange peel coming through without dominating the beer. Those ingredients are added during the boiling stage with hops, and are fairly common in Belgian breweries, while Americans have only started to use such ingredients amid the craft beer revolution.

CARTER'S BREWING CO.

2526 Montana Ave.-B • Billings, MT 59101 • (406) 252-0663
www.cartersbrewing.com • Established: 2007

SCENE & STORY

Constructed in an old railroad depot storage building in the center of town opposite Billings's old hotel row, Carter's is named for owner-founder-head brewer Mike Uhrich's son; Uhrich was a brewer with Yellowstone Valley Brewing Co. before getting the itch to brew his own styles. Carter's is the young turk of the Billings scene, with some sixteen taps from traditional kölsch to Belgian-style saisons and farmhouse ales, Imperial IPA and even an American-style sour. There are more than thirty oak barrels for wood-aging Belgian and other experimental styles strewn around the tiny 7 bbl brew house—a marvel of space management—and it's a popular gathering place for the local beer fanatics, who come in to chat, fill growlers, and catch the occasional game.

PHILOSOPHY

"Mike experiments and brews what he wants to brew and not necessarily what people want to drink," says Chuck Sowell, one of three assistants who bartends, and a dedicated advocate for Montana's growing craft beer scene. "It's an interesting approach," he adds. "We've met a lot of brewers who brew 'to style' or they brew to win medals, or they brew to meet demand for whatever sells the most or whatever people like the most. Mike brews what he wants to brew. He's really, really passionate about his beers."

KEY BEER

De-Railed IPA, at 6.5% ABV, is a big, piney, clean brew with a bitterness-to-body ratio that approaches the heartiest of West Coast IPAs.

DETOUR ➡ RED LODGE, Montana

A former Crow Nation redoubt and mining capital an hour out of Billings, the historic town of Red Lodge (established 1884) is the gateway to the Beartooth Highway, a famed 69-mile ribbon of switchbacks on Highway 212 that leads south from Red Lodge into some of the most beautiful corners of Yellowstone National Park, with high glacial lakes, alpine tundra, and year-round snow. Ringed by soaring 12,000-feet peaks in the Absaroka-Beartooth Wilderness, including Montana's tallest point, Granite Peak (12,799 feet), the town itself is quintessential Old West, with hundred-year-old homes and stone buildings dating from the 1880s looking over the main street (and a certain bank scoped-out—but never robbed—by Butch Cassidy, who worked the area). Despite a bit of particularly grim history—a mining accident outside of town in 1943 remains the state's worst ever, having killed seventy-four men—it's a vibrant place today. Make sure to stop and read the roadside attraction sign (which explains the disaster) heading into town from Billings, and stroll down Broadway, Red Lodge's main street. Red Lodge Ales hosts an Oktoberfest every September, and there are scores of other events (including annual hoe downs, a Red Lodge Festival of Nations for Native Americans, and assorted adventure races including 10K runs and a skijoring duel).

RED LODGE ALES & SAM'S TAP ROOM & KITCHEN

1445 N. Broadway • Red Lodge, MT 59068
(406) 446-4607 • redlodgeales.com • Established: 1998

SCENE & STORY

It's hard to miss the brewery along the road into Red Lodge with its jolly crimson paint job. On a busy day, depending on the season, you'll be on the heels of plenty of bikers and skiers, for starters. The taproom adjacent to the Red Lodge Ales brewery is Sam's Tap Room & Kitchen, a bright, sunny space that manages to feel both retro and modern at the same time. There are shiny metal stools and wall details of rusted and corrugated metal, a large woodstove, reclaimed barn wood, and historical photographs to warm things up. There are large viewing windows inside to the brewery, and outside space is plentiful as well, with a beer garden and separate lawn for weddings and concerts. It all feels easy-does-it and well designed, and the hops growing on all the fences outside are utilized in the brew house every fall. The coldest months bring some rowdy fun with a Winter Carnival (www.redlodge-mountain.com), complete with a local dog sled-pull contest.

Founder Sam Hoffmann, whose family comes from Germany, started out small, with a 500-square-foot facility, brewing tanks made of discarded dairy equipment, and a trio of German-style brews (alt, kölsch, and wheat), none of which are at all easy to make well. Now that the company has earned its local and regional fans and graduated to a much larger facility (on track to produce some 5,000 bbl in 2011), the approach is much the same, with some variations for seasonals and one-offs, and room for a new big seller, Bent Nail IPA. There are seven year-round beers, and nine to twelve seasonals, many of them lighter to medium in body, and generally mellow in hop character, all made with Montana-grown barley.

PHILOSOPHY

German precision meets eco-minded. Head Brewer and Director of Operations Justin Moore explains that while the range of beers is somewhat traditional, there's something for everybody. "We do have the IPAs and double IPAs that we get to have fun with as well," he assures. What's more, the methods of making Red Lodge's brews are anything but traditional. "We have Montana's largest solar array right now," explains Moore. Among other innovations: a "free air" system which utilizes sensors and the outside air to keep beer fresh inside up to nine months a year, and an in-house bio-diesel operation (to run company vehicles and delivery trucks). The brewers also crowd-source some of their own ingredients: locals are invited to bring in their own home-grown hops for use in a special fall brew called Harvest, which those same growers later enjoy at a discount.

KEY BEER

Bent Nail IPA, a juicy, piney brew at around 6.3% ABV is the biggest seller these days, but the original altbier, called Glacier Ale and pleasantly quaffable at 5% ABV, gives a look at what Red Lodge was built on. "I think it most represents us, our best year-round beer that is true to style," says Moore. Also try the 5% ABV Kölsch, known as Reserve Ale, cleanly made and made for sessions in the grassy beer garden out back.

Bozeman

MADISON RIVER BREWING CO.

20900 Frontage Rd., Bldg. B • Belgrade, MT 59714
(406) 388-0322 • madisonriverbrewing.com • Established: 2005

SCENE & STORY

Located a stone's throw from Belgrade's Gallatin Field Airport, which serves the Bozeman area, this unassuming taproom is the ideal place to unwind with locals before a flight (or after a bumpy arrival). While the warehouse exterior isn't much to look at, the interior is inviting and busy. Friendly drinkers chat quietly at tall tables and a small wooden bar beneath the tall ceilings. There's classic rock on the stereo, and a wall of ultracolorful hand-blown glass tankards belonging to the Mug Club members. It's for locals, but they're an amiable lot. "We get all kinds of people here," says owner Howard McMurray, the tall, gentle fellow behind the brew kettles. "We get fly fisherman, we get college students. A few days ago a little old lady came here from Butte for our Double IPA (which is a 9% ABV beer) and I actually questioned her—are you sure you want this one? And she said she'd driven an hour and a half just to drink it. It's great to see that."

PHILOSOPHY

There are six standard taps and two seasonals at any given time, and McMurray employs a workmanlike approach, researching styles and the ingredients generally used in each, to just "go with it." It's refreshing to hear a brewer speak of his own beers in this unpretentious way; too many seem eager to proclaim near-magical powers. But McMurray's straightforward approach doesn't mean MRBC's beers are boring. They're sturdy and solidly made.

KEY BEER

"The Hopper Pale Ale is a beer I've been making for ten years in the different places I've worked," says McMurray, adding that it's changed subtly over time as he's moved around in brewing positions. The most recent version, at 5.6% ABV, has a more ample body than many pale ales, the tang of juicy Centennial, Cascade, and Horizon hops, and a floral aroma. Copper John Scotch Ale is a style known as Wee Heavy (akin to a strong porter), and McMurray's version is made with roasted barley and a bit of smoked malts, which gives it an appealing char kick.

504 N. Broadway • Bozeman, MT 59715
(406) 585-9142 • bozemanbrewing.com • Established: 2001

SCENE & STORY

Ask anyone where to drink craft beer in Bozeman and the response is, inevitably, "Dude. *The BoZone*." The nickname has, admittedly, a catchy ring to it. Nestled in a former pea canning factory in Bozeman's northeast-of-center "warehouse district"—really just a line of buildings a few blocks off the main street—it's packed every night with locals clutching pints or goblets poured off of one of the eight taps. Mondays bring bluegrass jams, and the clubhouse feel lends an added buzz. This seems like the place Bozeman's most dedicated beer drinkers and ski bums come together when it snows outside, and with charming servers and walls that were literally painted with a sort of brewer's grain-infused paint, it's easy to see why. Bottle art was derived from a variety of historic Montana breweries, and overall the place has an unpretentious, friendly feel.

PHILOSOPHY

"When I started out here, it was on a shoe-string—borrowing against my house and the whole nine yards," recalls founder and head brewer Todd Scott, who brewed for the well-known (but ill-fated) Spanish Peaks brand, and scored much of its equipment after it closed. "And I was having a kid at the same time. I needed to come up with a beer that was going to start out selling well right out of the gate. I didn't have time to build a reputation for brewing awesome IPAs, or something like that. I needed a beer that was easy drinking, that people could drink three, four, five of, that was popular at the time—like Fat Tire. The idea was to brew something that looked like a Fat Tire, but didn't have that biscuity flavor. And that was our Amber."

KEY BEER

The malt-forward Bozone Amber Select is Scott's flagship today. "It's just such an easy drinking beer," says Scott. "There's nothing 'wow' about it necessarily, other than, 'I can have another one, and another one,' and that was by design." But don't skip the roasty, draught-only Plum Street Porter (six malts; no fruit added) and seasonals or one-offs, like a recent sour Belgian tripel-style creation called Funky Virtue; at 11% ABV, it is aged with cherries in port wine barrels for three years and was first released after Montana's state law changed in 2008, allowing the sale of beers of up to 14% ABV. It's got all the sourness and power and oaky notes one expects of well-made American wild ale.

611 E. Main St. • Bozeman, MT 59715 • (406) 587-7700
montanaaleworks.com • Established: 2000

SCENE & STORY

Spread out spaciously beneath the rafters of an 8,000-square-foot former train depot in the heart of town, Aleworks is packed nightly with locals, and its pool tables, cement bar, and outdoor patio accommodate crowds of around 300 at any given time. Still, with its cavernous wood ceilings and long layout, it doesn't feel like a madhouse even on a very busy night. The pepper-Parmesan fries have a well-deserved good reputation, and the fare centers around burgers and other steakhouse specialties like bison, Wild Alaskan salmon, and a superb eight-ounce tenderloin steak.

PHILOSOPHY

Upscale but not uptight. "We're not fine dining by any means, but we do a lot of really nice food, and one of the big things for me is keeping it affordable for locals—for everybody," says Executive Chef Roth Jordan. "We're really preaching that we take as much pride in a $9 hamburger as we do in a $36 Kobe rib-eye steak."

KEY BEER

There are thirty-two mostly local taps and eight rotating guest taps weighted toward regional brews from Belgrade, Missoula, and Big Sky. There's always a cask-conditioned beer (recently, Madison River Oatmeal Stout) and several seasonals like Bozeman Brewing Company's piney Harvestfest.

★ ★ ★

QUARRY BREWING CO.

45 W. Galena St. • Butte, MT 59701
(406) 723-0245 • wedigbeer.com • Established: 2007

SCENE & STORY

Chuck Schnabel and his wife, Lyza, opened a little brewery (seven-barrel system) in Butte against what some would call considerable odds. Butte was once home to five breweries at the turn of the last century (when "the Richest Hill on Earth" had made it a fantastically rich mining metropolis), but none survived past the mid-1960s, and the rough-around-the-edges town wasn't exactly the place to try anything too newfangled.

But today the Schnabel's airy taproom, built in a converted old garage, is a kind of testament to the steady community-building power of craft beer. It's comfortable and well lit, with brick walls and high ceilings, chalkboards and games for kids, and a wide wooden bar where Chuck or Lyza can usually be found tending bar. It's a good stopping point between Bozeman and Helena.

The only quibble is that Quarry's beers, which are named for types of local rock (basalt, granite, mica, calcite, etc.), were not (when sampled in late 2010) on par with other Montana brews in terms of quality. But they were not entirely lacking merit, and Schnabel is beginning to experiment with new recipes to meet the rising expectations and changing palates of beer lovers. (Note: In early 2011, Schnabel announced that Quarry was moving to a new location two blocks away, at 124 W. Broadway, in the old Grand Hotel, built in 1915 but gutted by fire in 1992 and vacant ever since. Plans for a ten-room bed and breakfast would make it Butte's first brewery B&B in the modern era.)

PHILOSOPHY

Schnabel is a pragmatist, even a bit curmudgeonly, and his beers reflect a utilitarian approach. "I try to keep it simple," he says. "There's no sense in overcomplicating recipes, overcomplicating brews. I don't even send beers to competitions. I don't believe in them. My biggest thing is this: If the beer sells, it's good. We have 157 members of our mug club and 260 on the waiting list. We gotta be doing something right." True enough. He's already risked a lot to get a craft brewery going in a macrobrew tavern town, and three years into it business is booming.

KEY BEER

Schnabel is particularly proud of his Gneiss IPA, made with Chinook and Cascade hops, and Galena Gold, a golden ale.

⟫⟫⟫⟫ A WILD RIDER'S PARTY TOWN ⟪⟪⟪⟪

Robert Craig Knievel, aka Evel Knievel, was born and raised in Butte (Oct. 17, 1938 to Nov. 30, 2007). Evel Knievel Days, a festival in his honor, occurs the last weekend in July, drawing some 50,000 every year. As the story goes, eight-year-old Knievel attended a daredevil show in town, and the rest is history—thirty-five broken bones later. On St. Patrick's Day, Butte, which has no open container law, becomes a massive open-air street party, and Quarry sells a great deal of beer every single second of it.

Helena

BLACKFOOT RIVER BREWING

54 S. Park Ave. • Helena, MT 59601 • (406) 449-3005
blackfootriverbrewing.com • Established: 1998

SCENE & STORY

Head Brewer Brian Smith and Brewer Brad Simshaw met while working at the state capitol (a big employer in town). "It's the exact same story many brewery founders will tell you," says Simshaw. "One day I walked home and got a catalog in the mail. It was James Page's Homebrew Supply out of Minneapolis. I walked back to the office and told Brian, 'I'm gonna order this!' And from there, we started brewing once a week for a couple of years, and just progressed from there." Today, their brewery in the heart of town is a popular, after-work spot, and the high tables for six encourage mingling. It cheerfully buzzes with servers, patrons, and conversation, and it's walking distance to Last Chance Gulch, the historic heart of downtown Helena.

PHILOSOPHY

Straight to style. It may not be terrifically adventurous, but it's effective, and the beers are uniformly tasty, fresh, and sessionable. They have a fourteen-barrel brew house, never pasteurize or package, rarely filter, and serve only on draught.

KEY BEER

Don't be confused: Blackfoot River's copper-hued Single Malt isn't a whiskey. It's an American IPA, and while it's heavily hopped with Pacific Northwest Simcoe and Cascade hops—packing a citrus punch at 6.9% ABV—it's quite a sociable beer, worth ordering twice. The name comes from the brewers' use of costly, 100 percent floor-malted Maris Otter malt from England, which, when brewed properly, yields complex beers with exceptional mouthfeel. Floor malting is when the grain has been dried and kilned and then raked on a wooden floor, a disappearing tradition.

►►►►►► Missoula and the Bitterroot Valley ◄◄◄◄◄◄

Southwestern Montana's Bitterroot Valley, a 100-mile stretch from Missoula in the north down to Lost Trail Pass (7,014 feet), straddling the Bitterroot River and flanked by the Bitterroot and Sapphire ranges, is not to be missed. With its world-class fishing holes and kayaking streams, jagged mountain vistas, easily accessible hot springs, swaths of cottonwood forest, historical attractions (Lewis and Clark paused in the area, and the Daly Mansion—a 24,000 square foot, 50-room palace—draw many visitors), it's one of Montana's prettiest corners. Missoula is home to a vibrant literary tradition (Norman Maclean, author of *A River Runs Through It,* was from here, and the yearly Festival of the Book is a major draw) and has a growing beer scene, nourished by the University of Montana, and featuring the Garden City Brewfest held every year on the first Saturday in May.

BITTER ROOT BREWING CO.

101 Marcus St. • Hamilton, MT 59840 • (406) 363-7468
bitterrootbrewing.com • Established: 1998

SCENE & STORY

In what used to be an old apple warehouse, this brewery in the sleepy former copper mining capital of Hamilton is bright and cheerful, with high wooden tables and metal stools—something of a Montana brewpub standard—and interesting old historical artifacts and photos, chalkboards, even a few big peacock feathers for good measure. Owner Tim Bozik, a commercial furniture manufacturer who moved to the area fifteen years ago, saw a wide-open opportunity to serve a thirsty local clientele who had few local options for craft beer. He utilized old dairy tanks and other hand-built equipment and began winning over the locals, crank by crank. "Old timers would come by and ask me, 'Are you gonna be brewing that dark sh—t?' Yep, I said. And most of those guys are still regulars." Bozik and his daughter, Nicol, are big music fans as well. There's a stage in the corner for live music twice a week; Huey Lewis (of famed 80s rock band) lives nearby, so if you're lucky you'll catch one of his impromptu appearances.

"There's such an eclectic crowd that comes in," says Bozik. "Walk in at any given time and you're bound to see the local pig farmer sitting next to the town judge and maybe a highway patrol guy."

PHILOSOPHY

"We're strictly about quality. I don't want someone coming in here and ordering a porter or IPA and hearing them say, 'You missed it,'" says Bozik. In other words, the brewing ethos is more or less directly to style, with an emphasis on clean, balanced beers. With the "whims," or seasonals, and experiments though, expect to see some more innovative styles like India Black Ale, smoked beers, and other departures. "The whims allow our brewers to try new things, try something that excites them. Sometimes we have guest brewers. And we do the same thing with our kitchen," says Nicol Bozik. Additionally, Bitter Root is one of the few breweries in Montana bottling at all, and what's more, they utilize the very sociable twenty-two-ounce bottle, great for sharing on a quiet night at home (or by the campfire).

KEY BEER

The juicy 6.2% ABV IPA is the flagship, but look for what's on the seasonal and whim list for a taste of what the brewery can really do. Additionally, the 5.1% ABV porter is especially interesting for its use of smoked malt, which gives it an almost leathery, earthy bite.

★ ★ ★

BIG SKY BREWING CO.

5417 Trumpeter Way • Missoula, MT 59808
(406) 549-2777 • www.bigskybrew.com • Established: 1995

SCENE & STORY

Two good friends who spent all their spare time home brewing and visiting breweries moved to Missoula in 1990 and met a third friend who was working in a ski shop. The trio got serious about beer (when not backcountry skiing) and their by-the-bootstraps creation, Big Sky, has grown so rapidly that today it brews more beer in one facility than the rest of Montana's twenty-three breweries combined. Not bad for "a bunch of yahoos up here having a good time," says cofounder Bjorn Nabozney. To certain Montanans who rue progress, the sudden success and size (around 40,000 barrels per year sold in Montana, Washington, Arizona, and twenty-one other states) can seem off-putting, but it's hard to begrudge their good-natured success. "We've sort of become the Schmidt Brewery of the craft scene with all of our animals," says Nabozney, whose mother designs the cartoon-like label art for the brewery. A visit to the bright, modern taproom is a fun affair, because every visitor is allowed four samples, which are no mere sips. Despite the location in an industrial park, there's often a sizeable crowd on hand.

PHILOSOPHY

Ultimately, Big Sky is in it for the beer. "We don't brew to get medals," says Nobozney. "We brew for ourselves. We brew what we like. Which is very similar to a lot of craft brewers. We don't brew a West Coast–style beer; we don't brew an East Coast–style beer. We're kind of monkeys-in-the-middle with regard to our hops and our malt characters. Our alcohols are pretty manageable; we don't brew a bunch of extreme beers. When I'm having a beer, I want to enjoy my third beer and not feel like I'm overly full or like I can't have another one. After I'm done skiing or getting off the river, I want to be able to have a couple."

That approach has paid off. "We know that because of our size, we're not the local beer anymore, we're more like Montana's beer. We're an apple in a basket of oranges—distinctly different," he says.

KEY BEER

The success of Big Sky has been built largely on the huge sales of Moose Drool, a slightly sweet-tasting 5.3% ABV American Brown Ale made with a tangy touch of Willamette hops from the Pacific Northwest, but the brewery's more ambitious barrel-aged barley wines, Belgian-style saisons, and other limited releases are worth trying, too.

LOCAL HERO

BRENNAN'S WAVE: Missoula and the Bitterroot area are famous for whitewater rafting, kayaking, and river boarding. In the taprooms and bars of Missoula, you'll inevitably hear of this man-made whitewater kayaking destination downtown on the Clark Fork River at Caras Park. Local Brennan Guth was a star high school athlete who later discovered whitewater and created a Montana-based kayaking school. He died in a boating accident in Chile in 2001, and a major community effort, including donations from Big Sky Brewing Co., resulted in the construction of this $300,000 play spot in the river (for experienced paddlers only), which was the site of the U.S. Freestyle Kayaking Championships in 2010. It's a meaningful local landmark.

BAYERN BREWING

1507 Montana St. • Missoula, MT 59801-1409
(406) 721-1482 • bayernbrewery.com • Established: 1987

SCENE & STORY

Think: Little Bavaria. Owner and head brewer Jürgen Knöller, who bought the operation from its original owners in 1991, is a born-and-raised Bavarian brewmaster, and he has taken great pains to create the atmosphere of a traditional German *bierstube* here, with wooden tables, German breweriana, hop garlands, and a barrel on the bar. The space is clean, with a wide bar and plenty of tables and stools inside. There are some traditional snacks available, like German *Landjaegers* (Bavarian beef jerky), and on Fridays, during the warm months, brats and sauerkraut are served outside. It's popular with firefighters in very dry years, reports Knöller, and there's a strong local contingent of fans as well.

PHILOSOPHY

"We're a lot different than the other breweries. For one, it's the good old way of brewing German beer, following the *Reinheitsgebot* [the German Beer Purity Law of 1516, still followed in spirit if not to the letter of the law in southern Germany]," says Jürgen. Which means the only ingredients used are malt, hops, yeast, and water, with nothing else in the brew. What's more, he's super dedicated to traditional styles like Pilsner and Dopplebock while adhering to extremely tight protocols for making and serving beer, but he's equally as vigorous in the fun department, sponsoring a raucous Oktoberfest and other events.

KEY BEER

Bayern Pilsner, at 5% ABV, is exactly true to style, and has a bready taste with good, ample, noble hop flavor, which is on the spicy side.

KETTLEHOUSE MYRTLE ST.

602 Myrtle St. • Missoula, MT 59801
(406) 728-1660, ext. 201 • Established: 2009

KETTLEHOUSE NORTH SIDE

313 N. 1st St. West • Missoula, MT 59802
(406) 728-1660, ext. 222 • Established: 1995

SCENE & STORY

The original location of Kettlehouse, a brew-on-premises facility where customers could make their own beer in small batches, has a gritty, backcountry ski hut feel, and newcomers are likely to find the crowd at least two-deep around the bar. It's there you'll find the magnificently named Al Pils—bartender, in-house philosopher, and the bearded inspiration behind a house beer bearing his own name. Pils and his cohorts serve an ultra dedicated fan base that sometimes refer to their favorite establishment as the "K-Hole," mingling as they sip on taproom-only offerings like the kookily named (but seriously brewed) Fresh Bongwater Pale Ale, Hemptober Spliff, and Discombobulator Maibock.

The newer north side location, necessitated by the company's steady growth, is a sleeker affair straddling the Orange Street underpass and built in an old train building, with high ceilings, exposed brick walls, and a wooden bar that must be one of the longest in Montana. It's a slightly more serene atmosphere, but not stuffy by any stretch of the imagination.

PHILOSOPHY

Tim O'Leary, Kettlehouse's founder, set out to match the quality of his beer to that of Montana's outdoor bounty. "I guess I don't call myself a brewmaster because I have a degree in physics," says the Helena native. "And I didn't go to formal brewing school, but we've taken recipes that I've created, and those that our staff has created, and refined them. A core principle of ours is to buy local ingredients whenever possible. The barley that we use is grown in Montana, across the divide. The hops come from the Willamette and Yakima valleys, and then we use pure Montana water. I spend most of my thinking, working, and worrying time on the quality of the beer. Montana's like a small town. If I put my name on a beer, I want to be proud of it, because I might see someone on the street, and they have no qualms about coming up to me to say, 'Hey, your beer's great!' or 'Your beer sucks.' If we're not making award-winning beer, I'm not doing my job. You've got to listen to people."

KEY BEER

"Cold smoke" is a skier's term for the sort of snow that forms with low humidity and low-temperature conditions, creating the best powder. It's light, buoyant, and rare outside the Rockies. Kettlehouse's award-winning beer of the same name isn't overly heavy, nor is it airy and light. It's a Scotch Ale that has fulsome, malty body with a slight smoky character. Spicy accents from East Kent Goldings hops (a British version also grown in the American West) balance it beautifully.

DETOUR ➡ BIG DIPPER ICE CREAM

631 S. Higgins • Missoula, MT 59801 • (406) 543-5722 • bigdippericecream.com

Not only is Cold Smoke the name for the best snow and a favorite local beer, it's now an ice-cream flavor, too. Big Dipper, a classic old-fashioned ice-cream stand which opened in the back of the original Kettlehouse brewery location in 1995, has become a staple in Missoula and achieved fame far beyond thanks to its retro feel. Cold Smoke ice-cream is made with Kettlehouse's signature Scotch Ale. Today, the company has a new location in Helena's Last Chance Gulch downtown, and added Big Sky IPA as a flavor, too. Other flavors (there are about forty total) include Pumpkin, Egg Nog, Chipotle Chocolate, Huckleberry Sorbet, and Strawberry Thin Mint Chip.

GLACIER BREWING CO.

6 10th Ave. East • Polson, MT 59860-3219
(406) 883-2595 • glacierbrewing.com • Established: 2003

SCENE & STORY

Located on the southern end of Flathead Lake (at 192 square miles the largest fresh-water lake in the United States), Polson is a town of some 4,000 year-round residents and is part of the Flathead Indian Reservation. It's also home to the nation's largest fiddle competition, and in the summertime the town becomes a major tourist thorough-fare. From the ground up, Glacier Brewing Company has a wonderful Old West feel, with swinging saloon doors and a historic brewery sign over the entrance (which came out of Montana's first brewery, the H.S. Gilbert Brewery in Virginia City), antique brewing posters, and wooden truss rafters. The owners expanded the taproom a few years ago, and today there's ample room for beer drinking both inside and out, in addition to a small wooden stage in the beer garden for all those fiddlers.

PHILOSOPHY

Unfussy and stylistically simple, hitting several major beer styles from Kölsch and pilsner to ältbier and stout, with friendly, smiling service.

KEY BEER

Cherries grow in the area, but the very popular, very sweet Flathead Cherry Ale is made with a grenadine-like cherry additive, which seasoned craft beer aficionados might have difficulty enjoying. Also try the Slurry Bomber Stout, at 5.5% ABV, a dry roasty sipper, and the Glacier Select Okto-berfest (6.7% ABV), a dark amber with some spicy hop character that is, despite the sea-sonal-sounding name, one of the company's most popular year-round beers.

TAMARACK BREWING & TAMARACK ALE-HOUSE & GRILL

105 Blacktail Rd., Ste. 1 • Lakeside, MT 59922
(406) 844-0244 • tamarackbrewing.com • Established: 2006

SCENE & STORY

Heading along the west side of Flathead Lake, it's a short drive onto Lakeside, with the turn for "The Rack," as locals call it, at the beginning of town. In the winter, this is a popular spot for skiers at nearby Blacktail Mountain Resort. The attractively modern two-level facility is situated on the side of Stoner Creek, and out back there's a shady patio that beckons in the summer months.

The operators, Craig Koontz and Joshua Townsley, sought to incorporate a number of touches from breweries they admire into Tamarack, such as an open viewing area from the second floor looking into the brew house and the lack of a barrier between the brewery tanks and the bar area itself (a feature borrowed from Four Peaks Brewery in Tempe, Arizona, where Northern California-raised brewer Koontz met business partner Townsley). With the beautiful copper-clad kettles and seven shiny fermenters, there's a cheery confidence about the place and a hum of activity even on weekday afternoons. One of the best features is a wood-burning indoor-outdoor fireplace with seating on each side—on the patio and inside the restaurant.

And while the Alehouse & Grill area is technically a separate business from the brewery, it's really only on paper that the two are distinct from each other. "You can hear it, and you can smell it," says Koontz proudly of the open-plan design. The food menu is extensive, from burgers to pizzas made with handmade beer dough and even a few Southwest items. Several beer dinners per year stretch the kitchen's repertoire with local Willow Spring Ranch lamb shanks, seasonal vegetable tortes, and cured meats.

PHILOSOPHY

Koontz is an eager experimenter with his ten-barrel facility, with recent forays into making pilsner with Sorachi Ace hops (developed in Japan), which have a distinctive lemongrass quality. But most of the beers are true to style. "There's stuff that sells for a reason," he says. With that in mind, the ten standards hew to familiar styles such as amber, wit, hefeweizen, and stout.

KEY BEER

Yard Sale Ale. "We describe it as a robust amber ale," says Koontz of his 5.6% ABV top seller. "It's bordering on a brown if you look at it in the glass, which separates it from the Fat Tires and Alaskan Ambers out there on the shelf," he says. "It's got heavy amounts of chocolate malt and a little roastiness to it, as well." Ask if Old Stache is available; it's a super limited-quantity porter aged in bourbon barrels.

★ ★ ★

THE GREAT NORTHERN BREWING CO. & BLACK STAR DRAUGHT HOUSE

2 Central Ave. East • Whitefish, MT 59937 • (406) 863-1000
greatnorthernbrewing.com • Established: 1994

SCENE & STORY

The mostly automated, 8,000-barrel capacity brewery itself is unmistakable; for one, it's the tallest building in town (three levels), and for another, it's more or less completely made of glass, which shows off a gravity-flow brewing setup (using few pumps) unlike any other in the state. It's a striking contrast to the less lofty wood clapboard buildings around it, and it means the brewers have the best view. A tour up and down the winding circular stairs is recommended, building a thirst for refreshment in the busy taproom, which is a popular hangout for locals.

PHILOSOPHY

Solid, malt-forward, cleanly made brews. Founder Minott Wessinger, the great-great-grandson of Henry Weinhard—whose own Blitz-Weinhard Brewery was a Portland institution from 1856 until it closed for good in 1999—built Great Northern Brewing in 1994 as a vehicle for Black Star Golden Lager, with a hoppy lager recipe akin to the great Weinhard's Private Reserve which had made his family's fortune. It's a hop-accented golden lager designed to appeal to discerning drinkers in both the macro and craft segments.

KEY BEER

"Black Star Golden Lager built this brewery," says General Manager Marcus Duffey, by way of explaining why they brought the 4.6% ABV brew back after a seven-year hiatus (see the "Detour" below for more on founder Minott Wessinger and his inventions). It's a slightly sweet, malty golden lager with some discernible, grassy hop character, good for a session down at the bar, but nothing particularly astounding.

DETOUR ➡ MINOTT WESSINGER

Whitefish, Montana—like Aspen, Taos, and Sisters, Oregon—is an ultra picturesque Western town that lures hordes of affluent, influential types to soak up the vibes and spread their empires. Minott Wessinger is one of those sorts himself. There are several very well-made beers in his lineup, and, taking cues from the Empire Builder train line that serves Whitefish, there is some dynasty-building going on that might come as a surprise to lovers of craft beer.

In 2001, Wessinger, who had struck gold developing St. Ides (a "malt liquor") under a contract arrangement with another brewery in the late 1980s by having rap artists including Snoop Dogg, Tupac Shakur, and Biggie Smalls expound on its qualities, decided to sell Great Northern Brewing Company and cease brewing Black Star Lager in order to pursue other projects, notably a youthfully marketed alcoholic soda pop called Sparks, which caused no little consternation among watchdog and parents groups. After launching it in 2002, Wessinger later sold Sparks to Miller in 1996 for a reported $220 million. Perhaps sensing his legacy and lineage—and sensing new opportunity in craft beer—Wessinger returned as a partner to Great Northern and helped relaunch Black Star Golden Lager in February 2010. Who knew craft beer and gangsta rap were bedfellows in Whitefish, Montana?

THE GREAT NORTHERN BAR & GRILL

27 Central Ave. • Whitefish, MT 59937 • (406) 862-2816
greatnorthernbar.com • Established: 1919

SCENE & STORY

Right across the street from the Great Northern brewery, this is the kind of place that every town needs but too often lacks: a classic old establishment with a beat-up old bar, cool old signage from days and businesses gone by, a patio, full menu, and a stage. It's got a roadhouse feel, with pool tables, shuffleboard, and ping pong, and the atmosphere of a glorious dive without too much of the grime. And because it's the social center of town in Whitefish, it's typically filled to the brim with Whitefish citizens and tourists young and old. The locals are appropriately proud of the day The Boss—Bruce Springsteen—jumped on stage with the band to play "Mustang Sally" way back when in August 1996.

PHILOSOPHY

Officially? "If we ain't got it, you don't need it."

KEY BEER

Of the tap brews, most are local to Montana, or at least the Pacific Northwest, so ask what's freshest and take your pick. Kettlehouse's Double Haul IPA is a mainstay, as is Big Sky's Moose Drool, and Blackfoot Organic Pale.

★ ★ ★

BEST of the REST: MONTANA

WORDEN'S MARKET
451 N. Higgins Ave. • Missoula, MT 59802-4522 • (406) 549-1293

Missoula's very first grocery store, now in its fifth location, originally opened in 1883 and has played a key role in the development of Montana's beer scene. For starters, it has long stocked a good selection of kegs, stoking many a local party, but more importantly, its owners have introduced locals to thousands of imports and American craft beers, which are lovingly curated by the talkative and knowledgeable Mark Thomsen. It's a friendly, bustling place. In October 2009 another of Montana's backward beer laws was amended, finally allowing the sale of beer up to 14% ABV, a threshold that is common with many of the most sought-after styles of Belgian and English beers.

BLACKSMITH BREWING CO.
114 Main St. • Stevensville, MT 59870 • (406) 777-0680 • blacksmithbrewing.com

Housed in an old buggy salesroom built in 1908 that later became both a Chinese laundry and a blacksmith's shop (until the year 2000!), Blacksmith is one of the latest additions to Montana's growing beer scene, opened in October 2008. Stevensville, on the other hand, is known as Montana's oldest community, founded in 1841, and the owners and fans alike see this as a kind of synergy capturing all that is good about the great state of Montana. The taproom is a visual nod to this pedigree, all exposed brick, vintage high backed wooden chairs, pine walls with cowboy branding-iron "graffiti" (discovered during renovations), and bare wooden rafters and beams. Right on Stevensville's main street, it ought to be on any Bitterroot Valley traveler's agenda. The beers are West Coast–style ales like Cutthroat IPA, at 6.2% ABV, a traditionally copper-colored brew that's dry-hopped for an extra citrus finish. A recent India Black Ale or "Black IPA" was excellent, too, with ample roasted bitterness and a fir tree's freshness.

FLATHEAD LAKE BREWING CO.
26008 E. Lake Shore Dr. (mile marker 26 on MT Route 35) • Woods Bay (Big Fork), MT 59911 • (406) 837-0353 • flatheadlakebrewing.com

Originally opened in 2004, this much-loved brewpub resides on the picturesque eastern shore of Flathead Lake in Woods Bay, and boasts views of the water and big mountains under the Big Sky. The company added a pub fare menu in 2010 and a second taproom location in Missoula in early 2011. Try the chocolaty 6.5% ABV Porter, which earned a bronze medal at the 2006 World Beer Cup.

Wyoming

★ ★ ★

SNAKE RIVER BREWING CO.

265 S. Millward St. • Jackson, WY 83001 • (307) 739-2337
snakeriverbrewing.com • Established: 1994

SCENE & STORY

The mere presence of great craft beer is not the first reason to go to Jackson—let's face it, the Grand Tetons are the real draw here, especially in the winter for skiers—but it does sweeten the deal considerably. Opened in 1994, Snake River has built an excellent restaurant and award-winning brewery. The brewpub itself is a spacious, well-lit, multi-level affair with lots of windows, and frequented by locals who avoid the tourist traps in town (i.e. the Million Dollar Cowboy Bar, which, truth be told, can be a fun pit stop). It turns into a serious party around holidays like Oktoberfest, Mardi Gras, Halloween, and Saint Patrick's Day, and the food earns high marks, especially "The Roper" sandwich: braised brisket, applewood-smoked bacon, caramelized onions, white cheddar, and horseradish mayo on a house-made bun.

PHILOSOPHY

Snake River's huge popularity could have led it down the path of mediocrity in a hurry. Instead the family-owned brewery seems to be getting better every year. Since 2007, the brewery has ramped up its brewing program considerably, adding bold new styles and experiments that are gaining notice.

KEY BEER

Snake River Brewing Company has traditionally excelled in one particular style that few manage to nail or even dare to tackle: Foreign (aka Export) Stout, which is characterized by a huge roasted malt profile, a higher than usual alcohol content, and malt-given flavors of caramel, cocoa powder, and coffee. Their 6% ABV Zonker Stout has won scads of awards over the years, helping make Wyoming's first brewpub something of a legend in craft beer circles, having won more than two-hundred prestigious medals. But it's Le Serpent and Le Serpent Cerise that have bitten hardest into the regional, and indeed, the entire national beer landscape. A pair of limited release, Flemish-style sour ales aged in French oak barrels up to eighteen months, these two beers made surprise appearances in the top ranks of the American and international craft brewing awards circuit in 2010. The Cerise version is aged in the barrel with whole Washington cherries; both burst with earthy, tart flavors of wood and fruit.

TEXAS *and the* SOUTHWEST

With its piñon-dotted highlands, sun-baked mesas, and labyrinthine canyon lands, the American Southwest is mesmerizing from 30,000 feet, the distance from which most travelers view it as they whiz by from LA or SF to the East Coast or back again. But the best way for a beer lover to experience its incredible bounty is to spend some time on the ground in the cities and small towns. The soulless casinos, strip malls, and tacky strip joints are just side effects, like jet lag, because a vanguard of hard-working beer lovers has suddenly propelled the Southwest's craft beer scene from tumbleweed to tornado, from Austin to Albuquerque, Reno, and even Sin City—Las Vegas. It used to be the kind of place where beer meant only a frosty can of Tecate with lime, the follow-up to a good tequila (which, to be honest, is still not a bad way to go). But beyond the old standbys there's now a new wealth of great American craft beer breweries and internationally savvy beer bars springing up like Christmas cactus in a dried-up arroyo, even along the iconic Route 66 amid the old adobe of New Mexico. In the end, there's nothing better than a brewery-fresh beer and a high desert sunset, but roadside tacos and Texas barbecue aren't far behind. Time to hit the road. Just don't forget the sunscreen.

Texas

★ ★ ★

THANKS IN LARGE PART TO WAVES OF GERMAN IMMIGRANTS WHO made Texas home, the Lone Star State has long been synonymous with beer, especially a couple of inexpensive, mass-produced lagers, Shiner Bock (from San Antonio's Gambrinus Corporation) and Pabst's Lone Star. No disrespect to those ubiquitous brews, but there's much, much more to discover in the new world of Texas craft breweries and beer bars today, especially in Austin, which has embraced pathbreaking brewing styles with the force of a Texas twister. These bold, natural beers go especially well with Texas Hill Country cuisine and languid afternoons with friends and great music.

Austin

THE GINGER MAN

301 Lavaca St. • Austin, TX 78701 • (512) 473-8801
aus.gingermanpub.com • Established: 1994

SCENE & STORY

Moved recently to its present location under pressure from real estate developers, this large, dimly lit bar consists of a long stone bar, couches, dark wood paneling and tables, a tasteful collection of beer trays on the walls, and a busy outdoor seating and stage area, well retaining the charm that made the original (close by and now called the Ghost Bar) one of Austin's most beloved spots. There are eighty taps and more than a hundred bottles to choose from, with a strong selection of American craft beers and choice international marks.

PHILOSOPHY

Founder Bob Precious took his inspiration for the Ginger Man family of bars from J. P. Donleavy's novel of the same name, in which the character of Sebastian Dangerfield is a young American abroad at Trinity College, a bon vivant *Time* magazine predicted readers would love for his "killer instinct, flamboyant charm, wit—and above all for his wild, fierce two-handed grab for every precious second of life." But thankfully, the maudlin shtick doesn't get the better of this loose-knit family of bars. Of the original Ginger Man, in Houston, Michael Jackson memorably wrote, "it is a true pub, where it is possible to indulge in conversation without having dubious entertainments or food pressed upon one. Despite its name, it has no oppressive theme, either as a literary bar or as an Irish tavern."

KEY BEER

Jester King's Commercial Suicide, a 3.3% ABV traditional English Mild, the sort of beer Michael Jackson (a Fuller's Chiswick Bitter man) might have sampled, and one that will not lead too quickly to reckless, Dangerfield-style debauchery.

DRAUGHT HOUSE PUB & BREWERY

4112 Medical Pkwy., No. 100 • Austin, TX 78756
(512) 452-MALT • draughthouse.com • Established: 1968

SCENE & STORY

Austin's most famous beer destination, The Draught House is an old Anglo-German-style bar with a Tudor half-timber exterior. Inside is a softly-lit, exposed-beamed space furnished with rough-hewn wood tables and straight-backed wood chairs, and a bar with seventy taps, eighteen bottles, and a few casks on at a time, along with pub grub like made-to-order pizza, nachos, and calzones. Outside, there's a massive beer garden that often fills with a chilled-out crowd.

PHILOSOPHY

The Old World meets Craft Beer Nation, U.S.A. Instead of lining up along the bar for the latest Victory, Dogfish, and Green Flash brews, locals know to form an orderly single-file line, as if purchasing train tickets in Munich or Piccadilly Circus, but they're quite happy in the process. You will be, too.

KEY BEER

There are always five or so house beers and one on cask, like a recent single hop IPA, Hop School Nugget (7% ABV), resinously grassy with a drying finish.

JESTER KING CRAFT BREWERY

13005 Fitzhugh Rd., Bld. B • Austin, TX 78736
(512) 537-5100 • jesterkingbrewery.com • Established: 2010

SCENE & STORY

Few breweries have to remind visitors to leave pets at home so as not to spook the livestock. Located fifteen miles outside of town on a ranch in the rolling Texas Hill Country, Jester King is a first for the American South: an ambitious farmhouse brewery working primarily in the rarified world of oak-barrel aging and second fermentations in the bottle. With a massive 8,000-square-foot barn next to the new stone-walled brewery, the owners opened for business with a rapid-fire release of highly rated beers including a collaboration with Dane Mikkel Borg Bjergsø of Mikkeller, the acclaimed globe-trotting gypsy brewer.

PHILOSOPHY

Belgium comes to Hill Country. By Texas standards these are wild, experimental beers, but the Belgian and French traditions at work here are time tested. The founders also espouse deep philosophical underpinnings of conservation, pledging to use organic and local raw materials at every turn, even rainwater in the brewing kettles.

KEY BEER

Boxer's Revenge Farmhouse Provision Ale (9% ABV) is a dry, Champagne-like farmhouse ale dry hopped with spicy Hallertau and floral Cascade and Centennial hops. The beer is refermented in French oak wine barrels with wild yeast for up to a year.

Fort Worth

RAHR & SONS BREWING CO.

701 Galveston Ave. • Fort Worth, TX 76104 • (817) 810-9266
rahrbrewing.com • Established: 2004

SCENE & STORY

"Fritz" Rahr Jr.'s great-great-grandfather William opened the first lager brewery in Wisconsin in 1847, but was killed due to burns suffered in a tragic brewing kettle fall. His descendant's brewery is already up to 6,000 bbl per year.

PHILOSOPHY

German-influenced beers with Texas twang and a sense of off-beat humor, as evidenced by beers named Ugly Pugg and Buffalo Butt.

KEY BEER

Look for the Iron Thistle, an 8.5% ABV Scotch Ale with hints of fig, raisin, chocolate, and smoke.

BEST *of the* REST: TEXAS

LIVE OAK BREWING COMPANY

3301-B E. 5th Street • Austin, TX 78702 • (512) 385-2299 • liveoakbrewing.com

Founded in a bare-bones two-room warehouse of a brewery in southeast Austin in 1997, Live Oak has gained a reputation for making some of Austin's—and the entire Southwest's—best beer, thanks to their luscious Live Oak HefeWeizen (4.1% ABV). The secret to their success? Ultratraditional old-world methods including open fermenters made from repurposed dairy tanks, secondary lagering (cold aging), and decoction mashing, a technique described in detail on a super popular, reservations-required ninety-minute tour.

THE FLYING SAUCER DRAFT EMPORIUM

815 W. 47th St. • Austin, TX 78751 • (512) 454-8200 • beerknurd.com/stores/

Six of the fourteen all-craft-focused Flying Saucer Draft Emporiums are located in Texas, which says a lot about the kind of beer Texans are getting into these days. With 70 taps, 140 bottled selections, and a couple of casks at any given time, this most recently added outlet's selection makes its mall-like exterior and college crowd eminently bearable. Early on, the servers were more eye candy than beer experts but the level of institutional knowledge has ramped up considerably in the last few years. Once akin to Hooters with better beer, the Flying Saucer, founded in 2008, is headed higher.

UNCLE BILLY'S BREW & QUE

1530 Barton Springs Rd. • Austin, TX 78704 • (512) 476-0100 • unclebillysaustin.com

Decent Texas-style barbecue, pulled pork sandwiches, fried chicken-and-waffles, and brisket share the bill with award-winning house brews. Brewer Brian Peters breaks out fresh cask beers on the first Tuesday of every month, and has recently been experimenting with smoked beers to go with all the mesquite-grilled fare. Try the Hell in Keller, a kellerbier (aka zwickelbier) which has earned two medals at the GABF. There's a sleek second location overlooking Lake Travis serving the same fare.

New Mexico

★ ★ ★

Albuquerque

MARBLE BREWERY

111 Marble Ave. NW • Albuquerque, NM 87102
(505) 243-2739 • marblebrewery.com • Established: 2008

SCENE & STORY

A hoppy oasis in a dusty warehouse area of Albuquerque not far from the main drag of Lomas Boulevard, Marble produces a modest, but growing, 6,000 bbl per year. The brewpub has hardwood floors, deep red walls, a forty-inch-wide bar, and a spacious, umbrella-equipped seating area outside. "It's a great scene," says founder Ted Rice. "We get blue-collar guys coming in from the machine shops that are right around the corner. But then we're also right next to the courthouse facility, so we'll get lawyers coming in, too. And we get the local beer nerds—all walks of life, all commingling and just gathering around a great local flavor." Try one of the ten beers available, including seven year-round brews plus the three Brewer's Specials, and fortify yourself with the Marble Nachos draped with a layer of homemade beef chili made with New Mexico red chiles. Casks are tapped Fridays, and tours are possible when the brewer's schedule allows (try calling ahead). Growlers go for a mere $7.75. This is a short drive from the airport, so it would make a great first or last stop in the Land of Enchantment.

PHILOSOPHY

Rice and Co. have helped New Mexico embrace the tang and bite of spicier beers. "We want the malt character and the residual sweetness to be low, to allow layers of hop flavors to shine through," Rice says. "So, when you have those layers of hop flavors and that low residual sweetness, the malt base is dry, and you have drinkability."

The water in Albuquerque is fairly alkaline and fluctuates depending on whether the city is drawing from surface or well sources; turning a potential liability into a strength, Marble runs brewing water through a reverse osmosis filter and then adds back in necessary minerals and salts, allowing them to mimic classic brewing styles.

KEY BEER

Marble Red is a chewy, 6.2% ABV sipper with ample caramel malt body enfolded by juicy Cascade, Crystal, and Simcoe hops.

★ ★ ★

Santa Fe

SANTA FE BREWING CO.

35 Fire Pl. • Santa Fe, NM 87508 • (505) 424-3333
santafebrewing.com • Established: 1988

SCENE & STORY

The road leading to New Mexico's oldest brewing company was known as a section of Route 66 as it passed through town during the 1920s and 1930s. Today it's known as Route 14, aka Cerillos Boulevard, and the Turquoise Trail National Scenic Byway. Time your visit (it's about a 15-minute drive from the city center) for sunset, because the taproom and its outdoor tables have ideal west-facing views overlooking the vast, high-desert plateau Bandelier National Monument.

The taproom is cozy, quiet, and congenial, with stools and high ceilings, and food is available next door at the related Santa Fe Brewing Pub & Grill, which also sells beer to-go and features a solid lineup of live concerts at night. Free, guided brewery tours are offered on Saturdays at 12 p.m., and there are ten house beers on tap plus one guest tap and growler sales. Once an almost unknown brand outside of Santa Fe, the addition of new tanks and a bottling line and canning capability for Happy Camper IPA and an Oktoberfest beer have revved up this brand to 11,000 bbl a year (it didn't hurt when the owners put the 6.6% ABV brew in a can comprised solely of the New Mexico state flag's red, stylized sunbeam "Zia" against a bright yellow field). Recently, the beers have gone from banal to barnstorming, incorporating barrel aging, wild yeasts, and other tricky techniques.

KEY BEER

Brewer Ty Levis's Zotte Berten series showcases the brewery's new experimental side, such as #5, a tart brew resembling the Belgian style of *geuze*, made from blends of aged and young lambic, or spontaneously fermented beer.

SECOND STREET BREWERY at SECOND STREET

1814 Second St. • Santa Fe, NM 87505 • (505) 982-3030
secondstreetbrewery.com • Established: 1996

SECOND STREET BREWERY at THE RAILYARD

1607 Paseo De Peralta, No. 10 • Santa Fe, NM 87501
(505) 989-3278 • Established: 2010

SCENE & STORY

Caught unawares amid the hordes of tourists Santa Fe is known for, it can be easy to want to run for the hills. Yet while 9,000-foot Atalaya Mountain just behind town makes a very good day hike, there is no brewery on the summit at present, so instead, hang with the laid-back locals who make Second Street a kind of second home. The original, housed in a warehouse-type structure next to some old train tracks with outdoor seating and a décor that might be described as 1980s meets 1880s: sponged sienna paint, wagon wheels for chandeliers, and arty photos on the wall. There's a more updated location, too, at the Railyard near downtown, home of Santa Fe's farmer's market (which supplies the restaurant in season) and the REI store, should you still need gear for that hiking escape. The patio makes a nice spot for al fresco beers when the temperature's right. Both locations have full menus; try something with green chile, like the juicy burger.

PHILOSOPHY

Strength in numbers. Brewer Rod Tweet has a huge repertoire, with about fifty different beers so far, though results are still a bit uneven.

KEY BEER

Start with a crisp Kolsch (4.6% ABV), which will put out the fire if the green chile takes you for a ride.

THE COWGIRL HALL OF FAME

319 S. Guadalupe St. • Santa Fe, NM 87501-2613
(505) 982-2565 • cowgirlsantafe.com • Established: 1993

SCENE & STORY

Known simply as "The Cowgirl," this darn-near-perfect bar is filled with creaky old wood floors, an incredible array of Western bric-a-brac, cowgirl photos, and the aromas of mesquite barbecue. Santa Fe's most popular watering hole, with nightly live music, a huge billiard parlor, private party rooms, and breezy brick patio, it's one of the West's perfect places to drink a good beer on a hot

afternoon. Based on a Southwestern barbecue restaurant opened in New York City under the watchful eye of the late Margaret Formby, the founder of the National Cowgirl Hall of Fame and Western Heritage Museum in Hereford, Texas, the Cowgirl is located in a hundred-year-old building in Santa Fe's historic Guadalupe district. Try for the Bob Dylan Brunch starting Sundays at noon, when local musicians jam on the iconic singer's material.

PHILOSOPHY

Beer, bluegrass, and barbecue, Annie Oakley–style.

KEY BEER

This isn't exactly a craft beer bar, but you won't go thirsty. Santa Fe Brewing Company's 6.4% ABV State Pen Porter is so good, so nutty, and so chocolate-like, you'll have to be careful not to drink too much of it, or end up in the clink yourself.

Founded in 1958 in nearby Española by the Atencio family, there are now seven locations in this miraculously talented family's minichain. Santa Fe's oldest (of two) is an unassuming little cinder block drive-through on Cerillos Boulevard; you may also walk in to order, which can be quicker when the cars are backed up or you've called ahead. The tender pork and beef tacos are sublime, but there's simply no way to adequately describe how good the burrito with roasted white meat chicken and guacamole with green chile tastes. Don't miss a bite of this New Mexico road food paradise.

Embudo

BLUE HERON BREWING CO.

2214 Hwy. 68 • Embudo, NM 87531 • (505) 579-9188
blueheronbrews.com • Established: 2010

SCENE & STORY

Housed in a tiny adobe overlooking the Rio Grande along the road up to Taos (the main road, not the "High Road to Taos"), this adorable little brewery was founded by dedicated home brewers in a building formerly used as a gas station, vet clinic, and art gallery. It's a teeny affair, with colorful framed art, track lighting, a little three-tap bar for the three beers on at any given time (brewed in a back room on a 100-gallon system), and at least three little kids with brewing in their futures. Parent-owners Kristin Hennelly and her husband, Scott, a biochemist, use locally grown hops.

PHILOSOPHY

This is community brewing with a sense of history—and humor. Scott Hennelly characterizes the clientele and the mission with a wink. "It's an art community, it's an old Hispanic community, it's a kind of a hippie community, and it's kind of a hipsters-escaping-the-world community. There's writers and artists from a couple of generations here. Kristin's parents have a winery—one of the earliest in New Mexico. It's probably one of the main reasons we're doing this, because they want to corner the local market in sin."

KEY BEER

Embudo Gold, using Perle and locally grown Cascade hops.

Taos

ESKE'S BREW PUB & EATERY

106 Des Georges Ln. • Taos, NM 87571
(575) 758-1517 • eskesbrewpub.com • Established: 1992

SCENE & STORY

New Mexico's oldest brewpub is still one of the oddest and most fun to visit. Founded by ski patroller Steve "Eske" Eskebeck in a little old adobe house a short walk from the plaza, it's just a few booths and tables and a small outdoor patio served by a nanosized brew house down some stairs next door. But there's something very comforting about the whole lack of pretense here. The food is good, homey, and cheap (try the green chile stew), and the best way to see what's been brewing is to order up a sampler and chat with the servers.

PHILOSOPHY

Eske is a local character who has seen the entire history of New Mexico's craft brewing industry unfold through recessions, booms, and waves upon waves of tourists. "I set out to capture what I thought would be a European-style brew pub or English brew pub, because I hated American bars," Eske says. "Dark and dingy and sometimes weird. We wanted a place where we could have friends and family over and have a good time. We still don't filter, we don't pasteurize, and with good healthy food, not too much frying going on, all ingredients are fresh, especially during summer from local markets. We have Hula-Hoops for kids out-side, a sandbox, ping-pong tables, and board games. Anybody can come in and you don't have to drink."

KEY BEER

A long-lost narrow-gauge railroad in the area was called the "Chili Line," running from Antonito, Colorado to Santa Fe, with a branch near Taos. Eske's homage to the local favorite tradition is Eske's Taos Green Chili Beer (4% ABV, a bronze medal winner at the 1993 GABF), made with whole roasted Sandia Hatch green chile added just after the yeast is pitched.

DETOUR ➡

RIDE ON THE WILD SIDE: THE SOUTH BOUNDARY TRAIL

Gearing Up Bicycle Shop • 129 Paseo del Pueblo Sur • Taos, NM 87571
(575) 751-0365 • gearingupbikes.com

Taos is world famous for mountain biking trails, none more vaunted than the South Boundary Trail, twenty-two miles of serpentine roller coaster bounding through steep glades of aspen, lush evergreen forest, and leafy meadows with widescreen views of soaring peaks and plunging valleys. Late September is prime season, just as the aspens reach their Technicolor best. To rent quality gear, hire a guide, or join a group, visit Gearing Up, right down the alley from Eske's. For $105, you can secure a seven-passenger van shuttle to and from the trailhead departing at 7 a.m. If you don't have a big group, call ahead to be added to a waiting list for your desired day, which ought be capped off with beers—where else?—on the patio at Eske's.

BEST of the REST: NEW MEXICO

CHAMA RIVER BREWING CO.

106 2nd St. SW • Albuquerque, NM 87103 • (505) 842-8329 • chamariverbrewery.com

An upscale brewpub with an ambitious steak house menu (petite sirloin; pan roasted striped bass) and even more ambitious young brewmaster, Justin Long, who paid his dues in Santa Fe and then worked at Marble before getting his chance to spread his wings. He took home Nevada's only gold medal in the 2010 Great American Beer Festival for his rich, roasty Baltic Porter, Three Dog Night.

MARBLE TAPROOM

60 E San Francisco St. • Santa Fe, NM 87501 • (505) 989-3565 • marblebrewery.com

With all the turquoise merchants of central Santa Fe's plaza area trying to get you into a serious bolo tie, the plaza can be a bit much. Fortunately, there's the Marble Taproom, located on the second floor of the Arcade building with a balcony overlooking the teeming park and market. Come here for views of the Cathedral and Sangre de Cristo Mountains and fresh pints of every Marble style.

Arizona

PAPAGO BREWING

7107 East McDowell Rd. • Scottsdale, AZ 85257
(480) 425-7439 • papagobrewing.com • Established: 2001

SCENE & STORY

Hidden among the car dealerships and dusty palm trees of Scottsdale Avenue inside a faux-adobe minimall is a real beer lover's dream, a solid brewpub that also stocks a massive tap row and more than five hundred varieties of beer in bottles carefully arranged in coolers. There's a couple of dartboards, some TVs, an overall mellow Western saloon vibe; the servers are hired to know their stuff on beer, which helps with a selection this vast.

PHILOSOPHY

The name refers to a local native tribe, a peaceful, agronomic group that anthropologists say were the first brewers in the region, making a corn beer called *tesquino* using woven baskets which are still in use today.

KEY BEER

There are several house beers that are contract brewed off-site. A 2005 bronze medal winner at the GABF in the nebulous "other strong ale or lager" category, Papago El Robusto Porter, at 8% ABV, is well above the standard English threshold of porter strength, but carries its weight well, with notes of nutty, burnt brown sugar and bittersweet chocolate.

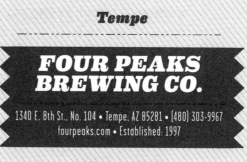

FOUR PEAKS BREWING CO.

1340 E. 8th St., No. 104 • Tempe, AZ 85281 • (480) 303-9967
fourpeaks.com • Established: 1997

SCENE & STORY

Just east of ASU's campus, Four Peaks Brewing Company (and a good percentage of ASU students on weekend nights) calls a huge 1892 Mission Revival–style barn home. Formerly housing a series of creamery businesses, it's got weathered brick walls and high wood ceilings with a 35-foot-high glass clerestory, the rafters festooned with banners for the Minnesota Vikings and ASU Sun Devils. There's a second location in Scottsdale, but this is the one to hit.

PHILOSOPHY

The All-American brewpub. Nothing wrong with that: expect eight tasty beers of a fairly standard lineup (Kölsch to stout), plus occasional seasonals and cask-conditioned beers, and the full complement of brewpub fare.

KEY BEER

If it's 110°F in the shade, go for the hazy, clovey 5.5% ABV Hefeweizen; any cooler, go for the Kilt Lifter, a 6% ABV Scotch ale with rich malt and smoky notes. Extra points for locating the Elvis shrine.

BEST *of the* REST: ARIZONA

TOPS LIQUORS & TASTE *of* TOPS

403 W. University Dr. • Tempe, AZ 85281 • (480) 967-2520 • topsliquors.com

What's better than a bottle shop with 1,000 selections comprising every foreign and domestic style and region imaginable? A bottle shop with a beer bar attached, drawing from its riches, that's what. The wood-paneled Taste of Tops bar has twelve rotating taps, over a hundred different bottled beers chilled in 750-milliliter, 22-ounce, and 12-ounce sizes, and a few small booths and two couches. There's a limited food menu, but the owners don't mind if you get takeout from Thai Basil or Tessio's Pizza next door.

Nevada

★ ★ ★

Reno

BUCKBEAN BREWING CO.

1155 South Rock Blvd., Ste. 490 • Reno, NV 89502
(775) 857-4444 • buckbeanbeer.com • Established: 2008

SCENE & STORY

With just a small seating area for a taproom and a couple of dartboards, the warehouse-like Buckbean HQ is a modest affair, but the cans-only brewery has big visions of supplying the region with craft beer in the mighty. The brewery offers free tours and tastes in a small taproom area with four drafts.

PHILOSOPHY

If you can it, they will come. Buckbean sponsored the first annual Reno International Canned Beer Festival—CanFest, for short—in November 2009, drawing dozens of brewing companies and hundreds of beer aficionados together just for the heck of it (www.canfestreno.com).

KEY BEER

Try the Original Orange Blossom Ale, an American amber ale made with Munich and caramel malts, American hops, and orange blossom water.

FREAKIN' FROG

4700 S. Maryland Pkwy. • Las Vegas, NV 89119
(702) 597-9702 • freakinfrog.com

SCENE & STORY

The Freakin' Frog is a three-mile drive or cab ride from the strip or downtown near UNLV, harkening back to a simpler era when there was no such thing as a roller coaster on top of a rotating hotel bar or the monstrous Wynne. It's dark as a dungeon; with no windows, the prettiest view is inside the walk-in beer cooler. There, in neat rows, are nearly 1,000 beers. The upstairs bar takes a similarly encyclopedic approach to whiskey and the pub grub is standard issue.

PHILOSOPHY

A good beer lover's retreat in a desert of tacky strip clubs and casinos, there's not one video poker machine in sight.

KEY BEER

The very un-Vegas-like Fantôm Saison D'Erezée, an earthy, rare Belgian farmhouse ale (8% ABV).

Utah

★ ★ ★

LITTLE KNOWN FACT: AS OF JULY 1, 2009, THE NOTORIOUSLY

conservative state of Utah's beer laws took a great leap forward. For the state's twenty-plus breweries and brewpubs, beers over the limit of 3.2 percent alcohol by weight (4.0% ABV) were made legal, though they must be bottled and sold in a place with the right license (which could be a brewpub, bar, or restaurant). The irksome "private club" law was dropped (it required drinkers to pay a membership fee for bars and sign a registry), but a few bars and other establishments still hew to the practice. "Taverns" must still sell only 4.0% ABV or weaker beer, and no wine or hard liquor. Keg sales are verboten, as is sampling at a brewery-only location, but home brewing up to 200 gallons per year per household is A-OK. It all makes perfect sense, doesn't it? So it goes. Time for a beer—might as well make it a strong one.

Salt Lake City

SQUATTERS PUB BREWERY

147 W. Broadway • Salt Lake City, UT 84101
(801) 363-2739 • squatters.com • Established: 1989

SCENE & STORY

Utah's most famous beer spot owes part of its fame to its central location in downtown Salt Lake City, which has of late gotten more fun to explore by night, thanks to the relaxation of state alcohol laws. There are nine taps and six bottled beers available (the excellent Reserve Series), with occasional casks, and a huge menu of good pub grub. It's big inside with exposed timber, corrugated metal details, tastefully modern lighting, and wide, polished blonde wood bars. Growlers are a mere $7.99, which makes them a good idea for après-ski libations up in the whisper-quiet Little Cottonwood Canyon.

PHILOSOPHY

Under the draconian limitations of the "3.2 laws" Squatters had to do a lot with a little for a very long time. But brewmaster Jenny Talley, in the role since 1994, has risen to the occasion, racking up a war chest full of medals for lower strength beers like her crisp 4% ABV Provo Girl Pilsner. Now she's stretching out into wilder terrain, with meatier old-world styles and New World variations thereof, like her 529, a Flanders oud bruin-style beer (or "old brown") aged for 529 days in oak barrels with wild yeasts (7.15% ABV).

The first brewer in Utah to venture into such tricky stylistic terrain, Talley was recognized in 2011 as the first female recipient of the *Russell Schehrer Award for Innovation in Brewing*, a prestigious honor from the Boulder, Colorado-based Brewers Association, which oversees the craft brewing industry nationwide.

KEY BEER

Black Forest Schwarzbier, Talley's authentically roasty yet light-bodied German-style black lager was recognized as the top example in the world in 2010, defeating thirty-seven rivals.

UINTA BREWING CO.

1722 Fremont Dr. • Salt Lake City, UT 84104
(801) 467-0909 • uintabrewing.com • Established: 1993

SCENE & STORY

From its catchphrase alone ("save water—drink beer"), this Salt Lake City microbrewery and brewpub a short drive southwest of downtown makes good beer without wrecking the neighborhood. Named for the soaring, east-west situated Uinta peaks in the north of the state, UBC is 100 percent wind powered and rewards customers that reuse six-pack carriers with swag from the gift shop, the Little Big Beer Store, which has seven varieties of beer to go. Inside the eight-tap bar, guests gather around wood tables, by the pool table or dartboard, and around the U-shaped bar, talking beer.

PHILOSOPHY

Uinta has been 100 percent wind powered since 2001, and all the spent grain goes to ranchers rather than landfills. Recently the brewery has also moved the beers in a more progressive direction. The minimalist labels of the Four+ series belie more complex beers within, such as the Wyld, a dry, citrusy, and faintly honeyish 4% ABV American pale ale. With somewhat mixed results, the 750-milliliter Crooked Series line wanders farther away from the old standards of pale, wheat, and stout, with an imperial Pilsner, double IPA, and 13.2% ABV black ale called Labyrinth, all labeled by hip local artists.

KEY BEER

Sum'r, from the Four+ series, is a 4% ABV blonde ale with a distinct lemony zing, excellent for a hot day.

★ ★ ★

BEST *of the* REST: UTAH

EPIC BREWING COMPANY
825 S. State St. • Salt Lake City, UT 84111-4207 • (801) 906-0123 • epicbrewing.com

The first high-strength brewery in Utah since Prohibition, Epic was established in 2010 to brew exclusively bigger beers like the Brainless Belgian series (around 9% ABV) which are strong golden ales, sometimes aged with cherries, peaches, and other fruit in wine barrels for added complexity. The beers come in three categories, Classic, Elevated, and Exponential, and are sold directly from the brewery in twenty-two-ounce bombers, but no sampling is allowed on the premises. No matter. Demand soared from Day One and Epic's distribution quickly spread throughout Utah, and into Idaho and Colorado as well.

THE BAYOU
645 S. State St. • Salt Lake City, UT 84111 • (801) 961-8400 • utahbayou.com

A busy taproom near downtown in an atmospheric old brick building with thirty drafts and some three hundred bottles to choose from (including some two dozen brews from Epic and another fifty-odd Utah-brewed beers), the massive selection is the real draw here, but a huge, Cajun-themed food menu, live jazz and blues performances, and free weeknight pool also draw hordes of locals.

EXIT 2

The Midwest ↗

The MIDWEST

he American heartland has long been the nation's beer cellar as well as its breadbasket. (And of course, the cheese counter, too.) But until very recently, nearly all the beer coming out of the lake-dotted countryside and prairies of Middle America was bland, industrial lager made with cheap adjuncts like corn, rice, and other profit-driven shortcuts, spending millions on ads instead of quality beer, even employing chemical foam enhancers. The craft beer revolution came on slowly here, but now more than ever, the area we sometimes call the Corn Belt—especially the Great Lakes region—has discovered the true joy of drinking all-natural craft beer. And if you haven't had the pleasure of drinking beer with native Midwest-erners, you're in for a treat.

The German and Central European immigrants who settled here certainly engrained a cultural thirst for the good stuff, and now breweries and beer bars are delving into life beyond—light years beyond—pale, watery lagers. It's a wild time: in 2011, Anheuser-InBev, the once proudly Midwestern but now foreign-owned makers of Budweiser, took control of the most famous craft brewery in the region, Goose Island, for a cool $39 million. Craft beer's march keeps gathering steam, and ambitious new breweries emerge almost monthly. From Chicago's world-famous Map Room bar to Nebraska and Missouri, where a bunch of rebel upstarts are helping remake the beer landscape from the geographical center of the nation, it's nothing short of a sea change. Or perhaps, wardrobe change is the better phrase: Beer Belt has a nice ring, doesn't it?

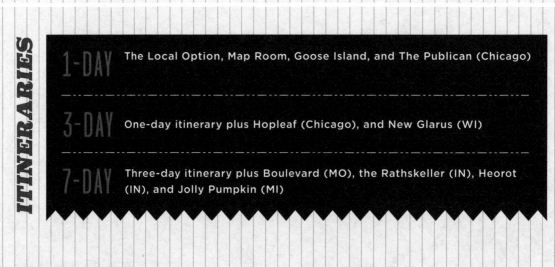

ITINERARIES

1-DAY The Local Option, Map Room, Goose Island, and The Publican (Chicago)

3-DAY One-day itinerary plus Hopleaf (Chicago), and New Glarus (WI)

7-DAY Three-day itinerary plus Boulevard (MO), the Rathskeller (IN), Heorot (IN), and Jolly Pumpkin (MI)

Illinois

Chicago

THE LOCAL OPTION

1102 W. Webster • Chicago, IL 60614 • (773) 348-2008
localoptionchicago.com • Established: 1988

SCENE & STORY

With black walls, a tattoo-like skull illustration on the wall, and a good-sized chalkboard of hard-to-find beers that unfailingly makes the savviest beer lovers weak in the knees, this Lincoln Park beer bar has another quality many of the top beer bars in this country haven't quite nailed: humility. Service is knowledgeable and friendly without being overly solicitous nor irritatingly aloof. There are twenty-five taps and fifty-five bottled brews drawn from the most eagerly savored American, Dutch, and Belgian brews, and the lineup often includes beers from Denmark-based Mikkeller, always an educational choice, as the beers are often formulated to highlight a single defining element, such as a hop variety or yeast strain.

PHILOSOPHY

As the motto in the skull says more colorfully in German, bad beer can be fatal.

KEY BEER

Jolly Pumpkin's Oro de Calabaza. Technically speaking, this is a *bière de garde*, or French for "beer to keep." It's earthy, oaky, spicy, floral, slightly tart and incredibly delicious.

THE MAP ROOM

1949 N. Hoyne • Chicago, IL 60647 • (773) 252-7636
maproom.com • Established: 1992

SCENE & STORY

True to its name, the Map Room is equipped with old issues of *National Geographic* and huge colorful topographic charts, and the 26 taps and 230 bottled selections (and one cask at all times) reflect the worldly outlook. A Bucktown neighborhood standby, the cash-only bar has high ceilings with black tin tiles hung with various flags, red walls and a half dozen round tables along a polished wood bar, and chalkboard tap lists that require a lot of attention, because beers turn over so often. The Map Room's owners freely admit they had no idea what they were doing when they started, but quickly fostered a community of committed beer lovers who held beer club meetings, brought back travelers' tales, and even taught "beer school" classes, a tradition that continues in the bar to this day, led by brewer Greg Browne of Mickey Finn's Brewery in Libertyville, north of the city.

PHILOSOPHY

The best kind of journey is one for the love of interesting beer. The Map Room's owners and staff go to great lengths to bring back treasures they can share. As founder Laura Blasingame writes on the pub's home page, the Map Room started out as a place "where ideas could be exchanged, where people could come to get some good social nourishment. What a better beverage to feature than beer?"

KEY BEER

Muncie, Indiana's Three Floyd's Dreadnaught, a 9.5% ABV Imperial IPA, a lush panoply of tropical and fruit flavors like mango and peach balanced with a hefty dose of resinous hops.

SHEFFIELD'S BEER AND WINE GARDEN

3258 N. Sheffield Ave. • Chicago, IL 60657 • (773) 281-4989
sheffieldschicago.com • Established: 1980

SCENE & STORY

With three distinct bar areas and a beer garden for fair-weather days, this well-established Windy City watering hole in the Lake View area of town is known for both its great beer lists and its "Backroom BBQ." The whole place has red tile floors, warm, mustard-yellow walls, antique trim, old craftsman-era light fixtures, and an incred-

ible selection of beers (38 taps; 150 bottles) from close-by favorites like Bell's and Goose Island to West Coast cult beers and abroad to Belgian, German, and Japanese imports such as Hitachino.

PHILOSOPHY

Options make the meal. Late founder Rick Hess worked hard to give diners the choice of the best Memphis-, Texas-, and Carolina-style sauces to dress the house-smoked ribs, brisket, and other barbecue fare, and the mostly American draft beer list reflects a similar attention to detail and quality, with cask-conditioned beers, growler sales to go, and a "new and notable" list for customers.

KEY BEER

Furious, from Surly Brewing in Minnesota is, a 6.2% ABV American IPA. It's perfect for cutting the tangy spice of the ribs.

THE PUBLICAN

837 W. Fulton Market • Chicago, IL 60607 • (312) 733-9555
thepublicanrestaurant.com • Established: 2008

SCENE & STORY

All together now! Among the most impressive aspects of the Publican is the huge square of walnut-hewn, communal table space in the center of the dining room, which seats one hundred and is ringed by tiered booths and walls glowing with an earthy ochre color and lit by striking, globe-like light fixtures. The space was designed by James Beard Award winner Thomas Schlesser, and the bar area is a marvel of polished steel and brass fixtures, chic wooden tap handles, and gleaming delicate glassware for the carefully curated list of twelve taps and eighty-five bottles. Impressively, all servers, managers, and bartenders have achieved at least level-one certification on the dauntingly long path to becoming Cicerones, the beer equivalent of master sommelier.

PHILOSOPHY

Beer and food deserve equal thought and care. Executive Chef Paul Kahan and Chef de Cuisine Brian Huston's beer-centric menus center upon sustainably sourced seafood, certified organic pork from Dyersville, Iowa (made into, among other things, terrines and charcuteries), seasonal vegetables and daily aïoli. Other beer friendly specialties include house-made black and white sausages, steak tartare, pork shoulder, pot-au-feu, and wood-roasted chicken with *frites*. Special beer dinners are common, with recent appearances by Los Angeles' the Bruery and American barrel-aging pioneer Allagash.

KEY BEER

Order up Thiriez XXtra (Brasserie Thiriez, of Esquelbecq, France), a wonderfully aromatic and spicily food–friendly beer in 750-milliliter bottles (4.50% ABV).

★ ★ ★

GOOSE ISLAND BEER CO.

1800 N. Clybourn • Chicago, IL 60614 • (312) 915-0071
gooseisland.com • Established: 1988

SCENE & STORY

The original Goose Island opened in Lincoln Park and has racked up over one hundred prestigious brewing medals for a huge variety of styles under brewer Greg Hall, whose father founded the company, and who attended the prestigious Siebel Institute of brewing before making several trips to Europe for inspiration. In the handsome wood-paneled pub with its huge central oval-shaped bar, there are at least twenty taps of Goose Island's highly rated beers available, many only available there (including occasional cask-conditioned ales), in addition to bottle and growler and keg sales to go, and merchandise. The pub grub consists of higher end pub fare including duck and rabbit, mussels, andouille, and cassoulet, among other hearty fare. There are often beers on tap that have been created as collaborations with local chefs including Rick Bayless and Paul Kahan of the Publican. A second brewpub, in Wrigleyville, opened in 1999. Tours of both locations ($7; about an hour) can be arranged on weekends at various times; reservations required.

PHILOSOPHY

Good, green, and innovative. In recent years the company has made strides with Belgian-style ales such as Matilda, a 7% ABV Belgian pale ale with earthy *Brettanomyces* yeast.

The 2011 takeover by Anheuser-InBev gave some in the craft beer industry pause, for fear the world's most powerful light-beer merchants might dumb down Goose Island's artful offerings. Let's hope not.

KEY BEER

Widely imitated, the first Bourbon County Stout was born after Hall met legendary Jim Beam distiller Booker Noe, who gave him some used bourbon barrels. Hall hoped to make a memorable beer for the Clyburn location's one thousandth batch; aged for a hundred days in the aromatic wood, the beer emerged opaque as coal, with a thick head of beige foam and mouthfuls of viscous, oak-tinged vanilla, dark chocolate, caramel, and smoke flavors (13% ABV).

BEST of the REST: ILLINOIS

DELILAH'S

2771 N. Lincoln Ave. • Chicago, IL 60614 • (773) 472-2771 • delilahschicago.com

The black, Old West exterior resembles a saloon a gunslinger might have preferred, but inside it's pure rock and roll. Dimly lit with an amber glow with punk, rock, ska, and alt-country blasting from a lovingly-stocked jukebox (plus pool tables upstairs), this bar (est. 1994) offers a refreshing break from the sometimes too-precious vibe of new-school beer bars. Owner Mike Miller proudly rotates a selection of 20 taps and 150 bottled crafts and imports, like Daisy Cutter Pale Ale (5.2% ABV), an American pale ale from Chicago's own Half Acre Brewing Company.

HALF ACRE BREWING CO.

4257 N. Lincoln Ave. • Chicago, IL 60618 • (773) 248-4038 • halfacrebeer.com

A group of bike-and-beer-loving friends living in Bucktown (home of the Map Room) started Half Acre as a contract brewing arrangement in 2006. Within two years, the crew was ready to move into a big converted brick warehouse and were soon brewing an impressive arsenal of beers, including the peachy, pungent, and eminently drinkable Daisy Cutter Pale Ale (5.2% ABV). Along the way the brewery has propelled the Half Acre's competitive cycling team to new heights. The beers are finding wider distribution in the area every day. Brewery tours are offered on Saturdays at 1 p.m. by reservation only, with a maximum of sixty adults per day.

HOPLEAF

5148 N. Clark St. • Chicago, IL 60640 • (773) 334-9851 • hopleaf.com

With warm weathered wood throughout, Hopleaf (opened in 1992) is broken up into three areas—a front bar, dining area, and loft-like seating area upstairs, offering 41 taps and 260 bottled selections. The beer selection is heavily influenced by Belgian styles, as is the menu: standout dishes include the mussels, frites, rabbit with dumplings, duck meatballs, and cod croquettes. Look for Lost Abbey beers (from California), such as the cloudy gold Carnevale on draft, a 6.5% ABV saison beer with hints of orange peel and a delicate floral aroma from ample Amarillo and Simcoe hops.

METROPOLITAN BREWING CO.

5121 N. Ravenswood Ave. • Chicago, IL 60640 • No phone number • metrobrewing.com

Out in the Ravenswood Industrial Corridor another upstart brewery is making waves in the Chicago beer market. Next door is Chicago's first microdistillery, Koval, which is both certified organic and kosher, making spirits with rose hip, ginger, pear, oat, spelt, wheat, rye, and even one of Metropolitan's beers. Metro (as it's sometimes called) is not a pub, and tours are by appointment only from the website, but for die-hard fans these are mere speed bumps on the road to trying some of head brewer Doug Hurst's genre-bending beers at the source. For example: Dynamo Copper Lager is a reddish and slightly nutty Vienna-style with clean, subtle hop character (5.8% ABV).

REVOLUTION BREWING CO.

2323 N. Milwaukee Ave. • Chicago, IL 60647-2924 • (773) 227-2739 • revbrew.com

Opened in 2010 with a vaguely Bolshevik attitude, this Logan Square brewpub roared into high gear under the leadership of former Goose Islander Josh Deth. With tin ceilings, contemporary-classic dark wood bar island, defiant fist tap handles, and locally sourced pub grub, it's cool enough for the young folk yet classy enough to take the parents (on a quiet afternoon that is; it gets mobbed at night). So quick and sure has the Revolution swept over Logan Square that they planned a production brewery for 2011 with room for barrel aging styles leaving chinks in the armor of macrobrew hegemony. Be sure to try the 4.4% ABV Paddy Wagon stout, an Irish dry stout along the lines of Guinness, but with more character.

TWO BROTHERS

30W315 Calumet Ave. • Warrenville, IL 60555 • (630) 657-5201 • twobrosbrew.com

Brothers Jim and Jason Ebel were obsessed with craft beer after living in Europe; when they returned home, they opened a home-brew shop, which led to plans to brew commercially. One brother completed a law degree while the other mastered brewing science; using borrowed money, gear, and some dairy tanks their grandfather handed down, Two Brothers was born in 1997 in the Western suburbs of Chicago, and has grown like a beanstalk ever since. Starting in 2009, the siblings acquired a pristine collection of wooden tanks called *foudres* for making far more complex beers than the hefeweizens (cloudy wheat beers) that put them on the map. Look for their flagship, Cane & Ebel Red Rye Ale, made with a bit of Thai palm sugar, rye malt, and unusually aromatic hops (7% ABV).

WINDY CITY BEER WEEK

The first annual Chicago Craft Beer Week kicked off in May 2010, with organized tastings, talks, and tours at dozens of beer bars, breweries, and beer-friendly restaurants, sponsored by the Illinois Brewers Guild. For more information log onto chibeerweek.com.

Indiana

★ ★ ★

Indianapolis

THE RATHSKELLER

401 E. Michigan St. • Indianapolis, IN 46204
(317) 636-0396 • rathskeller.com • Established: 1894

SCENE & STORY

There's something mightily satisfying about drinking from a thirty-two-ounce German stein while sitting underneath a mounted moose head. Of the many things The Rathskeller is, subtle isn't one of them. With history as rich as its oversized, dark wood décor, the Rathskeller is a like a true Bavarian castle encased in a massive nineteenth-century brick building (designed by, among others, Kurt Vonnegut's grandfather) in downtown Indianapolis. Once you head inside and take in the gorgeous interior of polished wood archways and creamy walls, it's time for a beer. There are twelve rotating imported drafts and fifty-some bottles of German, European, and American craft beer to choose from, along with a celebrated menu of authentic German fare, so the *gemütlichkeit* ("cheerful belonging") is not far behind.

In summer, don't miss the rooftop *biergarten*, featuring a widescreen view of the city, live music, and plenty of locals raising a stein or three. If you go on a weekend, chances are you'll get to ride the endorphins of somebody celebrating a wedding or class reunion in one of the banquet rooms. And if you're hungry, for the love of Klaus, do not leave without trying an oversized, pillowy pretzel coated in salt and served with a side of sinus-clearing hot mustard.

PHILOSOPHY

Auf freundes wohl! To the good health of friends! The Rathskeller is authentically German, with a side of Hoosier pride—check out the bust of the late author Vonnegut.

KEY BEER

Something German in a stein, naturally, like the Mönchshof Kellerbier; its creamy, caramel taste shines through the cloudy texture of this unfiltered, traditionally brewed lager (5.4% ABV).

HEOROT

219 S. Walnut • Muncie, IN 47305
(765) 287-0173 • No website • Established: 1994

SCENE & STORY

Named for the mead hall of heroes in the epic poem, *Beowulf,* this beer bar in the home of David Letterman's alma mater Ball State U. comes complete with a dragon sculpture curling in and out of the wall, stuffed animal heads, shields, skulls, various faux-medieval brick-a-brac, and Basil Pouledouris's soundtrack to *Conan the Barbarian* on the stereo. It's a bit hokey, sure, but when you have fifty-four-plus incredible taps and over six hundred bottles to choose from, including vintage ales in casks the likes of which are found almost nowhere else in the world—not to mention a sword on the wall lancing through cans of macrobrew for inspiration, with a house brewery planned for late 2011—who really cares?

PHILOSOPHY

Well, what is the air-speed velocity of an unladen swallow?

KEY BEER

Order up a Dogfish Head Midas Touch (based on a 2,700-year-old Turkish recipe found in the tomb of King Midas; 9% ABV) and call your Round Table to order.

THREE FLOYDS BREWING CO.

9750 Indiana Pkwy. • Munster, IN 46321 • (219) 922-3565
3floyds.com • Established: 1996

SCENE & STORY

Home-brewing brothers Nick and Simon and their father Mike Floyd started their brewery the old-fashioned way: with a kettle fired by a wok burner and some old, open Swiss-cheese tanks for fermenting the beers five barrels at a time (155 gallons). That was back in Hammond, Indiana. Four years later they were ready to move up to a larger facility, which is located behind an office park near a hospital. As far as their cultishly devoted fans are concerned, the Floyd brothers could have built that brewery three levels below the hospital in a moldy mop closet: in 2010, for the annual release party of Dark Lord, a buck-strong stout of 15% ABV topped in colored wax, eight *thousand* people showed up. Call it beer-geek Brigadoon.

Inside, the brewpub and taproom is equal parts stoner man cave and chef's pantry. Just when you expect to see corn dogs and tater tots come out of the kitchen, plates of cassoulet, duck-fat *frites* and whole roasted Wisconsin lake trout appear. Amid the psychedelic murals and flags, metal on the hi-fi, and projectors showing 80s movies like *The Karate Kid*, there are eleven excellent taps and twenty-one bottles to sample across the entire brewable spectrum.

PHILOSOPHY

Officially, the modus operandi is, "It's Not Normal." Three Floyds has unleashed dozens of intense beers pushing the envelope of hops, malt, and other flavor components. If they were to brew too many beers on the lighter side, their fans would be confused, even irritated. But refreshingly, they're not expanding at the maximum possible rate. Despite the wacky image and all the comic-book-inspired label art, etc., these brothers are obviously thinking straight.

KEY BEER

Gumballhead is an American pale wheat ale, and on the low end for FFF (5.5% ABV). But its lemony gold flavors and hemp-like aroma is no less desirable for the restraint.

BEST of the REST: INDIANA

SHALLO'S

8811 Hardegan St. • Country Line Shoppes • Indianapolis, IN 46227 • (317) 882-7997 • shallos.com

A cluttered, dimly lit and very old place on the south side of Indianapolis that's connected to the Old Time Pottery store in a desolated strip mall, Shallo's is the craft-beer bar as imagined by David Lynch, with smoke-darkened, wood-paneled walls, pressed tin ceilings, deep padded booths and a beer cooler with a neon sign reading INSURANCE. With three hundred bottled beers and forty drafts (presented on a perpetually outdated list) including the likes of Indiana's own Three Floyds, Mikkeller of Denmark, and San Francisco's He'brew ("The Chosen Beer"), it's a holy land for beer lovers if there ever was one.

UPLAND BREWING CO.

350 West 11th St. • Bloomington, IN 47404 • (812) 336-2337 • uplandbeer.com

Bloomington is a college town for Indiana University, and this sunny brick-sided brewpub draws them in with great burgers and an outdoor patio, where locals sip on cloudy gold glasses of Upland Wheat Ale, a 4.5% ABV Belgian *wit* (white beer), made with organic coriander, chamomile, and orange peel. Lately, the brewery has delved into more exotic Belgian and other brewing styles with strong results. Indiana still doesn't allow beer or alcohol sales on Sunday except from breweries or wineries, so during the summer, it's common practice for locals to buy a growler of the slightly tart and quenching Wheat and head to a local lake, sit in the sun, and sip beer straight out of the bottle—Indiana summer at its best.

Iowa

★ ★ ★

Des Moines

EL BAIT SHOP

200 SW 2nd St. • Des Moines, IA 50309
(515) 284-1970 • elbaitshop.com • Established: 2006

SCENE & STORY

For a bar with such a kooky mix of blue Formica, faux-wood paneling, retro video games, Maurice Sendak murals, and other late-period Greg Brady–era stylings (lacquered marlin; plastic grapes, assorted tchotchkes), El Bait Shop has an incredibly up-to-date beer list, with 105 taps and 115 bottles from over 30 countries. Especially strong is the draft list from the Midwest—Boulevard, Bells, and Goose Island.

PHILOSOPHY

The vinyl booths may be cheap, but there's no skimping on the beer, and the two-tiered tap row is a thing of organizational beauty. Neither college clown show nor meat market, this is a bar to love for one reason above all: almost everyone's here for the beer.

KEY BEER

This would be the perfect place to drink Boulevard's Long Strange Trip, a 9% ABV tripel that has a heady sweetness and a puff of delicate noble hop character.

BEST of the REST: IOWA

THE ROYAL MILE

210 4th St. • Des Moines, IA 50309 • (515) 280-3771 • royalmilebar.com

A glorious array of weathered old wood tables, English breweriana, stained glass, a Union Jack, and London Underground signs help make this the unofficial "living room" of Des Moines, an ideal place for storytelling among old friends. Along with a stream of special firkin nights from top craft brewers like Colorado's Left Hand and New Belgium, regulars gather inside (and out on a quaint brick patio) for hearty bites like English pork pie and bangers and mash, washed down with rare beers, including the delicately hoppy and refreshing Coniston Bluebird Bitter (4.2% ABV) from Cumbria, England.

Michigan

Ann Arbor

JOLLY PUMPKIN CAFÉ & BREWERY

311 S. Main St. • Ann Arbor, 48104 • (734) 913-2730
jollypumpkin.com • Established: 2004

SCENE & STORY

Ron Jeffries speaks softly but carries a big stick. Across the country American craft brewers have followed his quiet but confident lead, embracing tricky, Belgian-influenced techniques like the use of oak barrels and wild yeast strains that are lethal to beer in the wrong hands. He started his odyssey toward becoming one of the nation's best brewers of Belgian-style ales around 1991 with the goal of opening his own brewery. By 1995 he had made a name for himself in Michigan's emerging scene, and by 2004 he was ready to unleash his vision: a brewery dedicated to wood-aged artisanal beers. Trouble was, he hadn't settled on a name.

On a warm early spring afternoon with snow on the ground and ample heat in the air, Jeffries, who is tall and thin with the quiet, placid demeanor of a lit professor, thought of a name that encompassed everything he intended to do: Jolly Pumpkin Artisan Ales, a mishmash of concepts encompassing Halloween, pirates, his low-key, slow-paced Hawaii, and the kind of beer he wanted to make. He and his wife laughed. It grew on her. Jolly Pumpkin it was.

Today, Jeffries oversees operations of the original Dexter, Michigan, location (where a new pub was under way in 2011), a brewpub in Traverse City, and a brewpub in Ann Arbor, which has a lovely bar, roof deck, and full menu of beer-friendly cuisine. Both the Ann Arbor and Traverse City locations have Jeffries' beers on tap or in bottles, and both allow growler and bottle sales to go.

The beer that Jeffries has been brewing from the start is some of the most interesting and innovative in the country. These days it's relatively common to hear about wood-aging experiments, sour beers, bourbon barrels, and the like, but Jeffries is the only brewer to be fermenting all of his beer in huge wood fermenters from the start, which is incredibly risky—one runaway infection in a barrel and tens of thousands of dollars worth of beer can turn into something resembling vinegar. It's not easy to grapple with wild yeasts, which can bore into wood with the force of gamma rays and wreak havoc in a brew house, nor to bottle-condition the beer as if it were Champagne, but Jeffries doesn't going around crowing about it. He doesn't have to. The beers—complex, flavorful, original, by turns elegant and edgy—speak for themselves.

PHILOSOPHY

Traditional, small-scale production with deep, pleasing complexity as the ultimate goal. Not every experiment is perfect, but that's part of the beauty of Jolly Pumpkin.

KEY BEER

Luciernaga (6.5% ABV), and Luciernaga Grand Reserve (7% ABV). With a hearty helping of exotic spices like grains of paradise and coriander, Luciernaga is an annual spicy-tart Belgian pale ale arriving in summer, like the wondrous insect it's named for. It pours radiant, ruddy amber with a huge pillow of head. The Grand Reserve version is aged in bourbon barrels for fourteen months, deepening the flavors with curling, vinous notes of vanilla and smoke.

FOUNDERS BREWING CO.

235 Grandville Ave. SW • Grand Rapids, MI 49503
(616) 776-1195 • foundersbrewing.com • Established: 1997

SCENE & STORY

Like a lot of great American craft brewers, Mike Stevens and Dave Engbers started their dream company while working day jobs they couldn't wait to quit, and a giant loan from the bank. With beers that were balanced but frankly timid, they teetered on bankruptcy soon after opening the doors, so Stevens and Engbers decided to go all-in, releasing the sort of uncompromisingly bold beers that got them interested in brewing in the first place. After a remarkable turnaround, their brewery and airy taproom (a glorious space

of weathered hardwood floors, tall glass windows looking into the brewery, and a polished, serpentine mahogany bar), is one of America's top beer destinations, cranking out over 45,000 bbl annually.

PHILOSOPHY

The stated credo: "We don't brew beer for the masses. Instead, our beers are crafted for a chosen few, a small cadre of renegades and rebels who enjoy a beer that pushes the limits of what is commonly accepted as taste. In short, we make beer for people like us." Good call. By 2009 Founders was burning up the awards circuit and became the fastest growing American craft brewery.

KEY BEER

Founders' KBS (Kentucky Breakfast Stout) is an 11.2% ABV brew released annually on the Saturday closest to the Ides of March (the 15th), an event at the brewery that draws hordes of beer fans. It's got a massive quantity of chocolate and coffee and is cave-aged in bourbon barrels before bottling.

HOPCAT

25 Ionia Ave. SW • Grand Rapids, MI 49503
(616) 451-4677 • hopcatgr.com • Established: 2008

SCENE & STORY

With its seasonal outdoor patio, exposed brick walls, bare wood and pressed-tin ceilings, wood floors and tables, and narrow wrought iron support columns, HopCat is inviting before you even get to the bar. Then there's a series of inviting padded booths and tables and a loft-like seating area with couches upstairs. When you get to the bar, with its clover-honey-hued Italianate woodwork and mirrors and epic 48-tap row (featuring a slew of Michigan locals, 10 or more house brews, and 150 more bottles, not a macrobrew in sight), the hard part begins: What to drink? There's at least one thing you must order from the food menu: their house beer-battered Crack Fries (entirely as advertised though quite legal and only $4.95).

PHILOSOPHY

Experiment and learn. With beer education classes and an ever-changing list, HopCat is a gentle and rewarding master.

KEY BEER

Burly Belgo IPA, from North Peak Brewing Company in Traverse City, Michigan, is a 6.5% hybrid of an IPA with a citrus rind pop and a classic Belgian sweet-and-spice combination.

There are more than sixty-five breweries in the state of Michigan now, far too many to list here, and at least a half dozen active hops farms supplying them. For complete directories, details on Detroit Beer Week, and info on annual festivals statewide, go to michiganbrewersguild.org.

BELL'S BREWERY ECCENTRIC CAFE

355 E. Kalamazoo Ave. • Kalamazoo, MI 49007
(269) 382-2332 • bellsbeer.com • Established: 1985

SCENE & STORY

Larry Bell's operation is a household name in these parts, but it started as a mere Kalamazoo home-brew shop in 1983 and sold its first beer—quite literally made in a 15-gallon soup kettle—in 1985. Bell, a self-described failed jazz musician and occasional radio broadcaster, had started the first craft brewery east of the Rockies and by 1993 became the first brewer in the state of Michigan to serve beer on-site at a brewery.

Now the commercial production is housed in nearby Comstock, Michigan, cranking out a wide array of beers 24/7 on a system that brews 1,500 gallons per batch, around 170,000 barrels per year—or 5 million gallons, double the output of 2005. The original brewery location in Kalamazoo is home to the Eccentric Café, with a ten-tap bar, beer garden, and newly expanded, warehouse-sized music venue.

PHILOSOPHY

The official motto is "Inspired Brewing," but Larry himself is a no-nonsense kind of guy, more focused on the business of brewing beer than flights of commercial fancy. Inspired by the successes of Sierra Nevada and Anchor, his goal was to open a brewery that made at least 30,000 barrels a year. Mission accomplished, and a whole lot more.

KEY BEER

Bell's Expedition Stout is one of the early American versions of a Russian imperial stout, chewy and laced with flavors of black patent brewers' malt, chocolate, licorice, and stone fruit (10.5% ABV).

BEST *of the* REST: MICHIGAN

ASHLEY'S RESTAURANT & PUB

338 S. State St. • Ann Arbor, MI 48104 • (734) 996-9191 • ashleys.com

With seventy-two taps and fifty bottled selections, this cozy and often crowded college bar with an unremarkable interior has one of the best tap rows in the state. The sponsors of a Michigan cask ale festival (held at the newer Ashley's location, twenty-five miles away in Westland), Ashley's is credited with bringing the level of Michigan craft beer appreciation up overall since 1983, when it first opened. There's a rotating selection from the excellent Short's Brewing Company in Bellaire, Michigan, which ought to be your first choice.

ARCADIA BREWING

103 W. Michigan Ave. • Battle Creek, MI 49017 • (269) 963-9520 • arcadiaales.com

The centerpiece of Arcadia brewing company is the impressive wood- and brick-sided brewing system visible from behind glass in the British-style restaurant and T.C.'s Pub in the back, where you can snack on wood-oven pizzas and pita bread with hummus. Take a free tour of the brewery most Saturdays at 1 p.m. (and please call ahead). Built by influential British brewer Peter Austin, it's the birthplace of a wide selection of ales, like the 7.2% ABV Arcadia London Porter, which is sweet and full bodied with notes of cocoa and smoke.

Minnesota

★ ★ ★

St. Paul

THE HAPPY GNOME

498 Selby Ave. • St. Paul, MN 55102 • (651) 287-2018
thehappygnome.com • Established: 2005

SCENE & STORY

With its façade covered in climbing creeper vine, a spacious patio, vintage-inspired interior of plush brown leather booths, acres of dark and unvarnished wood surfaces, and framed poster art, the Happy Gnome is getting it right on multiple levels before you even sit down.

PHILOSOPHY

Beer is happiness. The beer and edibles will make you even happier, with seventy adventurous, fresh taps, four hundred bottle selections, and occasional firkins (the nine-gallon British vessels used to dispense cask-conditioned beers through a hand pump). There are monthly brewery dinners and a chef-driven menu daily, featuring expertly prepared fare like chestnut-stuffed quail with roasted squash puree, braised kale, and cherry-rye whiskey reduction.

KEY BEER

Look for the Furthermore Fatty Boombalatty Belgian pale ale (Wisconsin), which, besides being a lot of fun to order, is a 7.2% ABV brew of amber with wheaty, zesty notes and peppery bite.

Just like brewers in old Germany before the advent of mechanical refrigeration for brewing in the 1840s, the cleverest Minnesotans used to age their beer in caves. Dating back to the late 1800s, these vaulted sandstone caverns belonged to Wolf's Brewery, which used to lager (German for "store") beer here before and just after the repeal of Prohibition in 1933. Wolf's closed soon after The Great Mistake, but the brewery buildings were maintained, and in the 1990s housed a brewpub. Today, it's a mix of residential and commercial property. Take a 30-minute tour of the cool, atmospheric caves, and learn such chestnuts as why good brewmasters had bad teeth and the definition of a "cave kiss." Tours are scheduled weekends, every hour on the hour: Fridays 12 to 4 p.m., Saturdays and Sundays, 12 to 5 p.m. $5 per spelunker (no caving experience required).

BEST *of the* REST: MINNESOTA

SURLY BREWING CO.
4811 Dusharme Dr. • Brooklyn Center, MN 55429 • (763) 535-3330 • surlybrewing.co

After a trip to Oregon to tour breweries, founder Omar Ansari (a home brewer with big dreams) returned to build Minnesota's first new brewery since 1987. That was in 2006, and his beers and tours were so incredibly popular that by 2011 he was leading a pitched battle to get the state and local government to approve a destination brewery, bar, restaurant, and event center. Until then, visitors continue flocking to the brewery for tours and tastes of the beer, described as "for a glass, from a can." Tours are free and available most Friday evenings from 6 to 8 p.m.; register on the website and bring a nonperishable food item for donation. Furious is a 6.2% ABV American IPA brewed with five different malts and four tangy, grapefruity hop varieties working in surprisingly peaceful tandem.

THE MUDDY PIG
162 Dale St. • North Saint Paul, MN 55102-2028 • (651) 254-1030 • www.muddypig.com

An easy-to-find corner bar with a casual, neighborhoody feel and weathered old booths, books, a cozy outdoor patio, and lots of dark wood, the Muddy Pig has the best beer selection in the Twin Cities—around fifty taps and a similar number of Belgians. There's a limited food menu; stick to the beers like Flying Dog's 8.3% ABV Raging Bitch Belgian-style IPA, which has the peppery bite of a great Belgian and an aromatic whiff of Amarillo hops.

Missouri

★ ★ ★

Kansas City

2501 Southwest Blvd. • Kansas City, MO 64108
(816) 474-7095 • boulevard.com • Established: 1989

SCENE & STORY

John McDonald, a mild-mannered furniture maker, started with some used Bavarian equipment in a one-hundred-year-old converted warehouse. His modest goal was to turn out enough beer for the die-hard beer lovers in Kansas City, perhaps topping out at 6,000 barrels a year, but the local thirst for Boulevard Pale Ale and Unfiltered Wheat was seemingly unquenchable. Fifteen years later in 2005, he broke ground on a three-story, 70,000-square-foot expansion adjoining the original where Belgian-born brewmaster Steven Pauwels can really spread his wings. Boulevard is now among the largest locally owned craft breweries in the American Midwest (making over 600,000 barrels annually), with Unfiltered Wheat as the flagship. The Smokestack series, a line of experimental styles, many aged in wood, set tongues wagging in the beer-geek community.

To tour the operation is to see what happens when a fully modern brewery takes ancient techniques into action. The tour even includes a taste of beers in development along the fifty-minute stroll (free, including at least four samples; reservations required). On occasion Boulevard also works with local restaurant partners to create beer and food pairings for a tour and luncheon with brewmaster Pauwels for $38, which includes a tour, three-course lunch, and a souvenir pint glass.

PHILOSOPHY

Balance is everything. Pauwels brews so that countervailing sensory aspects in his beers—such as bitterness and residual sugars—play off and against one other, no matter how rudimentary the style.

KEY BEER

Tank 7 is an 8% ABV saison beer named for a fermenter that seemed to be giving Pauwels some problems for a new batch, but instead yielded one of the brewery's best beers yet. It's the color of hay with an aromatic fruit orchard of flavors and a peppery dry finish. Saison-Brett (8.5 % ABV) takes this superb beer one better: it's dry-hopped and bottle-conditioned with earthy *Brettanomyces* yeast, then aged three months before leaving the brewery.

St. Louis

SCHLAFLY BOTTLEWORKS

7260 Southwest Ave. • St. Louis, MO 63143
(314) 241-BEER • schlafly.com • Established: 2003

SCENE & STORY

There are about fifteen breweries in Saint Louis, home of The Big One, but Schlafly (pronounced schlaugh-lee) is the best. Built in an atmospheric old wood and brick building on the National Historic Register, it has gloriously worn-in floors befitting the original microbrewer in the state, the first to set up shop after Prohibition. It's a short walk away from both The Gateway Arch and City Museum, home of a massive, interactive monkey bars installation and the world's largest No. 2 pencil (citymuseum.org), and makes a great stop for unwinding after both.

In 2003 Schlafly took over the former home of an old grocery store to create Bottleworks, which boasts a cool little brewing history museum with historic cans and breweriana, a selection of beers to go in coolers, movie nights in a meeting room, and a farmer's market on occasion in the lot. There are twelve taps and a good little pub for eats, as well.

Tours (of Bottleworks) are free every Friday through Sunday from 12 to 5 p.m., and there's also a third Schlafly pub in Lambert International Airport if you'd just like a chance to try the beers en route to or from St. Louis.

PHILOSOPHY

Good local beer for good folks. To give you an idea of their scale, consider that The Big One (Anheuser-Busch) produces well over 100 million barrels of beer a year. The Bottleworks location produces just 40,000 (1.2 million gallons), making it 1/100th the size, and the Tap Room brewery is even smaller.

KEY BEER

Try the 4.8% ABV Pilsner for a taste of the style of beer Anheuser-Busch might have been making a hundred years ago. Also excellent: the 5.9% ABV Dry Hopped APA, or American Pale Ale, grainy and reminiscent of citrus and honey.

BEST *of the* REST: MISSOURI

INTERNATIONAL TAP HOUSE

1711 S. 9th St. • St. Louis, MO 63104 • (314) 621-4333 • internationaltaphouse.com

A mile and a half south of Busch Stadium (home of the Saint Louis Cardinals) "iTap" (as this sleek beer bar is known) has a spacious patio with Christmas lights hanging in draped rows outside and a long row of black captain's chairs inside facing the main event: coolers and forty-four taps totaling five hundred selections inside, with a world-class selection of craft brews, not a macro in sight. It's a long narrow space with exposed brick, low lighting, and frequent live acoustic music. Tuesdays feature Missouri brews, with extra rarities from Boulevard, Schlafly, and other local brews. There's a second location in Chesterfield, about twenty-two miles west—conveniently close to the Spirit of Saint Louis International Airport.

BRIDGE TAP HOUSE & WINE BAR

1004 Locust St. • St. Louis, MO 63101 • (314) 241-8141 • thebridgestl.com

With arty chandeliers, heavily framed black-and-white photos, polished wood, and a leaning library ladder behind the bar, this downtown St. Louis bar draws a young, casual crowd. Open every night until 1 a.m. (midnight on Sundays), it's the best place in the city to grab dinner from the chef-driven menu or just a bite of local and house-cured charcuterie, duck, pickles, and whole raw cheeses. In addition to a comprehensive wine and farm-to-table menu, there are fifty-five taps and more than two hundred bottled beers, with a full complement of Boulevard and a half dozen Founders taps, including Goose Island's food-friendly Sofie, oak-aged Belgian-style farmhouse ale aged with orange peel (6.5% ABV).

LITTLE YEOMAN BREWING CO.

12581 Dallas Ln. • Cabool, MO 65689 • 417-926-9185 • No website

An hour-and-a-half drive south of Springfield on a leafy farm in the Ozarks, Little Yeoman is a little eighty-gallon brewery with big dreams. For now, the only way to try the beers—ranging from cream ale to APA, IPA, porter, stout, and on up the intensity ladder to barley wine—is to drive out to the middle of the Mark Twain National Forest, look for a converted keg mailbox, and pay a visit. There, in a modest two-room barn, Chad Frederick (who commutes to work via a short walk in the woods and says he hopes to distribute his beer more widely), has made many fans in the area—and even some from abroad—who keep in touch via a (non-sanctioned) Facebook page to plan regular return visits, sometimes camping on the grounds, gathering around a woodstove, and sipping from homemade ceramic mugs, just $1.50 a fill.

Nebraska

★ ★ ★

Papillion

NEBRASKA BREWING CO.

Shadow Lake Towne Center
7474 Towne Center Pkwy., Ste. 101 • Papillion, NE 68046
(402) 934-7100 • nebraskabrewingco.com • Established: 2007

SCENE & STORY

Should you find yourself driving from the Midwest to Colorado across the vast expanse that is the Cornhusker state, it's just a short detour off of I-80 to the French-influenced prairie town outpost of Papillion (population: 24,000) outside of Omaha. Thanks to low unemployment, crime, and traffic it has been considered one of the best places to live in the United States by *Money* magazine. In 2007, life improved still more with the arrival of an adventurous brewery in a nondescript shopping center just down the sidewalk from T.J. Maxx and Bed, Bath & Beyond.

Inside, there's a beauty of a 10 bbl brew-house made in Japan behind glass and a spacious eight-tap pub with locals at the bar who look a lot like reformed lager-swilling college football junkies. But founder Paul Kavulak and his team of brewers have done more than just get the attention of the local drinking populace, they've found distributors willing to take a chance on their beer in markets as demanding as Oregon, and started winning awards in competitions, even pulling a bronze in the 2010 World Beer Cup in Chicago. Whoever said there's no good beer in the heartland hasn't been to Nebraska lately.

PHILOSOPHY

No risk, no reward. Nebraska Brewing undoubtedly raised some eyebrows in town when they started serving up beers aged in wood, like wines. But their timing was impeccable. Across the country the taste for barrel-aged beers was spreading like wildfire. The experiments continue, the fans and medals multiply, and the beers keep improving.

KEY BEER

Mélange à Trois Reserve Series, a 10% ABV strong Belgian pale ale aged in chardonnay barrels for six months, is full bodied in the mouth, mingling pear and tropical fruit with vanilla, spice, and a faint oaky woodiness.

★ ★ ★

Ohio

★ ★ ★

Cleveland

McNULTY'S BIER MARKET

1948 W. 25th St. • Cleveland, OH, 44113
(216) 274-1010 • bier-markt.com • Established: 2005

SCENE & STORY

Ohio's first Belgian beer bar set up shop in the center of the entertainment district, and stays open every day of the year until 2 a.m. The dark, alluring interior design is a feast for the eyes, simultaneously classic and futuristic, with red-trimmed windows against warm, earthy walls and jet black tin ceilings, elaborate paneling in other sections, and elongated Edison bulbs hanging over the curved main bar.

PHILOSOPHY

Meet the new boss: with brewery nights from the likes of Ommegang and Victory, a deep and mouthwatering list of gastropub fare, and a ninety-nine-label Belgian list, it's safe to say the Cleveland beer scene will never be the same again.

KEY BEER

Look for the Caracole Nostradamus, a deliciously complex 9.5% ABV Belgian brown ale.

GREAT LAKES BREWING CO.

2516 Market Ave. • Cleveland, OH 44113 • (216) 771-4404
greatlakesbrewing.com • Established: 1998

SCENE & STORY

The first microbrewery in the state of Ohio since the last of the old-line companies closed in the early 1980s, Great Lakes opened in 1998 in a massive Victorian complex. With its antique 1860s tiger mahogany bar, beer garden with retractable canvas roof, and atmospheric rathskeller belowground, it's a superb spot for an afternoon pint and a bite.

PHILOSOPHY

Proud and feisty. Raise a glass of Eliot Ness Amber Lager to the Untouchable himself, who drank here and might—just might—be responsible for a some bullet holes in the bar.

KEY BEER

Burning River Pale Ale is a great name; unfortunately it's also a reference to the worst days of the Cuyahoga River, once so befouled by coal plants on its banks that it periodically caught fire. But not to worry: there's nothing remotely toxic in this beer. It's a perfectly-carbonated pale ale of 6% ABV with the mellow sweetness of British-style pale ale but the flash and brightness of an American IPA.

Wisconsin

★ ★ ★

New Glarus

NEW GLARUS BREWING CO.

2400 State Hwy. 69 • New Glarus, WI 53574 • (608) 527-5850
newglarusbrewing.com • Established: 1993

SCENE & STORY

After the tiny New Glarus brewery was founded by Deb Carey and her brewer husband, Dan, something wonderful happened. Their little brewery in the countryside grew so quickly throughout the state and into several others that by 1998 the couple was rethinking a strategy of unchecked growth, and pulled distribution back to Wisconsin only, creating an uproar. The Careys were unfazed; they wanted their brewery to stay strong and local. And so the only way to drink some of the best beer in America is to go to Wisconsin, and ideally, New Glarus, to see where it's made.

It's a testament to ingenuity and the power of a brewery to pull together a community. Rather than stifling sales, limiting their sales market propelled sales higher, and by 2007, the Careys constructed one of the country's most appealing breweries, a 75,000-square-foot Bavarian-style brewery on a hill about a mile from the original location, which cost the couple $21 million. It's a fairy tale of steep pitched roofs, creamy exterior walls with exposed beams, stone stair approaches, and gleaming copper kettles inside. Free, self-guided tours are offered Monday through Sunday from 10 a.m. to 4 p.m.; "Hard Hat" tours depart every Friday at 1 p.m. from the original Riverside brewery location, where pilot batches are still developed and wood aged in some cases ($20 per person and reservations required).

PHILOSOPHY

Down to earth, experimental, fun, and delicious. As Dan puts it, "Some people paint, some sing, others write . . . I brew."

KEY BEER

Spotted Cow, a pale, mellow, and wheaty lager is the flagship, but it's the waxed-top, 750-milliliter bottles of Wisconsin Belgian Red that ends up in the trunk of the most choosey visitors. It's a racy, scarlet ale of 4.0% ABV brewed with a pound of whole sour Montmorency cherries per bottle, local wheat, and Belgian malt, then aged in oak tanks and balanced by German Hallertau hops which have been aged for a year in the brew house. It's as bright and jammy as a Wisconsin cherry pie.

La Crosse

THE BODEGA BREW PUB

122 S. 4th St. • La Crosse, WI 54601 • (608) 782-0677
bodegabrewpublax.com • Established: 1994

SCENE & STORY

Upon entering this magnificently cluttered bar, you may leave behind the plague of so many beer travelers—indecision. For among myriad other things before you is a 5 x 5-inch "beer wheel," which costs a flat rate of $3.25 per spin and gets the winner—everybody is a winner, actually—a frothy glass of whichever brew it lands on. Which means you could score a freshly tapped Wisconsin craft brew, or a delicious Erdinger Weisse beer from Bavaria . . . or perhaps something a little less lucky in the wet air category. But so it goes.

The walls and shelves are lined with old beer bottles, tap handles, and beer signs. With fourteen taps, plenty of local Wisconsin selections, and some four hundred international bottles (lovingly cramped in a lazy Susan–style cupboard), your pint glass soon runneth over. Food helps delay any damage. Try the Cubano sandwich with its thick amalgam of roast pork, ham, cheese, pickles, and mustard, or at least grab a handful of free popcorn.

PHILOSOPHY

Fortune favors the bold! The Bodega is a craft-beer-lover's paradise, and a great place to try eclectic brews. But the bottom line is you're here because being here is a kick.

KEY BEER

Oh, come on . . . spin the wheel.

Madison

THE OLD FASHIONED

23 N. Pinckney • Madison, WI 53703
(608) 310-4110 • theoldfashioned.com • Established: 2005

SCENE & STORY

Befitting its name, the Old Fashioned channels the feel of an old-timey supper club rich with Wisconsin history. It's located in the heart of Madison, with a view of the capitol building. Authentic Miller and Schlitz banners—along with maps of Wisconsin and a mounted walleye fish or two—adorn the walls, and dark, natural wood gives the spacious 100-seat dining room a convincingly homey, old-school vibe.

PHILOSOPHY

The Old Fashioned is Wisconsin, through and through. Their beer list—50 taps, 150 bottles—is stocked entirely by Wisconsin breweries, save one bottle of the oft-requested Grain Belt Premium from Minnesota—the sole "import." Their food menu follows suit: everything is made from local ingredients or picked up directly from local purveyors. They don't even have tomatoes when they're off-season in the Badger State. When it comes time to order, go for the fried walleye sandwich, or perhaps something involving the official state food, cheese. "The batter-fried cheese curds are out of this world," said waitress Jessica

Carrier on a recent visit, "and I'm not just saying that. I have literally had a dream about the cheese curds."

KEY BEER

Sprecher Black Bavarian Lager, an authentic, German-style black beer is a far more delicate brew than the hue would suggest (6% ABV).

BEST of the REST: WISCONSIN

TYRANENA BREWING CO.

1025 Owen St. • Lake Mills, WI 53551 • (920) 648-8699 • tyranena.com

A short drive from Madison leads to sleepy Lake Mills and the sleek Tyranena (pronounced tie-rah-nee-nah) brewery and taproom, opened in 1998. (The company is named for some mysterious rock formations at the edge of a nearby lake.) No one's quite sure who or what's behind their design, but no matter, the beer's good and the owners have a beer garden, steady live music, and a sense of humor, that translates to can't-miss events such as Sweater Vest Appreciation Night (really). There are free tours Saturdays at 3:30 p.m. and ten taps to sample (in addition to six-packaged beers, growlers, and specials). Chief Blackhawk Porter, named for the Sauk Indian chief who led the last armed conflict between Native Americans and Europeans east of the Mississippi, is a fulsome 5.5% ABV brew with notes of coffee, toffee, and chocolate.

EXIT 3

The Northeast ↗

The
NORTHEAST

While it's true that the West has a lock on modern craft brewing history and has long been at its leading edge, the Northeast offers tastes of both America's oldest, historical beer traditions, and its most delicious, innovative present tense all at once. From countryside breweries in rural Vermont and Appalachia making minor masterpieces to chic urban brewpubs in Boston and New York City, there's a new craft beer tapestry to explore that is every bit as dense and diverse as the population itself.

Once a region rich with local and regional breweries, nearly all died off during Prohibition. The comeback, starting in the 1980s and following the lead of West Coast path-breakers, didn't happen overnight. Thanks to their relative nearness to cosmopolitan Europe, cities like New York and Boston became hotbeds for pricey imports from England, Germany, and Holland starting in the 1970s. As innovative importers introduced Belgian ales and Eastern European Pilsners to choosey, sophisticated Northeasterners, their tastes for beer begin to wander. At the same time, ambitious British-style brewpubs and microbreweries began to thrive in the suburbs and even in rural towns. These weren't kids in a model U.N. or hippies going back to the land, these were brewers challenging the status quo and marching their fresh creations steadily into the best bars, restaurants, and quarters of town, opening a lot of minds in the process. Today, a once scrappy 1980s startup is America's largest craft brewery (Boston Beer Company). There's even a tiny artisanal brewery on one Manhattan rooftop (Eataly's La Birreria). No matter where you start or end up on a tour of the region, it's a beer lover's feast.

New York

★ ★ ★

TEN YEARS AGO, NEW YORK CITY WAS A CRAFT BEER BACKWATER.

There were a handful of bars with ambitious lists, sure, and some lovable eccentrics (like the original Blind Tiger Alehouse, a gloriously mildewed, Lilliputian tavern in the West Village). But it wasn't enough. A handful of craft breweries had struggled to their feet, some dying soon after, and there was a general sense around the millennium that New York might shrug off the craft beer renaissance and remain the alpha city that it is: expensive and above the fray. It was a place for cocktails, pricey wines, and power lunches, not rare farmhouse ales. New York City habitually ignores trends that do not spring from its culturally superior loins, and the crunchier-than-thou methodology of microbrew culture always seemed out of place.

But good local beer belongs here. New York City has beer in its very foundations: no fewer than three breweries called New Amsterdam home in 1612; in 1913, a man named Jake Ruppert built a $30 million dollar brewery and got himself a baseball team, the Yankees, along with Babe Ruth; Brooklyn produced one-fifth of the nation's beer by 1960, according to a recent *New York Times* story. But alas, by 1976, the number of local breweries had dropped to zero, and no one really cared about beer anymore. The best beers in town were standard-issue, mass-produced imports like Bass, Heineken, and Beck's.

All that's changed. It was only a matter of time perhaps, but the Slow Food-obsessed, pickle-your-own-cucumber inclinations (of Brooklynites, in particular) have ignited a new local beer scene. Several reputable small breweries now call the city home (with a total of fifty-four in the state), which means beer lovers get to drink far fresher beer, especially unfiltered, unpasteurized beers made in traditional styles, the kind in-the-know beer lovers seek out.

Naturally, the best action is found in the pubs, but for the beer traveler looking to splurge, several of the city's best restaurants have ambitiously scaled up their beer lists recently, too. Where beer was once an afterthought, it's now got its own menus—even beer sommeliers. Now truer than ever: New York is the city where you can get absolutely anything.

ITINERARIES

1-DAY Brooklyn Brewery, Spuyten Duyvil, the Blind Tiger, Whole Foods Bowery, Gramercy Tavern

3-DAY One-day itinerary plus Blue Hill at Stone Barns, Defiant Brewing Co., Captain Lawrence, Sixpoint

7-DAY Three-day itinerary plus Ommegang in Cooperstown

Manhattan

11 MADISON PARK

11 Madison Avenue, • New York, NY 10010 • (212) 889-0905
elevenmadisonpark.com • Established: 1998

SCENE & STORY

Only in New York could a restaurant with four stars from the *New York Times* and a 2011 win for Outstanding Restaurant in the country from the venerable James Beard Foundation count as one of the country's top beer destinations as well. And while it's not exactly the typical beer experience to sample artisanal beers and delicate market-driven cuisine in an elegant, hushed dining room, it's an experience whose time has come. The chef is among the best in the world, and if he says beer's acidity, residual sweetness, and sometimes oak barrel-given tannins work just as well with certain foods as the best wines, then who are we to protest? Pick a special occasion. Splurge, guiltlessly. The quieter the room, the louder you can hear your beer.

The beer list here is profound, with just four drafts but over 100 rare and vintage brews that are rarely seen in the United States—anywhere. In 2011, head chef Daniel Humm developed two unique collaboration beers with Brooklyn Brewery's Garrett Oliver and the Old Rip Van Winkle Distillery. Then to kick things up a notch, Humm and Oliver began to plan a series of dinners for which both the entire menu and the beers were created from scratch to work together for a single meal. When a single beer can take anywhere from ten days to three years to brew, this will be no small effort going forward, and you can be sure seats will be hard to come by.

PHILOSOPHY

Respect, consider, revolutionize. "We have been pushing the presence of beer in our dining room," says Kirk Kelewae, the restaurant's earnest young beer guru and Dining Room Manager. "I provide beer pairings to guests when they request it, and we've picked up a whole collection of crystal beer glasses from Spiegelau. We're working to redefine how beer is served in a fine-dining restaurant."

KEY BEER

Other than the Brooklyn collaboration beers? It just depends on what you're ordering for lunch—by all means ask for pairings from Kelewae or a member of his staff—but the restaurant's collection of beers from Brasserie Franches-Montagnes, an obscure but highly collectible producer, rivals any in the world.

RATTLE N' HUM

14 E. 33rd St. (between 5th and Madison)
New York, NY 10016 • (212) 481-1586
rattlenhumbarnyc.com • Established: 2008

SCENE & STORY

Rattle N' Hum makes midtown a destination. Instead of jostling with tourists carrying Macy's bags, though, you're hanging out in a craft beer oasis. Narrow and cozy with a grand, mirrored wood bar and forty beers on tap, the lines are routinely serviced (so the beer in your glass hasn't gone stale in the lines). There's also some one hundred bottles on the list, and a rotating bevy of cask-conditioned ales (twenty-four on a recent visit). Practice your best New York attitude when sidling up to the bar (it's all in the elbows). And in April—a nice, not too hot time to be in town—RNH hosts a cask ales festival, the back of the bar stacked high with firkins of delicate English-style ales. It's the best place to escape the hubbub of midtown, an ace up the sleeve.

PHILOSOPHY

This is a straightforward, narrow, and sometimes crowded bar with a serious beer list

and decent pub grub. The menu has a strong Northeast focus, plus specialty Norwegian and Belgian imports, and hard-to-find American releases on cask as well.

KEY BEER

American craft brewers are now besting Belgians at their own game, perfecting styles invented long ago in the Flanders countryside. Captain Lawrence Xtra Gold (10% ABV; $10 for 25 ounces), brewed in nearby Westchester County, is an American interpretation of the traditional "tripel," a hazy golden ale with a spicy backbone and notes of clove and lemon peel. It goes perfectly with the beer-battered fish-and-chips.

THE GRAMERCY TAVERN

42 E. 20th St. • New York, NY 10003 • (212) 477-0777
gramercytavern.com • Established: 1994

SCENE & STORY

The Gramercy Tavern is one of the most atmospheric and elegant eateries in the city. You just feel good walking in the place and handing over your coat on cold days, because the front of house staff is so well trained in the art of the welcome. But it's not just to make you feel at home before you've parted with your hard-earned money. High ceilings and acres of polished woodwork have a way of making everyday occasions feel big, but then you get to the real fun: eating (or at least a spot at the bar). Year after year, the stratospheric talent in the kitchen seems to work in more perfect synch with the attitude-less staff, a combination restaurateur

Danny Meyer has perfected in more than one place around town. The menu is seasonal and ever changing; recent beer travelers have dined on such dishes as a poached lobster with baby turnips, and daikon radish and lobster sauce paired with a spiced White Christmas Winter Lager from Moylan's Brewery of Novato, California. The angular, warming beer's acidity matched the shellfish's fulsome flavor perfectly. The Gramercy Tavern has earned accolades for treating beers with real respect by adding a strong list of aged beers to the menu and by training servers in suggesting matches for the high-flying cuisine.

PHILOSOPHY

Cosmopolitan, assured, and generous. The beers are cataloged in a deep, well-chosen, international list, and a featured specialty is aged beers. With higher than usual alcohol and sometimes tannins from oak-barrel aging (like big Bordeaux wines) certain strong beers last and improve with time; you'll find them here.

KEY BEER

Try the 2005 Ommegang Abbey Ale (8.5% ABV; $26 for 25 ounces), which is a New York–style interpretation of Abbey beer, a Belgian style. It's a rich, burgundy-colored ale with flavors of toffee, stone fruits, and coffee that pairs beautifully with poultry or beef dishes. Its added years of age lend it a dry, peppery bite less evident in the just-bottled release.

D.B.G.B.

299 Bowery (at E. 1st St.) • New York, NY 10003
(212) 933-5300 • danielnyc.com/dbgb • Established: 2009

SCENE & STORY

The Bowery neighborhood gentrified years ago, but it wasn't really a good beer lovers' destination until restaurateur Daniel Boulud added the chic eatery DBGB to the mix. While Boulud jokes that the name stands for "Daniel Boulud Good Beer," it's actually an homage to rock promoter Hilly Kristal's gone-but-not-forgotten downtown club CBGB & OMFUG, which stood for "Country Bluegrass Blues & Other Music for Uplifting Gormandizers." It's got fourteen kinds of house-made sausage, twenty-two taps of some of New York's best food-friendly beer (and an extensive bottle list) and three different burgers that might make you want to jump on the tables and scream like Joey Ramone.

True, with its glassy modern touches and copper cook pots hanging around there's nothing punk about Boulud's place, or the menu he's put together, but it's got mojo. The modern space bustles without getting deafening, and while it's easier to get a table in the outer section, make a reservation in the main room adjacent to the small L-shaped kitchen. Then turn to the beer list, and look for a pale smoked lager from Bamberg, Germany, called Aecht Schlenkerla, which pairs nicely with a selection of the salads, house-made sausages (including the Viennoise, made with moist pork and Emmenthaler cheese), or the Piggie, a six-ounce patty topped with pulled pork, jalapeño mayo, and Boston lettuce on a cheddar bun. This is comfort food writ large.

PHILOSOPHY

Artists only, to borrow the song title from CBGB regular and former Talking Head David Byrne. Boulud's beer list is packed with the best small-batch producers, including tiny Northeast startups and gems from southeastern Germany, among others.

KEY BEER

Collaboration beers between competing companies is all the rage in American craft brewing. Brooklyner-Schneider Hopfen-Weiss (8.5% ABV; $15 for 9 ounces) is one of the best examples so far. German brewmaster Hans-Peter Drexler came to Brooklyn and made this beer with Brooklyn Brewery's Garrett Oliver; it is dry hopped, but with American Amarillo and Palisade hops, giving it a something of a grassy pollen aroma and a spicy finish.

SPITZER'S CORNER

101 Rivington St. (between Essex St. & Ludlow St.)
New York, NY 10002 • (212) 228-0027 • spitzerscorner.com
Established: 2007

SCENE & STORY

This trendy bar is smack in the epicenter of the Lower East Side, which means this sleek brushed steel and burnished wood gastropub with communal seating is at times besieged by twenty-somethings wearing at least one piece of hipster-approved attire. But get past the very thorough bouncers (don't forget your ID, or forget coming), head to the back room and a seat by the window, and suddenly this place makes perfect sense. There are about eighty international and craft beers and a decadent list of treats including truffled mac-and-cheese and a Kobe beef cheeseburger (order the "fat fries," too, which come topped with sea salt and herbs de Provence). As long as the crowds are manageable, service is quick and attentive, if not incredibly knowledgeable about beer.

PHILOSOPHY

Social, not snobby.

KEY BEER

There are forty beers on tap with an American craft focus running the gamut from brewed in New York to rarely seen in New York. There are many more selections in bottles, not a stinker in the bunch. The Two Brothers Bitter End pale ale, often on tap (5.2% ABV), would be the perfect accompaniment to the decadently delicious Kobe beef burger.

DETOUR →

THE BLIND TIGER
ALEHOUSE
281 Bleecker St. • New York, NY 10014 • (212) 462-4682
blindtigeralehouse.com • Established: 1995

Beer, the drink of the people! Few New Yorkers understand this better than the owners of the Blind Tiger, a legendary New York City tavern that was relocated not long ago to the West Village. Dave Brodrick, its co-owner, was forced to close shop in late 2006, weakened by a long-running licensing battle involving the State Liquor Commission, 66th District Councilwoman Deborah J. Glick, and, by Internet petition, hundreds of the bar's most fervent fans.

For ten years, the Hudson street incarnation of the Tiger (as it was often called) had offered a vast selection of artisan-made ales from Europe and American microbrewers (nary a drop of Bud, Miller, or Coors was ever served). But the surroundings took some getting used to.

"The Blind Tiger Ale House is Dirty, Unhospitable [sic], Unpleasant, and served Terrible Beer," protested Brian Ó Broin, an assistant professor of linguistics and medieval literature in New Jersey, on a website he created expressly for this complaint. "Ambience: 0 [not a single redeeming quality]," he railed. To the uninitiated it seemed oppressively small and crabbed, especially on weekends, when regulars shied away. The list could seem by turns eccentric and expensive; there were rare bottles selling for $20, but if you somehow managed to get to the bar to order one, your feet were sticking to the floor. And a visit to its bathroom, a malevolent place at the bottom of a staircase (itself macabre) was not easily forgotten.

And so the Irishman wasn't much taken in by its charms. Nor was the Tiger's landlord, who hiked the rent in 2005, forcing the tavern to make way for Starbucks no. 374. Brodrick searched eight months for a new venue to house the Blind Tiger, settling on a former bar across from John's Pizzeria, but just before the new location opened, Deborah Glick—councilwoman for the neighborhood—wrote a letter to the State Liquor Commission urging denial of the the new Tiger's liquor license on the basis that it would be "a large bar that primarily serves beer." Say it isn't so, Glick! Brodrick launched a charm offensive, opening the new Tiger sans beer—but armed with unusual cheeses, pressed sandwiches, baked goods, espresso drinks, even birch beer (non-alcoholic). No Coyote Ugly, is this. Then he invited Glick to come see what the Tiger was all about. A little business trickled in, but no Glick. The stalemate wouldn't break, and eventually, Brodrick shuttered the doors. Fifteen hard months of exile began; New York's beer crowd glowered in their mugs somewhere else, and talked about the Tiger.

Like the Dove, the miniscule Hammersmith, London watering hole once favored by Graham Greene and Ernest Hemingway, or McSorley's Old Alehouse, the original Blind Tiger was dusty and cramped. It was, at its best, old-world squalor exalted. As the stalemate continued, Brodrick and co-owner Alan Jestice planned their new Tiger, nearly double the size of the original. It would be a beer boutique, a shrine to craft-brewed brews complete with wood-paneled walls and floors, custom bar, temperature-controlled cellar (for aging rare ales), and a selection every bit as Byzantine as the menu at Murray's Cheese Shop, just down the block. It wouldn't be easy. But the tigers were restless.

Vive la résistance! Starting in September 2006, a Tiger militia—hailing from the New York area and a handful of foreign countries—began circulating an e-petition aimed at the State Liquor Authority. Thomas Paine, who, 230 years ago cried out for fairness from the Crown on the taxation of beer— "the humblest drink of life"—might have been proud. "[The Blind Tiger] is far removed from those outlets who seek the sort of person that consumes cheap mass-produced drinks associated with binge drinking and uncouth behavior," wrote Alex Hall, of Brooklyn—the document's author and John Hancock. "Good beer is the new wine," wrote David Gould, signer no. 997, adding, a bit unhelpfully, that "drinkers of yellow beer should be drawn and quartered," a reference to both King George III's preferred form of execution and the sort of mass-produced dross unfit for the Tigerian palate. Others struck a more conciliatory tone. The Tiger "will be a nice quiet place where you can bring your mother," assured one.

Carry on, men! "Peace and quiet are to be found in the Catskills, not on Bleecker Street! Prohibition is over!" howled one insurrectionary. Another cited Jane Jacobs's 1961 manifesto, *The Death and Life of Great American Cities*, with its endorsement of civilized bars. "As a bouncer in good standing with local law enforcement," wrote Raymond Lopez, signer no. 999, "I can attest to the well-behaved manners of this crowd." One after another cast the closure in patriotic terms. "For a beer enthusiast, the closing of the old BT was as tragic as if they closed the Statue of Liberty," one gloamed. Peter Flanagan—the 1,385th partisan to commit his name—rattled his musket to end the debate: "Enough already; the people have spoken."

Indeed they had. The board eventually relented, and in March 2007, the Tiger reopened with a huge (but civilized!) party that hasn't really stopped. Infinitely cleaner, but no less fun, it's New York's most fiercely defended beer territory.

JIMMY'S No. 43

43 E. 7th St. • New York, NY 10003 • (212) 982-3006
jimmysno43.com • Established: 2005

SCENE & STORY

Most nights when you amble down the stairs into this amiable rathskeller (a bar below street level) the compactly stocky New York craft beer maven Jimmy Carbone is perched on a stool to greet you, along with the aroma of some very good food cooking—stick-to-your-ribs fare like ribs and gnocchi. Jimmy's got a twinkle in his eye and a beer in hand, and he's glad to see you. It's got a small, cozy dining room area, a narrow bar, and more or less feels like it was transported, inch by inch, out of Germany (those who have been lucky enough to travel to Aecht Schlenkerla, in Bamberg, will feel right at home). There's something wonderfully enveloping about the bar, or maybe that's just the way it feels when you huddle in cheek by jowl to sample beers and rap with Jimmy and his friendly crew.

PHILOSOPHY

With twelve ever-changing taps of beer, and some twenty-six in bottles, Carbone takes things coast-to-coast, and somehow he manages to score a lot of unique kegs other bars never seem to have, or are too chicken to put on tap.

KEY BEER

Jimmy loves his Belgian ales, from the mother country and our American counterparts, sometimes pitting them against one another in taste offs. Brasserie De Ranke's XX Bitter, a dry, bitter, and peppery Belgian pale ale inspired by Orval is sometimes on tap. It was brewed to be the hoppiest beer in Belgium and is not for the fainthearted, but rewards those who love earthy, intensely flavored brews.

LA BIRRERIA AT EATALY NYC

200 5th Ave. (top floor) • New York, NY 10010
Entrances on 5th Ave. and 23rd St.
(212) 229-2560 • eatalyny.com • Established: 2011

SCENE & STORY

Set in an 8,000-square-foot aerie soaring above Manhattan with views of the Flatiron and Empire State Buildings, La Birreria serves up the ultimate in Italian-style cask-conditioned ales (brewed on premises) paired with food by Mario Batali. The dream team in charge includes American brewing star Sam Calagione of Dogfish Head and creative Italian craft beer upstarts Teo Musso of Birrificio Le Baladin and Leonardo Di Vincenzo of Birra del Borgo. Brewer Brooks Carretta is at the kettles. That's a lot of hands in the brew house, but all very able ones indeed.

PHILOSOPHY

Old-world flavors and techniques mingle with unhinged experimentation, both in the kettle and on the plate. "This may well be the craziest and most amazing brewery in the world," says Di Vincenzo.

KEY BEER

All of the Birreria's beers are served on cask, with three cask beer engines featuring two year-round beers and one rotating seasonal. Staples include an English mild made with Italian chestnut powder and American pale ale made with dried thyme from Italy. In addition, there are eight draft taps with beers from Italian and American craft breweries.

THE HOPSICLE EXPERIENCE
DIABLO ROYALE ESTE
167 Ave. A (at 11th St.) • New York, NY 10009
(212) 388-9673 • diabloroyale.com

It gets really, *really* hot in New York during the months of June through September. Enter the Hopsicle Experience, a can of Tecate ingeniously spiked with simple syrup and lime, then frozen with a wooden stick—frozen-pop-style—for four days. Craft beer? Not so much. But here's the crafty part: order one, and the bartender saws the can open with a serrated steak knife—or a samurai sword, by one account—serves you the push-pop, and then asks if want a shot of tequila in there, too. Well, do you? Yes. Yes, you do.

VOL DU NUIT
148 W. 4th St. • New York, NY 10012 • (212) 979-2616
voldenuitbar.com • Established: 2001

SCENE & STORY

Vol Du Nuit is a bar in three parts: a dimly lit back room with a back bar made for slurping *moules frites* and Abbey ales, a courtyard in the middle for sitting sort of al fresco, and a tiny bar that most people breeze past as they enter the inner sanctum through a covered tunnel. But it's that one, the street side bar in its diminutive glory that makes this place worth a stop. And though there are plenty of West Village bars that have better beer lists and want to transport you to 1990s Paris or the University district of Brussels, this one succeeds the most convincingly. It's all about the atmosphere here, which is sort of *Ronin* meets *Amélie* minus the gnomes and gunplay. Don't be surprised if you suddenly want to bum a smoke from the NYU grad students hanging out, write in a leather-bound journal, and bike around some cobblestone streets humming a tune by Björk.

PHILOSOPHY

This no-frills bar is amiable and doesn't pretend to be more nor less than it is, a great place to have a good Belgian beer and some good, restorative food, and catch up with an old friend or two. It's an escape in the busy Village, a hideout from the hustle.

KEY BEER

The Belgian ales Orval and Saison Dupont

are available by the bottle, and they are both world-class, inimitable brews normal college kids can seldom afford, so you probably didn't drink them on your junior year abroad. Belgian ales are often better consumed by the bottle rather than on draft, so simply ask for the list and see what's in the cellar.

PONY BAR

637 10th Ave. • New York, NY 10036 • (212) 586-2707
theponybar.com • Established: 2009

SCENE & STORY

Hell's Kitchen has long been a hellhole of underlit, overpriced sports bars with dirty beer lines and questionable food—not a craft brew in sight. So the arrival of the Pony Bar was a very welcome change for the countless New Yorkers who live and work nearby. Inspired by an old black-and-white photo of Neil Young, there's exposed brick walls, a handsome bar, and snatches of Americana (wooden oars, a canoe on the ceiling, old wooden beer barrels, parade bunting, and a forty-eight-star Old Glory). The five-dollar, 14-ounce pours are quite fair (five dollars for 8 ounces on imperials and other big beers) and the vibe is friendly, if a little homogenous. All twenty tap beers are labeled with ABV and brewery; when a new keg comes on tap, the cellarman rings a bell and the patrons cheer "New beer!"

PHILOSOPHY

All of Pony Bar's craft beers are American and on draft (there are only two bottles, in fact—Budweiser and Bud Light, for the uninitiated). There are no dedicated tap lines; the selection continuously changes, with a preponderance of Northeast gems and a happy hour starting at 4:20 p.m. daily (subtle!). It's a bar for both the curious and committed craft beer drinker eager to try every new thing; the owners even organize tours to local area breweries. Regulars who try at least a hundred brews earn a cool Pony Bar short-sleeve button-down; and there have been a good many who've put in that hard work so far.

KEY BEER

There's a strong Northeastern regional presence, so look for new releases from Kelso, Sixpoint, Brooklyn, Ithaca, and Captain Lawrence, like a crisp Fresh Chester Pale Ale, to name a good session beer to go with a bite from the bar menu.

McSORLEY'S OLD ALE HOUSE

15 E. 7th St. • New York, NY 10003 • (212) 473-9148
mcsorleysnewyork.com • Established: Around 1860

SCENE & STORY

Every New York beer tour should at least stop, and maybe end, here. Joseph Mitchell's 1943 book *McSorley's Wonderful Saloon* describes this timeless place; Nothing much has changed, and though tourists predictably flock inside, they do so with very good reason. Open since about 1860 and reportedly unchanged inside since 1910, it's New York's oldest continuously operating saloon, and with its sawdusty floors and walls packed with ephemera, it's a time machine. To walk in is to follow in the footsteps of Abe Lincoln, Woody Guthrie, and John Lennon, among others. At McSorley's, frankly, it's not about the beer; it's about the place. It's about time spent with good friends, deep (or not so deep) conversations, and conjuring the easy elegance of a simpler time in the city.

PHILOSOPHY

"Be Good or Be Gone" and "We Were Here Before You Were Born" are the two house mottos; women were not allowed in until 1970. It can still be a bit of a boy's club (as in modern day Jersey boys), but on a good quiet afternoon it feels just as it should.

KEY BEER

McSorley's beer, first brewed by a long lost brewing company called Fidelio and later Schmidt, comes in two varieties, both quite light. Hop heads need not apply. Order one beer; two mugs are served. From time to time one hears of plans afoot to remake the recipe, for now it's a pair of Stroh's/Pabst creations, simply one "light" and one "dark" and nothing to write home about.

D.B.A.

41 1st Ave. (between 2nd and 3rd)
New York, NY 10003 •(212) 475-5097
drinkgoodstuff.com • Established: 1996

SCENE & STORY

When D.B.A. (a cheeky reference to a legal term referring to an assumed business name, "Doing Business As") opened, the Lower East Side was a touch edgier, but it's still got an appealing energy and street life. It's a New York classic, and its success has spawned two other outposts, one in Williamsburg, and one in New Orleans. Dimly lit with candles on copper-topped tables, an enormous chalkboard menu of beers and spirits available, and a small but comfortable back patio (with biergarten picnic tables imported from Germany), it's perhaps the best place to have a late-afternoon beer in New York City. D.B.A. is a weeknight or Sunday afternoon bar; take a bench in the small back garden area, or candlelit, copper-topped table near the back door, and let the time roll by.

PHILOSOPHY

Generosity is king. The late owner Ray Deter was a beer lover in the best sense, and he worked hard to keep the list rotating with unusual beers from both the region (Victory, Kelso, Southampton) and far, far away (St. Feuillien; Mikkeller; Ridgeway; De Ranke). It's not just a beer bar, though; Deter's stocked in some of the best single malts and other unusual spirits available in the States. He also serves Russ & Daughters bagels and lox—gratis—every Sunday afternoon until supplies run out. On Mondays, visitors who sit at the bar enjoy a complimentary cheese plate as well.

KEY BEER

Deter turned many a beer lover onto the true greatness of a beer called Taras Boulba, a 4.5% ABV Belgian Pale Ale from Brasserie De La Senne, a quenching, peppery, and light brew with a rocky white head and golden-amber hue.

THE HALF KING

505 W. 23rd St. • New York, NY 10011 • (212) 462-4300
thehalfking.com • Established:

SCENE & STORY

There was a sense, early on, that the Half King could have collapsed under the weight of its own lofty promise. Opened up by heavy-weight journalists Sebastian Junger and Scott Anderson as a bar by and for their fellow writers, there was some doubt whether it might prove that writers do their best work on the *other* side of the bar, draining kegs rather than changing them out every ten-minutes. But Junger and Anderson kept a close watch on things, hiring seasoned staff and talented but not showoffy cooks. The Half King has become a minor New York establishment, because of how effortless the old friends have made it all seem.

The three-room bar (plus a small back garden area and sidewalk patio area) is modeled on a traditional English pub, appointed in warm salvaged woods from a 200-year-old barn. The furniture is simple; the bar well-stocked and crisply run. Craft beer wasn't exactly in the heart of the matter at first, but recent beer dinners with the likes of Dogfish Head have pumped up the craft beer vibe. The best time to come here is for free Monday night readings by writers such as of *Vanity Fair's* William Langewiesche, *NYT* war correspondent Dexter Filkins, and novelist Jonathan Miles (to name a few recent appearances, in addition to sporadic events with Junger and Anderson). You'll be crammed in the small back room with a tinny microphone and little podium, sip a beer, hear some of America's best writers discuss their work, and have the chance to say hello afterward.

PHILOSOPHY

Every beer has a good story, and every good story deserves a beer.

KEY BEER

Blue Point Toasted Lager, at 5.3% ABV is low in bitterness for the style, easy-drinking yet refreshing, light, and well-suited to a long night of trading tales.

THE GINGER MAN

11 E. 36th St. • New York, NY 10016 • (212) 532-3740
No website • Established: 1996

SCENE & STORY

A New York standby and offshoot of the original Houston Gingerman (though only this location is still owned by founder Bob Precious), the beer list is truly incredible here, with some seventy taps and scores of truly obscure beers and a solid menu of upscale pub favorites. The Ginger Man is large and well lit, with varnished wood booths, white tile wall details, framed beer posters, and one of the first bartending female Cicerones in New York (if not the United States). Wise imbibers will avoid weekday happy hour, when the bar lines up three-deep with midtown and Murray Hill office workers clamoring for a brew.

PHILOSOPHY

Big and brash yet benign. Around the bar are lovely chalk murals by Julie Gaither, another bartender, attesting that this is a beer bar with its heart in the right place.

KEY BEER

Fluffy White Rabbits from Pretty Things Beer & Ale Project. An 8.5% ABV tripel style beer, it's hay-hued with layers of tropical fruit and spices like thyme and lemon grass.

GOOD BEER NYC

422 E. 9th St. • New York, NY 10009 • (212) 677-4836
goodbeernyc.com • Established: 2010

SCENE & STORY

David Cichowicz's amazing little beer shop is the latest reason for beer lovers to spend some extra time in Losaida (the Lower East Side). The vast selection (more than five hundred, heading toward nine hundred, he says) is organized neatly along old-timey wooden shelves and in glassed-in coolers, and best of all you're free to order pints while you shop or take growlers (with twelve taps running) to go. Cichowicz offers $6 pints and flights ($8 for four 4-ounce pours); snacks to keep you going include pretzels, organic grass-fed dogs, spicy or cheddar-filled kielbasa, and cheese plates.

PHILOSOPHY

The beers are divided regionally, with 80 percent domestic craft beer and 20 percent from overseas, and there's an especially strong mix from the Northeastern region.

KEY BEER

Look for a local specialty you might have missed, like Brooklyn Brewery's Cuvée Noire, a delicious, 8.7% ABV strong dark Belgian ale.

RESTO

111 E. 29th St. • New York, NY 10016 • (212) 685-5585
restonyc.com • Established: 2007

SCENE & STORY

The word *resto* is sometimes used as slang in France for a casual restaurant, but the sophisticated Belgian artistry here rises above the fray with sure-handed, nose-to-tail cooking served in a cozy refuge. *Moules frites* shine here, naturally: try the Dijon, house-made bacon, Parmesan, onion confit, and tarragon combo (the green curry, lemon grass, coconut milk, and kaffir lime combo is also excellent). What's more, there's a bit of bacchanalian sensibility when it comes to both beer and portions, which are available in ultra-large sizes. Fancy a delicious whole roast chicken for two ($60) and a 3-liter Jeroboam of luscious St. Feuillen Tripel ($165)? You've come to the right place. The great thing is that you won't feel like an idiot for ordering said jumbo spreads. It's what people do at Resto, and it's worth both the cost and effort. Dining at the bar is a great option if the tables kept open for walk-ins are already spoken for. Sunday dinners are institutional, and recently beer dinners have gotten more frequent. The slightly older crowd consists of well-dressed Manhattanites, but doesn't feel annoyingly business-like.

PHILOSOPHY

Chef Bobby Hellen worked for the likes of Jean-Georges Vongerichten but says his greatest influence is his grandmother, who made her own pasta and sausages and cured her own meats during his childhood on Staten Island. That about sums up the great dual nature of Resto. It's elegance and earthiness in equal measure—big measures.

KEY BEER

There are seven good Belgian ales on tap starting with Bavik Pilsner on the lighter side and heading all the way up the scale of liver impact to Koningshoeven's 10% ABV Quadruple, certainly a fine place to stop if you've had the five in between.

WHOLE FOODS

95 E. Houston St. • New York, NY 10002 • (212) 420-1320
wholefoodsmarket.com/stores/bowery/beer-room

SCENE & STORY

As worldly New Yorkers discover craft beer from around the world and what it can do alongside great food, Whole Foods has kept ahead of the curve with an ambitious beer program, exemplified by this Lower East Side location and its huge, 1,000-bottle-plus "beer room." There's also a row of six local taps for growler sales, and recently the store began selling homebrewing equipment and sponsoring a brewing contest with Kelso of Brooklyn—first place gets to brew at Kelso and see his or her brew on tap at this Whole Foods and around the city.

PHILOSOPHY

Back when the first Whole Foods opened in 1980, beer was not a priority. "We didn't sell much of it," says Doug Bell, one half of the beer-and-wine–buying team (with Geof Ryan) for the company, based in Austin, Texas. Fast-forward thirty years and beer now gets the same exhaustive treatment as cheese and heirloom vegetables. Working together, the duo oversees the 225 beer-selling locations in thirty-eight states, with the largest flagship locations boasting more than 800 offerings—including some rarities found almost nowhere else in the country. Because each store also employs at least one resident expert on beer with the authority to set the shelves, look for hometown—or home state—favorites to dominate. "Our local buyers have their fingers on the pulse," says Ryan.

KEY BEER

On draft, local powers such as Kelso, Brooklyn, Six Point, Captain Lawrence, Chelsea Brewing Company, and Sixpoint. In bottles, there's an especially strong grouping of British ales and oversize Belgian bottles. Shop away.

★ ★ ★

ZUM SCHNEIDER

107 Ave. C (at 7th Street) • New York, NY 10009
(212) 598-1098 • zumschneider.com • Established: 2000

SCENE & STORY

Small and quickly crowded, especially during its Oktoberfest, Zum Schneider is one of the most authentically German beer bars in the city. It's also among the nicest places to drink a sidewalk beer in summer in the East Village. There are excellent traditional specialties on the menu as well, from Blumenkohlsuppe creamy cauliflower soup to Schweinswürst'l, a plate of five grilled Nürnberg sausages with sauerkraut and fluffy mashed potatoes.

PHILOSOPHY

"Bier trinken ist ein gut essen (beer drinking is good eating)."—Immanuel Kant

KEY BEER

Look for unusual German seasonals such as the Traunstein Zwickel, an unfiltered lager from Munich's Hoffbräuhaus.

★　★　★

Brooklyn

BAR GREAT HARRY

280 Smith St. • Brooklyn, NY 11231 • (718) 222-1103
bargreatharry.com • Established: 2007

SCENE & STORY

A valid criticism of many of the late-aughts era bars of Brooklyn is that they try too hard—way too hard—to be cool, old, local, artisanal, *and* gastronomically innovative all at once. The endless iterations of gastropub-meets-speakeasy aesthetic (a Brooklyn epidemic) have become tiresome. Overdistilling the past, their suspendered mixologists slinging obscure sloe gin cocktails with house-cured maraschino cherries overreach to the point of absurdity.

Not so at Bar Great Harry. This is a beer bar, period, not a period bar. The tiny, no-frills, dog-friendly Cobble Hill beer lover's hideaway opened without fanfare, then proceeded to cycle through some 450 different tap handles in only two years, hosting brewmasters from across the land, like Carol Stoudt of Pennsylvania's Stoudt's. With low ceilings, a cozy, always-seated-with-regulars bar, and a recent back room addition, it's neighborhoody in the extreme, but that's what makes it so worthy. People cram in there, order rarities from Allagash, Bear Republic, Southern Tier, Troegs, and many others, and then repeat the process, as the sounds of Blur and Fugazi echo in the street. Dinner will have to wait. Sometimes there are Australian meat pies from DUB (Down Under Bakery) Pies, but it's really just about the beer.

PHILOSOPHY

Don't judge a beer bar—or a beer—by its size.

KEY BEER

Bear Republic's luscious, hoppy, strong Racer 5 IPA (7% ABV) is one of the few beers that seems to be on tap constantly. It's lush, piney, abundant, and stands with the best of the best IPAs in the world.

BROOKLYN BREWERY

No. 1 Brewers Row • 79 N. 11th St. • Brooklyn, NY 11211
(718) 486-7422 • brooklynbrewery.com • Established: 1987

SCENE & STORY

Once there were some four dozen breweries in Brooklyn, producing a fifth of the nation's brews, today, there are just a few in operation, and all of them are products of the modern craft beer era. The most famous of them is Brooklyn Brewery, a short hop on the L train into Williamsburg and by all means worth the beer traveler's efforts. Since former Associated Press journalist Steve Hindy and his downstairs neighbor Tom Potter founded the company in 1987 (with a ribbon cutting by Mayor Rudolph Giuliani), and especially with the arrival of brewmaster Garrett Oliver, the company's fame and acclaim have grown. The beers are distinctive, especially the small batch brews, which are in fact crafted in Brooklyn (the rest is brewed in Utica, New York).

Visitors mingle in a rustic tavern setting (opened in 1996) in view of the shiny tanks in the company's new 50 bbl brewhouse, where Monster (the brewery cat) is officially in charge. Friday nights have a raucous happy hour vibe and Saturdays and Sundays are for tours; many make the stop en route to other Williamsburg drinking destinations including Brookyn Bowl, Spuyten Duyvil, Radegast, Fette Sau, Barcade, the Diamond, and others.

PHILOSOPHY

Brooklyn's beers, under avowed foodie Garrett Oliver's watch, strive for dryness layered over a full malty backbone, and often hints of overt spiciness. Recently the company has released a slew of complex Belgian ales, collaborations, and experimental one-offs including beers made with bacon (!) and barrel-aged whimsies like Cuvée de la Crochet Rouge (his Belgian-style Local 1, a strong Belgian Pale ale, aged on botrytis-altered Riesling lees) that continue to spread Oliver's reputation for a steadily creative hand at the kettles. More than anything though, Oliver strives for what he calls "the four pint principle." It's simple: "If you don't want four pints, then I feel like there's something that you haven't really understood about the way the beer is supposed to be," he explains. Sounds like a principle worth putting to the test.

KEY BEER

Brooklyn Lager, the company's 5.2% ABV flagship (compare that to a standard Budweiser, at 5% ABV), is an unusual brew: it has the spice and fruitiness and body of many ales, but also the creamy but clean and palate-cleansing mouthfeel of German lagers (thanks to a long cold fermentation). Blast, an American-style double IPA that the brewery has quietly produced for years, is a delicious grapefruity hop bomb.

DETOUR → AN EVENING WITH BROOKLYN BREWERY'S GARRETT OLIVER

One of the most accomplished figures in the modern craft brewing world, Queens native Garrett Oliver is also among the most quotable. Over the course of an evening's tasting in Brooklyn on a chilly December night, Oliver, who was in the midst of finishing the editing of *The Oxford Companion to Beer* (a tome—not his first—with 1,150 different subjects and one hundred contributing editors on board), took time to elucidate his philosophies on being a brewmaster in New York City. And Oliver, as anticipated, was the perfect host.

Getting the Williamsburg operation off the ground, he recalled, was a dicey proposition, even for a seasoned local. "There was nothing. You went outside; it was dark; you were looking over your shoulder the whole time to make sure you didn't get clocked in the head," he said. "Brooklyn was 'Crooklyn' and the cabs wouldn't take you there." But the branding and the move to the budding scene of Williamsburg was incredibly prescient. "It's really only been in the last ten years or something that I would say that the name Brooklyn has become positive to people. It was always positive to us because we're from here, but in other places that we went, it was definitely kind of like, 'Uh, really?'"

But Oliver had very clear ideas about bringing craft beer to internationally experienced New York audiences, starting with their most notoriously decisive organ, the stomach. "Food came before beer," he reminisced. "My father was a serious cook." Oliver's love of food is evident in his book on the synergy of the two, *The Brewmaster's Table: Discovering the Pleasures of Real Beer with Real Food* (Ecco, 2003). Today, Oliver is a regular commentator on the delights of pairing food and beer, and has built a space inside the Williamsburg facility for special beer dinners.

Beyond the culinary aspects of beer that have helped Oliver brew for a New York mindset, he is most outspoken about craft beer's place amid the larger culture of New York, and America beyond. "My original background comes out of filmmaking," he said, "and people often ask me, 'How do you go from being a filmmaker to being a brewer?' In my mind, they are actually almost exactly the same. They are disciplines where you need 50 percent technical ability and 50 percent inspiration and art. Now, you can have a career with only one half or with an imbalance of those two things, but we have all been to movies where all the explosions and car chases are perfect, and you walk out of there and that's just two hours of your life you'll never get back. Basically Anheuser-Busch is Jerry Bruckheimer."

As we moved from the lemon verbena-like Sorachi Ace Saison to the racy, aromatic Blast IPA to the maltier, Belgian Abbey–style Brooklyn Local 2 and Cuvée Noire, a complex, roasty stout, Oliver explained that unlike the nation's truly mass producers, he sees brewing in more writerly terms.

"A beer is like a story. It has a beginning, a middle, and an end, and it should be interesting throughout, and it's supposed to have a structure that beckons to you to say, 'I would love to have a bunch of that'."

To achieve this sort of drinkability, Oliver went on to explain, is to manage a factor that many winemakers also must confront: attenuation. How much residual sugar should remain? "I think dryness is vastly underrated," he says. He's right. What goes for wit in conversation works as well with wheat beer, wild ale, or whatever beer you like: more often than not, less is more.

The genius of restraint is that then you want more of it, achieving perhaps what Oliver calls, "The Four Pint Threshold." "That's what I'm always trying to do . . . [the beer] falls into a place on your palate that causes you to say, 'You know what? I could sit down and get really comfortable with this'."

DETOUR ➡ **THE BROOKLYN INN**
148 Hoyt St. (at Bergen St.) • Brooklyn, NY 11217
(718) 522-2525 • Established: 1880s

It has no sign; it has never needed one and never will. Regulars and neighbors fretted in 2009 when The Brooklyn Inn, a perfect little jewelbox of a bar on a quiet Cobble Hill street was rumored to be near closing, then remodeling to expand its seating, then appeared as a set for post-adolescent angst in the *Gossip Girl* TV show. It was surely headed for the rocky shoals of history, smashed to bits amid the glare of such misguided attention.

But not so. History has been good to the Brooklyn Inn, open for the last 120 years or so in various incarnations, and with its creamy craftsman light fixtures, high windows, tin ceilings, dark wood walls, massive polished mirror bar (imported from Germany in the 1870s), eclectic jukebox, good local beers, and back room pool table, it's got all the ingredients for perfection for centuries to come.

Perfection, it's true, has its drawbacks. Like many of New York's most vaunted bars, it's to be avoided on Friday or Saturday nights, when the crowd seems to have wandered out of New York's most flavorless, résumé-obsessed quadrants and drunk kids are sitting on the pool table instead of running it. It's far better on a quiet afternoon, especially Sunday, ideally when it's snowing and the only sounds in the bar are soft voices and the creaks of a barstool on the old wooden floors.

THE GATE

321 5th Ave. (between 3rd St. & 4th) • Brooklyn, NY 11215
(718) 768-4329 • thegatebrooklyn.blogspot.com
Established: 1997

SCENE & STORY

Channeling old-world hospitality, the Gate has become many a Brooklyn craft beer lover's home away from home. The main reason for this is a brilliant beer selection. But it's more about the down-to-earth ambiance. With dark wood walls and a wide wooden bar, it's got the perfect Brooklyn mix of edge and coziness. The bartender has a speed metal group that plays on Halloween ("Smokewagon"), but the jukebox will spin Patsy Cline when you need it, too.

The Gate is also beloved for its patio, which, spread out on an airy Park Slope street corner, is, hands down, the borough's best place for an afternoon beer. As soon as the warm weather hits, the Gate is a hive of activity, and the hefeweizen's always fresh. Best of all, when hunger hits, simply ask the bartenders for the takeout bible, a three-ring binder with about 1,000 menus from nearby restaurants that will deliver sustenance directly to you. (Bonny's Burgers is the best bet.)

PHILOSOPHY

Not too serious, not joking around. Local Brooklyn micros share the tap row with European classics like Augustiner. And the tap dating, written on a pair of chalkboards, is a welcome addition.

KEY BEER

Ithaca Gorges Brewing Company, in the Finger Lakes region of upstate New York, has been making inroads into the crowded New York beer market. Look for their Smoked Porter (6.3% ABV), an American take on the German tradition of using malt smoked over beechwood fires, which lends a briney edge nicely reminiscent of campfire smoke.

PACIFIC STANDARD

82 4th Ave. • Brooklyn, NY 11217 • (718) 858-1951
pacificstandardbrooklyn.com • Established: 2007

SCENE & STORY

The arrival of this friendly, exposed-brick taproom a stone's throw from the Atlantic-Pacific subway hub helped usher in a renaissance for this section of Nowheresville, Brooklyn, a windblown patch of asphalt along 4th Avenue between the brownstones of Park Slope and the delis and boutiques of Boerum Hill, Carrol Gardens, and Cobble Hill a bit further West. Suddenly the area has several good bars with excellent vibes and beer lists, and it would be easy to spend an evening traipsing around this sector of Brooklyn, which is essentially the setting for Jonathan Lethem's novel *Fortress of Solitude*. The Brooklyn Inn, Bar Great Harry, the Gate, Mission Dolores, and 4th Avenue Pub are all reachable by a short walk, as are Southpaw, Barbés, and the Bell House, three excellent music venues with solid beer lists of their own.

Tuesdays are three-dollar-pint nights; on Sundays, regulars cram in for a tricky pub quiz at 8 p.m. There are readings in the spring and fall and storytelling nights three times a month, and the list of well-established writers and poets who have appeared in the slightly ramshackle but nevertheless comfy couch- and booth-filled backroom is impressive, from Colson Whitehead and Philip Levine to Joseph O'Neill and Joshua Ferris.

PHILOSOPHY

A refuge for West Coasters grinding it out in go-go New York, without being too affected; it's just a regular, comfortable, friendly bar, the kind of place to hunker down in and plan a road trip, and then cap it off on the tail end, too.

KEY BEER

Of the sixteen taps, six are typically dedicated to the West Coast craft brewers like Rogue, Lagunitas, Anchor, Sierra Nevada, and 21st Amendment, and casks make regular appearances as well. Somehow the angular, fulsome bite of Lagunitas Pils seems like exactly the right beer here every time.

SPUYTEN DUYVIL

359 Metropolitan Ave. (between 4th St. & Havemeyer St.)
Brooklyn, NY 11211 • (718) 963-4140
spuytenduyvilnyc.com • Established: 2003

SCENE & STORY

To many a resident of Gotham, Spuyten Duyvil—by its location in hipster-infested Williamsburg alone—always seemed too precious to be true: a craft beer bar built in a narrow old railroad apartment with a wide old wood bar, lovingly scripted chalkboards, creaky wood floors, pressed tin ceilings, and apothecary knickknacks, all completely dedicated to the enjoyment of "rare and obscure" Belgian and other European beers. *Fuggheddaboutit.* The upshot is that by leaving the bar alone to the "rare and obscure" sorts of folks—beer geeks and assorted *arrivistes* equally content with a PBR or rare Flemish *geuze* in hand, whatever seems cooler at the time—New Yorkers *have* given the bar a break, and the concept works just about as well as the marriage of chocolate and peanut butter. Which is to say, as New Yorkers sometimes do, it's "freaking awesome." Today Spuyten Duyvil (loosely, "spitting devil" or "in spite of the devil" in Dutch, depending who you ask) has earned its rightful place among the great craft beer bars of the nation. A round of beers here with the cheese plate and its Brooklyn-made pickles would make the perfect stop before hitting Brooklyn Brewery, Brooklyn Bowl, and local BBQ palace Fette Sau.

PHILOSOPHY

Rare and obscure—what else matters?

KEY BEER

Start with shared bottles of De Ranke's Kriek, then work your way up through a flask of Wostynjte Mustard ale, which is actually made with mustard seeds, giving it a delicious kick. Graduate to a 750-milliliter Cantillon Lou Pepe Framboise, and finish it all off with the world-classic Trappist monastery-brewed Rochefort 10. Who's cool now?

BROOKLYN DOES BBQ
FETTE SAU

354 Metropolitan Ave.
Brooklyn, NY 11211
(718) 963-3404 • fettesaubbq.com

Pork belly much? If you're in the area long or late you owe it to your self to seek out some incredible dry-rub barbecue from heritage livestock smoked over red and white oak, maple, beech and cherry wood; a huge American whiskey list; and craft beer taps from the likes of Kelso (with growler sales to go).

BEER TABLE

427-B 7th Ave. (between 14th St. & 15th St.)
Brooklyn, NY 11215 • (718) 965-1196
beertable.com • Established: 2008

SCENE & STORY

A tiny Park Slope eatery with a ballooning reputation (and a new growler filling shop in Grand Central Station), Beer Table aims to make up for what it lacks in square footage what it offers in terms of flavorful cooking and a tightly curated international beer list built for pairing. Its exposed brick walls, smooth, handmade wooden tables, and jars of pickled and dehydrated vegetables are instantly embracing. The main reason to be here is the kitchen, which issues forth hearty, inventive, and broadly European flavors—think smoked eel, Grafton village cheddar melted on toast, caramelized pork belly, hashes and veal, white beans, and waffles (at brunch) with assurance. It's an ideal place for quiet conversation beneath the tufts of mugwort and Mason jar light fixtures decorating the overhead space. Stop here en route to Park Slope's Prospect Park or the historic Greenwood Cemetery, one of Brooklyn's least-visited but most worthy points of interest (and eternal resting place of Duke Ellington, Margaret Sanger, William "Boss" Tweed, Leonard Bernstein, and countless other noted Gothamites).

PHILOSOPHY

Owners Justin and Tricia Phillips and chef Julie Farias are dedicated to raising the place of beer in fine dining one small inventive plate and tableside conversation at a time, and they're all friendly and approachable.

In many ways it's a perfect little scene, but while the beers change almost daily, the prices are on the high side (drafts for $7 to $12; bottles up to $100 and over). That quibble aside, it's definitely worth seeking out. Ask about their prixe fixe, which has been a great deal in years past.

KEY BEER

Dieu du Ciel! is one of North America's best micros, but since it's up in Montreal, the beers aren't exactly common in New York. Beer Table however, seems to get their beers with some regularity, so when you see Corne Du Diable, a rich and spicy red-hued IPA of 6.5% ABV, order it right up.

THE BRAZEN HEAD

228 Atlantic Ave. • Brooklyn, NY 11201 • 718-488-0430
brazenheadbrooklyn.com • Established: 2000

SCENE & STORY

A friendly, traditional Irish pub modeled after Dublin's most famous (and oldest), Brooklyn's version is a good approximation, with yellowed tin ceilings, darts, a wide wooden bar, and a small outdoor area in the back. The vibe here is relaxing and unpretentious, which is a welcome quality in the sometimes cooler-than-thou Borough of Kings. Brooklyn's first real ale festival (celebrating cask-conditioned beers) was staged here, an annual event that returns each November, which is worth attending, provided you arrive good and early.

PHILOSOPHY

People first. This is more a beer bar to hit with friends than an educational experience with every visit, but that doesn't mean the beers aren't good.

KEY BEER

There are typically fifteen beers on tap with two casks, so look for recent releases from New York area brewers including Chelsea, Captain Lawrence, and Brooklyn.

THE DIAMOND

43 Franklin St. (between Quay St. & Calyer St.)
Brooklyn, NY 11222 • (718) 383-5030
thediamondbrooklyn.com

SCENE & STORY

A lighthearted den where craft beer meets pop art and rock and roll, the Diamond is a little out of the way, a little bit kooky, and a lot of awesome. With its bright lighting, contemporary art, horseshoe bar, high metal stools, shuffleboard, and back patio equipped with an old ski gondola car, it's a refreshing change of pace from the Ye Olden Days vibe that pervades so many bars and taverns in New York these days. It makes a superb afternoon stop on the way into Williamsburg's other great beer destinations like Spuyten Duyvil, Radegast, and Fette Sau. The bar sponsors a Shuffleboard Biathlon, and "Brew n' Chew," a homebrew and home cooking competition, as well as occasional beer dinners, such as a recent sausage event.

PHILOSOPHY

The fact is, you're not going to come here for lectures on hop growing, but the beer list is no less worthy, and if you're really lucky, you might get to hear Van Heusen, owner "Diamond Dave" Pollack's Van Halen cover band.

KEY BEER

With seven taps, about thirty-four bottles, and a few cans, the selection is organized into "session beers," "middleweights," "strong," and "extra large." Look for obscurities like White Birch Wrigian, a rich, 7% ABV brown rye beer made with spicy Belgian yeast.

BIERKRAFT

191 5th Ave., No. 1 • Brooklyn, NY 11217 • (718) 230-7600
bierkraft.com • Established: 2001

SCENE & STORY

Former mortgage broker Richard Scholz opened Bierkraft on a stretch of 5th Avenue that wasn't exactly screaming "craft beer." This, of course, was exactly the genius in his move. The area was on the cusp of rapidly gentrifying and soon he had steady business. Despite high prices, the assortment of over 1,000 beers as well as 14 fresh beers on tap in growlers has made it a go-to for beer lovers. It's a narrow horseshoe-shaped space with a long beer cooler, stacks, and shelves of various sundries, the growler filling station, and enough meat, cheese, and chocolate racks to make the mind reel.

PHILOSOPHY

Beer is food. The store has expanded to include an incredible array of edibles: 250 artisan cheeses, more than 100 gourmet chocolate bars, rustic charcuterie, and other specialty foodstuffs are piled high from end to end. This would be the place to create the ultimate picnic or gift basket.

KEY BEER

Bierkraft carries more than 250 Belgian beers and nine beers on tap, available to go. Store employee Benjamin Granger built a counter-pressure filler so growlers stay fresher longer (as long as three months unopened, he claims, but it's better not to wait so long). Taps tend to be devoted to local beers not available in bottles. They also have their own "Randall," which for the uninitiated, is a kind of filter packed with fresh hops; beers on draught are pushed through it, picking up even more fresh hop aroma, though little bitterness.

EAGLE PROVISIONS

628 5th Ave. • Brooklyn, NY 11215
(718) 499-0026 • Established: 1940s

SCENE & STORY

The neighborhood around this cluttered old institution is alternately referred to as Windsor Terrace, South Slope, South Park Slope, and Greenwood Heights. It's a crossroads of sorts, but also a premiere destination because of the Old White Eagle Market, aka Eagle Provisions, a historic Polish grocery specializing in house-smoked meats:

wursts, great kielbasa, sausages, and the like. It also boasts what is likely New York City's biggest retail beer selection: 1,500 varieties and counting.

The entrance is cluttered with house-plants beneath the hand-painted sign with its martial-looking red eagle, and once inside, visitors are greeted by a statue of the Virgin Mary, various Polish flags, pictures of at least one pope, and cute and always-bored checker girls in their candy stripe aprons. Then co-owner John Zawisny or his brother guides you from there to the front right corner with its imponderable number of bottles, organized by country, looming floor to ceiling. It's not all refrigerated, but it's not far too dusty either—a sign that the beer moves with some regularity (still, check dates for lesser-strength bottles). And there you will wander around until the cows come home. It's a joy to visit (and is also en route to the verdant vistas of Green-wood Cemetery), not least because it offers a glimpse of that long ago time before groceries became all too perfect, hawking every shade-grown tofu and organic wheatgrass-infused whim of the moment.

PHILOSOPHY

Produce? What's that for, again? Fruits and vegetables play second, maybe third fiddle here. Both fancy and everyday Eastern European foods shine instead, from dark breads to potted pork products, pickled veg-etables, sauerkraut, pierogi, sodas and juices and other assorted mysteries in jars and cans of all shapes and sizes.

KEY BEER

With rarities in all shapes (even some mini-kegs) and beers from obscure breweries like Haandbryggeriet and Nøgne Ø (Norway), and Oude Beersel, Hanssens, Fantome, and Cantillon (all Belgian), not to mention a superb selection of U.S. craft brews, and Czech, Lithuanian, Polish, and even strange South American and Caribbean beers, this is nothing less than a beer geek smorgas-bord. Budget some extra time for a visit here, and make sure to bring some kielbasa and mustard to the party afterward, okay?

RADEGAST HALL & BIERGARTEN

113 N. 3rd St. • Brooklyn, NY 11211 • (718) 963-3973
radegasthall.com • Established: 2007

SCENE & STORY

This Austro-Hungarian style beer hall, built into a couple of transformed old warehouse spaces by Slovakian friends Ivan Kohut and Andy Ivanov, is named for an ancient Slavic deity of hospitality, and its interior seems like it was airlifted out of nineteenth-cen-tury Budapest. In the darkened entry room is a unique, polygonal bar with high stools and gleaming taps and atmospheric chande-liers overhead. But it's out in the next room, a great-hall-type affair with communal benches and skylights overhead, that most evenings seem to unfold. With a smoking grill station in the back and dirndl-clad bar-maidens weaving around the room, steins in hand, it's easy to feel transported. It gets absolutely packed on weekend nights, so the thing to do is to come in the afternoon for some fortifying fare, and stake out some territory—the tables fill up quick. At the same time, it can be a nice way to meet other New Yorkers.

PHILOSOPHY

It might appear to be a mere nostalgia fest, but the owners have made sure to lay in much more than the obvious in terms of beer, too. There are thirteen drafts on tap and fifty-eight beers by the bottle, with some pretty adventurous choices. This is an excellent place for larger groups to convene and settle in for some brats and beer, provided it's not Friday or Saturday night at 10:30 p.m.

KEY BEER

Schlenkerla Helles (in bottle). It's a fairly standard, straw-colored lager from Bamberg, Germany, but because it's brewed where smoked malts are used for other, bigger beers, it picks up a slight but super pleasant smokey note that pairs perfectly with a good venison sausage and some sauerkraut. If they're out, Köstritzer Schwarzbier on draft is a good, light-bodied but full-flavored option.

BROOKLYN BOWL

61 Wythe Ave. (between N. 11th St. & 12th St.)
Brooklyn, NY 11211 • 718-963-3369 • brooklynbowl.com
Established: 2009

SCENE & STORY

In addition to sixteen state-of-the art alleys, Brooklyn Bowl has ten local craft brews on tap, cool punk-inspired art, mega-size flat-screen TVs, swank black leather Chesterfield couches, a DJ platform, and legendary talents from Questlove to the Funky Meters appearing on a main stage practically every night. Pushing it right over the top, the local culinary wizards behind Blue Ribbon (with locations in Park Slope and Manhattan) have reinvented the typical ten-pin alley menu around haute soul food staples such as fried chicken, collard greens with bacon, baby back ribs, blackened Cajun catfish, and pork rinds served with cilantro, jalapeño, red onion, and queso fresco. It's all a bit pricey, but where else are going to find all of these things under one roof?

PHILOSOPHY

Goodness and plenty of it. This LEED-certified shrine to the ultimate leisure sport is surely the only set of lanes in America with 200-year-old reclaimed wood floors, tables made from old bowling alley lanes, and 100 percent wind-powered air conditioning, which keeps it White-Russian-cool even on the hottest summer night.

KEY BEER

There are ten draft beers, including five from Brooklyn Brewery next door, three from Six Point, and two from Kelso. Brooklyn's Blast Double IPA should encourage just the right amount of swagger to make those post-spare dance routines unforgettable.

MISSION DOLORES

249 4th Ave. (between President St. & Carroll St.)
Brooklyn, NY 11215 • (718) 399-0099
missiondoloresbar.com • Established: 2010

SCENE & STORY

From the owners of Bar Great Harry on nearby Smith Street comes an urbanite's shrine to rare and recherché craft beer, classic pinball games, and reclaimed building materials. Owner Mike Wiley says he wanted the interior to look something like a huge Vol du Nuit (see Manhattan entries), with luminous natural light coming through skylights so visitors can luxuriate in all the textures of wood, metal, cement, glass and other materials that were used to form the interior, benches, and bar. Like Bar Great Harry this is a place for drinking beer, but should hunger strike, you can order a savory meat pie from the same bakery (DUB) that supplies Bar Great Harry.

PHILOSOPHY

The owners' own site refers to it as "that weird bar at 4th and Carroll," which is understating how incredibly cool this place looks on the inside, and how pleasant it is to pass some time here among committed beer lovers, or the merely curious. A bar for the adventurous, Mission Dolores hosted a "Where the Wild Beers Are" festival in October 2011 for wild and sour ales.

KEY BEER

There are twenty tap lines, about three-quarters of them American craft beers; the remaining are Belgian or German, and there's always usually one cask. Standout offerings include several hard-to-find West Coast brews from Green Flash, Ballast Point, and Firestone Walker. Another recent score: the rare, 9.5% ABV Mikkeller/Brew-Dog collaboration DIPA (Double, or Imperial IPA), Hardcore You.

GOWANUS YACHT CLUB

323 Smith St. (at President St.) • Brooklyn, NY 11231
No phone, No website, no worries

SCENE & STORY

Forewarning: the G.Y.C. is a ramshackle sidewalk affair in Carroll Gardens with rickety picnic tables, uneven service, a bunch of smart-aleck rules (sometimes enforced, e.g. "no patchouli"), little protection from the elements, and all stripes of tragic hipster. But no matter. This seasonal (May through October) Brooklyn afternoon drinking rite rife with nautical airs, named for a Superfund sluice of toxic waste a few blocks south, is "garage-sale chic meets Gilligan's Island," according to the owner, who owns some other, less cool bars. Think: plastic cups and grilled frankfurters with kraut, a buck fifty. And here's a quiz: Who are you most likely to meet there at 2 a.m. on a stormy summer night, huddling under an umbrella as "Exile on Main Street" wails away? Is it a) a researcher just back from Antarctica, b) a *New Yorker* cartoonist, c) a well-known folk-rock singer winding down after a show, d) a stewardess from Japan Airlines, *in uniform,* or e) all of the above?

The answer is (e). It could only be (e).

PHILOSOPHY

Three sheets to the wind, lads!

KEY BEER

Jever Pilsner, which isn't too bad, and there's sometimes a hefeweizen. Come to think of it, there are a few craft beers to choose from, now and again. Or you could drink PBR. Don't worry about it too much. Worrying is bad for you.

SUNNY'S

253 Conover St. • Brooklyn, NY 11231
(718) 625-8211 • sunnysredhook.com • Established: 1890

SCENE & STORY

There is, at the end of a desolated, cobblestone street in the neighborhood of Red Hook, a bar seemingly cut from pure sailcloth, burlap, denim, and time. Opened in 1890, Sunny's is one of the last, best, most authentic New York places; to spend some hours there is to understand what makes the unhip, untrendy New York so appealing to a certain sort of drinker. The owner, Sunny's grandfather, opened up the place, and it doesn't seem like it's changed much, ever. There are electric Christmas light strands and maritime knickknacks left over from its days as a longshoreman's bar. An old green Willy's Jeep sits parked in front; the wood floors slope, and at night (it's only open Wednesday, Friday, and Saturday, from 8 p.m. to 4 a.m.), you crowd in and listen to really good musicians play Western Swing, dancing if you feel like it.

Sunny's just might be my favorite bar in the world. It's not for everyone. For starters, Sunny's is not easy to find. There's no subway close by, and the bus service is sporadic. Close to the harbor, you can smell the water, and the piers seem eerie. And even though there are some new bike paths and a fancy Fairway grocery store not too far away, on arrival, one immediately understands the meaning of the term Brooklyn Noir, which was invented for long-shadow streets like this. You can't use a credit card. You bring dollars, and you drink out of the bottle or a can. The bartender does not make faux old-timey cocktails or pretend he's a character in *The Great Gatsby*. It's not a place for the critic. It's also not really for cowboys, but the bluegrass jam session on Saturday nights makes you feel like you might have been one in a past life. You might just want to spend this life there, too.

PHILOSOPHY

Micro-what? Hey, in 1844, Pabst Blue Ribbon, named for a German ship captain, was a sort of craft beer, too. This is not beergeek country, but that's exactly what is so refreshing about coming here.

KEY BEER

The spicy, grainy Brooklyn Lager (5% ABV), if it's on. It's a standby throughout the borough. Truth be told, this is a Budweiser longneck kind of place, but Sunny often brings in Italian (mass-produced) lagers like Peroni, too.

Queens

BOHEMIAN HALL & BEER GARDEN

29-19 24th Ave. • Astoria, NY 11102 • (718) 274-4925
bohemianhall.com • Established: 1910

SCENE & STORY

Founded in 1892 in Astoria, Queens, to support Czech and Slovak immigrants to the area, as well as people of Czech and Slovak ancestry, the Bohemian Citizens' Benevolent Society is housed in "Bohemian Hall" and its tree-shaded beer garden outside is the oldest continuously operated beer garden in New York City, opened in 1910. It can fill up early, so head over early as part of an East New York (i.e. Brooklyn) trek.

PHILOSOPHY

As the Czech proverb says, "a fine beer may be judged with just one sip, but it's better to be thoroughly sure." Come for the traditional Czech and Bohemian food like goulash and dumplings, live music, open-air movies, or just beers in the open air. Sundays bring a small arts-and-crafts market, too.

KEY BEER

You can also opt for New York–area craft beers from Blue Point, Ommegang (Hennepin), Chelsea, and Captain Lawrence, but the great, golden-hued Czech import Pilsner Urquell would be the classic choice, and it's fairly priced at $5 for a half liter (16.5 ounces) or $15 for a pitcher. It's light and sparkly but packed with malt flavor, and wonderfully quenching from juicy, spicy hops, as well.

Southhampton

SOUTHAMPTON PUBLICK HOUSE

40 Bowden Square • Southampton, NY 11968
(631) 283-2800 • publick.com • Established: 1996

SCENE & STORY

Hitting the Hamptons doesn't have to mean dodging the tourists getting plowed in cheesy bars. The first and only craft brewery on the East End of Long Island (which once boasted scores of hops farms), Southampton Publick House calls a weathered former juke joint home and has the soulfulness to prove it. Inside a hedge area there's a bar-serviced patio, and inside, a bar and tables amid wood-paneled Yankee décor and nautical knickknacks. The beer is the main draw. Founding brewer and former engineer Phil Markowski is the author of a seminal 2004 book on farmhouse ales (*Farmhouse Ales: Culture and Craftsmanship in the Belgian Tradition*) and he excels with the earthy, spicy, and unfiltered end of the spectrum of beer, as evidenced by his tart, award-winning, low-alcohol Berliner Weisse (2% ABV) and a strong (9.5% ABV) Belgian pale ale called Grand Cru, among others. He also experiments with fresh hop ales, made with "wet" hops that are brewed within hours of picking on the same day each fall. With the prefect crop (rain can intervene), these beers are more aromatic and delicate than typical beers using hops that have been dried and stored, exploding with mouthwatering aromas of citrus, pine, and powdery floral notes.

PHILOSOPHY

Farm-to-brewery. "There's an unfortunate disconnect between brewers and their ingredients," Markowski said recently as he picked through loaded vines at the hopyard of local farmer Gian Mangiere, located at the western edge of Southold Town on Long Island. One of the few farmers growing hops anywhere in the Northeast, Mangieri says he does it for the love of beer. His tiny patch of Cascade, Nugget, and Fuggles hops—the delicate green flowers that give beer its aroma, bitterness, and aftertaste, sticky with lupulin, a resinous substance resembling pollen—were decimated by over twelve inches of windy rain that June, but they still managed to gather about six pounds of Cascades, which they immediately transported to the brewery and added to a special one-off 330-gallon batch of ESB. Mangieri has plans to double his hopyard.

KEY BEER

A strong Belgian-style Pale Ale, Southampton's 9.5% ABV Grand Cru is Markowksi's best beer to date, undlerlining how he's one of the few Americans that can pull the Belgian game off year after year. With appealing hints of anise, coriander, and orange peel, this is your ultimate special occasion beer at an everyman's price.

Pleasantville

99 Castleton St. • Pleasantville, NY 10570 • (914) 741-2337
captainlawrencebrewing.com • Established: 2005

SCENE & STORY

Captain Lawrence's cozy, sage green taproom draws a steady stream of locals and their guests who know that tours and samples are both free. In tony Westchester county, the straight-talking head brewer Scott Vaccaro and his father (often helping out in the taproom) and other crewmembers (many related to the father-son duo) come off as refreshingly down-to-earth. Not so long ago the younger Vaccaro was getting his butt kicked as a freshman in Villanova's accounting track, largely because he spent all his time home brewing with anything he could get his hands on, even plastic gasoline canisters. He graduated up to junior college in Cupertino, California, his last step before attending the fermentation science program at U.C. Davis, from which he catapulted into externships in Connecticut and England and finally an actual job at Sierra Nevada. The rest is history, and today Captain Lawrence (named for the street the Vaccaros lived on when Scott was a boy) is among the best-known and most accessible New York area breweries. As of late 2011 Vaccaro had planned to move his operation to 444 Saw Mill River Rd., Elmsford, NY 10523.

PHILOSOPHY

Vaccaro is a pragmatist, and while the beers are a bit uneven, he doesn't seem too concerned. "I just brew beer I like to drink and hope other people like it," he says. "Start with a traditional product and give it your own twist. Extra Gold, for example, is brewed after a Belgian triple, then we dry hop it like an American IPA."

KEY BEER

The bright, brassy 5.5% ABV Fresh Chester American Pale Ale has a solid New York area presence, but committed beer pilgrims will want to try and get their hands on something rarer like Vaccaro's annual Smoke from the Oak release, generally a porter which undergoes extended aging in port, bourbon, red wine, or even apple brandy barrels.

DETOUR → THE BEST BEER LUNCH IN AMERICA

Blue Hill at Stone Barns (restaurant) • 630 Bedford Rd.
Pocantico Hills, NY 10591 • (914) 366-9600 • bluehillfarm.com • Established: 2004

SCENE & STORY

Built amid soaring, remodeled 1930s stone buildings on what was once part of a Rockefeller family estate, the Inn at Stone Barns is more than just a restaurant; it's the apogee of farm-to-table gastronomy in the New York area and maybe the entire United Sates. Simply put, together with his staff chef Dan Barber has created what has been called the most important restaurant in America, and thanks to the hard work of beer sommelier Michael Greenberg, it's also an absolutely incredible place to indulge in a beer lunch for a very special occasion (starting at $85 per person, before drinks or gratuity). To get there you simply go to Grand Central, jump on the train to Tarrytown up the glorious Hudson Line, grab a ten-minute cab ride, and then, for most living persons, step off the face of the known culinary landscape.

There's no way to predict what you'll eat in the elegantly appointed, fifty-five-seat former dairy barn other than by glancing as you walk in at the list of what's seasonal, which is going to be a long one, even in early December. One merely indicates any contraindicated foods in your diet and the rest is up to Barber and his band of thirty or so extravagantly talented chefs, who interpret vegetables, especially, with a creativity bordering on the gonzo, to do the rest. On the day I visited with a cousin we gazed out the windows at verdant farmland and meandered through at least twelve courses paired carefully with a half dozen beers, mainly from the immediate area.

Some of the edible, and imbibed highlights:

- tender micro vegetables (including beets, radishes, and carrots) garnished with *ficoides glaciale* (an ornamental edible from the southern hemisphere), and flakes of smoked Tuscan kale
- cloudy-blonde, 8% ABV saison beer from Brouwerij Hof Ten Dormaal, in Tildonk, Belgium, with wheaty notes of apricot, lemon, and black pepper
- "vegetable sheets" of liquefied and dried wheat, parsnip, and beet edible stained glass hung from little mini wooden clothesline clips
- Kelso Pilsner, Brooklyn, NY (infused with lemon verbena and Blue Hill Farm's honey)
- a tiny "burger" of pureed, citrusy beets on a sweet minibrioche with sesame seeds
- a round of tastes of Kelso's cocoa-powdery Chocolate Lager, spicy Christmas Ale from nearby Defiant Brewing Co., in Pearl River, New York, and Keegan's superbly light and smooth Mother's Milk Stout
- delicate brook trout with a spicy fall vegetable and Maine crab sauce
- homemade ricotta from Dan Barber's farm in the Berkshires
- a deliciously herbal 7.4% ABV Saison Deluxe from Southampton Brewery
- tender pasture-raised venison tenderloin with Brussels sprouts and pistachios
- bread pudding in a mini cast iron skillet with house-made vanilla ice cream

Greenberg is truly a champion of the local craft beer industry, and he's already ushering along the cultivation of at least nine varieties of hops on the property for future collaboration batches of beer. "If we're not supporting these local brewers, and putting our money behind it, they're never going to get to that point of the Schneiders or Rodenbachs of the world," he says with typical generosity. "I really started to rethink our beer list and the form it took was from the Mississippi and the East."

Greenberg fosters a close rapport with the brewers and his distributors who are in synch with the overall culinary goals of Stone Barns. One highlight for beer lovers, surely, is the annual Sausage & Beer Dinner; in 2011 Barber and Greenberg worked with an area maltster, and local breweries to showcase five malts (rye, spelt, emmer wheat, triticale—a hybrid of wheat and rye—and roasted barley) alongside fresh sausages and cured meats followed by a five-course tasting menu featuring Blue Hill Farm pork, local grass-fed venison, beef, and lamb, and Stone Barns Bourbon Red turkeys.

PHILOSOPHY

Farm-to-table cooking meets local Hudson Valley brewing in the name of art, no stone unturned. "It's know your farmer, know your brewer," says Greenberg. That collaborative relationship extends to diners who come in on a Sunday, as I did, with an interest in beer. Greenberg (or any of his fellow servers, who are all highly trained on the beers available) take diners on a journey with beers that spread beyond a single course. "Because it's carbonated, there's a little bit more going on with the beer than the wine, and can be more filling, so I'll pick a bottle that will stretch over maybe one or two, maybe three courses, depending on the size of the bottle and what Dan and Greg have written as far as the menu, and I try to find something that is a little more versatile." Beer is often used in the kitchen as well, from soups and broths to deserts. Will brew tanks ever grace the halls of Stone Barns, I ask? He nods and smiles wryly, indicating a room adjacent to the hayloft structure where the beer-and-sausage pairing dinners are held. "We had to put a giant generator in the bay there. That would have been perfect," he says. In other words, it would not be wise to rule it out.

KEY BEER

Local New York area brewers shine here, obviously, especially Kelso of Brooklyn (also called Greenpoint Beerworks), constantly at work on a number of experiments for the restaurant including brews infused with farm-grown lavender, lemon verbena, farm-fresh honey, house-made apple-mint tea, chocolate mint, fall harvest honey, and roasted beet puree.

Pearl River

DEFIANT BREWING CO.

6 Dexter Plaza • Pearl River, NY 10965 • (845) 920-8602
defiantbrewing.com • Established: 2006

SCENE & STORY

In a narrow old artillery factory built "before electricity" and currently lined with gleaming copper tanks, Bronx native and head brewer Neill Acer holds court over one of the most distinctive and worthwhile little brewpubs in America. The crowd, a mix of office professionals, firemen, police, and other locals, is loyal and friendly, drawn by the good beers and house-smoked barbecue, which alone is worth a drive from New York. Served heaped on platters, this is some of the best pulled pork, brisket, and dry-rubbed ribs (served with pickles and mac-and-cheese) you will find anywhere in the Northeast.

Perched on a stool behind the bar, Acer stokes a vibe of easygoing misbehavior among patrons. "We work pretty late and we like to brew in front of people. There is a convenience level to being a microbrewer . . . just be in a little room with your favorite people and music playing in the background." It's clear he dearly loves his chosen path. "When I discovered how to make beer, it was like someone taught me how to make fire," he laughs.

PHILOSOPHY

Thanks to rigorous training at the Siebel Institute and stints setting up several different brewpubs, Acer has a capable hand with a huge swath of beer styles, from pre-Prohibition-style lagers to 15% ABV Imperial Stouts. And while he can rather effortlessly brew across entire stylistic valleys, he hasn't lost sight of his mission. "There is a level of David and Goliath to doing what we do as brewers," says Acer of the Defiant name. "You are really fighting for huge powers. Right here in the Northeast, this is the jewel in the crown; this is the Manhattan triangle. It is the largest beer market in the world."

KEY BEER

Acer's best beers are also his biggest, so look for the 9% ABV triple, various stouts, and his pièce de résistance, Death, a coal black monster with the complexity of an old vine Bordeaux and heft of a dump truck. Despite its huge profile, it's got an incredibly smooth, decadent palate of chocolate, dark fruits, and vanilla notes.

Cooperstown

BREWERY OMMEGANG

656 County Hwy 33 • Cooperstown, NY 13326
(607) 544-1800 • ommegang.com • Established: 1997

SCENE & STORY

The roots of Ommegang are tightly intertwined with the history of Belgian beer appreciation in this country. American Don Feinberg headed to Europe after Yale to do his MBA in 1978, ended up in Brussels, and fell in love with Belgian beer. He was also in love with Wendy Littlefield, his college sweetheart; the two of them eloped to Brussels and ended up spending three years there. To make a long story short, when they returned, they started organizing to bring in some cases of Duvel Golden Ale as an import project, and one of the U.S.'s most prestigious beer import companies was born, Vanberg & Dewulf, later responsible for introducing American beer lovers to Affligem, Rodenbach, and Brasserie Dupont's Saison lineup, among many others.

In 1997, the couple collaborated with Affligem, Scaldis, and Moortgat (brewers of Duvel) to launch Ommegang, dedicated to classic Belgian styles of brewing. The brewery itself is incredibly beautiful: an homage to eighteenth-century Wallonian farmstead architecture, the creamy white structures were built on a former hops farm on the banks of the Susquehanna River. With a portfolio of superb, award-winning beers and tours every day, Ommegang has become a true beer lover's destination.

PHILOSOPHY

Ommegang is dedicated to making Belgian beers with superb balance and appropriately decorous packaging. The company stands out in a sea of imitators with its consistent image and beer formulation.

KEY BEER

There are five year-round beers and five seasonals and the occasional one-off or experimental brew, always a hot commodity. Hennepin, a 7.7% ABV unfiltered golden farmhouse style (aka Saison), is perhaps the most emblematic of Ommegang's year-round brews. It's a delightful melody of grainy toast flavors, mild banana, lemony tartness, and spicy notes of clove and pepper, and a great introductory beer to non-craft beer drinkers. Lately the brewery has been releasing more daring beers with spices and added barrel aging, such as the excellent Zuur, a 6% ABV Flanders oud bruin, or old-style brown ale.

BEST *of the* REST: NEW YORK

AGAINST THE GRAIN
620 E. 6th St. • New York, NY 10009 • (212) 358-7065 • grapeandgrain.net

Against the Grain is a near-perfect secret spot for a quiet afternoon pint en route through Chinatown, the Lower East Side, and East Village. This teeny space around the corner from D.B.A. has a narrow, warmly lit bar, a few stools, flickery Edison bulbs, and knowledgeable servers that don't condescend. The beer list is eclectic and long, with hard-to-find brews from Achel and Thiriez, among many good domestic craft beers as well.

THE STANDARD HOTEL BIERGARTEN
848 Washington St. (near. Little W. 12th St.) • New York, NY 10014 • (212) 645-4646 • standardhotels.com

A short walk from New York's ethereal Highline park, Andre Balazs's Standard Hotel boasts an airy urban beer garden offering all the comforts of Bavaria and Bohemia in both liquid and sausage form, with ping-pong tables and serious people watching, too.

THE SPOTTED PIG
314 W. 11th St. • New York, NY 10014 • (212) 620-0393 • thespottedpig.com

Chef April Bloomfield's see-and-be-seen (especially late night) Greenwich Village gastropub isn't exactly a craft beer shrine per se, but the upstairs bar is perhaps the best place in Manhattan to take down some ultra-fresh Victory Prima Pils with some even fresher bluepoint oysters.

BARCADE
388 Union Ave. • New York, NY 11211 • (718) 302-6464 • barcadebrooklyn.com

Opened in 2004, Barcade is a shrine to two things: fresh (mostly local) craft beer and old-school, 25-cent videogames from the 70s, 80s, and 90s. Which makes it cool, if not a place to bring your parents, lest they be reminded of your irrecoverable years spent playing Super Mario Brothers instead of studying.

REBAR

147 Front St. • DUMBO, Brooklyn, NY 11201 • (718) 766-9110 • rebarnyc.com

Rebar has the feel of an artist's loft, if all artists were rich and could afford vaulted brick ceilings, recessed lighting, and plush couches. There's a deep list with eighty bottles and fifteen rotating taps; specialties include Belgian ales (Trappists are well represented), beer cocktails, and upmarket bar food. Since 2006, this has been the perfect spot to refresh while on a Dumbo gallery tour or after walking across the Brooklyn Bridge from Manhattan.

4th AVENUE PUB

76 4th Ave • Brooklyn, NY 11217 • (718) 643-2273 • myspace.com/4thavepub

With rarities from Pretty Things, Allagash, and Jolly Pumpkin, 4th Avenue Pub is narrow architecturally but fat as a prize pig when you factor in its twenty-seven taps and a cask beer on at all times, not to mention a deep bottle list and a pleasant backyard space for hot days.

STUDIO SQUARE BEER GARDEN

35-33 36th St. • Long Island City, NY 11106 • (718) 383-1001 • studiosquarenyc.com

This expansive, 20-tap, birch-tree-shaded beer garden shares an urban setting in Queens with Kaufman Astoria Studios, the Contemporary Art Center PS1, and the Museum of the Moving Image, making it an ideal destination drinking spot for culture vultures. Excellent beers include Green's Discovery (a gluten-free beer) and Bear Republic's juicy Racer 5 IPA.

LAZY BOY SALOON

154 Mamaroneck Ave. • White Plains, NY 10601 • (914) 761-0272 • lazyboysaloon.com

A trusted Westchester County beer-lovers outpost with huge international tap row, four casks (with fresh casks added Thursdays), deep bottle list, and vaunted hot wings in unusual flavors like Caribbean jerk and tequila citrus.

MAHAR'S PUBLIC HOUSE

1110 Madison Ave. • Albany, NY 12208 • (518) 459-7868 • itsonlybeer.com

Small, renowned, crowded beer-geek hideout with an ever-changing list and four to six casks at a time, and a bit of local edge, so order with authority. In the words of the owners, there's "no juke box, no bands, no beer specials, little or no food, and no tolerance for bad attitude or bad manners."

EMPIRE BREWING CO.

120 Walton St. • Syracuse, NY 13202 • (315) 475-4400 • empirebrew.com

These brewers of highly regarded barley wines also sling solid burgers and onion straws in a contemporary, subterranean space. There are ten house taps, three for New York state brewers, and one macro for the misinformed.

THE BLUE MONK

727 Elmwood Ave. • Buffalo, NY 14222 • (716) 882-6665 • bluemonkbflo.com

Opened in 2010, this ode to Belgian beer culture boasts *frites* cooked in duck fat, mussels steamed in Ommegang or Delerium Tremens (a strong golden ale from Belgium), and thirty-two taps of *very* hard-to-find Belgian and craft brews along the lines of Glazen Toren Saison d'Erpe-Mere, a hazy, pale gold Belgian beer with earthy, bright and tart fruit notes and a snow-white head. There's also the option of Blaugies Darbyste, a 5.8% ABV Belgian pale ale brewed with figs.

Connecticut

★ ★ ★

Middletown

ELI CANNON'S

695 Main St. • Middletown, CT 06457
(860) 347-ELIS(3547) • elicannons.com • Established: 1994

SCENE & STORY

First thing's first: Eli Cannon's, built in a historic old brick building, is absolutely crammed floor to ceiling with brewery ephemera, antiques, old TVs (some on, some off), barber chairs, tap handles, road signs, motorbikes—you name it. That it is also a bar and grill with good food and thirty-three taps of constantly rotating microbrews, a smart bottle list, visiting brewery nights and tap takeovers, a cool outoor patio drinking area, and a fun, youngish crowd makes it all the reason to clamber in and see where things go.

PHILOSOPHY

The more there is, the better.

KEY BEER

Harpoon's lemony, spicy UFO White (4.8% ABV), a Belgian-style witbier (white beer) would make the perfect libation for a session in Eli's leafy beer garden out back.

BEST *of the* REST: CONNECTICUT

PRIME 16 TAP HOUSE & BURGERS

172 Temple St. • New Haven, CT 06510 (203) 782-1616 • prime16.com

With exposed bricks, pressed black tin ceiling, sumptuous wood bar, and large wood tables beside burgundy walls, this friendly bar offers free beer tastings every Wednesday night starting at 9 p.m. The 20-tap, 45-bottle beer list is smartly varied, with almost half of the drafts less-common Northeastern beers like New England Brewing Company's 668 the Neighbor of the Beast, a 9% ABV Belgian pale ale, and the burgers get high marks.

Vermont

★ ★ ★

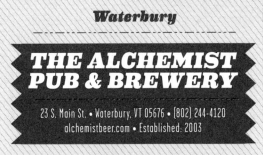

THE ALCHEMIST PUB & BREWERY

23 S. Main St. • Waterbury, VT 05676 • (802) 244-4120
alchemistbeer.com • Established: 2003

SCENE & STORY

Founder John Kimmich fell in love with brewing during his senior year of college at Penn State and after nine months of working in a home-brew store took his savings of $4,000, packed up his Subaru, and headed to Vermont. His goal was to work with the late Greg Noonan, a legendary writer of several influential beer books and a professional brewer who had founded Vermont Pub & Brewery. Under Noonan's guidance, Kimmich eventually became the head brewer there. Now he heads up his own Alchemist Pub & Brewery, set in a historic building in Waterbury, just a short drive from Burlington and the Stowe Mountain Resort.

PHILOSOPHY

Kimmich is a borderline neurotic perfectionist and (not inconsequently) a hell of a brewer, and his creations have become highly sought after, earning medals and a reputation for real mastery. He doesn't allow growler sales because he fears the beer being consumed in less than optimum conditions. Even deciding to can Heady Topper, his critically acclaimed 8% ABV DIPA, was agonizing. "It will be difficult for me to give up so much control and release it out into the wild, but I just really want to be able to take some Heady Topper on a long hike in the woods," he explained.

KEY BEER

Heady Topper, just one of several Double IPAs that Kimmich has brewed well, is the flagship (and is now available regionally in cans), but it's his Celia series that is most remarkable, named after celiac disease, or gluten intolerance. When Kimmich's wife developed a gluten allergy, he decided to try sorghum as a barley substitute (rural sorghum-based beers are common in parts of Africa). Kimmich started with an IPA and then a wild ale made with red raspberries and fermented with Brettanomyces yeast; both beers were awarded medals at the 2009 Great American Beer Festival (GABF). When he turned his attention to saison, the resulting beer would earn a gold at the 2010 World Beer Cup, and another gold at the 2010 GABF.

HILL FARMSTEAD

403 Hill Rd. • Greensboro Bend, VT 05842 • (802) 533-7450
hillfarmstead.com • Established: 2010

SCENE & STORY

Eighth generation Vermonter Shaun Hill recommends you do some Google mapping or consult an onboard GPS before trying to locate his remote, freestanding barn down a dirt road in the countryside where he's leading a revolution of the Vermont brewing scene. It's worth the trouble because it's exceedingly tricky to find his award-winning beers anywhere else. In a tale oft recounted in craft beer circles, Hill worked entry-level jobs in a pair of breweries in Vermont after college and then gained increasing responsibilities in three firms in Europe. Among them was Danish craft brewery Nørrebro Bryghus, led at the time by Anders Kissmeyer, a brewer who had taken a revolutionary road of his own by pioneering experimental styles in Carlsberg-saturated Denmark. The partnership was an incredibly fruitful one: three beers Hill brewed with Kissmeyer earned two golds and a silver at the 2010 World Beer Cup in Chicago.

Hill returned and using borrowed equipment and loans from fans and friends he got his own brewery up and running on land not far from the spot where his great-great-grandfather had opened a tavern on Hill Road. The beers have ranged from Belgian wit beer (Florence) to Black IPA aged in pinot noir barrels and dry-hopped with Simcoe (Jim), a release of a mere twenty-five cases. Ephraim, a 10.3% ABV Imperial IPA, contains five hop varieties and off-the-chart IBUs (International Bittering Units, measuring hop bitterness levels), but has dazzled the relatively few beer lovers who have been able to taste it.

PHILOSOPHY

Brewer as Super Man? Hill has released beers he says were inspired by Danish philosopher Søren Kierkegaard and Friedrich Nietzsche, and working within the arch-individualistic underpinnings those associations suggest, he aims to please. "All of my decisions, related to the present and future of Hill Farmstead Brewery, are calculated, rational, and existential," Hill says. Starting out, he blogged, sporadically: "We love hops. The majority of the beers that we brew are greater than 85 IBUs and dry hopped. We also love oak barrels: the aroma of the oak in the brewery, the added softness and roundness that the beer develops from its extended aging in the barrel."

KEY BEER

The Ancestor series is an ongoing celebration of Hill's forebears in the area including Edward (an APA that is his best seller). The Collaboration series was launched with a beer Hill called Fear and Trembling (there's the Kierkegaard), a smoked Baltic Porter aged in French oak cabernet barrels. Kissmeyer himself traveled from Denmark to assist his former pupil, hand smoking the malt over maple wood chips outside the barn, resulting in a powerfully smoky 9.3% ABV brew with chocolate- and espresso-like flavors and a vinous finish.

Burlington

THE FARMHOUSE TAP & GRILL

160 Bank St. • Burlington, VT 05401
(802) 859-0888 • farmhousetg.com

In a turn of events perhaps indicating some important cultural wind direction, the building that houses this new (2010) gastropub used to be home to a McDonald's—for thirty years. Today, the space is dedicated to a classic farm-to-table eatery with a beer list every bit as curated as its menu of grass-fed beef, free-range poultry, and heritage pork dishes accented by local cheese, charcuterie, and produce. Regional and local brewers, including Hill Farmstead, Otter Creek, Trapp, Rock Art, and Wolaver's, are all well represented, as are many of the top American and Belgian small batch and farmhouse-style producers.

Brattleboro

FORTY PUTNEY ROAD

192 Putney Rd. • Brattleboro, VT 05301
(802) 254-6268 • fortyputneyroad.com

Tim and Amy Brady, the thirty-something owners of this charming little six-room inn and pub are self-described beer geeks; they host tastings in their pub every Saturday night at 5:30 p.m. (seven beers paired with cheeses and other snacks for $19). The inn—built in 1929 as the superintendent's home for the Vermont Asylum for the Insane—was

established in 2007; it's got a luxurious carriage house option and an attached pub where Tim curates a nice little three-tap tower and bottle list including foreign gems like Rochefort and Orval. Starting in 2011, Tim and Amy are offering two-night "Meet the Master" weekends, during which guests mingle with noted brewmasters and participate in tastings of their beers.

Best of the Rest: Vermont

THREE PENNY TAPROOM

108 Main St. • Montpelier, VT 05602
(802) 223-8277 • threepennytaproom.com

A craft beer bar on Montpelier's Main Street, Three Penny Taproom has twenty-four taps and forty-five bottles available, including craft-brewed Belgian, American, and particularly Northeast beers such as Hill Farmstead, Southern Tier, and Trapp Family, paired with local cheeses.

★ ★ ★

New Hampshire

★ ★ ★

WHITE BIRCH BREWING

1368 Hooksett Rd., Unit 6 • Hooksett, NH 03106
(603) 244-8593 • whitebirchbrewing.com • Established: 2009

SCENE & STORY

New Hampshire's first nanobrewery, founded by dedicated homebrewer-turned-pro Bill Herlicka in a plain industrial space, started with half-barrel (about 15 gallon) batches that became so popular he was almost immediately planning a 7 bbl brew house to meet demand. That expansion now complete, Herlicka is still running a small operation dedicated to making excellent beer in unusual styles, many of which are barrel-aged British– and Belgian–style beers. There's a small tasting room area for samples and growler sales, with tours by appointment (calling or e-mailing ahead is recommended).

PHILOSOPHY

White Birch is no-frills but innovative, a classic successful craft brewer combination. It's not that he lacks ideas, he has said, it's that he suffers for a shortage of time and fermenter space—the two most expensive ingredients in brewing.

KEY BEER

Look for the Hooksett Belgian IPA, an intense, spicy, hop-suffused bomb of a beer at 9.5% ABV.

Best of the Rest: New Hampshire

WOODSTOCK STATION INN & BREWERY

135 Main St. • North Woodstock, NH 03262
(800) 321-3985 • woodstockinnnh.com

The Woodstock Station Inn opened its little copper, wood, and brick-clad seven-barrel brewery in 1996 and soon began booking guests deeply interested in the process of brewing itself. Offered in April and May for $125 (not including room cost), Brewery Weekend guests enjoy a reception Friday night and beer dinner Saturday, breakfast each morning and lunch on Saturday, and the chance to try out some aspects of the process during hands-on sessions in the brew house.

Maine

★ ★ ★

Portland

ALLAGASH

50 Industrial Wy. • Portland, ME 04103
(800) 330-5385 • allagash.com • Established: 1994

SCENE & STORY

Rob Tod's Allagash Brewery helped usher in the American craze for Belgian brewing styles with its first of many insanely drinkable beers, Allagash White, a traditional 5% ABV wit containing wheat (in place of barley), coriander, and other spices, and curaçao orange peel. Since then, Tod, along with brewmaster Jason Perkins, have created an array of new standards and superb bottle-conditioned beers. It's not much to look at on the outside, but the beer is extraordinary in every way, and has influenced and inspired countless young American brewers.

PHILOSOPHY

Of all the American craft breweries inspired by Belgium's unorthodox brewing practices, Allagash has made some of the boldest leaps, utilizing herbs, spices, and starchy vegetables usually only eaten on Thanksgiving. Some are wood aged and then bottle conditioned, meaning the beers have rested quietly in oak barrels before bottling with some

yeast and a small measure of special brewing sugar to carbonate in the bottle. Inspired by Belgian classics but going in new directions too, these beers boast wine-like complexity and higher alcohol levels, pushing the limits of what's considered sane and desirable in American microbrewing. Incredibly time-consuming and expensive to produce, barrel-aged beers expand the sensory horizon of beer almost exponentially, and Allagash has been at the forefront of this practice, inspiring countless imitators.

KEY BEER

Part of the (not barrel-aged) Serie de Origine experimental series, Confluence (7.5% ABV) combines the house Belgian yeast strain with *brettanomyces*, two kinds of traditional English hops, and a transatlantic medley of grains (including German-style Pilsner malts) for a totally deracinated, fully delicious evening sipper. This is a beer that shouldn't work—it sounds like the recipe came from a few rolls of some cloak-wearing home brewer's twelve-sided dice—but does. It's tart and wine-like on the front end, warm and creamy on the back end, and delicious throughout.

THE COOL SHIP REVOLUTION AND THE SLOW BURN OF AMERICAN WILD ALES

For some craft brewers innovation means slowing down—way down. Instead of finding ways to get more people to buy their beer faster, they're aging ales for months or even years with monkish consideration. You've heard of Slow Food? This is Slow *Brewed*.

In 2008, following Founder and Brewmaster Rob Tod's trip to Belgium and tours of several artisanal operations, Allagash installed what is thought to be the first modern *koelschip*, or "cool ship" in the United States. A shallow-bottomed steel vessel used to cool a rich wheat-, barley-, and aged-hops-infused wort (unfermented beer), expose it to the outside air, and kick off a spontaneous wild yeast fermentation, cool ships are still used in a handful of breweries in Belgium (including Cantillon, the granddaddy of them all) in the making of *lambic,* the traditional sour beers of the Zenne Valley outside of Brussels.

It's a remarkable process to observe. With freshly brewed beer moved into the *koelschip* following a four-hour boil of a mash using unmalted wheat (to facilitate a superlong fermentation), the brewer opens louvered vents or windows to allow ambient air to cool and to let naturally occurring yeasts to settle in the beer. The next day the now-inoculated beer is racked into pre-used wood barrels (often formerly containing red wine), whereupon the wild yeasts begin—very slowly begin—to chew on the starches inside. Anywhere from hours or days to several months later the fermentation erupts and the beer begins a voyage of drying, souring, and evaporation through the oak walls of the barrels, leaving behind a more tart and more complex beer as time goes on. It's a mysterious, near-mystical process, one far more gnostic than most traditional brew masters can stomach. Later those beers are sometimes blended with younger beers to make what Belgians call *geuze,* or aged again with fresh fruits to make *kriek* (cherry), *framboise* (raspberry), *cassis* (currant), and other tart-sweet creations.

Allagash's bold experiment succeeded, and in so doing challenged long-held beliefs. There are many who still object that the Allagash beers (and subsequent, similar projects) can't be called Lambic, an appellation akin to Champagne or Parma ham. Tod and Russian River's Vinnie Cilurzo (among others) who are leading the American revival of the style (and variations thereof) prefer to call them wild ales or spontaneous fermentation beers, a solution which seems respectful and useful, especially as the beers—owing to the difference in local microflora—are unique, even if the methods are similar. Now the excellent Allagash beers are trickling out (the aging and blending period can take up to three years). Tod and Perkins have proven that Americans can make wild ales without physically adding yeast, a development the most enlightened Belgian producers—such as Cantillon's Van Roy—applaud and support. And thanks to the success of Tod's *koelschip*, other breweries are trying them out, too.

NOVARE RES BIER CAFÉ

4 Canal Plaza • Portland, ME 04101 • (207) 761-BIER (2437)
novareresbiercafe.com • Established: 2008

SCENE & STORY

With 25 rotating taps, 2 hand pumps, and some 300 bottles on its list, Novare Res is a craft beer lovers' refuge down an alley in the Old Port area of town off of Exchange Street. Inside the bar is an array of beer signage, warm wood tones, exposed brick, oak barrels, and tin ceilings. Outside there's an elevated wood patio area, which fills up on sunny days. Every May, an annual Belgian Beer fest brings nothing but Belgian beers to the taps for three weeks, and the owners—who were inspired to open the bar after extensive travels in Europe—organize frequent events year-round with noted brewmasters and extremely hard-to-find beers. The combination has resulted in a beer bar with something of a special reputation: seemingly no matter where you travel in craft beer America, people are either talking about a recent visit to Novare Res, or planning to go. According to Dan Shelton, the outspoken writer and importer of Cantillon and over a hundred other very special European beers, owner Eric Michaud is running "the best beer bar in Maine," which, coming from the famously Europhile Shelton, is no faint praise. There's a menu of relatively simple but hearty fare (stew, sausages, artisan meats and cheeses, hot sandwiches), and ambitious desserts cooked with sought-after Belgian ales like Cantillon.

PHILOSOPHY

Novare Res means "to start a revolution" in Latin, and the owners cheekily define the bar by what it is *not*. It's neither British pub (though there are dartboards and cask ales), nor German biergarten (though there are the appropriate picnic tables outside), nor Belgian bière café (though Belgophiles will love its selection). It is instead a hybrid of approaches dedicated to great beer, no matter where or how it may have been brewed. Founder Eric Michaud previously managed the Moan & Dove, and there's a fond fellowship between the two bars.

KEY BEER

Marshall Wharf and Allagash are two local brewing companies especially well represented. The Belgian list is deep; the creamy bodied Moinette Blond from the makers of Saison Dupont is an enormously complex but sociable pale ale (even at 8.5% ABV) with yeasty, fruity notes up front and a snappy hop finish.

★ ★ ★

Belfast

MARSHALL WHARF BREWING CO. & THREE TIDES

2 Pinchy Ln. • Belfast, ME 04915
(207) 338-1707 • marshallwharf.com
Established: 2003 (bar) and 2007 (brewery)

SCENE & STORY

Located smack on the pier next to the tugs of Belfast—a fishing village first settled in 1770—the Marshall Wharf brewery was built in the town's original granary in 2007. A combination patio- and bocce-court-equipped beer bar, seven-barrel brew house with 8-spigot taproom and lobster pound (so you can buy some fresh-caught on summer mornings to take home), and a twelve-tap seasonal beer garden, Marshall Wharf is truly a one-stop affair. Brewing around thirty unusual styles and aging certain brews in Heaven Hill distillery barrels with increasingly assured results—especially in the IIPA, brown, stout, and Baltic Porter genres—founder David Carlson and brewer Danny McGovern have been helping remake coastal Maine's beer scene for some time. McGovern, the former owner of Lake St. George Brewing Company and brewer for Belfast Bay Brewing Company (and a trained butcher), brought Carlson's operation a number of interesting recipes. And Carlson's waterfront Three Tides bar next door (which now serves seventeen Marshall Wharf beers and is sometimes known by locals as the "Lampshade Bar") had been

the first bar in Maine to serve beers from Anchor, Unibroue, and Ayinger on draft.

PHILOSOPHY

Good beer, fresh seafood, and a bocce ball court are the only necessities of life.

KEY BEER

Cant Dog, an Imperial IPA released in 2004, was one of Marshall Wharf's early beers, and came about when Carlson and McGovern scored a haul of Simcoe hops from an Idaho brewer in distress. It's a golden amber, 10% ABV hop bomb with such dangerous drinkability that patrons are limited to two per day.

Lovell

EBENEZER'S PUB

44 Allen Rd. • Lovell, ME 04051 • (207) 925-3200
ebenezerspub.net • Established: 2004

SCENE & STORY

One of the country's most celebrated beer bars, Ebenezer's—named for a late-eighteenth-century trapper said to have survived a duel with a bear but lost an arm—is located in the attached barn of an old farmhouse on a rural golf course, meaning it will take some planning (and driver's GPS) to reach. With its screen porch, copper-topped bar, thirty-five taps (about two-thirds Belgian) and more than seven hundred labels in the cellar, it's a bucket list beer bar with well-regarded food and a reputation for impromptu, eye-popping cellar tours. It's not just that the list is long, it's ridiculously deep, varied, and unusual. The location makes it a pilgrimage (and it's easy to part with a great deal of money here), but those who make the effort are richly rewarded.

PHILOSOPHY

"We may be located in a small Maine town, but we've always dreamed big. From day one, it was our goal to build the best beer pub in the world," says owner Chris Lively, who, with his wife, Jen, is a constant presence in the bar. This translates to cheerful service and a massive selection, care for the beer on hand, and a tradition of over-the-top events and beer dinners.

KEY BEER

The house beer is Black Albert, a resinous, roasty, coal black 13% ABV Russian Imperial Stout brewed by De Struise of Belgium. Lively's selection of large-format bottles will no doubt be tempting too, especially for groups who make this pilgrimage, and the draft choices are beyond unusual, like a recent tapping of 2006 Cantillon Kriek, a sour Belgian ale aged with whole cherries in oak casks for up to three years before it is released.

BEST of the REST: MAINE

THE LION'S PRIDE
112 Pleasant St. • Brunswick, ME 04101 • (207) 373-1840 • lionspridepub.com

Open since July 2009, the sister pub to Ebenezer's has a similarly incredible draft selection in an easier-to-reach location. Owners Chris and Jen Lively have stocked it with a copper-topped bar, hand-blown glass tap handles, dark wood and brewery signage throughout, "Beer 101" tasting classes on Wednesday nights, and a pilot brewing system for special guest brewers to take for victory laps (with the results available in the bar later).

THE GREAT LOST BEAR
540 Forest Ave. • Portland, ME 04101 • (207) 772-0300 • www.greatlostbear.com

A dimly-lit British-style pub packed with ephemera and breweriana, the Great Lost Bear opened in 1979 and arguably helped Maine's nascent brewing industry take shape throughout the 1980s. With some 70 taps, 50 of which are from the Northeast (including 15 from Maine), it's still a favorite destination for beer lovers in the area and tourists, and its "Allagash Alley"—a tap row proudly dedicated to the local brewer's beers—is a nice touch.

Massachusetts

★ ★ ★

GOING BACK TO THE DAYS OF THE MAYFLOWER AND THE FOUNDING

Fathers, beer has long played a central role here. Today the earliest breweries are long gone but thanks in part to Jim Koch, the energetic founder of Boston Beer Company, the homegrown tradition is alive and well. "Boston was one of the original brewing centers in the United States," explains Koch on a recent afternoon visit to his South Boston headquarters, a renovated, 25,000-square-foot brewery that gets about 150,000 thirsty visitors per year. "The first brewery in the English colonies was built here in Boston, in 1635, the year before Harvard was founded," he says. "I guess you can't have college if you don't have beer."

Koch, a sixth-generation brewmaster who holds BA, MBA, and JD degrees from Harvard, describes why beer has always been so important to Boston life. "From the day the Pilgrims landed, beer was a part of the social fabric here," he says. "For one, it was a nutritional necessity; water was polluted. By the 1600s, one of the duties of the president of Harvard was for his wife to brew beer—for the students. Today there's a street in Cambridge called Alewife. There was even one president who got kicked out—because his wife made bad beer," Koch says.

Flash-forward a hundred years, at which point Boston was welcoming waves of European immigrants, including scores of brewers. "At the turn of the twentieth century, there were thirty-one breweries inside the city limits, mostly in this area," says Koch. Inspired by Samuel Adams's story, Koch decided on the Boston area to carry on the family tradition. An article in an old magazine tipped him to a vacant brew house in which to sink capital he'd raised working as a high-powered consultant, but the neighborhood gave him second thoughts.

"It was an eyesore," recalls Koch. "There were trees growing all over; there was a squatter; there were gangs. We couldn't get people to work here. It was a real problem."

Working with a neighborhood association, Koch and his band of brewers became an anchor tenant and were soon delivering fresh beer to the managers of old Boston pubs. "The whole idea was insane. No one had heard of microbrews," Koch remembers. "Back then, the whole beer world was mass-produced domestic beers: Bud, Miller, Coors, and imports. There was nothing else."

Today there are more than fifty-four breweries and brewpubs in the Commonwealth of Massachusetts, along with some of the finest beer bars in the country.

DETOUR → THE BOSTON BOY: Jim Koch on Drinking Beer in Boston and Doyle's Café

"Boston's a great beer town because it's a community that combines so many different elements. It's a basic, blue-collar town, with the neighborhoods like Southie and Charlestown that you see in the movies—those are real places. You've got *Good Will Hunting* going on there. And Boston's also the world's center of higher education. Boston is able to put them together in this extraordinary way.

"That's the essence of beer. Beer is democratic; beer is the alcoholic beverage equivalent of Andy Warhol's Coke bottle. People asked him, 'Why a Coke bottle?' And he said, 'This is an icon that is uniquely American.' Because in America no matter who you are—you can be Bill Gates, you can be Barack Obama, or you can be the janitor at the elementary school—everybody in the country gets the same Coke. Beer is that way, too. No matter who you are, you cannot get a better Sam Adams Boston Lager than anybody else.

"If you have to leave the brewery and find another place to drink, you don't have to go very far. We're in a blue-collar neighborhood, Jamaica Plain. It's the home neighborhood of James Michael Curley, the famous rascal mayor of Boston. He actually lived near our brewery and wanted his own parish, so now, around our brewery is a parochial school and Our Lady of Lourdes, a church—Mayor Curley's parish.

"Just down the street is a bar called Doyle's. Doyle's has been a bar since the 1880s, so you're drinking at a place that's been a bar for almost 130 years. It's owned by a family of Irish guys—wonderful people—the Burkes. They grew up running bars, and their dad had the beer concession at the zoo. All they ever wanted to do was run a great bar, and they've done that. It's this complete, wonderful melting pot, what a bar should be. That's where Ted Kennedy used to spend St. Patricks's Day. Mayor Flynn [Boston mayor from 1984 to 1993] went to Doyle's. I was there once when Mayor Flynn was tending bar on Saturday night. If there were a real *Cheers* bar, it would be Doyle's."

Jamaica Plain

BOSTON BEER COMPANY

30 Germania St. • Jamaica Plain, MA 02130
(617) 983-9036 • bostonbeer.com • Established: 1984

SCENE & STORY

A tour of Boston Beer Company paints the picture of what is perhaps America's most remarkable craft brewing story. Starting in 1984, Jim Koch has built what is now the nation's largest craft brewing company. The Boston facility operates as a test brewery and barrel aging facility; the firm's commercial beers are brewed elsewhere. Through a remarkable combination of a great story and a standout recipe (the recipe for Boston Lager was based on a recipe created by his great-grandfather, Louis Koch), quality control, timing (the microbrewing wave was simmering nationwide), ready investment capital, hard work (he pounded the pavement and learned to drive a forklift himself), Koch and company created a barnburner of a brand and haven't looked back.

Today, more than eight hundred local bars serve the company's beers (and thousands nationally). The company's lineup has expanded to dozens of styles, including one bi-annual release that ranks among the world's strongest, Utopias, a costly elixir aged for years in oak barrels and costing hundreds of dollars per bottle. Visitors wend through display cases brimming with medals, accounting sheets from the early days, and prototype bottles before settling in with some tasters at a small bar area. It's

hard to believe how much has changed in America's brewing scene in just twenty-seven years. A Cincinnati native, Koch is proud of the role he's played in the advent of craft-brewed beer in Boston and around the country. In 1989, Boston Beer Company was cranking out some 60,000 barrels of beer. In 2011, that number stands at more like 2.25 million annually.

"In a lot of ways, American craft brewers have become sort of the Noah's Ark of the world's brewing traditions," Koch says. "We are preserving and developing them here at the same time as they are dying out in their home countries," he says. "I'd like to think that we're one of the few pioneers of the industry left that still has that passion for innovating, experimenting, and pushing the envelope."

PHILOSOPHY

No stone unturned. There are plenty of Sam Adams beers that aren't all that good, but for all the experiments and misfires, there's an overall ratio of excellence. A couple of years ago, Koch had a five-hundred-pound bale of fresh hops delivered, literally picked off the vine earlier in the day, which is a remarkable feat (the flower-like cones, which are best when fresh, give beer its bitterness, aroma, and aftertaste, and must be carefully kiln-dried and packed into bales for shipment).

Even more remarkable? Koch only uses delicate European noble hops. As the vividly fresh, spicy, tangy smell of Hallertau Mittelfrüh hops infused the room, Koch described how the Stanglmair clan, a hop-growing family in Bavaria supplying the hops used in Boston Lager, had helped him arrange an unprecedented air drop so he could be the first American brewer to brew with European hops picked *the same day*. It was a stunt, sure, but one that underscored his daring side, and one that guaranteed an extraordinarily aromatic finish to a batch of Pilsner already steaming out of the copper-clad kettles. Chalk it up to old-fashioned Yankee optimism, and Koch's flair for marketing the craft of brewing.

"It's a lot of work for seven hundred cases of beer," he added, making an obvious point, but one that truly illustrates what separates craft brewers—the revolutionaries of beer making—from the old guard. "To me, it's like a responsibility. We're big enough so we have the resources to try something like this, yet we're still small enough to be crazy. That's what makes it fun."

KEY BEER

Koch has overseen the development of some one hundred different beers of almost every conceivable style and some that didn't really exist before, for better or worse. But it's still the Samuel Adams Boston Lager, a smooth, 4.9% ABV lager now ubiquitous in the United States that has held up the best since it was introduced in 1985, when it won a GABF gold medal mere weeks after Boston Brewing Company opened for business. It's a spicy, malty, and faintly nutty-fruity elixir with a gorgeous, new-penny color, fluffy white head, and smacking dry finish.

BEST *of the* REST: MASSACHUSETTS

DEEP ELLUM

477 Cambridge St. • Allston, MA 02134 • (617) 787-BEER (2337) • deepellum-boston.com

With its light beige walls, beautiful polished bar and dark wood accents, white tile floors, airy garden patio, and reasonably priced upscale comfort fare (meat loaf, mac-and-cheese), Deep Ellum would be a go-to spot even without its excellent, even world-class tap and bottle list. But what a list. There are twenty-eight taps and about a hundred bottled varieties at any one given time (with matching logo glassware); look for beers from such insiders-only producers as High and Mighty and Pretty Things, both of Massachussetts, and Belgium's De Ranke (Belgium).

SUNSET GRILL & TAP

130 Brighton Ave. • Allston, MA 02134 • (617) 254-1331 • allstonsfinest.com

With an eclectic, breweriana-stuffed interior, four handsome ceramic bar-top tap towers, 112 total handles, and some 380 bottles on offer, selection is definitely not an issue. But with so many beers on tap, and so many lines to look after, beer emporiums such as this one can overreach, letting beers stale and mix in the lines. Early on, freshness was an occasional problem here, but today the Sunset gets high marks for service, decent pub grub, quality glassware, and tapped-on dates that tell you which kegs are freshest.

REDBONES

55 Chester St. • Somerville, MA 02144 • (617) 628-2200 • redbones.com

A dependable, down-to-earth barbecue place open since 1987 and serving up big heaping piles of Memphis–, Texas–, Arkansas–, and St. Louis–style ribs, Redbones has always had a strong beer list. And with beer bars all over the country raising the bar to unheard-of heights in terms of hard-to-find beers, this affably rough hewn two-story place has kept pace, adding a total of twenty-eight taps, a smart little bottle list, and cask-conditioned ales. Recent drafts included California cult beers, such as Lost Abbey and Ballast Point, two makers of big-hearted beers that go well with the spicy, juicy barbecue feast coming off the grill.

LORD HOBO

92 Hampshire St. • Cambridge, MA 02141 • (617) 250-8454 • lordhobo.com

Lord Hobo took over the space of B-Side, a fabled cocktail bar in Inman Square, in late 2009. With forty taps balanced between obscurities and crowd-pleasers, three hand-pump lines, regular appearances by well-known craft brewers, a small but connoisseur-ready bottle list, and a few bar-top casks, the beer bona fides are absolutely solid. The beer selection is complemented by an ambitious (and accordingly priced) menu of haute-comfort food (*boquerones,* pan-seared scallops, grilled rib-eye) served in a dark, arty environment.

DOYLE'S CAFÉ

3484 Washington St. • Jamaica Plain, MA 02130 • (617) 524-2345 • doylescafeboston.com

Low tin ceilings, acres of dark wood, Kennedy campaign posters, and fresh Sam Adams brews—this was Jim Koch's first account in 1984—make this stop essential for anyone touring the nearby Boston Beer Company. There's a small draft list with Sam Adams and Wachusett seasonals, the obligatory Guinness, and bottles of Samuel Smiths and Chimay, among others.

THE PUBLICK HOUSE

1648 Beacon St • Brookline, MA 02445 • (617) 277-2880 • eatgoodfooddrinkbetterbeer.com

With 36 taps and about 150 bottle selections the Publick House has garnered rapturous reviews since 2002 from beer geeks and casual fans alike, drawn in by its vast menu, candlelit interior, and broadly Belgian-influenced pub-grub menu. The beer list is divided into Belgian, Belgian-style, Here (domestic craft) and There (imported craft), and yields some very unusual treats, such as a recent sour, dark Flemish red beer called Cuvée Des Jacobins Rouge (5.5% ABV) from Brouwerij Bockor.

THE MOAN & DOVE

460 West St. • Amherst, MA 01002 • (413) 256-1710 • moananddove.com

The Moan & Dove serves no food except peanuts, and then maybe only if you're lucky. The strip-mall-like location is random, near a gas station. And yet, this is not a problem: to a certain stripe of beer lover, it wouldn't matter if this beer selection were for sale *inside* that gas station. You're here for the beer. There are twenty-three taps and over a hundred bottles on offer—a smart and wide American and European array—and a tribe of loyal, mug-club member locals to share beer stories with. Order up a Mahr's Ungespundet Hefetrub (unfiltered lager, served by the half liter for $8) and see what happens next.

EXIT 4

The Mid-Atlantic

The
MID-ATLANTIC

THERE IS NO MORE HISTORICALLY SIGNIFICANT BEER SCENE IN AMERICA

than in and around Philadelphia, Pennsylvania, going all the way back to founder and brewer William Penn himself (who tied up his boat on arrival next to a pub, the Blue Anchor) and the Founding Fathers, many of whom were avid brewers and regulars in the area taverns and public houses, those "nurseries of liberty." By the early twentieth century, Pennsylvania was home to a world-famous beer brewing industry and America's oldest brewery, Yuengling (founded 1829), still in operation. Thanks to the work of a new wave of enterprising small breweries and hardworking tavern, bar, and brewpub owners, it's an absolutely superb place to explore beer, just as it was in America's earliest days.

And there's something else about Philly. The conversations, the approach to bar keeping—it's a no-nonsense town. You ought to discover and drink craft beer and craft-beer cuisine without worrying about it all too much. And getting to know it will take repeated visits, because you will meet more than one tour guide who'd like to show you his or her favorite watering hole, and before you know it, you've discovered ten new perfect places you never knew existed. That's Philly beer.

Today, there are some ninety breweries in the state, with about twenty in the Philly vicinity, and countless places to enjoy their creations. There are more than six hundred beer-friendly bars, including some of the very best in the country, in Philly alone. And then there's that famous Philly "attytood," the bluster and tough talk about the neighborhoods before they cleaned up, giving it soul, authenticity, and depth. In a way—and no disrespect to the excellent breweries—Pennsylvania feels like it is even more of a craft beer *drinking* state than it is a brewing state, and beer travelers will undoubtedly face many tough choices on a swing through.

Another reason Philly is such a great beer-drinking town is the trifecta of Monk's Café co-owner and Belgian beer guru Tom Peters, the *Philadelphia Daily News* columnist Don Russel, and the late Bruce Nichols of Museum Catering

Company. Nichols first brought the writer Michael Jackson to Philadelphia in 1991 for a tutored beer-tasting dinner at the University of Pennsylvania Museum of Archeology and Anthropology, a smash success followed in years hence by some dozen others, during which time he joined forces with Peters and Russel to create Philly Beer Week, an annual ten-day June bacchanal drawing thousands of visitors to over a thousand events throughout the city and the first such event in the nation, which has spawned scores of similar fetes. The only limit is time. Maybe we should call it the City of *Brewery* Love?

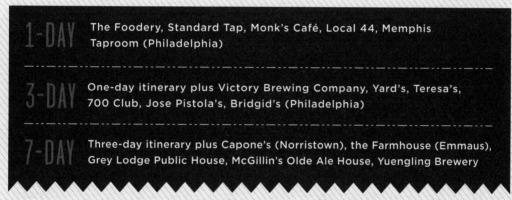

ITINERARIES

1-DAY   The Foodery, Standard Tap, Monk's Café, Local 44, Memphis Taproom (Philadelphia)

3-DAY   One-day itinerary plus Victory Brewing Company, Yard's, Teresa's, 700 Club, Jose Pistola's, Bridgid's (Philadelphia)

7-DAY   Three-day itinerary plus Capone's (Norristown), the Farmhouse (Emmaus), Grey Lodge Public House, McGillin's Olde Ale House, Yuengling Brewery

THE STANDARD TAP

901 N. 2nd St. • Philadelphia, PA 19123 • (215) 238-0630
standardtap.com • Established: 1999

SCENE & STORY

In a charming three-and-a-half-story structure dating back to at least 1810, the Standard Tap's headquarters has been a bar many times over, as well as a pharmacy and drugstore. It's also been an apartment, at least on the third floor, when former Samuel Adams brewer Will Reed lived there while working with his partner Paul Kimport to help revitalize Philly's stricken Northern Liberties neighborhood. They'd thought about brewing beer there, too, but the spaces were a bit confining, so they decided to open a beer bar instead. The building had the right bones, and was also just a half block from the site where a brewer named John Wagner became the first American to successfully produce lagers. Reed and Kimport have built a distinctive two-story pub with an ambitious menu (duck confit, anyone?) and solid reputation for taking care of their beer and their customers.

PHILOSOPHY

Good beer and food for locals, by locals. Reed and Kimport felt the area breweries weren't being well represented, and that the city needed to get behind its own residents working hard to remake the area's historic brewing scene. So the beers are exclusively from eighteen local and state breweries and always on draft or cask. "We looked at places like Portland and Seattle, and we wanted people to be really proud of where their beer came from," Reed recalls. "So we're just going to do all local beer and we're going to do all draft beer. I love the Belgian stuff and everything, but I don't want to be a Belgian or a British pub. I don't want to be an Irish pub. I want to be a Philadelphia pub."

KEY BEER

There are twenty taps, two cask engines, and a single bottle: Lord Chesterfield, an antique recipe still brewed by Yuengling. Avoid it unless you're just one of those irredeemably curious cats. Troëg's is a favorite tap handle; look for the piney, 6% ABV Simcoe dry hopped Hop Back Amber on cask. It's soft, dry, quenching, faintly sweet, and bitter all at once, just as a good cask-conditioned beer should be.

THE FOODERY

837 N. 2nd St. (across the street from Standard Tap)
Philadelphia, PA 19123 • (215) 238-6077
fooderybeer.com • Established: 2006

With more than eight hundred labels of beer available and a vaunted deli, The Foodery also has an especially good selection of large format bottles from U.S. and Belgian craft brewers. The Northern Liberties location is across the street from Standard Tap, so there's no reason not to take a spin through. There are picnic tables inside and the owners sponsor frequent tasting events.

KHYBER PASS

56 S. 2nd St. • Philadelphia, PA 19106
(215) 238-5888 • khyberpasspub.com
Established: late 1970s

SCENE & STORY

The Khyber Pass, which has been a drinking establishment since the 1850s, takes its name from a remarkable story about its Maryland-born owner, Serrill Headley. As the story goes, Headley, daughter of a University of Maryland football star, fled Pakistan and her marriage to a Pakistani diplomat over the Khyber Pass in the early 1970s, moved to Philadelphia, and bought the old bar in a rush of freedom.

In 1987 new owners took over the space, nestled in an unassuming corner of the historic but tourist-clogged zone of Old City, and continued its tradition of live music. Over the next twenty-two years and at least one more change of ownership it would become a venerated indie rock venue featuring the likes of Guided By Voices, Iggy Pop, the White Stripes, Liz Phair, and the Strokes, with locally legendary shows up until 2010. At the same time, the owners were slinging bottles of Chimay, and Philly's young tastemakers were simultaneously sampling some of the best rock music of the era and bottles of world-class beer to boot. Today the Khyber (as it's known) has settled into a quieter groove as an appealingly ramshackle craft beer bar with excellent soul food and an impessive list of beer served by superknowledgeable bartenders. There's a gorgeous old wood bar adorned with twinkling Christmas lights and a dining room where the bands once rocked, and a peaceful vibe throughout.

PHILOSOPHY

The Khyber treats its beer list like record collectors treat vinyl, prizing rarities. Look for unusual American Saisons from Pretty Things, St. Somewhere, and Stillwater. At the same time, it's not too stuffy to stock BMC (Bud, Miller, or Coors), though one suspects such options are merely concession to the Jersey-Shorish crowd that makes Old City (and this bar, alas) a no-go on weekends.

KEY BEER

There are twenty taps and two casks; this would be an excellent place to sip a fresh Stoudt's Pils, or something along the lines of a Port Brewing Mongo, a recently-on-tap IIPA (aka DIPA or Double IPA) named for a brewery cat who lived out all its nine lives, not unlike the Khyber Pass bar seems to be doing.

GRACE TAVERN

2229 Grays Ferry Ave. • Philadelphia, PA 19146
(215) 893-9580 • gracetavern.com • Established: 2004

SCENE & STORY

A beloved local institution, this narrow apartment-like space is just wide enough for some stools and a rail to line up some beers or throw a few dice around and eat baskets of spicy blackened Cajun green beans and remoulade, which is mandatory and only $2. It's not a shrine to craft beer with an encyclopedic list, nor an annoying sports bar; it is a tavern for people to relax in, and its layout and architecture encourages conversation. A joint effort by Monk's Café founder Tom Peters and local publican Fergus Carey, it's got battered tin ceilings and a gorgeous built-in 1955 refrigerator called a Bevador and an abiding sense of time well spent. Don't miss it.

PHILOSOPHY

The Grace fosters a sense that a life well lived necessarily involves hours upon hours of sometimes aimless conversation over beers with friends in a local bar. At some point in your life, make this that bar.

KEY BEER

With about nine taps and forty-five well-chosen bottles, there's an ideal blend of crafts and everyday sippers from Monk's Flemish Sour to releases from Sly Fox, Nottinghead, Yard's, and Miller Lite for good measure. Start it off with Troëg's crisp and medium-bodied, straw gold 5.3% ABV Sunshine Pils and go from there.

MIDATLANTIC RESTAURANT & TAP ROOM

3711 Market St. • Philadelphia, PA 19104 • (215) 386-3711
midatlanticrestaurant.com • Established: 2009

SCENE & STORY

This modern, brightly lit eatery in University City—a diverse area of West Philadelphia close to the river populated by Penn and Drexel students—offers a contemporary twist on the beer café with its stylish interior, adorned throughout with reclaimed building materials amid shiny steel and arty chairs and chandeliers, and its menus are no less curated.

PHILOSOPHY

Good beer deserves good food, and vice versa. The local, nose-to-tail, haute-rustic comfort food options (house-cured pickles; all-beef house-made hot dogs; crab scrapple served with a savory waffle and spicy pepper marmalade) earn positive reviews, and there are also occasional beer dinners and tastings, especially during Philly Beer Week.

KEY BEER

Along with dozens of beers from its namesake region, the 8-tap, 50-bottle list features New Jersey's Flying Fish (with its Exit 4 American Trippel). Tripel, as it's usually spelled is a brewing term from Belgium that signifies that a massive dose of grain has been added to the "mash" (a key early stage in the brewing process), resulting in the legendary high-octane golden ale that has made the homeland of Jean Claude Van Damme a must-visit destination for alcoholics worldwide. Too often the abundance of grain translates to a cloying sweetness; not Exit 4, which has ample hop bitterness balancing the fruity, grain-given heft (9.7% ABV). Even better, this one's the first in a series named for exits on the New Jersey Turnpike (not that you could drive after finishing one).

EULOGY

136 Chestnut St. • Philadelphia, PA 19106
(215) 413-1918 • eulogybar.com Established: 2002

SCENE & STORY

Built in a narrow old four-story townhouse with a Belgian-flag themed red, black, and yellow paint job, Eulogy has a light, spicy house brew on tap (Busty Blonde, a Belgian pale ale beer brewed by La Binchoise), a decent tap row and long bottle list, reputable *moules frites*, burgers, and wings. Because of its location, Eulogy makes a smart early afternoon stop after paying respects to the Liberty Bell, but according to the owner himself—an American and former resident of Belgium—it is to be avoided on weekend nights. The bartenders are knowledgeable, but if the place is packed three-deep you won't get to ask any questions or sample the kegs one by one before you make the choice. On any weekend, this is a first beer of the day sort of bar, one for wiling away an afternoon before heading to quieter quarters.

PHILOSOPHY

Owner Mike Naessens has channeled the Old World with a cozy but not too cramped "brown bar" feel. In particular, his bar seems to be a manifestation of the quizzical nature of Belgians, who love dark humor as much as they love strong beer. With that in mind, make sure to check the upstairs "coffin room."

KEY BEER

On tap, the tart-sweet Duchesse de Bourgogne, a 6.2% ABV Flanders Red Ale from Brouwerij Verhaeghe is the perfect choice to go with an order of garlic and leek crab cakes.

THE 700 CLUB

700 N. 2nd St. • Philadelphia, PA 19123
(215) 413-3181 • the700.org • Established: 1997

SCENE AND STORY

This Northern Liberties hangout is without a doubt one of the happiest and most cheerful places in Philly to drink craft brews. With its easygoing bar staff, vinyl-spinning DJ, solid tap row and bottle list, and reputation for sweaty late-night weekend dance parties (the Rutger Hauer Power Hour is held on the fourth Wednesday of each month to get you in the mood), it manages to exude good vibes without really trying, and its laid-back clientele is made up of a menagerie of local artists, musicians, and writer types, more often approachable than not.

PHILOSOPHY

Dog friendly. No bouncer, no attitude, no cover. Just good people, good tunes, and usually a soccer game on the tube.

KEY BEER

There are ten drafts and two casks, plus a big old vintage refrigerator full of crafts in bottles. Philadelphia Brewing Company's Kenzinger Kölsch will keep the party local and, and at just 4.5% ABV, rolling strong.

THE BELGIAN CAFÉ

601 N. 21st St. • Philadelphia, PA 19130
(215) 235-3500 • thebelgiancafe.com • Established: 2007

SCENE & STORY

Blackboard with an ever-changing tap list—check. Wooden bar with an armrest lip and a brass pipe foot rail—check. Elegant back bar and mirrors stacked with glassware—check. Located in the arty, affluent Fairmont neighborhood, this is one of Monk's Café founder Tom Peters's many establishments (this one a joint venture with fellow Philly publican Fergus Carey), and it has the deep Belgian beer list and nourishing haute-rustic pub menu to match their legendary appetites. But unlike Monk's (most of the time, at least), it lacks constant crowds, and with its amber-hued walls, lustrous dark wood and wainscoting, and classic Victor Horta–style flourishes, the bar possesses an uncanny resemblance to good beer bars in Brussels. Peters even commissioned a local artist to do a series of five Art Nouveau–style paintings in the main dining room area, and they infuse the space with a color and energy not found in many beer bars. The chef is serious about cooking with beer—even tofu dishes are marinated in it—and standout options include the vegan barbecue wings, wasabi-dusted sea scallops served with Duvel beure blanc (Duvel is a classic strong Belgian golden ale), and the Monk's Burger, with caramelized leeks and bleu cheese.

PHILOSOPHY

This is a classic, dark, cozy bar, with excellent food and drink on offer, and a serious but not needlessly pedantic approach to beer. It would make a great lunch spot or venue for catching up with an old friend.

KEY BEER

Glazen Toren brewery's Ondineke (on tap) is a yeasty, deeply golden triple from Belgium that tastes of grass, spice, and apricot, deceptively light for a beer of 8.5% ABV, and a great match with mussels.

THE GREY LODGE PUBLIC HOUSE

6235 Frankford Ave. • Philadelphia, PA 19135
(215) 856-3591 • greylodge.com • Established: 1996

SCENE & STORY

Opened with a distinctive oval bar in the 1950s (under a different name) this Northeast Philly institution has a dark red walls and stained wood trim throughout, with an old-school first floor bar (dart boards and flat screens) and a more quiet and updated second floor dining room and whiskey-stocked bar, which also has eight taps of its own. More than familiar pub stylings, though, it possesses a hefty dose of Philly heart, less easily quantifiable but undeniably part of the character. That means that locals rule the roost here but in a good-hearted way, for the most part. Events take on a quirky feel, with "Quizzo" on Wednesdays, Friday the Firkinteenth (any Friday the 13th) being dedicated to twenty-five or more firkins on draft, and Groundhog Day, when everyone shows up in Hawaiian shirts and gets well and duly hammered. The food options earn raves, especially the wild boar tacos and cheesesteak.

PHILOSOPHY

This is a beer bar with a bit of edge and off-kilter personality with serious beer cred to boot. Be sure to check out the restrooms, which are elaborately tiled in red, green, and blue mosaics with various bon mots. Beer lists are published online under the rubrics "currently on tap," "on deck," "due in this week," and "barrels being saved for a special night," which helps stoke anticipation for return visits, while tap lines are ceremoniously cleaned on Mondays in front of patrons. Attention all beer bar owners: please follow Grey Lodge's example and do the same.

KEY BEER

There are eleven taps and a cask, plus forty or so bottles and fourteen cans available. Look for nearby New Jersey's Flying Fish, which always has a seasonal release available, or Victory's eminently sessionable Dark Lager.

MEMPHIS TAPROOM

2331 E. Cumberland St. • Philadelphia, PA 19125
(215) 425-4460 • memphistaproom.com • Established: 2008

SCENE & STORY

Four words: beer-battered kosher dills. That's just one of the delicious bites that makes this Kensington area pub shine, along with ten beer-geek-approved taps (always rotating brands) and a beer engine for cask ales. Top rank offerings range from rarities such as De Ranke to Bear Republic and Ridgeway. A co-owner is the outspoken former Khyber Pass barman Brendan "Spanky" Hartranft, who also operates Local 44 and Resurrection Alehouse, making him, like Tom Peters, Will Reed, and Fergus Carey, one of the prime movers in Philly's good beer scene. Starting a craft beer bar in a tough neighborhood wasn't easy. "It was a total renovation; it took four months," recalls Hartranft. "My dad was on the ladder doing some electrical work about three weeks into it one day, and this guy comes over and grabs the bottom of the ladder and goes, 'Drop your wallet or I'm pulling out the ladder.' My dad goes, 'Uh, *no*,' pulls out his hammer, and drops it right on the guy's head. Skull fracture—we called the cops and an ambulance. After that, everyone that had been walking by calling us a yuppie bar beforehand were starting to say, 'Hey, when are you guys opening up?'"

PHILOSOPHY

The bar is "on a mission" to prove that certain dusty, aged bottles of beer deserve equal respect, if not more, than brewery-fresh bottles, and has the deep menu of options to prove it.

KEY BEER

2007 Oude Beersel Geuze ($14), a lemony-tart, dry geuze with notes of unripened fruit.

LOCAL 44

4333 Spruce St. • Philadelphia, PA 19104
(215) 222-2337 • local44beerbar.com • Established: 2009

SCENE & STORY

Ever since Brendan Hartranft and his wife, Leigh, opened this gem of a beer bar in the leafy Port Richmond area of West Philly on New Year's Day in 2009, it has been busy. With its deep red walls, Edison bulbs, and metal fire door, the space is striking and enveloping. The goal was to create a welcoming, upscale dark bar with twenty taps, each with a distinct style. The well-made fare is "boardwalk cuisine": riffs on comfort food like corndogs, Reuben sandwiches, and mahi-mahi fish tacos.

PHILOSOPHY

No pretense here. Just good beer and a fair shake. "My price structure is based on what my dad would think if he came in here," says Hartranft. In other words, he tries to keep it affordable, and even opened up the bar with the precious Cantillon Lou Pepe kriek on draft for a mere $8 (it is often sold for $12 or $13).

KEY BEER

The international list of rarities changes daily, but one beer is always available no matter what: Orval, a Belgian Trappist "world classic." It is, in fact, the *only* bottled beer for sale at Local 44. And if you get a chance to ask Hartranft about his passion for this beer, be prepared for some colorful commentary. It's a beer that inspires, to say the least.

MONKS CAFÉ & BELGIAN BEER EMPORIUM

264 S. 16th St. • Philadelphia, PA 19102
(215) 545-7005 • monkscafe.com • Established: 1997

SCENE & STORY

In the religion of *Seinfeld*, Monk's Café—the fictional coffee shop where the main characters gather—is its tabernacle, the cherished brick-and-mortar corner of the universe where Jerry, George, Elaine, and Kramer and some of their most memorable stories unfold and intertwine. In a way, one could say the same thing about the real-life Monk's Café: it's a tabernacle for craft beer lovers—it even has its own "Beer Bible"—but Fergus Carey and Tom Peters's Center City Philadelphia version has far superior food. Among the best-known beer bars in the United States—along with San Francisco's Toronado and Portland's Horse Brass—Monk's Café is more than a tavern where beer is served. It's an institution, and as such, it's to be visited with planning and forethought. To have the best experience, try Monk's on a weeknight or during the day on weekends, or be prepared for a wait of an hour or two.

But that wait, should you have to endure it, is worthwhile: what beer travelers find when they come here is a narrow, wood-paneled front bar area with fabric-covered walls, then an area of a few snug booths and some smaller tables. Assorted breweriana and maps and paintings are carefully displayed throughout; beyond the middle dining area is the darker back bar, with more elegant wood paneling and a different tap list. The crowd is made up of Philly locals, beer pilgrims, and the odd musician in town for a gig. Recent artists to stroll in include Danger Mouse, James Mercer, and members of both Beirut and Broken Bells. It's surely one of the only craft beer bars in the country that can claim Questlove, drummer of the Roots, as a regular.

Beer is the main focus, but not by much. Food options run the gamut from the delicious, wing-style frog legs to mussels steamed in Saison Dupont beer with parsley, caramelized leeks, bacon, bleu cheese, and garlic. Beer options are extensive, naturally, which is where the 20-page "Beer Bible" comes in: besides the 6 taps in the front bar and eight in back, it adds some 200 rarities to your decision-making process.

PHILOSOPHY

La vie Belgique. Any beer traveler knows, as Belgians have proven, that a great beer café can be the lifeblood of local community. With Monk's, Carey and Peters have created a gathering place for lovers of craft beer, and sometimes their causes. When the great beer writer Michael Jackson—a regular visitor to Monk's and dear friend of Peters—died in 2007, Peters was among the organizers of a nationwide toast to raise money for Parkinson's (the illness that Jackson battled bravely and privately for ten years before his death).

KEY BEER

In search of the perfect proprietary ale, Peters traveled to Van Steenberge, the last brewery in the Meetjesland (East Flanders) region of Belgium, where Monk's Café Flemish Sour, his superb, ruddy-red house

beer, would be born. At 5.5% ABV it's a Flemish Oud Bruin–style ale, aged in oak and fabulously complex, with wild but pleasing blasts of leather, tart fruit, and woody tannins. "I told [Van Steenberg's brewers] the basic parameters I was looking for. I wanted a sour beer with not much sweetness. I wanted a relatively light body, with low to moderate alcohol, a thirst quencher in the summertime," says Peters. He got it. You should, too.

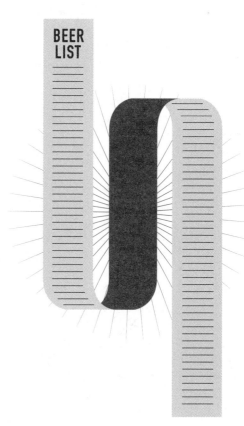

BEER LIST

DETOUR → THE MONK'S CAFÉ'S TOM PETERS

In the early 1980s, during the protoplasmic days of Belgian beer appreciation (Merchant du Vin and Vanberg Dewulf had only started bringing in their specialties in 1978, and then only in bottles), Tom Peters began converting one local drinker at a time to Belgian ales. One fateful evening at a bar called Café Nola on South Street, Peters promised a couple of patrons he'd pay for a bottle of Chimay Grand Reserve out of his own pocket if they didn't like it. He'd tried the delicious, tawny brown ale at the recommendation of a barman in Brussels in 1984, and, electrified by its flavors, worked on getting it into his bar, despite the owner's concerns that the brew would fizzle. By the end of the first night he'd sold the whole box, and though he'd failed to keep one for himself ("I'll never make that mistake again," he quipped) a movement was born. Eventually Peters would help bring in a number of Belgian specialties to the United States for the first time ever in kegs, including such iconic brews as Kwak, Houblon Chouffe, Lindeman's, and Corsendonk. When a craft beer lover goes into a bar and sees native Belgian beers actually on tap, Peters is the man to toast.

Peters wasn't always obvious craft beer material, as it were. A dedicated long-distance runner and drummer, he first tried the law, then military life. By the time Philly beer culture came alive in the late 1980s and 1990s—Stoudt's, Penn Brewing, and Dock Street were all ramping up production, as was Home Sweet Homebrew, an incubator of later talents like Bill Covaleski of Victory—Peters was making plans for Monk's, which he opened with his friend and business partner Fergus Carey in 1997. A couple of years before he'd brought in a pallet of Kwak beer kegs to a bar called Copa Too!, his next managing gig after Café Nola and they'd sold like hotcakes. The vision for Monk's was vividly apparent. Today their bar sells vast quantities of Belgian beer, and his cellar is easily one of the biggest repositories of rare Belgian ales anywhere in the world. In 2004, he was made a Knight of Honor in *Chevalier du Fourquet des Brasseurs*, the 400-year old Belgian brewers' guild, in Brussels, and one of the only *Ambassadeurs d'Orval* in the United States, an honor extended by the famed Belgian Trappist brewery.

Philly, with its blue-collar roots and deep beer history, was the perfect town for Peters to help cultivate the Belgian ale craze, which continues unabated. "The beer culture runs really deep for the whole country, but I think it runs deeper in Philadelphia than anywhere else," says Peters. "There's no other city in the world that has the current beer culture we have here. You can go to any restaurant, new or established. Or to the Phillies stadium, Citizens Bank Park, and you can find good beer at almost every stand." Today he marvels at the new generation of beer drinkers and brewers who started with unusual craft beers right off the bat, and wonders where they'll take the genre—and the market share—for craft brewing. "I think the possibilities are limitless," he says.

With typical humility, the affable Peters is quick to share kudos with others. He points out that bar manager Chris Morris at Khyber Pass was already selling good beers when he had his own aha! moment. "A lot of credit has to go to Craig LaBan too, our *Philadelphia Inquirer* food reviewer," adds Peters. "He's into beer, and every time he reviews any restaurant he talks about the beer selection, so nobody will dare to open without giving serious consideration to beer."

When you get to Monk's Café, and you have to if you love Belgian beer and food, look for Tom, who may be, if the night is winding down, sipping an Orval or his house beer. He is still enthralled with what has unfolded around him: Belgian beer is more than an oddity now, it's practically a new norm of eating and drinking. "I love my bar," he says. "You have people in New York and all these cities that have the same passion I have and they can't get the culture to take hold. Well, maybe now they can, but twenty-five years ago it wasn't working." But then again, it was never about fashion at Monk's, nor was it about Tom. It was about keeping good company. "I never look at trends. You know, I taste something that I like and then I want to share it with somebody."

RESURRECTION ALEHOUSE

2425 Grays Ferry Ave. • Philadelphia, PA 19146 • (215) 735-2202
resurrectionalehouse.com • Established: 2009

SCENE & STORY

Another Hartranft venture, this modestly sized, clean-cut, two-level beer bar is in a mostly residential Graduate Hospital area of Philly. With thirteen taps and about forty-five hard-to-get mostly European bottles—from La Rulles to Smisje and Russian River—the beer options would be impressive on their own, but also square quite nicely with a menu of Southern revival cuisine including renowned twice-fried chicken served with a spiced honey drizzle.

PHILOSOPHY

Quality, not quantity. The beer lists are short and very sweet. Often as it should be.

KEY BEER

Brasserie De La Senne Zinnebier, a 6% ABV Belgian style pale ale that is honey-blonde with a great balance of spice and breadiness.

SOUTH PHILADELPHIA TAP ROOM

1509 Mifflin St. • Philadelphia, PA 19145
(215) 271-SPTR (7787) • southphiladelphiataproom.com
Established: 2003

SCENE & STORY

Just the words "South Philly Taproom" have a good ring. With fourteen taps along the lines of California's sought-after Russian River, along with Founders and Sly Fox, this well-established corner bar deep in South Philly sponsors "Meet the Brewer" nights (Rob Tod, of Allagash, was a recent guest) and earns notice for its upmarket bar food, like a $10 grass-fed bacon cheeseburger.

PHILOSOPHY

Neighborhood hangout with the best possible beer and beloved bar food.

KEY BEER

Stoudt's Karnival Kolsch, a crisp 4.8% ABV beer with a light body and dry finish.

McGILLIN'S OLDE ALE HOUSE

1310 Drury St. • Philadelphia, PA 19107
(215) 735-5562 • mcgillins.com • Established: 1860

SCENE & STORY

Philly's oldest continuously operating pub and one of this country's best Irish pubs, McGillin's opened as the Bell in Hand during the waning days of the Buchanan administration (the only U.S. President from Pennsylvania, alas). Its name came from William McGillin, the publican who ran the place and lived with his thirteen children upstairs. Crammed with dark wood paneling and exposed beams, brewery signs, parade bunting, iron chandeliers, plaques, and bric-a-brac, it's everything you'd hope to see in a 150-year-old pub.

PHILOSOPHY

Hey, where ya from? Friendly and sometimes a bit wild, McGillin's inspires cheer.

KEY BEER

Try a McGillin's IPA, brewed for the pub by Stoudt's, which also brews a real ale and lager for this Philly institution. Other craft standout taps include Yard's, Flying Fish, Victory, Sly Fox, and Dogfish Head.

DOCK STREET BREWING CO.

701 S. 50th St. • Philadelphia, PA 19143 • (215) 726-2337
dockstreetbeer.com • Established: 1985

SCENE & STORY

Built in the historic Cedar Park neighborhood, Dock Street was Philadelphia's first craft brewery and one of the earlier firms to get up and running nationwide. Housed in an historic firehouse, the taproom/pizzeria is known for being a beacon of friendliness in a slightly sketchy neighborhood.

PHILOSOPHY

Unfiltered, unpasteurized, and unpretentious.

KEY BEER

The spicy Rye IPA (7.2% ABV) would make a good accompaniment to the brick oven, wood-fired pizza or calzone, with a snifter of Prince Myshkin's Russian Imperial Stout for dessert.

BRIDGID'S

726 N 24th St. • Philadelphia, PA 19130 • (215) 232-3232
bridgids.com • Established: 1989

SCENE & STORY

Even an unassuming neighborhood bar can be memorable, even if just a pit stop on the way to bigger beer lists. Located in the Fairmount area, close to the Philadelphia Art Museum, Bridgid's is small, comfortable café-style bar with an eclectic Euro-Cajun menu and ten taps (plus more than 60 bottles). It also has a unique "gravity tap" emanating from the second floor ceiling that comes down and hovers over the bar like a too-short fire pole but always has a beer from Yard's brewery. If you're lucky, that beer is Yard's Love Stout. It's quite conducive to conversations at the small, J-shaped bar.

PHILOSOPHY

Where is the love?

KEY BEER

Yard's Love Stout (5% ABV), a creamy, light-chocolaty wonder made with actual oysters.

JOSE PISTOLA'S

263 South 15th St. • Philadelphia, PA 19102
(215) 545-4101 • josepistolas.com • Established: 2007

SCENE & STORY

A couple of local bartenders took over a former restaurant in this two-story, Center City space to create a shrine to good Latin/Southwest cooking and American craft beer in 2007. Amid its exposed brick walls, skull-adorned back bar mirror, and wide bar, the patrons are here to drink beer, see friends, and talk amongst each other, not look at the China patterns. Expect knowledgeable staff, excellent Mexican fare, and a deep list of unusual American and Belgian micros.

PHILOSOPHY

Come one or all. Jose's has a steady crowd of beer pilgrims and industry members gathering for a bit of late night R + D. This is a great fallback plan if Monk's Café is too crowded, or for a nightcap after touring the area's other bars and eateries.

KEY BEER

Walker's Reserve Porter, from California's Firestone Walker (5.8% ABV), on the fresh and light side for porter, and delicious.

★ ★ ★

YARD'S BREWING CO.

901 N. Delaware Ave. • Philadelphia, PA 19123
(215) 634-2600 • yardsbrewing.com • Established: 1994

SCENE & STORY

The makers of excellent beers like Philly Pale Ale and the silky Love Stout, Yard's also offers shuffleboard and free tours on Saturday afternoons, and perhaps best of all it's walking distance from Northern Liberties (making the Foodery, Standard Tap, and 700 Club easy next stops). Pints are $5 (a buck or two more than you'll find in many Philly pubs) but it's worth it if you take the tour, play some leisurely pool or shuffleboard, and have a grilled cheese.

PHILOSOPHY

Gritty and fun-loving: kind of like the whole city of Philadelphia. Started by two college wrestling buddies, the Yard's brewery (Philadelphia's largest) is a marvel of DIY spirit: with bar tops made from reclaimed bowling alley lanes and salvaged mahogany trim in the taproom, it's also running one hundred percent on wind power, an achievement in itself.

KEY BEER

Yard's eminently drinkable Extra Special Ale (6.3% ABV) was the favorite of the late British beer writer Michael Jackson when he would visit town.

VICTORY BREWING CO.

420 Acorn Ln. • Downingtown, PA 19335
(610) 873-0881 • victorybeer.com • Established: 1996

SCENE & STORY

Built in a former Pepperidge Farm factory about an hour west of Philly, just east of the rolling Amish countryside, Victory Brewing Company was founded by locals Ron Barchet and Bill Covaleski. The two childhood friends trained in Germany and in other U.S. breweries and searched across the country for a spot to build their own. After nearly picking the Lake Tahoe area, they settled on their home region, which proved a smart move. With little marketing, the company quickly became one of the most powerful players in the craft beer landscape, with 110,000 barrels of brewing capacity (and 60,000 bbls output currently, and trending upwards). A visit to Victory affords a chance to try twenty of their current brews on tap in immaculate condition (and a half dozen more on hand pumps) and to soak up some Philadelphia beer culture in the making: the company is only fifteen years old (as of 2011) but already feels institutional, part of the fabric of things. This was by design. Covaleski has an eye for populist imagery, and together with the archival WWII photos in a dining room area of the pub and the old copper brewing kettle tops that decorate the main bar space, he's managed to make a space that feels authentically lived in.

PHILOSOPHY

The Old World exalted. Using mostly whole flower hops and an "uncommon" number of yeasts, Victory melds traditional brewing methods with new technology in the brew house to create distinctive styles of beer. In other words, once-moribund styles sparkle with new depths and dimensions in the able hands of the brewers.

KEY BEER

Victory's Prima Pils, a floral-accented, full-bodied golden sipper, has converted many a skeptic from domestic to craft, but it's the Braumeister series of Pilsners exhibiting different hop varieties (including grassy Tettnang and spicy Saaz so far) that truly show what Covaleski and his cohorts are capable of.

TERESA'S NEXT DOOR

124 North Wayne Ave. • Wayne, PA 19087 • (610) 293-9909
teresas-cafe.com • Established: 2007

SCENE & STORY

With twenty-four taps and several hand pumps (in addition to a vast two-hundred-plus bottle list) this beer geek's hideaway opened in 2007 in the affluent enclave of Wayne (just outside of Philly), drawing immediate acclaim. It's a long, sleek space with stone accents, recessed lighting, brewery-specific glassware, a long bar, and padded booths along the back wall. The bar organizes taps by style, so regulars know that number five, for example, will typically feature Belgian blondes and Belgian pale ales. There are frequent beer events and tastings, including a spring dinner utilizing tangy spring hoop shoots, an asparagus-like delicacy used in Belgian cuisine.

PHILOSOPHY

Beer is treated with the proper respect here, but not pretentious solemnity. There's always a sour beer on, and the bartenders, chefs, and owners are all passionate about craft beer.

KEY BEER

The unofficial house beer is Russian River Damnation, a deliciously spicy-strong Belgian-style pale ale from California (7.75% ABV). Or try Petrus Aged Pale Ale (7.3% ABV) on tap from Belgium's Brouwerij Bavik, a medium-bodied and not-too-puckering sour with vinous, woody notes and a bracing acidity. It would make a nice complement to the rich kitchen offerings, which include braised rabbit and wood-fired baby back ribs.

YUENGLING

501 Mahantongo St. • Pottsville, PA 17901
(570) 628-4890 • yuengling.com • Established: 1829

SCENE & STORY

Founded in 1829 by German immigrant David G. Yuengling in Pennsylvania coal country, this is America's oldest brewery, and has enjoyed a surge in popularity in recent years, propelled by its easy-drinking flagship brew and nostalgic image. Pronounced "Ying-Ling," the company produces seven beers, and is still a privately-held, family-run organization, helmed by Dick Yuengling Jr., the fifth generation of Yuenglings to run the show and the father of four daughters, all of whom work for the company.

Touring the Yuengling plant is not remarkable in any technical, beer-making sense; there's no wood or stone fermenters like you'd find in certain old Belgian or British firms. But you're here for the history. Its traditional *rathskeller*, or cellar bar, opened in 1936, and is the end of the line for popular free tours offered on weekdays, after which visitors are treated to a pair of free drafts. The company hit 180 years in 2009, and has surged from producing 127,000 barrels of beer in 1985 to over 2 million in recent years.

PHILOSOPHY

Yuengling's sturdy American image isn't cultivated through marketing or hype. It's the real deal: an old American company getting by with perseverance and hard work, and relatively conservative expansions into new territories.

KEY BEER

A cult beer in the Northeast, Yuengling Premium Lager is an affable amber sipper of 4.4% ABV with a touch of light caramel sweetness and faint citrus from hops on the tail end. Ideally, this beer is consumed while cleaning crab, fishing, or shooting pool.

BEST *of the* REST: PENNSYLVANIA

TRIA CAFÉ
123 S. 18th St. • Philadelphia, PA 19103 • (215) 972-TRIA (8742) • triacafe.com

This is a sleek Center City café opened in 2004 that earns praise for small food and cheese plates complementing a beer list divided by categories: "Invigorating," "Friendly," "Profound," and "Extreme." With one-of-a-kind beers like Victory Braumeister Pils Tettnang on draft and an owner who leads beer appreciation classes (held in another Tria location), beer is very much on the table.

EARTH BREAD & BREWERY
7136 Germantown Ave. • Philadelphia, PA 19119 • (215) 242-6666 • earthbreadbrewery.com • Established: 2008

Tom Baker became a craft beer hero when he unleashed a beer called Perkuno's Hammer Imperial Porter out of his Heavyweight Brewing Co. in New Jersey around the millenium. It was among the first really, *really* big beers available in the region and the Baltic Porter style was rare, not to mention Imperial versions thereof. Despite critical hosannas his little brewery could not stay open in the brutal 2000s. Since 2008 Baker and his wife have been operating this eco-minded flatbread bakery in the Mt. Airy neighborhood of Philly, with bars and dining areas on two levels. Baker started with session beers but has ably returned to bigger beer styles more recently.

CAPONE'S

224 W. Germantown Pike • Norristown, PA 19401 • (610) 279-4748 • caponesdraftlist.blogspot.com

It looks a lot like a drab family-style restaurant, but with thirty draft lines crowded with obscure one-offs and at least five hundred bottles available for retail (not to mention growler sales) this unassuming beer haven about twenty-five miles north of Philadelphia has one of Pennsylvania's biggest and best-kept beer selections.

STOUDT'S BREWING CO. & THE BLACK ANGUS RESTAURANT & BREWPUB

Rte. 272 • 2800 N. Reading Rd. • Adamstown, PA 19501 • (717) 484-4386 • stoudtsbeer.com

Just off the Pennsylvania Turnpike in Adamstown, the makers of many well-made beers including the 4.7% ABV Stoudt's Pils—an aromatic and flavorful standby session beer in the Northeast for years now—offer free tours (by co-founder Ed Stoudt) and nourishment in their attached *gasthaus*-style restaurant.

TRÖEGS

800 Paxton St. • Harrisburg, PA 17104 • (717) 232-1297 • troegs.com

Founded in 1996 by brothers Chris and John Trogner, Tröegs has emerged as one of Pennsylvania's most iconic brewing companies on the strength of beers like Nugget Nectar, HopBack Amber Ale, and Mad Elf. The sleek tasting room offers some eleven more, and there are free guided tours every Saturday afternoon (reservations all but required). The brothers broke ground on a new 90,000 square foot brewery and tasting room location in Hershey in 2011.

THE FARMHOUSE

1449 Chestnut St. • Emmaus, PA 18049 • (610) 967-6225 • thefarmhouse.com

Located outside of Allentown in Pennsylvania's Lehigh Valley, this nineteenth-century stone-farmhouse-turned-destination-restaurant boasts two draws for beer lovers. One, it has an English-style pub on a lower level, laid in with distinctive American craft beers on tap (Smuttynose, Terrapin, Southern Tier) and more than 160 bottled selections, including dozens of vintage ales and oversize bottles. There are beer-and-food pairing dinners on the third Thursday of every month; Javan Small, the chef, has worked in Europe and favors a farm-to-table approach with European techniques. There's also an even older stone barn structure adjacent to the building where beer dinners featuring top tier brewmasters are held from time to time as well.

New Jersey

Milford

THE SHIP INN

61 Bridge St. • Milford, NJ 08848
(908) 995-0188 • britishbrewpub.com

SCENE & STORY

The Ship Inn has the distinction of being New Jersey's first brewpub, and resides along a sleepy creek which forms the border with Pennsylvania. It was built as an atmospheric 1860s Victorian home that had formerly housed a bakery, bowling alley, and ice-cream parlor with a backdoor speakeasy during The Great Mistake. The 7 bbl brewery was added in 1995 (making it the first New Jersey business to legally brew and sell its own beer since Prohibition), and it's a traditional brick-and-copper-clad affair with open fermenters, a rarity in the United States (tours by appointment).

PHILOSOPHY

The poetic pub. The interior is quiet and relaxing, with deep green walls, weathered wood floors, pewter mugs, exposed beams, antique brickwork, tin ceilings, and best of all, no televisions.

KEY BEER

There are three house beers on at all times (Golden Wheat Light, ESB, and Best Bitter) plus a porter, brown, or stout and a seasonal, but even the biggest beer doesn't go much higher than 6% ABV. Why not try them all?

BEST of the REST: NEW JERSEY

ZEPPELIN HALL

88 Liberty View Dr. (near Grand St.) • Jersey City, NJ 07302 • (201) 721-8888 • zeppelinhall.com

This is a massive watering hole with traditional biergarten stylings outside and somewhat corny medieval trappings inside. No matter, it's got a craft-enhanced beer list, with Ommegang, Victory, and Dogfish Head brews on tap alongside some German classics.

HIGH POINT BREWING

22 Park Pl. • Butler, NJ 07405 • (973) 838-7400 • ramsteinbeer.com

Established in 1994 by Germany-trained brewer Greg Zaccardi as America's only brewery doing exclusively German-style wheat beers (under the Ramstein label), the operation has loosened up some of late, stylistically speaking, but wheat is still the go-to grain. It's a low-key affair, hardly on New York City's craft beer radar, but no less an authority than Michael Jackson deemed Zaccardi's 9.5% ABV Winter Wheat (a dopplebock) "powerfully enveloping, deep and complex." The small industrial-style facility is open for tours on the second Saturday of every month from 2 to 4 p.m.

THE COPPER MINE

323 Ridge Rd. • North Arlington, NJ 07031 • (201) 428-1223 • thecopperminepub.com

The Copper Mine may have named itself for too common a metal. With twenty rotating taps and some fifty labels from U.S. and imported craft beers, the bar opened in November 2008 and specializes in Northeast craft brewers such as Defiant, Flying Fish, High Point, Saranac, and the recently launched New Jersey Beer Company.

Delaware

★ ★ ★

DOGFISH HEAD BREWINGS & EATS

320 Rehoboth Ave. • Rehoboth Beach, DE 19971
(302) 226-2739 • dogfish.com • Established: 1995

SCENE & STORY

Named for a spit of land on the craggy Maine coast, Dogfish Head is the brainchild of Sam Calagione, who grew up in a wine-making family in Massachusetts and was once kicked out of prep school for unruly behavior. According to Burkhard Bilger's infamous 2008 *New Yorker* profile, this included the following: "flipping a truck on campus; breaking into the skating rink and playing naked hockey; 'surfing' on the roof of a Winnebago, going sixty miles per hour down I-91." (Not to mention selling shoulder-tapped cases of beer he hid in his hockey bag to students for a profit.)

Today the company he leads (along with his effusive wife, Mariah) has become, along with Sierra Nevada and the Boston Beer Company, one of the best-known craft breweries in the country, widely imitated and envied by competitors. Once touted as the smallest in the nation, it now hovers around 11th out of over 1,700.

The success of Dogfish didn't always seem to be in the cards. After stints in graduate school in New York and a bit of modeling—and having only brewed perhaps ten batches of beer—Calagione headed to Delaware to open that state's first brewery since Prohibition using a tiny pilot system and a bunch of commercially untested and unconventional—even haphazard—recipes. The state laws still forbade brewpubs at the time (a situation he successfully helped lobby to change) and the early years were financially sketchy. But the pub and nanobrewery took off, and Calagione's timing proved impeccable.

Out of the ashes of a nationwide slowdown in the craft beer sector around 1996, Dogfish emerged as a creative juggernaut as the industry regained its composure and the sector returned to double-digit growth, which makes it sound more business-like than it really was. To list the various attention-grabbing (and occasionally award-winning) semi-stunts released since then—sometimes referred to as "extreme brewing," using such ingredients as African honey, muscat grapes, chrysanthemums, even algae—would be a long and thirst-provoking task involving footnotes. But amid the wacky, sometimes deliberately provocative libations ("Golden Shower" was one ill-advised label) have emerged a few slightly more sober-minded experiments reinterpreting ancient recipes, a track that Calagione and company have spent a great deal of time pursuing around the world. Along the way Sam has written a few books, raised a family, and high-fived his way into an ever-brighter spotlight with each new release, making it all look easy. Of course, it's not. Madness, meet method.

Beyond the experiments, Sam's Dogfish crew crafted recipes appealing to wider audiences, too, and it was perhaps inevitable that Calagione and his Dogfish would be ready for a close-up. In 2010, the Discovery Channel created a new show, *Brew Masters*, centered around his globe-trotting recipe hunts and daily business challenges played as life-or-death countdowns to disaster or critical acclaim.

Dogfish offers free tours of the nearby main brewery (reserve ahead by calling 302-684-1000, ext. 0); make sure to look out for the bocce courts and treehouse board-room. A combination brewery tour and trip to the original two-story pub location in the center of Rehoboth makes for an excellent long afternoon and evening. There are always more than twenty Dogfish brews and a cask (including pub-only drafts). There's also a micro-distillery project gathering steam on-site, solid pub grub, and live music on occasion. If Sam's there (and he often is), he'll be rapping with the young guy washing dishes. Despite all his fame and acclaim, he knows everyone who works with him at the company by name.

PHILOSOPHY

Dogfish Head is a seamless meld of restless beer-geek thinking plus market savvy and a hearty dose of punk rock attitude, a winning and incredibly unique combo. Its official M.O. has long been "Off-Centered Ales for Off-Centered People," but "controlled chaos" might be a more succinct description. The beers are designed to make you think, but not at the expense of actually drinking them again and again and again.

KEY BEER

The best experimental beer? Take your pick, but the recent Miles Davis–inspired Bitches Brew, made with brown sugar from the island of Mauritius, raw unfiltered Ethiopian honey, and "an a—load of dark, roasty grains to balance the sweetness of the honey," as Calagione explained it to me (with typical gusto), is a great example. The company's top-seller is 60 Minute IPA, first brewed in 2003 and a graham-cracker-like feast Calagione has described as being "super pungent, citrusy, and grassy, without being crushingly bitter."

★ ★ ★

BEST of the REST: DELAWARE

IRON HILL

147 E. Main St. • Newark, DE 19711 • (302) 266-9000 • ironhillbrewery.com

OTHER LOCATIONS:

Wilmington, DE (710 S. Madison St., 302-472-2739)
Media, PA (30 E. State St., 610-627-9000)
West Chester, PA (3 W. Gay St., 610-738-9600)
North Wales, PA (1460 Bethlehem Pike, 267-708-2000)
Phoenixville, PA (130 E. Bridge St., 610-983-9333)
Lancaster, PA (781 Harrisburg Pike, 717-291-9800)
Maple Shade, NJ (124 E. Kings Hwy., 856-273-0300)

Now the flagship of a minichain with eight locations in the area and brewing medals with surprising speed (nine major categories in two prestigious competitions during 2010), the original Iron Hill location is near the University of Delaware. There are five house standard beers ranging from a light lager to a 5.4% ABV porter, plus an always-on seasonal Belgian ale, several other seasonals, and about seventeen bottled reserves (including some vintage-dated beers). The house beers are acceptably solid, but the action for committed craft mavens is in those ever-changing offerings from month to month. The interior is sort of "modern library," with reddish wood paneling and deep green walls beneath a vaulted modern Quonset hut ceiling. The menu reaches for a higher culinary plane than most brewpubs, too, with respectable results.

Maryland

Baltimore

ALEWIFE

21 N Eutaw Street • Baltimore, MD 21201 • (410) 545-5112
www.alewifebaltimore.com • Established: 2010

SCENE & STORY

Built in the glorious old Eutaw bank building in West Baltimore with handsome tile floors, soaring ceilings, art nouveau leaded glass windows, heavy Craftsman-looking chandeliers, and a spiral staircase leading to a high balcony, the home of Alewife had been sitting empty for a year after housing a tavern when woodworker-turned–bar manager Bryan Palombo and his business partner took on the challenge of overhauling the much-decayed space. The goal was to launch one of the best craft beer spots in the mid-Atlantic. "We walked in and we're like, 'Oh yeah: it's a beer hall. It's perfect. Let's do it.' We got this place ready in five weeks. It was record-breaking. Everything was broken," recalls Palombo. The result? Bulls-eye. With an ambitious menu of pub grub (try the artery-clogging but oh-so-worth-it Smoked Burger and fries cooked in duck fat; $15) and a huge, ever changing list (40 taps, around 100 bottles), it's certainly one of the best things going in Baltimore for the craft beer scene, and a nice, convivial environment for traveling beer lovers.

PHILOSOPHY

Initially, the goal was no compromise ("Find the best beer in the world— done!") Palombo reports, but the reality check of one too many slow-moving beers has prompted a more down-to-earth list, though one that's hardly plebeian.

KEY BEER

Often on tap, the herbal, drying, aromatic Belgian pale ale Zinnebir (Brasserie De La Senne; 6% ABV) would make a great accompaniment to the rich smoke burger and fries.

THE BREWER'S ART

1106 North Charles Street • Baltimore, MD 21201
(410) 547-9310 • www.thebrewersart.com • Established: 1996

SCENE & STORY

Built in an elegant old three-story Mt. Vernon area town house, the Brewers Art is easily one of the most famous brewpubs in the country, thanks to lakes of dedicated ink in the *New York Times, Esquire,* and scores of drink magazines. With all its hype one can be forgiven for worrying about a letdown, but the fact is that it's a true original, well worth a special trip. However, do *not* show up on Friday at 7 p.m. and expect to waltz in—it's extremely popular, and service varies from chipper and friendly to "And you are . . . ?" What you'll find on arrival depends: upstairs, just above street level, there's a bustling bar crowd in the front window crowded around a black-and-white Greek Revival bar area, beyond which is a mezzanine and finally a spacious seated dining room area. Down-stairs the vibe is classic *rathskeller*, with a dimly lit horseshoe bar and alcoves for huddling over the well-crafted beers.

PHILOSOPHY

American-style Belgian café, no excuses. "They did not compromise from day one. They did not brew sh-tty beer just to stay with the masses," says Thor Cheston, manager and beer sommelier of Washington D.C.'s Brasserie Beck. "I mean, with some of their beers like the Green Peppercorn Triple—when they first came out—people were like 'What the h-ll are you thinking?' But you know, it's amazing. Their beers are phenomenal."

KEY BEER

With four house ales, a cast of some twenty rotating seasonals, a strong international bottle list including a few lambics, and other new releases coming on line, there's much to choose from. Resurrection, a sweet, malty Abbey style of 7% ABV, is the most popular beer, but it's the Ozzy that stands out. Inspired by the classic Belgian pale ale Duvel, it's a clear golden sipper of 7.25% ABV with a huge rocky head and a yeasty, peppery bite, thanks to a devilish dose of Styrian goldings hops.

MAX'S TAPROOM

737 South Broadway • Baltimore, MD 21231
(410) 675-6297 • www.maxs.com • Established: 1986

SCENE & STORY

Fell's Point is Baltimore's cobblestoned former Colonial seaport boasting over 160 National historic register buildings, a flotilla of historic tall ships tied up along the shore, and alley upon alley of laid-back bars where brothels and old-time boarding houses used to be. It's also home to Max's, one of the best beer bars on the East Coast. Max's organizes a huge Belgian beer festival, for starters, so the Flemish/Wallonian contingent runs deleriously high. With a long bar lined by 140 rotating taps, 1,200 different beers in coolers, bar top casks, and a wild collection of breweriana, it's absolutely chockablock on weekend nights with a mixed crowd of college kids (and occasionally their parents), hordes of tourists (especially in the summertime), and tourists who end up partying with those college kids and their parents.

PHILOSOPHY

The bigger the beer list, the more fun you're having—right? Or, sometimes, maybe that's "the bigger the *cup*". Friday is "big ass draft" night—$6 for 32 ounces of anything on tap (except for big Belgians and other crafts), served in beer pong-ready *plastique*. In other words, avoid Max's on Friday nights, unless your inner collegian wouldn't have it any other way. Tuesdays, on the other hand, are dedicated to the "Beer Social" at 6 p. m. when brewers and members of the local craft crowd mingle upstairs. And you're more likely to get on the pool tables downstairs later, since no one is drunkenly sprawled across it.

KEY BEER

Beers from Baltimore's own Clipper City Brewing Co./Heavy Seas Beer line like Loose Cannon (a 7.25% ABV AIPA) are big favorites, but the chance to drink the even rarer local Stillwater Brewing Company's one-offs (such as "Our Side" saison, a recent 7.5% ABV collaboration with Danish "gypsy brewer" Mikkel Bjergsø) should not be passed up.

THE WHARF RAT

801 South Ann Street • Baltimore, MD 21231
(410) 276-8304 • www.thewharfrat.com • Established: 1982

SCENE & STORY

Walking into the late-1700s building that houses the Wharf Rat pub instantly conjures the time when Fells Point was still so teeming with privateers just off a square rigger from some port afar that the British called it a "Nest of Pirates." Low-ceilinged and cluttered with valuable nautical memorabilia, a solid tap row of Northeast and mid-Atlantic craft ales, and several Oliver's English-style ales from Pratt Street Alehouse, this is one of Baltimore's most beloved spots, if not for the food then for the massive stone fireplace in the back of the bar and the incredible atmosphere. Legend has it the place is haunted too, notably by a gentleman who was shot for playing "The Star-Spangled Banner" far too often

(and too loudly) on his gramophone. Ask a bartender or bouncer for the tale.

PHILOSOPHY

Cask-conditioned beers, good friends, and a roaring fireplace is all that matters on a cold winter's night.

KEY BEER

Oliver's Best Bitter, an amber, smooth, gently carbonated traditional sipper of 4.8% ABV.

Best of the Rest: Maryland

THE QUARRY HOUSE TAVERN

8401 Georgia Ave # B • Silver Spring, MD 20910-4486
(301) 587-8350 • www.quarryhousetavern.com

A classic, cash-only dive ("Beer. Burgers. Basement.") down a steep stairway underneath an Indian restaurant called Bombay Gaylord with an improbably long list of import and craft brews, the Quarry House has been around nearly 80 years and generates about as many differing opinions on its merits, most of them positive. It's dimly lit, the walls are lined with cases of beer, it gets packed. You're here for a huge beer list, 9 on tap and about 300 bottles (Allagash, Dogfish, Clipper City), perhaps a bit of greasy pub grub (½ lb. cheeseburgers, Old Bay tater tots, battered pickles, fried Oreos *ala mode*), and occasionally live bands.

District of Columbia

★ ★ ★

BIRCH & BARLEY CHURCH KEY

1337 14th Street NW • Washington D.C., DC 20005
(202) 567-2576 • www.birchandbarley.com • Established: 2009

SCENE & STORY

Located in D.C.'s up and coming Logan Circle area, this is two establishments served by one truly incredible beer selection with the result being one of the United States' top craft beer destinations, hands down. Downstairs, in the chic, low-lit street level space, young chef Kyle Bailey—at 30, already a veteran of New York power-player restaurants Blue Hill and Allen & Delancey—prepares Birch & Barley's entire New American menu expressly for enjoyment with the place's selection of 550 different beers. There's a nightly seven-course tasting menu, including beers for $77, which has included such entrées as a strip loin of beef with balsamic-braised cabbage, parsnip gnocchi, and glazed pearl onion, served with Great Divide Grand Cru from Denver. You could do much, much worse.

Upstairs is the more casual, high-ceilinged Church Key bar, with high brick walls, a long banquette and line of stools, cozy raised booths, and a small section of couch and low padded stools in a sort of chill-out area. But there's not much of that.

Helping usher in something of a D.C. nightlife renaissance, both businesses have been incredibly busy since day one, and...well, you know the drill. Arrive early; on weekend nights, the upstairs is a first-come, first-serve, three-deep scrum. If you make it in early, stake out your territory, pounce when you can, and play fair by ordering all night long as the hordes surround. Expect a mixed crowd of beer geeks (lining the bar, having arrived early), K Street lobbyists and young lawyer types crowding in. The food is fatty and sometimes a bit too clever by half, but there are winners (the tots). The flatbread pizzas are a mixed bag: crispy figs, prosciutto, and melty gorgonzola? More, please. Mushy, salt-less pulled pork, no thanks.

PHILOSOPHY

Both rooms are served by the same beer supply, and here's where things get interesting: beer Director Greg Engbert has assembled an upstairs selection of over fifty drafts (organized on menus under categories along flavor lines, i.e. crisp, hop, malt, roast, tart & funky, and fruit & spice) that are stored in a series of temperature-controlled coolers and served according to their ideal temperature: 42, 48, 50-52, and 54 degrees Fahrenheit (in quality house glassware, naturally). All the other bottles, kegs, and casks (about 10-15 per week) are organized meticulously as well, likewise stored in their own designated coolers. Even the beer lines themselves run through glycol-cooled pipes to keep the beer at the desired temperature before it hits a freshly rinsed (and yes, then re-cooled) glass. Engbert leads twice-weekly staff meetings to explain what's coming on tap, and longer seminars once a month to drill servers on the nuances of the beers they're serving. It's incredibly, almost insanely anal, but the fact is that beer does best express itself in the temperature range with which it was created, and Engbert's costly accomplishment is nothing if not admirable (if unlikely to be widely imitated, alas). These coolers supply the rocking bar area; downstairs, a gleaming row of copper pipes ("The Beer Organ") descend from the ceiling and into the taps serving the dining room.

KEY BEER

With all the taps turning over regularly and lines meticulously monitored, freshness shouldn't be a problem, and you can order $1.50 taster sizes to sample a variety. Look for Delaware's own newcomer, Evolution Brewing, which makes Rise Up Stout, Caribbean-style (slightly stronger, at 6.7%) and cold-steeped in the brew house with organic coffee (6.8%, 48 degrees).

★ ★ ★

THE MERIDIAN PINT

3400 11th Street NW • Washington D.C., DC 20010
(202) 588-1075 • www.meridianpint.com • Established: 2010

SCENE & STORY

With a clean-lined, garage-doored space, wood floors, and tin ceilings, this is a two-level beer bar with exclusively American craft beers, some of which are available by the ounce in a pay-as-you-go arrangement from six basement table taps (reservations recommended). It draws a mostly young crowd, especially on weekends and for big games, but there have been a number of events with craft brewing industry rock stars Sam Calagione, Jim Koch of Boston Beer Co., and Ken Grossman of Sierra Nevada.

PHILOSOPHY

The earnest reasoning for the U.S.-only list is that it's better for the environment, as is the wind power, local-dwelling staff (Columbia Heights), and aggressive composting and recycling programs in place. Can't argue with any of that.

KEY BEER

Dogfish Head's neo-Berliner Weisse style Festina Pêche (4.5%) and bottles of the 9%ABV Weyerbacher Double Simcoe IPA ($8) for dessert.

BRASSERIE BECK

1101 K Street NW • Washington D.C., DC 20005
(202) 408-1717 • www.beckdc.com • Established: 2007

SCENE & STORY

Acclaimed Belgian-born chef Robert Wied-maier opened this airy, marble- and white tile-filled bistro in D.C.'s McPherson Square neighborhood in 2007 to strong reviews. Washington professionals took to the sumptuous dining scene and dramatic open kitchen setting (and its private dining area, for bigwigs and events) while the craft beer and raw seafood-stocked grey marble front bar area quickly became a hot after-work spot. Today, thanks to the affable Thor Cheston—who proudly left behind med school to pursue his love of craft beer and eventually worked his way up to the job as General Manager and beer sommelier here—it's got the deepest Belgian beer list in D.C. (150+ labels), a superb house-brewed ale from Belgium, and a growing reputation treating beer like Belgians do—with a deep and joyful respect. To make Belgophiles feel even more at home, there are some plastic woven chairs like you see in Brussels' Grand Place bistros and a large clock displaying the time there, too.

PHILOSOPHY

Proper is the operative word. "It's all about service," says the effusive Cheston, who in 2009 was inducted into the Knighthood of the Brewers' Mashtaff, an honorary cadre of Belgian beer supporters coordinated by the Belgian Brewers' Guild. "It's proper service, taking care of the beer, everything from proper temperature for the bottles to proper storage. Everything needs to be held cold and then run through a proper draft system, always running the proper mixture of gas, and the proper amount of pressure on the kegs. I'm an absolute stickler for the proper glassware, a proper pour—the whole presentation. All the servers know how to do a perfect Hefeweizen pour, where you dump the bottle in the glass, pour it out and make it really sexy. What I want to do is put the beer into context, really train servers so they know everything about the beer." It sounds a bit stuffy, but Cheston is having serious fun, and his beer cellar and list is the proof. Come winter, Cheston even serves La Dragonne (from the Swiss brewery Brasserie des Franches-Montagnes a.k.a. "BFM") at 120 degrees F in a steaming bucket of water with a large snifter for $45 "so that the aromas of anise, syrupy brown sugar, raisins and plums wrapped around thick sweet malt infused with cinammon, star anise, orange peel, cardamom, cloves, coriander, and juniper berries can be appreciated fully," he says, practically giddy at the thought.

KEY BEER

With eleven drafts and Cheston's voluminous bottle list (not only Belgian; there are excellent American, German, and French brews as well), beer is an absolute fixture here, with events, tastings, and beer in the kitchen, too. Antigoon, the hazy-golden 6.8%abv house pale ale, hails from Belgium's Brouwerij De Musketiers and is named for the mythical giant once lording over the town of Wiedmaier's native Antwerp. It's pleasantly bready and yeasty, with a delicate fruity aromas of tulip, pear, and fresh sliced apple, and finishes with a brisk white pepper crack. It's superb with food, and the bottle it's served in has some of the most interesting label art ever created, illustrating the tale of Antigoon's demise. Brabo Pils, a German style kellerbier (unfiltered lager) and the second house beer brewed for Brasserie Beck (from by Huyghe, makers of Delerium Tremens) made its debut on tap in the final days of 2010.

BIRRERIA PARADISO

3282 M Street NW • Washington DC 20057
(202) 337-1245 • www.eatyourpizza.com
Established: 2002 (Georgetown location)

SCENE & STORY

This cozy 16-tap, 10-stool, 20 seat beer bar with fireplace is located in the basement of a sunny, bustling wood oven Georgetown pizza eatery with superb pie (and crowds to show for it). The night to go is Tuesday or Wednesday when the fracas mellows and there are both pizza and draft beer specials from 5-7pm. Manager/Beer Chief Greg Jasgur maintains a massive bottle list as well, and, like his predecessor Thor Cheston, gets the cream of the crop when highly allocated beers become available from brewers with cult followings. The Atomica (tomato, salami, black olives, hot pepper flakes, mozzarella) is an excellent choice for beer, and with such a varied and rotating selection of brews (and pizza specials) it's practically inconceivable to go wrong.

PHILOSOPHY

The MO here is simple: pizza and beer were made for each other, so why not go for the absolute best of both worlds? The ingredients, food preparation, beers, prices, and service are all exceptional. As usual, go on a quieter night for the best possible experience.

KEY BEER

Del Borgo Re Ale, a nutty, caramelly, citrus-tinged American style pale ale from central Italy's Birra Del Borgo brewery, if it's available. It's a 6.4% brew absolutely made for pizza. Barring that, look for Stoudt's bready, gold and grassy Karnival Kölsch (4.8%), if available, which would make a nice palate-cleansing start; then move up to a Flying Dog Raging Bitch Belgian IPA (8.3%).

★ ★ ★

Virginia
★ ★

MODERN CRAFT BREWING IS RELATIVELY NEW TO THE APPALACHIAN REGION,

but it's more than at home already. Five Virginia breweries so far have signed on to the state-sponsored "Brew Ridge Trail" initiative (brewridgetrail.com), to spur interest in and travel through the homegrown scene, which is growing by leaps and bounds. From Blue Mountain Brewery in Afton to Devil's Backbone Brewing Company, there's a groundswell of new brewing afoot that's long overdue.

Roseland

DEVIL'S BACKBONE

200 Mosbys Run • Roseland, VA 22967 • (434) 361-1001
dbbrewingcompany.com • Established: 2008

SCENE & STORY

Devils Backbone, a two-and-a-half story mountain-lodge-style brewpub in a tiny town in the Blue Ridge Mountains of Nelson County, Virginia, burst onto the national craft brewing radar at the 2009 Great American Beer Festival and 2010 World Beer Cup in Chicago by racking up no less than twelve medals, including Champion Brewery and Brewmaster at the WBC (in the Small Brewpub category, 2010). Despite having only opened some two years ago, the brewery was suddenly Virginia's most award-winning brewery, and the little 8 bbl brewpub near the Wintergreen ski area in a town of less than 2,000 was sharing the stage with some truly heavy hitters in the industry. Those 2,000 locals were ecstatic, naturally, and plans to expand with a second location with a 30 bbl brewhouse and packaging line near Charlottesville came together rapidly. The original location is a handsome structure made of materials repurposed from a 1900s dairy barn, a horse farm, and a tobacco plantation barn.

PHILOSOPHY

Brewer Jason Oliver tends to brew and naturally carbonate subtle twists on sessionable old-world styles that might seem tame compared to the fare on draft in some craft beer destinations, but are well made nonetheless.

KEY BEER

There are ten beers on tap at all times including four year-round beers and six rotating seasonal beers created by Oliver. Gold Leaf Lager, a 4.5% ABV international style Pilsner, the brewery's flagship, is a good place to start. Lately Oliver has been working on bigger styles, from Wheat Stouts to Black IPAs and Imperial Coffee Stouts. Surely there are more medals to come.

Afton

BLUE MOUNTAIN BREWERY

9519 Critzers Shop Rd. • Afton, VA 22920 • (540) 456-8020
bluemountainbrewery.com • Established: 2007

SCENE & STORY

As the name suggests this is another brewery with a proud connection to the Blue Ridge Mountains of central Virginia, and resides in a beautiful white building outside of Charlottesville along the Monticello Wine Trail. But the connection to the land here goes even deeper: Starting in 2006, owner and head brewer Taylor Smack began growing his own hops, and is now wrangling some five hundred plants of Cascade and Centennial, which are irrigated with brewery runoff and used in the brewing process.

PHILOSOPHY

Innovative brewing with a Southern touch— and a green heart. Smack is keeping an eye on Virginia Tech experiments aiming to develop strains of barley that could flourish locally, and the brewpub is serving beef from cattle raised on his spent grains.

KEY BEER

Look for his Summer Haze, a lush and fruity, dry-hopped 8% ABV brew approximately the color of a lazy Appalachian sunset.

DETOUR ➡

JEFFERSONIAN ZYMURGY:

931 Thomas Jefferson Pkwy. • Charlottesville, VA 22902
(434) 984-9822 • monticello.org

It's a relatively minor point of interest among historians but one enormous point of pride for craft beer aficionados that Thomas Jefferson was highly involved in brewing. Beer was considered one of the "table liquors" traditionally served with meals, and there was a dedicated cellar for aging the house ales before they'd be served upstairs. Beer was in the picture early on. According to records from 1772, Jefferson's wife, Martha, was used to brewing 15-gallon casks of small beer every two weeks. (Small beers can be made with the spent grain of stronger batches or simply with less grain; either way the technique results in a lower alcohol brew.) By 1794 he'd planted hops, and Monticello, which had been conceived with a brewery in the elevation drawings, was on its way to becoming a full-fledged estate brewery—even a malt house would be added much later, in 1820. In 1815, Jefferson wrote in a letter to Joseph Coppinger (himself a brewer): *"I am lately become a brewer for family use, having had the benefit of instruction to one of my people by an English brewer of the first order."*

Jefferson's teacher was Joseph Miller, a British expatriate who also trained one of Jefferson's slaves, Peter Hemings (brother of Sally), how to malt and brew with raw materials grown on the 5,000-acre hilltop estate. Hemings was a quick study, and would eventually undertake the brewing of a hundred gallons of ale every spring and fall.

By 1814, a sturdy brew house was in place, and Hemings and Jefferson began malting estate grains to avoid having to buy them, enough to turn out 60-gallon batches of brew at a time. Jefferson preferred to bottle condition the ales, decrying local brews from the "public breweries" as "meager and vapid" and was fixated on cork quality. As he served the finished ale to friends, family, and visiting dignitaries, his fame as a brewer spread, and neighbors were soon asking him how they could get into the act, too.

To celebrate Jeffersonian Zymurgy (the art and science of brewing), nearby Starr Hill Brewery founder and brewmaster Mark Thompson and brewer Levi Hill collaborated with the Thomas Jefferson Foundation in late 2010 and early 2011 on the launch of Monticello Reserve Ale, the official beer of Monticello, inspired by what was produced and consumed by the third president and his guests. Today, Monticello Reserve Ale is sold in 750-milliliter bottles at the brewery and served on tap at local restaurants. It's extremely light in body and bitterness by today's standards, but offers a taste of what life as a brewer might have been like in Jefferson's day.

BEST *of the* REST: VIRGINIA

THE BIRCH
1231 W. Olney Rd. • Norfolk, VA 23507 • (757) 962-5400 • thebirchbar.com

It's fitting that the neighborhood in the Navy town of Norfolk that this new beer bar calls home is West Ghent—as in the Flemish city—Belgium looms large here. Since they opened in January of 2011, Malia Paasch and Ben Bublick have graffitied the floor-to-ceiling chalkboard with incredible selections for the twenty-one taps. There's another 100 in the bottle, and with Belgian rarities like De Glazen Toren, St. Feuillien, Brasserie de Blaugies, and Pico-brouwerij Alvinne (and American-born craft specialties from Allagash, Stillwater, and Weyerbacher), Norfolk's first full-fledged craft beer bar has established a lofty tradition in a very short time.

RUSTICO
827 Slaters Ln. • Alexandria, VA 22314 • (703) 224-5051 • rusticorestaurant.com

A wood oven pizzeria with a mean beer selection (thanks to Greg Engbert, who worked at the famous Brickskeller Bar and went on to put Birch & Barley and Church Key on the map) Rustico is a spacious modern eatery with 30 taps and around 250 bottled selections from such esoteric producers as De Hoevebrouwers and Brouwerij Girardin (Belgium) and Birrificio Troll (Italy). One nice touch: beers are served in the proper glassware, such as snifters for stronger ales, which help aromas waft out of the glass.

CAPITAL ALEHOUSE
623 E. Main St. • Richmond, VA 23219 • (804) 780-ALES (2537) • capitalalehouse.com

The original of four locations in the area, this well-established beer bar was opened in 2002 in the heart of downtown Richmond within walking distance of Brown's Island, the Richmond Ballet, and the Virginia State Capitol. Constructed with sweat equity by a group of beer fanatics in a 108-year-old building, the bar boasts more than fifty taps, two cask beer engines, more than two hundred bottled beers from around the world, and a varied pub grub menu. On a lower level there's a pool table, four dart boards, and a beer garden area with communal seating and a fountain for al fresco beer drinking.

The SOUTHEAST

weet tea, jambalaya, barbecue . . . and Belgian ale? With Prohibition-era laws still on the books in parts of the region, keeping the beer weak and home brew kettles dry (Alabama and Mississippi are the last two U.S. states to still ban home brewing as of 2011), it seemed good beer might never really arrive in the Deep South, much less reweave the social fabric as it has in cities like Philly, Portland, and San Diego. There was—and surely still is, in some dustier corners—a sense that craft beer might not really make sense. There's something about the South that calls for beers to come in a red plastic cup, very cold and very light, or, lacking such a distinguished vessel, simply canned and at least half cold, especially on a hot day. The late, great Mississippi writer Larry Brown's imagery (and preferred method) of drinking beer—while blasting Robert Earl Keen with empties clanging around in the back of an old beater and hauling down some country road—seems more apt.

And yet the art of craft beer *has* well and truly arrived in the South. Brewing is nothing if not social, and there's no better match to a spicy pulled pork po'boy than a crisp craft-brewed Pilsner. From ambitious new breweries in Asheville and new beer bars in New Orleans, the former "brewing capital of the South," to the anodyne, palm-lined byways of South Florida, it's becoming one of the country's most interesting regions when it comes to craft beer.

Louisiana

★ ★ ★

THE REBIRTH OF LOUISIANA'S BEER SCENE IS THE SOUTH'S STRONGEST

evidence for the good beer revolution. What had been gathering steam before the deluge of Katrina—the growth of a home-brewing scene centered around Brew Ha Ha, a supply shop owned by a man named Mike "Elvis" Karnowski; Cooter Brown's beer bar (a multi-tap tavern widening horizons); and the regional presence of Abita Brewing Company—was destined to come back, even if Elvis himself was no longer in the building (he moved North).

Even as government bureaucrats bicker about alcohol strength caps and home-brewing laws, the land of fizzy yellow water is going big for the good-beer gumbo—and reviving a proud brewing past. Warning: There is a distinct danger of packing on a few pounds. If the beers don't give you some extra padding around the middle, the soulful food will. And that's perfectly all right.

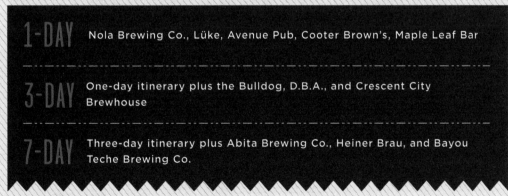

ITINERARIES

1-DAY Nola Brewing Co., Lüke, Avenue Pub, Cooter Brown's, Maple Leaf Bar

3-DAY One-day itinerary plus the Bulldog, D.B.A., and Crescent City Brewhouse

7-DAY Three-day itinerary plus Abita Brewing Co., Heiner Brau, and Bayou Teche Brewing Co.

New Orleans

THE AVENUE PUB

1732 St. Charles Ave. • New Orleans, LA 70130
(504) 586-9243 • avenuepub.com • Established: 1989

SCENE & STORY

It's not necessary to call ahead or plan your visit to New Orleans' best beer bar because it never closes—ever. It has been said that the world-class beer bar in the Lower Garden district, open 24-7 every day of the year, doesn't even have locks on the doors. Owner Polly Watts took over and rechristened the place in 2006 after her father died and turned this once seedier spot into a real destination for beer lovers everywhere. The charming, slightly ramshackle building overlooking St. Charles dates back to the 1840s and boasts a huge wraparound upstairs porch, making it a coveted spot during Mardi Gras, as the parade passes directly by. On the first level several black chalkboards dense with American craft beers (and some truly wonderful imports) frame a relatively narrow bar area with seating nearby. A stairwell leads up to a coffee house–esque room with antique furniture, framed pictures, and the second bar area with its own menu.

The selection of a few dozen bottles is the most inspired in Louisiana, and there are real finds among the tap list of forty-seven rotating brands. Then there's the friendly, ultraknowledgeable staff and chilled out locals enjoying a quiet drink at the bar. Last but not least is the excellent—and very affordable—bar food, which is far more advanced than the quotidian menu item names would suggest. The grilled cheese turns out to be a ridiculously gooey-good combo of drunken goat cheese, sharp cheddar, and feta grilled in sourdough with sage, herb pesto, bacon, and tomato. It's hedonism on a plate.

PHILOSOPHY

Enlightened. Watts is an unabashed craft beer maven, but neither she nor her staff will condescend to another's taste. This is New Orleans: self-serious puffery is ill advised. Knowledge, on the other hand, is power. The bar offers classes for the Cicerone program, a beer expertise certification course, and she keeps her tap beers fresh using a costly system that dispenses beers under a mixture of CO_2 and nitrogen that is calibrated according to each beer's ideal mixture. Her staff cleans the lines every two weeks, inhibiting the bacteria growth that can contribute to terribly off flavors in beer. This is a (woefully) rare and yet essential practice.

KEY BEER

Watts recently put the seldom seen Cantillon Lou Pepe Kriek on tap; it's a tart lambic brew from Belgium that is spontaneously fermented with wild yeasts, aged in Bordeaux barrels for up to three years, and refermented with the juice of local cherries before bottling. With its unremittingly tart flavor it would be the perfect combo for the rich artisan cheese board from St. James Cheese Company, a noted Garden District merchant.

NOLA BREWING CO.

3001 Tchoupitoulas St. • New Orleans, LA 70115
(504) 896-9996 • nolabrewing.com • Established: 2008

SCENE & STORY

With the sultry weather it would seem unlikely that craft beer—with its sometimes intense, attention-demanding flavors and hefty alcoholic punch—would gain much of a foothold in New Orleans. But it has. This is, after all, the city that invented the cocktail, elevating simple spirits to something higher, and, at one time, the former brewing capital of the American South.

Those days may be coming back. It's a short drive from the French Quarter down to Tchoupitoulas Street to get to one of the most remarkable success stories—in beer, or any local business—since Katrina. With the void left by Dixie, the New Orleans Lager & Ale Brewing Company, universally known as Nola Brewing, is poised to become the city's preeminent craft brewery, first by putting super distinctive batches on draft around town and then by packaging.

Native son and founder Kirk Coco and head brewer Peter Caddoo have set up shop in a hangar-like former metal shop just south of the Garden District overlooking the Mississippi River. Standing beneath the soaring eaves in view of their compact 20 bbl system of kettle and tanks (sure to expand) with the freshest possible brew in hand, it's easy to think the sky's the limit.

Coco, a former lawyer with wily enthusiasm, was working as a surface warfare officer in the U.S. Navy during Katrina, while Caddoo, a shyer sort but often wearing a contented, wry grin, had been sous chef under Emeril Lagasse at Commander's Palace before working at Dixie—until all the brewers were laid off a few months before Katrina as the company foundered. Both men watched from a safe distance as the storm took its terrible toll on the city and on Dixie, its last proud brewery, and, slowly, as the city picked up the pieces in 2007, began to plan their venture.

PHILOSOPHY

Quintessentially local. Coco and Caddoo are experimenting with some local ingredients like watermelon and say they want to stay small (they did about 1,300 bbl in 2010, and say they'd top out at 10,000). "More than any other city—except maybe Seattle or San Francisco—New Orleans supports local products so strongly," says Coco. "That's why there are no chain restaurants around. It's very hard to find one.

KEY BEER

The IPA has come a long way, from oddity to everyday brew, but the trouble is, too many are haphazard affairs defined by a long and face-contorting aftertaste. Not Caddoo's 6.5% ABV Hopitoulas IPA, a blend of six malts and six hops, which is then dry hopped with two different hops beyond that point. It's balanced, with notes of pine, grapefruit, and caramel.

DETOUR ➡ THE MAPLE LEAF

8316 Oak St. • New Orleans, LA 70118 • (504) 866-9359 • mapleleafbar.com

Open since 1974, the old Leaf is the paradigmatic New Orleans music bar, with shows and jam sessions seven nights a week and regular standing gigs for many incredible artists calling New Orleans home. To walk into its small space and take in its dilapidated floors, red tin walls, and deep crimson lighting is to become a part of the Crescent City itself. A photo of poet and "Maple Leaf Laureate" Everett Hawthorne Maddox ("in residence 1976–1989") and a bottle of his Famous Grouse bourbon hang on the wall; poetry readings are traditional here, too. Musically speaking, it's pure New Orleans, with nightly performances by the likes of Rebirth Brass Band, Papa Grows Funk, the Radiators, members of the Funky Meters, and surprise appearances by artists of icon status (aka Springsteen; Beyoncé filmed a video here . . .).

You don't come to the Maple Leaf to drink elaborate cocktails (mixers beyond ice get dicey); you don't come here to analyze Belgian ales. You come here to soak up soul deeper than the roots of a live oak. After the storm, Walter "Wolfman" Jackson played the first (publicized, at least) New Orleans concert on an emotional night. With the famous Jacques-Imo's restaurant next door one could make an easy night of it. Just get there.

LÜKE

333 St. Charles Ave. • New Orleans, LA 70130
(504) 378-2840 • lukeneworleans.com • Established: 2007

SCENE & STORY

Mid-city native and James Beard award-winning chef John Besh's Lüke (one of a half dozen eateries he owns) has gorgeous tile floors and high, shiny tin-clad ceilings and a mouthwatering menu of dishes like 25-cent oysters, redfish "court-bouillon" (with crab, shrimp, oysters, and rice); and shrimp "en cocotte" (with creamy white-corn grits and andouille). But it's the succulent Lüke burger that sings, with juicy tomatoes, smoky bacon from Madisonville, Tennessee, perfectly caramelized onions, and Emmentaler cheese with seasoned, thick-cut fries. That gloriously rich ensemble is worth the trip alone. But Heiner Brau, up in Covington, across Lake Pontchartrain, brews Besh's house beers, which have included Lüke Fru (a delicate Kölsch), Lüke Export (a pils with Austrian hops) Lüke Alt (an aged, Düsseldorf-style lager, well matched with meatier fare), and Mardi Gras Festbier, a smooth, potent bock, make the whole package even tastier.

PHILOSOPHY

Nostalgic. Besh sought to make Lüke an homage to the grand old Franco-German brasseries that once reigned in New Orleans, and it succeeds beautifully.

KEY BEER

Bok, or bock (German for "goat") is a strong lager brewed in the winter to drink in early spring. If your timing is right (December to February), go for the medium-bodied Festbier version of this style, which is copper-hued with a smooth malty profile and just enough acidity and bitterness to complement the rich flavors of the burger.

CRESCENT CITY BREWHOUSE

527 Decatur St. • New Orleans, LA 70130
(888) 819-9330 or (504) 522-0571
crescentcitybrewhouse.com • Established: 1991

SCENE & STORY

Overlooking the busy pedestrian area of Decatur Street in the French Quarter, the oldest brewpub in New Orleans features a handsome oval-shaped wooden bar, oyster bar, and musicians' area overshadowed by copper German kettles and a huge sign reading OYSTERS and below that "air conditioned," the two best reasons to come here. Dating to 1794, the building is fairly huge, and in addition to the ground and patio levels there's a small garden terrace and airy patio upstairs overlooking the street. While the food earns good marks, the best way to experience this bar may be by popping in for a look at the copper work, then buying a beer in a plastic cup from the street-level bar, and heading on your way uptown in a taxi.

PHILOSOPHY

Traditional. House brews from the 17 bbl system include a Pilsner, Vienna-style lager, Munich-style dark, and unfiltered wheat beer, all basic and to some degrees boring;

hopefully the brewers will take a look at Nola, Tin Roof, and Bayou Teche and step up their game.

KEY BEER

Black Forest, a Munich-style dark lager, is a medium- to light-bodied brew with roasty notes of caramel and dark chocolate.

THE BULLDOG

3236 Magazine St. • New Orleans, LA 70115 • (504) 891-1516
bulldog.draftfreak.com • Established: 1994

THE BULLDOG MIDCITY

5135 Canal Blvd. • New Orleans, LA 70124 • (504) 488-4191
bulldog-midcity.draftfreak.com • Established: 2004

SCENE & STORY

Magazine Street, in the area generally referred to as uptown (and bordering the Garden District) is lined with cool old bars, shops, art galleries, and eateries, and makes a nice change from the French Quarter, which varies from magical to insufferably touristy. The original Bulldog on Magazine Street has fifty beers on tap and a hundred in bottles, standard pub fare, and a spacious patio out back featuring a fountain made of beer taps. The mid-city location is a bit more upscale; both bars offer easygoing environments that make them worth a stop on a pub-crawl. The Bulldog has two other locations as well: Baton Rouge (where you can try the latest brews from Tin Roof,

Louisiana's most recent craft brewery to fire up), and Jackson, Mississippi.

PHILOSOPHY

Good fun for good causes. There are generally a lot of Tulane and Loyola students, and it's dog friendly, donating often to the local Humane Society and ASPCA. Wednesdays are popular as everyone gets to keep the pint glasses, or, by leaving them, donate to the causes.

KEY BEER

Nola Blonde, an easygoing, light-bodied brew first released in March 2009, is grainy, pale gold, and has an angular hop attack for the style.

COOTER BROWN'S TAVERN, GRILL, & OYSTER BAR

509 S. Carrollton Ave. • New Orleans, LA 70118
(504) 886-9104 • cooterbrowns.com • Established: 1977

SCENE & STORY

The gloriously dive-y Cooter Brown's, in the Riverbend area of uptown New Orleans, is the eccentric granddaddy of New Orleans beer bars, with a vast hoard of beer (358 bottles and 42 taps), pool tables, pressed tin walls, wood slatted ceilings, and a gallery of ceramic caricatures of "dead celebrities," clutching beers related somehow to their careers ("Jimmy Dean, an unfulfilled acting career cut short by tragedy, grips a bottle of Golden Promise," explains the website). It's a classic, plain and simple.

PHILOSOPHY

No frills. You'll hear it described as a good beer bar and a place to mingle with drunken Tulane students and eccentric locals, and it is indeed both, as well as a decent place to go for oysters and crawfish.

KEY BEER

A deliciously safe bet is Duvel in a 12-ounce bottle, the classic 8.5% ABV Belgian strong pale ale. It's a big, refreshing, kicky beer with fine effervescence and Champagne dryness that can stand the extra shelf time that comes for beers in bars with huge lists.

DETOUR ➡ RUINS & RESURRECTION

Not so long ago, of course, all the laughter ended in The Big Easy. When the floodwaters of Katrina breached in August 2005, the area's breweries took a serious hit along with the rest of the beleaguered city. Hardest hit was Dixie Brewing Company, opened in New Orleans in 1907. A familiar landmark in town for 98 grand years, Dixie was inundated with 8 or 9 feet of water.

Today the wracked shell of a building stands as a grim reminder of what the region suffered in the great storm. Visible from I-90 over on Tulane Avenue, the red brick behemoth stands scarred, its windows blackened and broken out, the interior emptied, the brewing equipment long looted and sold for scrap. After the storm, the owners talked of coming back, but costs were prohibitive, and today the ruins gloam over 3rd Ward streets with an abiding sadness. Once the largest brewery in town and the pride of the region, the catastrophic storm reduced it to an empty hulk.

As of mid-2011 there are competing plans to either redevelop or raze the ruins. So if it's still there, make sure to drive past it a few times, perhaps slowing down for a picture or two (it's not currently a safe area to walk around on foot), and apprehend a powerful reminder of what New Orleans once was—the brewing capital of the South. Locals seem resigned to the fact that the wrecking ball can't be far off, but perhaps someone whose heart beats for an old brewery will find a way to make it work.

It's a heavy thing to take in—a real specter of death and destruction—so the best thing you can do next is to head to nearby Mandina's, on Canal Street, for some Italo-Creole comfort food (3800 Canal St.; 504-482-9179). Its quaint pink-with-white trim exterior and front porch conceals thirteen-foot-high ceilings, bow-tied waiters, and a clientele of cheery, well-dressed locals and policemen chatting away. On the day I visited, it felt like a scene from *Back to the Future*.

Refreshingly, there were no tourists whatsoever. I took my seat in the first dining room and ordered an iced tea. Over my left shoulder I spotted a faded old *Times-Picayune* story about how the place was opened in 1932 by the sons of Sebastian Mandina, from Palermo, Sicily. He'd opened it as a shop in 1898, and was briefly jailed for selling home brew, hidden in a false window in the store. It became a neighborhood—and, indeed, citywide—institution, and stayed in the Mandina family.

Katrina tried to silence this place too, deluging the dining room up to about six feet. But because the restaurant is raised up from street level, the water came up to just below the tabletops, which were found eerily still set when Cindy Mandina first ventured back inside about six weeks after the storm. Now restored to its 1930s luster by Cindy and her family, the food is excellent and the portions hearty. The catfish po'boy is one of the best sandwiches I've ever eaten, in any city. And a word to the wise: the "whole loaf" is huge; the "half loaf" could feed two people, and the quarter loaf is just right for one.

DETOUR ➡ NEW ORLEANS' BEST COMFORT FOOD

Central Grocery (deli & market) • 923 Decatur St. • New Orleans, LA 70116 • (504) 523-1620
& Café du Monde (café) • 800 Decatur St. • New Orleans, LA 70116 • (504) 587-0831

Unless you have superhuman powers of self-control, exploring the beer bars and eateries of the French Quarter in New Orleans will lead to foggy mornings, your brain, body, and soul crying out for sugar, caffeine, and fatty Italian meats on bread. First, proceed to the wonderfully decayed Café du Monde, a traditional coffee stand open since 1862 (and open every day except Christmas). One order of beignet per person (say "behn-yay") means three puffy warm dough fritters gloriously dusted with powdered sugar. The joe is strong and not too terrible, though the chicory version is an acquired taste, a blend of coffee and dried endive plant root that was favored during the Civil War.

Just down the block is Central Grocery, an Italian market opened in 1906 and home of the muffaletta, the signature New Orleans sandwich. The concept is simple: it's a circular loaf of soft Italian bread sliced horizontally, layered with top-quality sliced ham, salami, and provolone cheese. That trio is then capped with a layer of olive salad—chopped green and black olives minced with anchovies and garlic. A half feeds two adults handily, and if there's room in the back, you can sit at a little lunch counter and tuck in, or head back outside and try for a bench in front of St. Louis Cathedral in Jackson Square. With the perfect sandwich, the riverboats, and the former home of Jax Brewery (now a shopping area) in view, you're suddenly, completely whole again.

BAYOU TECHE BREWING CO.

1106 Bushville Hwy. • Arnaudville, Louisiana, 70512
(337) 303-8000 • bayoutechebrewing.com • Established: 2010

SCENE & STORY

It's a family affair. Early in 2010 the brothers Knott (Karlos, Byron, and Dorsey) opened the doors on their little train-car-turned-taproom on farmland once used for growing beans, a good-sized patch of earth maintained by the Knott family since the 1800s. Karlos and his brothers grew up in a Cajun French–speaking home, and their father Floyd writes about Acadiana, the traditional Cajun name for the area. The only beers around when the boys were growing up in the area were Jax (defunct), Budweiser, and Falstaff, all industrial lagers. Later Karlos served in the military in Germany and then at Fort Lewis in Washington State, and loved the good beers he drank in both locations. On Saint Patrick's Day 2008, they decided to brew professionally. After all, they had a place to do it: the family farm.

To find that farm you drive west and a hair north out of New Orleans for about two-and-a-half hours and wend along LA-31 beside the serpentine Bayou Teche, the 125-mile waterway leading from Arnaudville to the Gulf. As Karlos puts it, the next part involves a T in the road, a Piggly Wiggly store, and "left turn at the twelfth station of the cross." One way or another you'll find their Bayou Teche Brewery, once a nano-sized, 1 bbl project with modest ambitions,

and today a vital presence in Southern craft brewing. "The local Budweiser distributor told us locals didn't want craft beer," recalls Karlos, who has a grey-flecked beard, dark eyes, and a genteel manner. "I said 'well, maybe they haven't been offered it,' and sure enough, the beer we'd planned for three months sold out in three days."

It has been a wild ride since then for these bayou brothers, who were hit so hard with demand that Lazy Magnolia Brewery in Kiln, Mississippi agreed to help them meet it by contracting some extra capacity. This is Cajun country, and you'll hear some great music in the taproom, perhaps even from the musically talented brothers. In 2011, the Knotts broke ground on a new 8,000-square-foot facility to house their 15 bbl brew house, but the train car taproom will stay intact.

PHILOSOPHY

Low Country craft with a side of Southern ease. Karlos and his brothers had been home brewing batches for crawfish boils and gumbos for years when the idea took hold to step things up and invest in a pilot brewery. "We thought it would be best to brew beers to complement our low country style of cuisine, and with some hoppier flavors, too, to go with all the pork fat we use," Knott recalls.

KEY BEER

LA 31 Bière Pâle, their Belgian-inflected pale ale named for the state highway, was intended to be the flagship, but Grenade (pronounced grah-nod), a wheat beer brewed with passion fruit juice (another local wild fruit) quickly overtook it. The most unique is Boucanée ("smoked"), a lightly smoked wheat beer. As the story goes, there's a local species of wild cherry tree, and when the Knotts were kids, their grandparents would cut one tree down per year. The women would make a liqueur called "cherry bounce" and the men would cut up the branches for smoking andouille and tasso and sausage. This beer is their homage to that tradition. Thirsty yet?

ABITA BREWING COMPANY

21084 Hwy. 36 • Abita Springs, LA 70433 • (985) 893-3143
abita.com • Established: 1986

ABITA BREWPUB

72011 Holly St. • Abita Springs, LA 70420
(985) 892-5837 • Established: 1994

SCENE & STORY

Abita was the first southeastern craft brewery to emerge and today, with both a modern brewery and the original brewpub, has an epochal feel, like a shiny new stadium in a town with the old bleachers down the road. To get to the new 49,000-square-foot brewery from New Orleans you drive the straight 30-mile shot across Lake Pontchartrain toward St. Tammany Parrish and Covington and veer right toward Abita Springs. The brewery owners settled on their location due to the presence of the five-million year-old aquifer of soft artesian water, a celebrated font that happens to have a perfect pH for brewing and requires no spendy chemical adjustment. The local Chocktaw Indians used this water for medicinal purposes, and turn-of-the-century tourists traveled there to recover from yellow fever. You can—and should!—drink it from water fountains inside the brewery on the tour.

Visitors (minor hordes actually, with over 18,000 clocked per year at present) convene in a large, porticoed taproom with a wide mahogany bar and watch a surprisingly thorough video before taking a tour amid the brewery's enormous 400 bbl tanks the size of school buses. It's a sociable place, and it's hardly surprising that one of the main tour guides is an affable brewer by the name of Sonny Day II, a well-respected veteran of Dixie Brewing Company now helping run the show.

The original brewery location just down the road has, since 1994, housed a 100-seat brewpub where you can sample a few house beers Abita doesn't bottle, like a recent Black IPA. Behind its white picket fence and cypress window frames, it's a nice enough place to spend some time after the tour. Expect above average southeastern pub fare, though the kitchen hasn't done much cooking with Abita beer.

PHILOSOPHY

Abita has grown like a beanstalk since the day it opened in 1986 with a capacity for 1,500 bbl, and modernized operations considerably, including the installment of a unique brewing kettle device called the Merlin, a massive steel heating agent more common in Europe and prized for efficiency. Along the way the company has headed north of 80,000 barrels produced annually, but managed to keep a somewhat soulful image. In the aftermath of Hurricane Katrina, Abita launched a beer they dubbed Fleur de Lis Restoration Pale Ale and raised over half a million dollars for hurricane relief, having been spared themselves from major physical damages, and in 2010 released SOS Pilsner to raise funds for the BP Gulf Oil recovery efforts. The brewery is run by David Blossman, a longtime craft beer enthusiast and original shareholder.

"People say there's no beer culture [here], and I just have to disagree," says Blossman. He ties craft beer's success in the Crescent City to the incredible food scene, with its ambitious chefs and a panoply of influences. "We owe a lot of our success to the chefs who took us under their wings," he explains, echoing a point often made in the city's taprooms: the beer scene is intertwined with dining, a central facet of life. Ambitious chefs working from farmer's markets have helped open the city palate wider, expanding on the already wide spectrum of Cajun, Creole, French, North American, and African American traditions. And of course, it's The Big Easy: people like to drink here. "It's a different lifestyle. People like to slow down. We're very social," Blossman adds.

KEY BEER

Abita is best known for its caramel-colored and light-bodied amber (4.5% ABV), but the company has six other year-round beers in all, in addition to five seasonals plus occasional one-offs for the pub brewed on Sonny Day's one-barrel pilot system. The best for daytime drinking is Restoration Ale, a deep gold, lightly dry-hopped ale with Cascade hops, or Purple Haze, a light and cloudy American style wheat ale (4.2% ABV) blended with raspberry puree post-filtration, giving it a fruity zing.

HEINER BRAU

226 E. Lockwood St. • Covington, LA 70433 • (888) 910-BEER
(985) 893-2884 • heinerbrau.com • Established: 2005

SCENE & STORY

Just off the town square in quiet Covington, one of the South's most unusual breweries—one which wouldn't look out of place in the Alps—is Heiner Brau. There, German-born, bred, and trained brewer Henryk "Heiner" Orlik holds court, having left his native home to brew in the United States in 1994 with nary a glance back. The irrepressibly friendly Bavarian came to this country to get in on the burgeoning craft beer industry; the trade in Germany has been slowing down for decades. After stints in Cleveland, at nearby Abita, and in North Carolina, he opened up Heiner Brau in Covington's barn-like old passenger rail station in 2005.

The brewery itself is one of the most photogenic in the South, a copper clad 15 bbl system set by two rows of low copper-clad tanks by big windows (the better to show off the gear, with lighting on the tanks after dark). There are brewing photos and artifacts arranged throughout, giving it a quaint museum feel.

"I'm really blessed for great conditions in America," says Heiner, who has raised four kids with his wife and seems to have a permanent grin on his face along with the brisk, helpful manners of a Bavarian. He's brewing around 2,500 to 3,000 bbl per year, and contract brewing a couple of projects beyond the three main beers of the Heiner Brau line. Heiner, to put it in American vernacular, is loving it. "For me, it's a dream come true to start a small brewery. The best time in my life has been in America. I'm a lucky person." Tours are free on Saturdays at 10, 10:45, and 11:30 a.m., starting with German precision.

PHILOSOPHY

By the books—mostly. Orlik trained at Doemens Academy in Germany, and like all trained brewers in Germany, is most comfortable (and quite proud) to be working within the strictures of *Reinheitsgebot*, a medieval German "purity" edict that holds brewers to four base ingredients (malt/wheat, hops, yeast, and water), using naturally generated carbonation, and a variety of other strictures.

KEY BEER

In addition to his contract beers and seasonals, Heiner does three main brews: Maibock, Hefe-Weisse, and Strawberry Ale, his most popular brand and also his least traditional (and one he would hesitate to brew in hidebound Germany). After a festival for the red fruits in the area, Heiner began experimenting with adding the berries to beer, eventually settling on a method of adding the berries into a conditioning tank after removing yeast so the alcohol level wouldn't spike. The result was a sensation locally; customers wanted the first kegs—the slushiest ones—full of all that berriness. To the hop head, it's hard to swallow, but a thirsty traveler can get into the spirit. "I'm very proud about this one," says Orlik. "In the summer, when you work in the garden, it's very refreshing." Yep—just about as refreshing as finding a traditional German brewery in rural Louisiana.

BEST of the REST: LOUISIANA

DBA NEW ORLEANS

618 Frenchmen St. • New Orleans, LA 70116-2002 • (504) 942-3731 • dbabars.com/dbano

Opened in 2000, The Big Easy outpost of good-beer maven Ray Deter's trio of good beer bars (along with one in Manhattan and one in Brooklyn), DBA New Orleans is located down on Frenchmen Street in an historic building far enough from the touristy Quarter to keep the yahoos out but not so far it feels dangerous or too quiet (still, it's best to travel in groups or cabs at night). Expect high ceilings and walls made of cypress, exposed brick, black chalkboards with beer and whiskeys well organized, and a steady stream of impressive bands like the Dirty Dozen Brass Band, with occasional appearances by the likes of Jimmy Buffett and Stevie Wonder.

COLUMBIA STREET TAP ROOM AND GRILL

434 N. Columbia St. • Covington, LA 70433 • (985) 898-0899 • columbiastreettaproom

The home of Heiner Brau and a good little oyster bar (Buster's Place), Covington (population: 9,000) has a sleepy Mayberry feel. Still, it comes alive on occasion, especially when the frequent live bands fire up at "the tap room," as this craft beer bar opened in 1996 is commonly called. It's got classic old bar appointments, with exposed brick walls and high ceilings, old Dixie Beer signs, and a wide, handsome antique bar. Built in 1906 by the Seilers, a prominent family in town, the building operated for years as a tavern-inn with lodgings on the second floor. Of the thirty taps, about half are Louisiana brews from the likes of Heiner, Abita, and Bayou Teche, with some better imports such as Blanche de Bruxelles thrown in for good measure. The draught lineup is complemented by a smallish but solid bottle list, as well as a selection of burgers and soul food.

THE BARLEY OAK

2101 Lakeshore Dr. • Mandeville, LA 70448 • (985) 727-7420 • thebarleyoak.com

Located at the end of a residential road on the north shore of Lake Pontchartrain, the Barley Oak (est. 2009) is a new British- and German-themed pub with a patio-equipped upstairs bar drawing from a selection of 47 taps and 120 bottles. The service is warm and friendly; the view from the patio on a clear day, looking south toward New Orleans over a Spanish-moss-draped live oak and miles of blue water, is unbeatable. Beer prices run high on rarer brews; still, there could be no better place to catch a sunset and an inexpensive bite (nothing over $11) before heading back into NoLa for the evening. The draught list represents locals with pride, and among the mostly conventional bottle list are some goodies from Blaugies, Brooklyn, Jolly Pumpkin, and Mikkeller.

North Carolina

★ ★ ★

Asheville

What makes a beer city come of age? It seems that when towns of a sociable size (say, 50,000 to about 500,000) gain a certain preponderance of outdoorsy young and college folk, a jamming-good music and craft beer scene cannot be far behind. Along with Boulder, Colorado; Portland, Oregon; and San Diego, California, leafy Asheville, North Carolina (and the surrounding area) has become a hotbed of brewing over the past few years—especially since the state legislature raised the limit for beer's alcohol content from 6 percent to 15 percent in 2005 after a campaign led by brewer Sean Lilly Wilson, who went on to found Fullsteam Brewing Company in Durham—and shows little sign of slowing down. Then there's the famous Southern food and hospitality, which, of course, is charming.

HIGHLAND BREWING

12 Old Charlotte Hwy., Ste. H • Asheville, NC 28803
(828) 299-3370 • highlandbrewing.com • Established: 1986

SCENE & STORY

Asheville's original craft brewery launched under the watchful (and patient) eyes of brewer John Lyda and Oscar Wong, a retired engineer, using retrofitted dairy equipment. Located today in a converted warehouse atop a hill just a short drive from the center of town, it's one of Asheville's top craft beer draws and brews some 20,000 bbls a year, making it a good-sized operation. In the taproom (open Monday through Saturday from 4 p.m. to 8 p.m.), revelers gather for tours amid converted container ship units that serve as offices, a music stage, plenty of seats and tables, and a draft bar with year round-releases and seasonals. The tours and samples are free, but donations of food and cash are accepted for local charities, a nice touch. Visitors gather in the taproom for $3.50 pints afterwards and during the blues, bluegrass, and other Americana-inspired shows.

PHILOSOPHY

Highland's beers broke early ground, but could be maddeningly uneven at first. After about eight years of trial and error, the outfit began to turn the corner with a lineup of assertive beers. It's a rather conventional lineup, from light wheat on up to stouts, porters, and other strong ales, but recent brews have shown a more experimental side, with amped up dry hopping regimes, oak barrel aging, fruit additions, and Belgian styles entering the mix.

KEY BEER

The amber-hued Gaelic Ale (5.8% ABV) with its graham cracker sweetness and kiss of Cascade and Willamette hops is something of a flagship, but it's the roasty, mocha-tinged Highland Oatmeal Porter (also 5.8% ABV) that shows off Highland's brewing chops most consistently.

BARLEY'S TAPROOM & PIZZERIA

42 Biltmore • Asheville, NC 28801 • (828) 255-0504
www.barleystaproom.com • Established: 1994

SCENE & STORY

Every beer bar should have the luxury of this much room. In a renovated, 8,000 square foot 1920s former appliance store in the heart of Asheville's arts and entertainment district, Barley's is more than a beer bar. It's also a restaurant and music venue, with New York-style sourdough pizza made from the spent grains of local breweries (and other pub fare) to go with all the live Americana music on offer several nights a week. Better yet, there's no cover. The twenty-four-tap ground floor is a deep space of weathered wood floors and tables, handsome wooden bar with high "captain's chairs," and tinned and carved timber ceilings. For a game of pool, head upstairs to a room of regulation slate billiard tables available by the hour, plus darts and nineteen additional taps.

PHILOSOPHY

This is a shrine for the Southern craft beer awakening: of the approximately one hundred total beers available on draught or in bottles, just under half are from the South, while the rest are mostly from American brewers.

KEY BEER

Pisgah's hazy orange organic Pale Ale (5.5% ABV) is the perfect pizza beer: crisp, a touch sweet, and finishing with enough bitter bite to stand up to the zip of the sauce and meats.

★ ★ ★

THE THIRSTY MONK

92 Patton Ave. • Asheville, NC 28801
(828) 254-5470 • monkpub.com • Established: 2008

SCENE & STORY

The first thing you'll notice about the Monk, provided it's daylight, is that the outside of the bar is painted a funny color: purple. Then you enter the place by way of a long ramp, which seems a bit odd, and drop into a narrow space with cream walls and high ceilings. And there you are: one of the more recent additions to the Asheville scene, the Thirsty Monk happens to be one of the best in the country, with 44 taps and 220 bottles of American and Belgian craft specialties. The deep and thoughtful beer list is complemented by innovative beer-friendly foods sourced from local purveyors including farm lamb, bakery breads, cheese, mustard, and trout, which provides for smoked trout sandwiches. It's a happy and bright place with a steady stream of special events, brewer appearances, and other beer-centric gatherings. A second location, nicknamed Monk South by locals, opened in the Gerber Village shopping center in late 2009 with its own 30 tap/200 bottle combination.

PHILOSOPHY

Belgian-style beers and hospitality with Southern soul.

KEY BEER

If the Monk's house beer is available, order it. Otherwise start with a palate cleansing SweetWater Road Trip, a 5.3% ABV German-style Pilsner, then wade into a Gnomegang, a 9.5% ABV collaboration beer made by New York's Ommegang with La Chouffe of Belgium that is rich, complex, citrusy, spicy, and earthy all at once.

The BREWGRASS FESTIVAL

Held each year on the third weekend of September in the big grassy expanse of Asheville's Martin Luther King, Jr. Park (the 2011 event is the fifteenth annual), the Brewgrass festival draws around 120 selections from forty top-tier craft breweries—including regional favorites like Pisgah, Catawba Valley, and Nantahala Brewing Company. Those liquid treasures accompany and celebrate a world-class lineup of bluegrass bands from the old-school masters like J. D. Crowe and Norman Blake to high-intensity jamgrass acts like the Yonder Mountain String Band. Time to break out the tie-dye and sandals. *brewgrassfestival.com*

PACK'S TAVERN

20 S. Spruce St. • Asheville, NC 28801-3745
(828) 225-6944 • packstavern.com • Established: 2010

SCENE & STORY

Just a couple of blocks east of Barley's Taproom, the Hayes and Hopson building (a historic property on Asheville's Pack Square Park) has housed merchants of lumber, auto parts, barbecue, and most notoriously moonshine, but today the newly renovated structure contains a classy-casual beer-focused eatery. The interior is airy, spacious, and decked out with comforts like church pews in the waiting area, plush leather banquettes, and cool tile floors under the bar.

PHILOSOPHY

There are some thirty or more local, national, and international craft beers, and the owners have pledged to work with area brewers to tap one-off and other limited quantity releases, such as recent cask night with Victory Brewing Company of Downingtown, Pennsylvania. The draft list features the latest from Craggie, Highland, and French Broad Brewing (all from Asheville) in addition to a good but not pointlessly large selection of other crafts (and a few macros to boot).

KEY BEER

Look for Craggie's Toubab Brewe, a slightly tangy 4.2% ABV *kellerbier* (unfiltered lager) that would pair well with much of the pub grub on offer.

>>>>> SWEET SPOT <<<<<

Don't leave town without hitting Tupelo Honey Café (12 College St., 828-255-4683; tupelohoneycafe.com) for their signature dish, a large buttermilk pancake flavored with cinnamon and sweet potatoes, topped with whipped peach butter and spiced pecans. Tip: Add Grandma's Maple Granola for extra crunch. Your waistline may not thank you, but your taste buds will.

LEXINGTON AVENUE BREWERY

39 N. Lexington Ave. • Asheville, NC 28801
(828) 252-0212 • lexavebrew.com • Established: 2010

SCENE & STORY

With color-shifting night club illumination on brewing tanks behind curving glass and a serpentine bar snaking amid mixed exposed brick, polished and distressed metals, wood paneling, and other trendy stylings, the LAB opened in 2010 and seems at first glance more cocktail den than beer bar. But the special effects are restricted to the bar area, while the larger seating section is open, communal, and rather traditional for a brewpub. It's all a refreshing change of atmosphere from old weather-beaten wood, and the Kobe beef sliders and burgers fly out of the kitchen.

PHILOSOPHY

Crowd pleasers. While the "L.A.B." nickname and brewhouse lighting announces a futuristic approach, the actual beer list is presently rooted in the Reagan years.

KEY BEER

Nitrogen-powered taps ("on nitro") give certain beers added silkiness and a densely creamy head; try the 6% ABV Chocolate Stout to see what it's all about.

125-B Roberts St. • Asheville, NC 28801 • (828) 505-2792
wedgebrewing.com • Established: 2010

SCENE & STORY

It takes extra effort to find the Wedge taproom, located in the lower level of a dilapidated old warehouse in Asheville's French Broad River Arts district (just keep the number handy or call, should you get lost). Once used for meatpacking and food storage, the brewery, taproom, and arty patio area overlook a rail yard, and the beer produced there is, like Pisgah's outside of town, fast becoming sought after by beer-savvy locals.

PHILOSOPHY

Beer, the best form of art. There are multiple sculptures and artworks on the grounds and inside the pub area, adding to the overall progressive, community-based good vibes.

KEY BEER

Try the Golem, a 9% ABV strong Belgian Pale Ale with a hazy gold color and rich notes of apricot, wheat, and a lingering spiciness reminiscent of cinnamon and white pepper.

150 Eastside Dr. • Black Mountain, NC 28711
(828) 669-0190 • pisgahbrewing.com • Established: 2004

SCENE & STORY

Part of the proud American tradition of accomplished brewpubs in downright weird places, Pisgah resides in a nondescript industrial park about twenty minutes outside Asheville with absolutely no pomp and circumstance—the sign is smaller than a spider's eye, with approximately one-inch lettering. All of the energy goes into the organically brewed beers, produced on a small system. There's also an outdoor fire pit, pool table, some picnic benches, and an outdoor stage for blues, rock, and reggae acts as talented as the legendary Steel Pulse. Who needs a spendy tap room in the middle of town?

PHILOSOPHY

Green is the color. Pisgah was the first certified organic brewery in the Southeast.

KEY BEER

Look for the Vortex II Russian Imperial Stout, a devilishly smooth and drinkable 11.7% ABV elixir of roasted black malt flavors.

BRUISIN' ALES

66 Broadway St. • Asheville, NC 28801 • (828) 252-8999
bruisin-ales.com • Established: 2006

SCENE & STORY

The presence of a truly great comprehensive bottle shop can propel a small city to find its craft beer feet and take off running for the good stuff. By making available a wide range of international and domestic craft beers to locals, the store stokes a thirst for homegrown breweries and quality beer bars. Bruisin' Ales fills that essential role in Asheville, with over nine hundred beers handsomely and carefully presented in a bright, clean space (with two taps as well).

PHILOSOPHY

"Teach a man to fish . . ." It's a hub of Asheville's craft beer scene, offering events and classes, brewer appearances, meet-ups of the Asheville Brewers Alliance, which is working to promote beer tourism and area festivals.

KEY BEER

The deliciously named (and made) Conduplico Immundus Monachus, from South Carolina's Thomas Creek Brewery (10% ABV). It's a mouthful of dark brown sugar, cocoa, and caramel tastes with a fruity edge.

Farmville

THE DUCK-RABBIT CRAFT BREWERY

4519 W. Pine St. • Farmville, NC 27828 • (252) 753-7745
duckrabbitbrewery.com • Established: 2004

SCENE & STORY

"The dark beer specialists" at Duck-Rabbit have grown their business into a small regional brewery, producing around 3,700 barrels annually and steadily rising. Based in the sleepy town of Farmville (which lives up to its name), it's really only a small, packaging-only operation built in a light industrial garage, but there's a cozy new taproom for guests to sample brewer Paul Philippon's much-lauded creations, like his 9% ABV Baltic Porter and a variety of other stouts and dark beers (he prefers the darker end of the spectrum).

PHILOSOPHY

Dark beer, light heart. Philippon is a former philosophy teacher, and wanted to honor his past by illustrating labels with a classic Gestalt shift diagram, which appears as either a duck or a rabbit, or something else entirely depending on how many beers you've had.

KEY BEER

Well, is it a duck or a rabbit? Try the 5.6% ABV Brown Ale, which is nutty, smooth, and chocolate-y without being too sweet.

Raleigh

THE RALEIGH TIMES BAR

14 E. Hargett St. • Raleigh, NC 27601 • (919) 833-0999
raleightimesbar.com • Established: 2006

SCENE & STORY

The hip nonsmoking bar known as the Raleigh Times goes back to 2006 but the building's history is a hundred years older, having housed the august *Raleigh Times*—the newspaper—up until its last edition ran in 1989. Part of a small complex of interconnected businesses with a breakfast counter (Morning Times), eatery (Dining Times), and hipper bar (RTBX), the atmospheric Times Bar has high tinned ceilings, old exposed brick walls, and hardwood floors next to a wide, burnished wood bar. It's timeless; one half expects Atticus Finch to walk in here clutching a story to take up with the editors in righteous fury.

PHILOSOPHY

All the beer that's fit to drink. While there are only eight draft beers at a time (mostly from area producers), the bottle list has more than a hundred selections, half of which are American craft releases (especially from North Carolina and the surrounding states), and half Belgians.

KEY BEER

The list includes sours and other oddities like Drie Fonteinen Kriek, a Belgian sour beer made with cherries.

Charlotte

GROWLER'S POURHOUSE

3116 N. Davidson St. • Charlotte, NC 28205 • (704) 910-6566
growlerspourhouse.com • Established: 2010

SCENE & STORY

The pace of the Southern craft beer revolution quickened in 2010 with the arrival of Growler's in Charlotte's arty NoDa area (North of Downtown). With impressive antique Chinese doors, heavy wood tables, hardwood floors, and chic track lighting, it strikes a classy pose. But the beer and "beer food" are more than window dressing. Choose from fourteen taps and one rotating cask served from a nineteenth-century hand-pump engine, house-made hot dogs, sausages, and an oyster bar with rotating varieties; treats like peel-and-eat shrimp and tableside marshmallow roasting make this place even more fun.

PHILOSOPHY

House-made or bust. Even the potato chips are fried in the kitchen.

KEY BEER

Foothills Brewing Co. from Winston-Salem ought to be on tap; look for their Sexual Chocolate (9.75% ABV), a burly Russian Imperial Stout.

Durham

FULLSTEAM

726 Rigsbee Ave. • Durham, NC 27701

(919) 682-BEER or (888) 756-9274

fullsteam.ag • Established: 2010

SCENE & STORY

Just north of downtown Durham near the corner of Geer and Rigsbee, start looking for a huge backwards "F," the symbol of this upstart brewery in a spacious, beige brick warehouse with a pub inside. Consider it your duty: North Carolina beer travelers owe a lot to the founders of Fullsteam. For one, Sean Lilly Wilson is the man whose "Pop the Cap" campaign successfully raised the state's allowable beer alcohol limit to 15 percent in 2005); he joined with former Abita head brewer Brooks Hamaker and über home brewer Chris Davis to launch one of the South's most ambitious breweries.

The trio's R+D Tavern (on-site, enclosed in a boxy red room inside the brewery) is a family-friendly tavern/indoor beer garden featuring Fullsteam beer, guest taps of North Carolina beers, music and events, and dining options via food trucks (the website features a calendar of events, which is helpful).

PHILOSOPHY

Originally launched under the banner of "plow-to-pint beer from the beautiful South," Fullsteam is brewing beers that seem unusual not only in said sunny region, they're newfangled for the whole Craft Beer Nation. There are three categories: Workers' Compensation, a group of session beers led by Fullsteam Southern Lager (5.5% ABV); Apothecary, for "radical, farm-focused" beers including Hogwash, a hickory-smoked porter, and Summer Basil; and the Forager series, which utilizes fruit and other fermentables that members of the community are invited to sell to the brewery at a fair market price in exchange for some of the finished beer (and bragging rights, of course). Local persimmons and pears have already made it into the rotation. Other brews either already out or in development make use of parsnip, kudzu, rhubarb, and sweet potato, even grits. All these adjuncts, of course, are part and parcel of the Southern abundance, and one has to wonder, what next?

KEY BEER

Summer Basil, the first beer brewed on Fullsteam's commercial system, is a 5.5% ABV summer seasonal with fresh local basil added. The idea was born when Wilson plunged a grip of fresh leaves into a can of Budweiser while at a house party. The resulting beer is a hazy, peachy gold ale with a bready body and green herb overtones.

BEST *of the* REST: NORTH CAROLINA

JACK OF THE WOOD PUBLIC HOUSE
95 Patton Ave. • Asheville, NC 28801 • (828) 252-5445, ext. 105 • jackofthewood.com

Asheville-go-bragh. A hippified Celtic beer bar in downtown Asheville, Jack of the Wood was the original location of Green Man Brewing and still serves five of its beers, with a small selection of brews from beyond town (even Brooklyn!). There are popular jam sessions on Wednesdays (from 6 p.m.), Thursdays (bluegrass, after 9 p.m.) and Sundays (Irish, starting at 5 p.m.), and frequent weekend bands for little or no cover charge.

GREEN MAN BREWERY
23 Buxton Ave. • Asheville, NC 28801 • (828) 252-5502 • greenmanbrewery.com

A hard-to-find, soccer-friendly brewery first established in 1997 at the current location of Jack of the Wood and later moved to its current, garage-like incarnation, Green Man is also known as Dirty Jack's. With a wide blond-wood bar, a range of well-made, American-inflected British-style ales (pale, bitter, IPA, ESB, stout, etc.), its light industrial setting is leavened by a roll-up garage door for nice days, along with a covered side porch for al fresco sipping.

THE BIER GARDEN
46 Haywood St. • Asheville, NC 28801 • (828) 285-0002 • ashevillebiergarden.com

A family-friendly, casual, and sports-oriented bar established in 1994, the Bier Garden features about ten North Carolina beers among its thirty taps and some two hundred bottles, one of the best selections in all of Asheville. It's not an actual biergarten, though, being housed partly in an atrium-like space in an office building. Still, it's a good place to try a selection of beers, upscale pub grub, and take in a ball game.

South Carolina

★ ★ ★

Greenville

THE COMMUNITY TAP

205 Wade Hampton Blvd. • Greenville, SC 29609
(864) 631-2525 • thecommunitytap.com • Established: 2010

SCENE & STORY

A top-tier bottle and growler station for beer (and wine, on tap!) that has helped usher in a new era of craft brew appreciation for the city of Greenville, the Community Tap opened in 2010 with ten taps, some 150 breweries in the arsenal, and weekly tastings. It's helping expose locals to an incredible selection of American and imported beers, all carefully kept and displayed. Unlike a lot of bottle shops, it's clean and well organized, not chaotic and dusty.

PHILOSOPHY

Beer shopping should not be like going to a garage sale, with dusty stacks of boxes. Beer shopping should be *exactly* like this.

KEY BEER

What's freshest? Look for South Carolina brewery R.J. Rockers, which makes the intensely flavorful Black Perle (9% ABV), with pinecone like aromas and an opaque black body of roasted malt.

Tennessee

★ ★ ★

Nashville

YAZOO BREWING CO.

910 Division St. • Nashville, TN 37203 • (615) 891-4649
yazoobrew.com • Established: 2003

SCENE & STORY

With founders named Linus and Lila and a beer named Sue, Johnny Cash fans and craft beer lovers alike will want to seek out this craft brewery a short drive from the center of Music City. Brewery tours in the warehouse-like space run on Saturdays only, starting at 2:30 p.m. and continuing every hour until 6:30; $6 with complimentary Yazoo pint glass and beer samples. There's also a cozy taproom open for growler fills only, Wednesdays from 4 to 8 p.m. and Thursday through Saturday from 2 to 8 p.m.

PHILOSOPHY

Linus apprenticed with Garrett Oliver in Brooklyn, and loves to experiment with single-hop varieties and more recently, barrel aging.

KEY BEER

Mexican lagers like Bohemia (the best available) are often descendants of the Vienna-style lager, tending toward a reddish hue, light to medium body, and crackling dry finish. Yazoo's Dos Perros, a superlight American Brown Ale (at just 3.5% ABV) is a great example of the style. And the aforementioned Sue? It's a smoked Imperial Porter on the other end of the intensity spectrum at 9% ABV, a bomber of roasted malt flavor with flavors of nutty caramel and charred bacon fat. In other words, it's a beer that hollers, "My name is Sue! How do you do?"

Kentucky

★ ★ ★

SERGIO'S WORLD BEERS

1605 Story Ave • Louisville, KY 40206 • (502) 618-BEER
sergiosworldbeers.com • Established: 2006

SCENE & STORY

Sergio Ribemboim is a globetrotting Brazilian with an obsessive love for beer, and his man-cave-like shop and taproom in Louisville is a cluttered shrine to beer in every imaginable form from every corner of the planet. With 43 taps and over 1,300 bottles on offer, the correct phrase to describe this cash-only beer-geek destination is "mind-numbing"—there are more than 500 from the United States and 600 from Europe, for starters. Along with the L-shaped bar lined floor to ceiling with coolers, cases, empties, and other ephemera, there's a small seating area and kitchen serving an eclectic menu (fajitas, cheesesteak, spaghetti). The food is often very good, but you're really here to wander among the country's oddest, biggest, and best selections of craft beer from around the globe.

PHILOSOPHY

Ribemboim keeps the outside low profile and the website a bit cryptic; he's not aiming to convert skeptics or please the general consumer, but to delight and awe the aficionado, and he's eager to help when approached.

KEY BEER

There's no itch that cannot be scratched at Sergio's, so take a half hour to peruse the insanity and, if still stumped, ask Sergio for some recommendations.

Best of the Rest: Kentucky

THE BEER TRAPPE

811 Euclid Ave. • Lexington, KY 40502
(859) 309-0911 • *thebeertrappe.com*

Only recently opened (2010), Lexington's top craft beer destination has eight quickly rotating taps, over four hundred bottle selections, leather couches, and walls decked out with brewery signage. The bar also graciously provides tastings, flights, growler fills, and classes, making it a hub for Lexington's growing craft beer community.

★ ★ ★

Mississippi

★ ★ ★

THE MAGNOLIA STATE HAS THE LOWEST LEGAL BEER ALCOHOL TOLERANCE

in the country at 5 percent (alcohol by volume) and, insanely, still outlaws home brewing. Fully half of the counties are still dry. Until the political community sees craft beer for what it is—an enlightened movement toward moderate drinking habits that can bring a state billions in tax dollars when breweries are promoted—craft beer will languish. But for locals, there are a couple of places to gather, sip craft brews, and plot the campaign to get Mississippi at least in line with neighboring states. Recently, a series of beer festivals (Top of the Hops) have been gathering sellout crowds, which sends a strong message. It's only a matter of time. Mississippi, Craft Beer Nation is 100 percent behind you.

Kiln

LAZY MAGNOLIA BREWING CO.

7030 Roscoe-Turner Rd. • Kiln, MS 39556
(228) 467-2727 • lazymagnolia.com • Established: 2005

SCENE & STORY

It's a classic love story, but with a twist (or two). Boy meets girl. Girl buys boy home brewing kit. Boy brews decent beer; girl falls in love with brewing, takes over, goes to brewing school; couple starts brewing company (and boy designs the label). That's the short version for Leslie and Mark Henderson, who met in college and and opened for business in 2005 in an industrial facility in

tiny Kiln (population: 2,000). A crossroads of a town not too far from the Gulf of Mexico and formerly famous only for the presence of Brett Favre's high school, it's not terribly far from New Orleans (about one hour, without traffic). There are free, no-reservation-required tours every Saturday morning, but state law forbids sampling on-site (post-tour, pick up a list of local bars serving the beer). In other words, it's a pilgrimage.

PHILOSOPHY

Named for the flowers that grow along the banks of the nearby Jordan River (and one malnourished, hence "lazy" specimen on the couple's back porch), Lazy Magnolia uses everything from sweet potatoes to roasted pecans and honey from an uncle's bee-keeping operation in the brewing process.

KEY BEER

Beer nuts are usually on the side, but not in the case of Southern Pecan, a caramel-tinted brown ale flavored with whole roasted pecans. It has a sweet, nutty body and easy-drinking alcohol content of just 4.25% ABV.

Hattiesburg

THE KEG & BARREL BREW PUB

1315 Hardy St. • Hattiesburg, MS 39401
(601) 582-7148 • kegandbarrel.com • Established: 2005

SCENE & STORY

The beating heart of Mississippi's craft beer scene, this is a bar in a refurbished 100-year-old house with a wraparound porch and tables in the yard and a good list for a state that is completely backward with regards to beer laws. Due to distribution issues, the bottle list relies on familiar American crafts and everyday imports (though there are some good brews among those, like Samuel Smith's Oatmeal Stout and Franziskaner Hefeweizen). On draft, sought-after kegs run dry with alacrity. It's just not easy to get beer all the way to Hattiesburg.

That is, unless it's made on-site. The Keg & Barrel is also the home of an upstart nanobrewery, Southern Prohibition, now a legal resident in a side room (unlike the early days, when one imagines all sorts of interesting excuses for the aromas wafting around Hattiesburg). With about sixty taps and thirty bottles, the selection is the best around for nearly a hundred miles, absolutely worth a trip for any beer lover in the area. And you won't go hungry: choose from Southern comfort food staples such as fried chicken and waffles, fried green tomatoes, and chicken-fried steak (did someone say fried?).

PHILOSOPHY

This is a friendly little oasis trying to do the right thing for the locals and for the state. For now, the right thing means bringing as many good beers to the area as possible under the limit, which excludes a huge number of beers, but doesn't mean you can't get a good one.

KEY BEER

From Flying Dog to Anchor and Sierra Nevada, there are some familiar and excellent drafts on the list, as well as the whole Lazy Magnolia line. So whatever Southern Prohibition's little nanosystem has kicked out most recently, put it in your glass and tell everyone you meet in the state they need to try it, too.

Oklahoma

★ ★ ★

Tulsa

JAMES MCNELLIE'S PUBLIC HOUSE

409 East 1st St. • Tulsa, OK 74120 • (918) 382-PINT
mcnellies.com • Established: 2004

SCENE & STORY

Also known for its Scotch selection, this huge, two-story beer bar in Tulsa's booming Blue Dome District was inspired by the owner's travels in Ireland and gleams with a huge brass-clad tap row, copper accents, and other old-world flourishes. Today it boasts two spin-off bars—one in Oklahoma City, and one in the town of Norman—but this is the original and Oklahoma's best beer spot. It has 62 beers on tap, two casks on Oklahoma's only beer engines, another 290 bottled brews, and great sweet-potato fries from the long and varied pub menu.

PHILOSOPHY

Classic Irish. The bar draws a mixed crowd of locals, collegians (upstairs is a more raucous smoking area), beer geeks, and families whose kids perform in fiddle jams. (Present company included! My talented nieces Isabella and Sophia have performed there.)

KEY BEER

Drink local. Tulsa's own Marshall Brewing Company typically has two or three brews on draft, like the Pawnee Pale Ale and a resinous, tangy Revival Red. Try those before ambling into the long bottle list, which has some very good options.

Georgia

Athens

THE TRAPPEZE PUB

269 North Hull St. • Athens, GA 30601
(706) 543-8997 • trappezepub.com • Established: 2007

SCENE & STORY

Every beer town worth its salt needs a marquee draw, be it a bar, brewery, bottle shop, or that home-brew store stoking the early sparks. Fortunately for Athens, which has a lively art scene, bike culture, and energetic food-and-drink vibe, the Trappeze Pub pulls off a 33-tap, 200-bottle high-wire routine without breaking a sweat. It can't be easy to maintain such a selection, but in this brightly lit and crisply run bar—all warm terra-cotta-hued walls, big windows, tasteful breweriana and a vast collection of appropriate glassware—but the owners make it seem that way, pulling in vaunted brewers from companies like Belgium's Urthel and Colorado's Left Hand for tasting nights. Inventive pub grub, such as spent-grain breads and beef dishes braised in beer, round out the bill.

PHILOSOPHY

Good beer is not just something to attract customers; it's in the foundations—it really matters here. Which is why the place is often slammed, and why you should go, too.

KEY BEER

The tap row runs heavy on regional favorites from Sweetwater, Terrapin, and Wild Heaven Brewing Company, a Decatur upstart for which Trappeze founder Eric Johnson is the consulting brewmaster (the brand-new company is in expansion phase now, looking to put Decatur on the map as a brewing town). Look for Wild Heaven's Invocation, an 8.5% ABV Belgian Strong Pale Ale, a powerful blend of lush, ripe pear-like fruit flavors from pale malts with spicy noble hops in the background.

Savannah

THE DISTILLERY

416 W. Liberty St. • Savannah, GA 31401 • (912) 236-1772
distillerysavannah.com • Established: 2008

SCENE & STORY

The Volen family honored a colorful bit of local lore when they overhauled this historic former distillery, drugstore, soda fountain, lunch counter, and rumored bathtub gin dispensary. It's full of atmospheric exposed brick surrounding a glorious mahogany back bar, oak bar, old copper still, and artifacts discovered on-site, from musket balls to old liquor bottles, clay pipes, dishware, and bleached bones. The menu features inspired comfort foods, such as fried pickles, wild Georgia shrimp, and a beer-battered cod po'boy sandwich among other goodies, but save room for the Double Chocolate Deep Fried Moon Pie and Beer Float, made with stout, lambic, or other fresh draft brew.

PHILOSOPHY

Officially: "No crap—just craft."

KEY BEER

Ode to Mercy, a rich and toffee-ish 8.2% ABV American Brown Ale from Decatur's new Wild Heaven Brewing Company, making waves throughout the Deep South with adventurous, well-crafted beers.

Decatur

THE BRICK STORE PUB

125 E. Court Square • Decatur, GA 30030 • (404) 687-0990
brickstorepub.com • Established: 1997

SCENE & STORY

The Brick Store in downtown Decatur (a short drive from the center of Atlanta) is one of those beer bars you hear about in conversation described as a hallowed place, a sanctuary, the end of the rainbow in humankind's quest for the perfect beer bar. Of course, we all know nothing's perfect (or

why keep searching?), but it has got more than a few checks in the win column. The interior downstairs has the paradigmatic blend of exposed brick and creaky wood floors, cool lighting, 18 rotating taps and about 100 bottles, all superb, centered on local, regional, and nationally acclaimed American craft beers, with a good mix of German and English specialty beers and vintage and reserve bottled beers as well. There's an upstairs bar, too, the Belgian Room, which is as advertised and one of the main reasons to visit, with 8 taps and over 120 bottles laid in.

There's a good and varied food menu, too, with beer snacks (like house-made pretzels and ale-battered chicken fingers), burgers, salads and some beer-friendly entrées such as shepherd's pie and fish-and-chips, and the prices are very reasonable: there's nothing on the menu over $9.

PHILOSOPHY

Beer appreciation is the focus here. To allow and encourage conversations and cater to the naturally curious drinker, there are "no televisions, no neon, no obnoxious music and no major domestic beers." This is the beer enlightenment in action, but it's not dull or pretentious.

KEY BEER

This is surely one of the only places in the entire American South where you could find a beer like De Proef Signature Ale, a collaboration between Lost Abbey/Port Brewing's Tomme Arthur and Dirk Knaudts of the famed De Proef brewery in Belgium. Their 8.5% ABV golden-colored ale is tart, big, and funky, and as Michael Jackson described it,

"Everything promised by the brewers, and more. Aromas fresh as a forest. A hint of green wood. Firm, smooth, rounded body. Lemongrass, lemon zest, and cedar. A suspicion of sulfur and sweat. A long and distinct finish—you don't want it to end."

Atlanta

THE PORTER BEER BAR

1156 Euclid Ave. • Atlanta, GA 30307 • (404) 223-0393
theporterbeerbar.com • Established: 2008

SCENE & STORY

This diminutive Little Five Points area bar is small in layout but mighty in stature. Along with Decatur's Brick Store, this is one of the premiere beer bars in the South, and the interior is a home run, with long wood benches, cool metal tables, white-tiled walls, and a collection of retro plastic and vinyl suitcases. With thirty taps and four hundred bottle selections to choose from, the owners go out of their way to print pairing suggestions for the haute-rustic bar bites like pork empanadas with golden raisins, adobo almonds, and cocoa pineapple-jalapeño sauce, hush puppies with applewood smoked bacon, and Fuji apple sauce, and wild Georgia shrimp po'boys.

PHILOSOPHY

Thorough. With both a food and beer blog, a beer list updated "daily by 6 p.m.", beer flights, and other considerations, this beer bar is going the extra mile.

KEY BEER

Hitachino XH, a Belgian-style brown ale, brewed in Japan and aged for three months in shochu casks—the kind of beer-world curiosity that is generally far tastier in concept than in execution. But this strong, spicy, frothy oddity is delicious, with a wine like bite that would work well with those bacon and apple-kissed hush puppies (7% ABV).

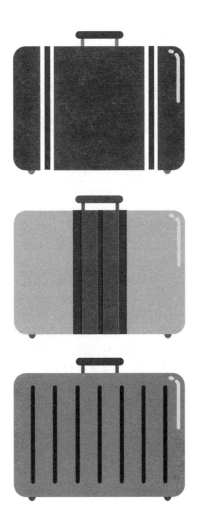

BEST *of the* REST: GEORGIA

TWAIN'S BILLIARDS *and* TAP

211 E. Trinity Pl. • Decatur, Georgia 30030 • (404) 373-0063 • twains.net

Brewer Jordan Fleetwood is ramping up the fresh tap offerings at this popular pool hall and lately, brewpub, with various Belgian-style, smoked malt, fruit-enhanced, and barrel-aged experiments to go with his popular pales, IPAs, and brown ales. The interior has cool teal-and-blue tile floors, copper pool table lamps, local art, green wooden chairs, and exposed gray brick.

TERRAPIN BEER CO.

265 Newton Bridge Rd. • Athens, GA 30607 • (706) 549-3377 • terrapinbeer.com

Opened in 2002 by friends John Cochran and Brian "Spike" Buckowski, this is a young brewery growing fast (18,800 bbl and climbing) with ever more adventurous styles and interpretations. Tours of the 40,000-square-foot space turn festive with live music in the taproom. (Tours are offered Wednesday through Saturday from 5:30 to 7:30 p.m.; $10 tasting glass fee.) Look for the Side Project beer series, such as Monk's Revenge, a superstrong (9.6% ABV) Belgian IPA with intense flavors of sweet and ripe citrus with an herbal, hoppy finish.

YOUNG AUGUSTINE'S

327 Memorial Dr. • Atlanta, GA 30312 • (404) 681-3344 • sites.google.com/site/youngaugustines

A chic and airy haven of variegated wood paneling and polished cement floors, this bar was a service station before it became a beer-focused gastropub with highbrow beer snacks (gourmet hot dog combo, pork sausage sliders with pickled carrots and Thai chili mayo, and the like). The thirty-tap list includes some truly inspired and wonderful finds, such as Hofstetter's 8.3% ABV Hochland Bio Organic Bock, a crackery, honey-tinged lager from Austria that is spiced with flowers, exceedingly rare, and delicious.

Alabama

★ ★ ★

Birmingham

J. CLYDE HOT ROCK TAVERN & ALEHOUSE

1312 Cobb Ln. • Birmingham, AL 35205 • (205) 939-1312
jclyde.com • Established: 2007

SCENE & STORY

Full of classic beer-bar appointments (exposed brick, wood rafters, beams, and tables), J. Clyde has some forty-three taps and another two hundred bottles on offer, in addition to a late-night menu with items like steak au poivre and fried green tomatoes.

PHILOSOPHY

Cask and ye shall receive. On most days, and infallibly every Friday at 4 p.m., something notable happens here in the state's best beer bar: a vessel of the only cask-conditioned ale in the state is tapped (and then drained in short order). Generally, the term "cask conditioned" refers to lighter British-style ales fermented and then "conditioned" or rested for a period of time at temperatures around 50°F–55°F with some natural fining agents in the beer, resulting in clarity, softness, and a delicate carbonation. (I say "generally" because cask conditioning is migrating into other, not-exactly-British styles, like the Italo American experiments at Eataly New York's rooftop Birreria.)

KEY BEER

Look for Coffee Oatmeal Stout from Birmingham's Good People Brewing Company on draught (and maybe cask). It's a 6% ABV sipper with deep roasted coffee and cocoa flavors.

★ ★ ★

Florida

★ ★ ★

THE SUNSHINE STATE HAS EMBRACED CRAFT BEER WITH THE FORCE

of a tropical storm. It seems hard to imagine that in the soporific land of blue hair retirees, Disney rides, and plastic nightclubs that earthy, DIY craft brewing would take such hold, but in fact it has, with some sixty (!) breweries and brew-pubs open and several more in planning stages. And loungey, Latin-inflected South Florida has a world of its own, a curious but worthy mix. The following is but a fraction of what's worth exploring.

Tampa

CIGAR CITY BREWING

3924 W. Spruce St., Ste. A • Tampa, FL 33607
(813) 648-6363 • cigarcitybrewing.com • Established: 2009

SCENE & STORY

Beer writer and Tampa native Joey Redner was immersed in beer—selling it, writing about it, running a bar, and generally loving the entire craft beer scene. Wayne Wambles was a home brewer gone pro; he had discovered the wonders of craft brews during 1996's Hurricane Opal, when a friend shared home brews with him over the course of three days as they waited for the power and water to return. When Redner and Wambles met, the die was cast for Cigar City, a company quickly remaking the entire Florida beer scene with innovative, award-winning beers. There are tours Wednesday through Friday from 11 a.m. to 2 p.m.; reservations are required, so e-mail info@cigarcitybrewing.com to schedule.

PHILOSOPHY

Brewery-as-melting pot. Redner is an aficionado of Tampas's culinary brew that melds Sicilian, Spanish, Puerto Rican, traditional Southern and soul food, and especially Cuban traditions. The mission driving Cigar City is to create ales and lagers that pair perfectly with Cuban dishes, such as boliche and picadillo, and Wambles is a tireless experimenter, employing everything from additions of apricot, mango, pomegranate, scuppernong grapes, and peppercorn to various sorts of barrel-aged beers with cedar chips, lavender, and heather.

KEY BEER

Wambles's favorite beer, the bombastic 7.5% ABV Jai Alai IPA is a walloping beer with a fat caramel malt backbone and six different hop varietals, including Simcoe, used only in dry hopping. It's hugely citric and resinous with the waves of tang and fruit in the balance that are required of great IPAs.

Oldsmar

300 State St. East, No. 107 • Oldsmar, FL 34677
(813) 855-9181 • oldsmartaphouse.com • Established: 2008

SCENE & STORY

Foosball anyone? That's if you can bear to put down the beer. The best craft bar in the Tampa area has thirty-six taps and more than eighty bottles, a mix of great American and Europeans from New Hampshire's Smuttynose to Belgian legend Saison Dupont. There's a small selection of sandwiches, sausages, and cheeses to tide you over.

PHILOSOPHY

For the aficionado with a heavy beer blog habit.

KEY BEER

Cigar City's 5.5% ABV Maduro Brown, a sweet, slightly nutty and fulsome beer.

★ ★ ★

DeLand

117 N. Woodland Blvd. • DeLand, FL 32720 • (386) 734-4545
abbeydeland.com • Established: 2006

SCENE & STORY

This upscale beer-and-wine bar about twenty minutes from Daytona Beach has parchment-colored walls, handsome terracotta tile floors, recessed lighting, and eighteen taps with a focus on the rare and hard-to-find Belgian variety. There are 150 beers in bottles including the six Trappist beers available in this country (the seventh, Westvleteren is well-nigh impossible to obtain without traveling to Belgium).

PHILOSOPHY

The owners focus on recommending pairings, including vintage ales and other specialties, to go with a rotating menu of sandwiches and other simple fare.

KEY BEER

Where else will you find the extraordinary Dupont Avec Les Bons Voeux? A strong saison from Belgium (9.5% ABV) that is hazy gold in color, fruity, and vinous in flavor, with a dry earthy kick in the finish, it's worth a trip inland from the beach.

ABRAXAS LOUNGE

407 Meridian Ave. • Miami Beach, FL 33139 • (305) 534-9005
myspace.com/abraxaslounge • Established: 2007

SCENE & STORY

In club-filled South Beach a hop skip and a jump from Ocean Drive, the last thing one expects to find is a beer serving rare Belgian farmhouse ales, much less a beer scene taking shape. But that's exactly what ponytailed Colombian beer lover Diego Escobar has created with Abraxas (named for the classic Santana album), a hidden lounge with a serious beer list and Modish 70s vibe (white couches—bold choice, amigo).

PHILOSOPHY

It's dark and candlelit, but no Biscayne Bay, where the Cuban gentlemen sleep all day (to paraphrase the classic Steely Dan song Dr. Wu). Expect nightly crowds keyed up on jazz, indie, rock and a well-balanced beers as sought-after as Dupont, Russian River, and various Mikkeller one-offs.

KEY BEER

Saison Athene, at 7.5% ABV, is Tarpon Springs brewery Saint Somewhere's contribution to the mustardy-gold style. Brewer Bob Sylvester is getting it right: fermented at higher temperatures (thanks, Florida), it's got big, interesting layers of fruity complexity.

★ ★ ★

BEST *of the* REST: FLORIDA

DATZ
2616 S. Macdill Ave. • Tampa, FL 33629 • (813) 831-7000 • datztampa.com

A combination bottle shop, deli, gourmet market, and beer bar with chef demonstration classes, fabled sandwiches, and twenty-six rotating taps including Soggy Loaf, a spicy, roasty pumpernickel rye porter brewed expressly for the bar by Cigar City Brewing, Datz is one of Florida's top beer destinations.

RED LIGHT, RED LIGHT
745 Bennett Rd. • Orlando, FL 32803 • (407) 893-9832 • www.myspace.com/theredlightredlight

The hometown of Disney World is also home to a world-class but ultra down-to-earth beer bar with a supercurated beer list comprised of American micros and special European finds. Established in 2005, its location recalls the setting for a 1970s movie car chase, but inside the bar is cozy, with brewery-sign-dotted dark walls and a vividly tiled back bar. The tap row runs to twenty-three taps and two engines, plus another hundred or so in bottles at any given time, like Kulmbacher's roasty Mönchshof Schwarzbier, light but flavorful (4.9% ABV).

TEQUESTA BREWING CO.
287 S US HWY 1 • Tequesta, FL 33469 • (561) 745-5000 • info via FaceBook.com

With its club-like Windex blue night lighting, jostling weekend crowds, and flat screens, Tequesta eschews the olden days vibe for a club-like narrow tasting room and growler filling station attached to the brewery, which is helping bring craft beer to South Florida in a bold way. Look for beers like Big Hitter Double Black IPA, Honey Badger, and the cleverly named, hop-blasted This Ain't Your Momma's Double IPA (8.7% ABV).

THE LODGE
200 S Federal Hwy • Boca Raton, FL • (561) 392-5003 • thelodgeboca.com

In a land where bars tend to be either translucent disco floor affairs teeming with spray tans and tube tops or a Latino-Mediterranean grab bag of stucco and pastel, The Lodge goes a lot more Hazzard County, with wall-to-wall unfinished wood walls, antler chandeliers, sports on TV and waitresses in short shorts and plaid blouses. There are 24 taps (with new releases from the likes of Stone, Dogfish Head, and Cigar City, recently), but the focus isn't only on brews, sports, and bouts of beer pong. The menu features bar bites like truffle oil fries with parmesan, an $8 pint, burger, and fries deal, and homemade chipotle-barbecue chicken nachos that come piled deliciously high.

BEST CRAFT BEER AND A BURGER PLACE:

Brouwer's Café, Seattle, WA

DBGB, New York, NY

The Falling Rock Taphouse, Denver, CO

Father's Office, Santa Monica, CA

The Laurel Tavern, Los Angeles, CA

Lüke, New Orleans, LA

Montana Aleworks, Bozeman, MT

The Porter Beer Bar, Atlanta, GA

Quinn's, Seattle, WA

Verdugo Bar/Grill 'Em All Food Truck, Los Angeles, CA

BEST DATE SPOTS FOR BEER LOVERS:

Blue Hill at Stone Barns, Pocantico Hills, NY

Bouchon, Beverly Hills, CA

Brasserie Beck, Washington, D.C.

Eleven Madison Park, New York, NY

Gramercy Tavern, New York, NY

Higgins, Portland, OR

Lüke, New Orleans, LA

The Publican, Chicago, IL

Resto, New York, NY

The Spotted Pig, New York, NY

BEST (WITH ALL DUE RESPECT) DIVES:

The Alaskan Hotel Bar, Juneau, AK
Cooter Brown's, New Orleans, LA
The Gowanus Yacht Club, Brooklyn, NY
Max's Taproom, Baltimore, MD
The Quarry House Tavern, Silver Spring, MD
Red Light Red Light, Orlando, FL
Shallo's, Indianapolis, IN
The Stumbling Monk, Seattle, WA
Toronado, San Francisco, CA
Zeitgeist, San Francisco, CA

OLD-SCHOOL TAVERNS:

The Brooklyn Inn, Brooklyn, NY
The Goose Hollow, Portland, OR
The Horse Brass, Portland, OR
The Parkway Tavern, Tacoma, WA
The Raleigh Times, Raleigh, NC
The Rathskeller, Indianapolis, IN
Saraveza, Portland, OR
Sunny's, Brooklyn, NY
Tony's Darts Away, Burbank, CA
The Wharf Rat, Baltimore, MD

OVERALL BEST BEER CITIES:

Asheville, NC
Chicago, IL
Denver, CO
Los Angeles, CA
New York, NY
Philadelphia, PA
Portland, OR
San Diego, CA
San Francisco, CA
Seattle, WA

BEST ANNUAL FESTIVALS:

Big Beers, Belgians, and Barley Wines, Vail, CO
Brewgrass, Asheville, NC
CanFest, Reno, NV
Deschutes Brewery Street Fair, Portland, OR
The Great Alaska Beer & Barley Wine Festival, Anchorage, AK
Great American Beer Festival, Denver, CO
Jupiter Craft Beer Festival, Jupiter, FL
Oregon Brewers Festival, Portland, OR
Tour de Fat, Fort Collins, CO
Where the Wild Beers Are, Brooklyn, NY

BEST BOTTLE SHOPS:

Beer Revolution, Oakland, CA
The Beer Trappe, Lexington KY
Belmont Station, Portland, OR
The Bier Stein, Eugene, OR
Bruisin' Ales, Asheville, NC
Datz Deli, Tampa, FL
Eagle Provisions, Brooklyn, NY
Saraveza, Portland, OR
Sergio's World Beers, Louisville, KY
Worden's Market, Missoula, MT

BEST BELGIAN LISTS/BELGIAN STYLE BARS:

The Brick Store, Decatur, GA
Brouwer's Café, Seattle, WA
Cascade Barrel House, Portland, OR
Higgins, Portland, OR
Jimmy's No. 43, New York, NY
Local 44, Philadelphia, PA
McNulty's Bier Markt, Cleveland, OH
Monk's Café, Philadelphia, PA
Novare Res, Portland, ME
Spuyten Duyvil, Brooklyn, NY

BEST OUTDOOR DRINKING:

Bohemian Hall, Queens, New York, NY
Eataly Birreria, New York, NY
Edgefield, Troutdale, OR
Lagunitas Brewing Co., Petaluma, CA
Marshall Wharf Brewing Co., Belfast, ME
Ouray Brewing Co., Ouray, CO
Pagosa Springs Brewing Co., Pagosa Springs, CO
Rathskeller, Indianapolis, IN
The Standard Hotel, New York, NY
Terminal Gravity, Enterprise, OR

BEST OFF-THE-BEATEN-PATH CRAFT BEER DESTINATIONS:

Diamond Knot Brewing, Mukilteo, WA
Dogfish Head, Rehoboth Beach, DE
Ebenezer's, Lovell, ME
Haines Brewing Co., Haines, AK
Jetty Fishery, Rockaway Beach, OR
Little Yeoman Brewing Co., Cabool, MO
Ourayle House, Ouray, CO
Prodigal Sun, Pendleton, OR
The Ship Inn, Milford, NJ
Silver Gulch Brewing & Bottling Co., Fairbanks, AK

BEST RARE BOTTLE LISTS:

Birch & Barley/Church Key, Washington, D.C.
Brasserie Beck, Washington, D.C.
Ebenezer's, Lovell, ME
Eleven Madison Park, New York, NY
The Falling Rock Taphouse, Denver, CO
Heorot, Muncie, ID
Max's Tap Room, Baltimore, MD
Monk's Café, Philadelphia, PA
The Porter Beer Bar, Atlanta, GA
Toronado, San Francisco, CA

Postscript

★ ★ ★

EVERY DAY I WRITE, OR DRINK A BEER, AND ESPECIALLY WHEN I'M

doing both, I think of Michael Jackson. Not 'that one', as he would say, but the Yorkshire journalist whose life and career was defined by a glorious world tour of beer. The towering hero of craft beer appreciation since the late 1970s, Jackson—author of sixteen seminal works including The World Guide to Beer (1977) and The New World Guide to Beer (1988), The Great Beers of Belgium (1991), and many others—took me under his wing starting in late 1996. With a seemingly bottomless reserve of graciousness, he helped me get started as a beer writer after I won a post-graduate fellowship that allowed me to delve into beer brewing techniques around the world for a year right out of college. Those encounters and that year changed my life.

It was August, 1996. I was twenty-two, and I had arrived in England just a few days before to start a wandering independent study on brewing for the Watson Foundation. After a needlessly nervous phone call to his office I traveled by train from Shawford, a village outside Winchester, to visit Jackson in his London home, in Hammersmith. We headed to his local, and then The Dove, a gloriously weathered old pub along the Thames, and drank for an entire evening. That day he became a mentor, writing to me (and once, to my amazement, about me, in a story about the Belgian beer Orval, a mutual minor obsession), and even promised me he would write the foreword to my first beer book. Alas, I failed to have this one ready for him in time.

I saw Michael infrequently after my year of research, not entirely by choice. Shortly after we'd met again in Portland, Oregon at the 1998 American Homebrewers' Association's National Conference, I moved to New Mexico for my first national magazine job, then decamped to New York just two days before 9/11 to pursue my luck as a writer. Though we spoke by telephone and corresponded by e-mail intermittently, Michael didn't make many appearances in Gotham, and what's more, I'd drifted away from the craft beer scene a bit in pursuit of New York–based travel writing work, which didn't call for my craft beer expertise nearly enough (yet). It would take five more years in the trenches for me to earn the right to call myself a full-time writer, and I'll never forget how he would always inquire, in the most honestly inquisitive and supportive manner imaginable, if I was getting there. "Keep writing," he wrote to me in a dedication in one of his books he'd given me as a gift. I did.

The last time I saw Michael was at D.B.A., the classic New York beer bar, on a limpid spring night on March 23, 2007. He was in town for a special tasting at a hotel in midtown, and D.B.A. owner Ray Deter and an assortment of other beer lovers who knew him well had arranged for a late-night session to taste rare Scandinavian ales. By candlelight, around 1a.m., we watched as Jackson arrived. He was walking with companions including the lovely Carolyn Smagalski, beer importer Dan Shelton, and his wife, Tessa (Dan had called to invite me to join, for which I am eternally grateful), and Monk's Café owner Tom Peters. I was shocked when I looked at my old mentor: he greeted me warmly, but his eyes were weary, his frame hunched. It was not the Michael I once knew. Dan Shelton pulled me aside and told me what was going on; it was then that I learned he had been severely weakened by a decade-long battle with Parkinson's, a closely-held secret for years, but something Jackson had begun to discuss bravely.

This was devastating news for me—and as Deter opened up his back patio area for the gathering, I struggled to find words, to feel at ease. We piled in shoulder to shoulder at a picnic table as samples made the rounds, and soon Jackson was bantering like his old self. Though his eyes were glassy and his head swayed gently from side to side, he was in his element. I felt both profoundly sad and grateful all at once.

There we stayed into the early morning, candles flickering and oozing all over the tables, sampling the beers Dan Shelton had discovered during his journeys. As glasses and bottles crisscrossed the table for inspection, Jackson—ever the journalist—spoke of the Norse tradition of home brewing a beer for your own approaching death, so that your loved ones may send you off in proper style. There was no pathos in his tone, but I detected a glint in his eye as he broached the topic—that of death, and his own, by extension—as he looked around at the brood over his wire-frame glasses perched at the end of his nose. The words ached; I was a little bit afraid of his state. But I didn't need to be. He had been writing about beer for as long as I'd been alive, and though the eeriness of the moment hovered in the air like smoke—this part, we heard in echoing silence—he wasn't being maudlin; he was doing what he always loved to do the most: talk about beer, drink, and laugh among old friends.

It's a bitter irony that in his final years, like the beverage he loved, Jackson was often misunderstood. Many mistook the effects of his illness for excess. He joked that his next book was going to be about Parkinson's: "I'm Not Drunk," he thought of calling it.

It was the last time I ever saw him; Jackson died five months later, on August 30, 2007, in his home. Shelton called me to tell me the news while I was out in New Mexico visiting old friends and colleagues at Outside magazine. It was a teary phone call for us both: Dan was one of the lucky people who was able to spend a lot of time with "The Bard of Beer," and even filmed a set of extraordinary interviews with him in England. In September, as shock surrendered to sorrow, beer lovers, including at D.B.A., participated in organized tributes worldwide. It's an annual tradition for me on his birthday (March 27) to salute the man and what his efforts have inspired in me and in so many others. As a beer lover, writer, and friend, I will always owe him the world.

Acknowledgments

★ ★ ★

THIS DREAM PROJECT REQUIRED THE WILLING WORK AND GRACIOUS

assistance of many, many people, more than I could possibly recall, but I will try. From friends, family, brewers, beer bar owners and beer writers to chefs, servers, and myriad others who work in the craft beer industry across the country, I'm truly grateful for having had the chance to meet and learn from so many inspiring people. I could never, ever have done this without their help. THANK YOU ALL.

A special first thank you to my joyful parents who have believed in me and in this book forever; and entire loving family, especially my brothers, Michelle, and Laura and Richard: thank you. To the late writer Michael Jackson, for his shining example of scholarship, wit, and wisdom. Thank you for taking me in that day back in 1996 and helping light the way every day since. You are sorely missed. Jonathan Miles, for the life-changing recommendation to top all others—I've got the next round, and the one after that. To McCormick & Williams and Alia Habib, my brilliant, tenacious agent, who stood side by side with me to create this book and to whom I am eternally grateful for advice, insight, support, and inspiration. To Jennifer Kasius, for expertly and efficiently bringing this book to life with Running Press, Monica Parcell, copyeditor, for her wit and élan, Ryan Hayes for his cool jacket design, and Nicole DeJackmo for working hard to promote it. To Garrett Oliver, for writing the elegant preface and believing in this project at first word. To Nancy Newhouse, for years of warm and caring hospitality, guidance and sage advice on all things literary and professional, especially this book, and to Mary and Tony Smith and Barky Pennick for their gracious support, hospitality, and burger- and beer-research expeditions. To the lovely and fearless Megan Flynn, for endless patience, unforgettable road trips and on-site research, draft reading and big picture dreaming, late-night pesto, pizza, Thai, and scrumptious green chile stew deliveries, and impromptu Blazer games, thank you for sharing this adventure with me. To Dana Cowin, Pam Kaufman, Ray Isle, and the heroic Jennifer Murphy of *Food & Wine* for believing in me and in craft beer travel and for assigning the all-important story on San Diego beer culture that led to this book. To Avery Houser, O.G., aide-de-camp, wingman, brewer, fixer, *flâneur*: I'd brew with you any day. To the brilliant Georgia Perry, for her Hoosier-style heroics, malarkey detection, virtuosic press release defilement, eagle-eye fact checking, and ability to say "whatever" at critical junctures: thank you for saving my bacon. To John Rasmus, who championed this journey all along, especially when the wheels came off, and for his steadfast backing during and after my days at *National Geographic*. To Sarah Rosenberg of ABC for always caring and making me laugh and look incredibly lazy by comparison. A very special thanks to Zoya Ihnatovich for bringing me the delicious borscht so many times, and to Joanna Agee of the Hive for making me so welcome. To Amanda Pederson for her tireless and timely research under the gun and both Bessie Seeley and Prakash Patodia and Gina Smith of Cabbage Tree for superb transcription work. A major note of thanks to Seth Fletcher and Abe Streep, for innumerable calls, insights and encouragements, visits, cold beers, hospitality, and editorial advice in the final hours. To willing galley readers Jane and Michael Stern, Mike Benoist, Mark Adams, William Bostwick, Hampton Sides, Ken Wells, Sebastian Junger, Corey Seymour, Bill Gifford, Kevin Fedarko, Brad Wieners, Jack Hitt, Liesl Schillinger, Elizabeth Hightower-Allen, Nick Fauchald, Tyghe Trimble, and Jordan Mackay: thank you. To Kasey Kordell, Brian Barker, Rachel Ritchie, and Randy Gragg of Portland Monthly, thanks for cheering me on. To dear friends Max and the rest of the Hallin Clan, especially Ingrid and Kurt, Abe and Denise Sorom, Charlie Redd, Courtney and Leather Storrs, C. Brown, Ryan Yaden, Gabriel Sherman, James Jung, The Brothers Eshak, Brian Ursino, Andrew Langham, Josh Boulange, and Huy Nguyen for easing the load. To Stephanie Dos Santos and Teresa Molitor for your calls and letters. To George Quraishi, Josh Hersh, Julian Smith, Fred Reimers, and Cliff Ransom for much needed breaks involving the consumption of beer without undue levels of note-taking. To Margo True for that unforgettable lunch at Higgins; to Greg Higgins for cooking it! To Lisa Morrison for her enthusiastic, perfectly timed encouragement and her own great book, a superb resource; to Tom Dalldorf for a great report from Alaska. To Juliet Lapidos of *Slate* for a thrilling first assignment on beer in the thick of it. To Christine Muhlke for her kind words and Julie Coe and Richard David Story of *Departures* for taking me aboard, and for assigning a story that informed this book. Lockhart Steel and Raphael Brion for the deliciousness that is *Eater*. To *Men's Journal* for letting Seth Fletcher and I run with the annual beer package for the beer part of a decade, which helped make the case for this undertaking. To *Outside* and Chris Keyes for letting me dream big, A.J. Jacobs for the same reason, and to Brad Wieners and Elizabeth Hightower Allen for helping me put the rubber to the road.To Kate Lacroix for so-bad-it's-good poetry, timely puns, IM wisdom, and book party-planning zeal. Lisa Donoughe for years of cheerful support, promotion, tips, talks, and fun book launch party plans: Thank you. I could not have done this without you. To Banks Tarver, Scott Carlin, and Gabriele Wilson for visions of small screen glory and artistic achievement. Hallie Beaune, Ray Daniels, Joshua Bernstein, Geoff Van Dyke, Susan Greene, Don Russell, Jim "Dr. Fermento" Roberts, Robinson Mills, Michael Pfohl, Christian Hattemer, and John Carlson for inside tips, assessments, and ideas. To Kevin Brooks for encouragement and help in my Pennsylvania touring. To John Foyston, Jeff Alworth, Fred Eckhardt, Lew Bryson, Lucy Saunders, Marisa Huff, Rachel Bleiweiss-

Sande, Arianne Cohen, Bree O'Connor, and Lessley Anderson, thanks for advice and spreading the good word near and far, even to lofty critics who only drink light beer in Chinese restaurants. To James Andrew and Harvey Claussen of Zythos Project for the spark of our shiny new endeavor, and to Leon Yeh for teaching me how to market something after years of having no clue.

Amid the craft beer and restaurant industry, a mere sliver of names to thank personally for help on this project includes Dan Shelton, for being heroic, hilarious, and half-crazy, and the ingenious Tessa Shelton for keeping him that way. A very warm thanks to Tom Peters and Will Reed for showing me the City of Brotherly Love and bringing it truly alive for me; to Julia Herz and Charlie Papazian of The Brewers Association, for years of support and promotion, especially at the outset of my writing project. To Bill Covaleski, for running red lights when it matters. To Bill Owens, for paving the way. Christian Ettinger, and Van Havig for keeping Portland on its toes. The dear Charles and Rose Ann Finkel, Dave Brodrick and Alan Jestice of the amazing Blind Tiger, Mike Greenberg and Irene Hamburger, the late, great Ray Deter, Mike Wiley, Shaun Hill, Brendan "Spanky" Hartranft, Sang Yoon, Don Feinberg and Wendy Littlefield: thank you for sharing your establishments, your secrets, and your remarkable beer stories. To Phil Markowski, Larry Bennett, Craig Hartinger, Fritz Maytag, Geoff and Marcy Larson and Donovan Neal, Jim Meehan of P.D.T., Sean Z. Paxton, Ron Jeffries, Matt Dinges, Eric Michaud, Marty Jones, Ben Weiss, Jamie Smith, Jerald O'Kennard and Chad Wulff, Dan and Deb Carey, C.V. Howe and Adam Avery, Chris Cochran, Brian Butenschoen, Chris Crabb, Charlie Deveraux, Greg Koch, Katie Powell, Anne Sprecher, Carol Stoudt, Peter Zien, Shaun O'Sullivan, Tony Forder, Adam Carbonell, and Dr. Bill Sysak. To Kirk Kelewae and Will Guidara of the peerless Eleven Madison Park; to Tony Simmons, Morgan Miller, Dale Katechis, Ike Manchester, Mike Hale, Eric Wallace, Paul Long, Chad Kennedy, Rob Tod, Patrick Rue, Pat McIlhenney, Gary and Carol Fish, Steven Pauwels, Jamie Floyd, Brian Hunt, Tomme Arthur, Lee Chase, Nick Arsner, barn-burners Jim Koch and Sam and Mariah Calagione, Gabe Fletcher, Kevin Burton, John McDonald, Matthew Brynildson, Preston Weesner and Ron Gansberg of Cascade, Steve "Eske" Eskebeck, Greg Engert, Kirk Coco, Peter Caddoo, the Knott Brothers, "Heiner" Orlik, David Blossman, Sonny Day II, Taylor Rees, Will and Mari Kemper, the dapper Thor Cheston, Jimmy Carbone of the great Jimmy's 43, Bill Opinsky, Alan Sprints, Sarah Pederson, Allison Wagner, Jennie Hatton, David McLean, Josh Schaffner, "Hutch" Hutchison, Marie Melsheimer, Constance Aguilar, Clayton Scrivner, Mark Jilg, Chris Swerzey, Kris Oyler, Chad Melis, Chris Quinn, Sandra Evans, Chris Nemlowill, Casey Parker, Chris Black, Bryan Simpson, Neill Acer, Brad Lincoln, Alana Jones, Mark Jilg, Scot Blair, Vinnie Cilurzo, Carol White, Mike Lawinski, Robert Hodson, Matt Cutter, Tomme Arthur, Garrett Marrero, Amanda Johnson, Volker Stewart, Shawn McCasland, Liz Melby, Ken and Brian Grossman, Chuck Stilphen, Bill Manley, Jamie Smith, Matthew Arata, Ron Lindenbusch, Alex Ganum, Adam Carbonell, Paul Gatza, Evan Rail, Julie Bradford, Jesse McCann, Amanda Hathaway, Ted Lane, Scott Vaccaro, Terry Usry, Jeffrey Stuffings, Julie Weeks, Ashley Hawkins, Jess Cutler, Daves Welz and Thibodeau, Christina Clabbers, Kate Goldstein-Breyer, Max Gellman and too many others to list, for opening up your businesses and schedules.

For travel, logistical, promotional, and other forms of support along the way thanks to Jane and Michael Stern, the fabulous Colu Henry and Andrew Knowlton of *Bon Appetit,* Scott Dolich, Stephanie Boettner, Katie Schneider, Marke Rubenstein, Jenny Tallis, Laura Herbert, Kelly McCandless, Barbara Neilan, Lisa Jones, Jan Metzmaker, Cara Schneider and Donna Schorr, Jack Bonney, Jeffra Clough, Glen Hemingson and the Copper Whale Inn, Caitlin Sullivan, Katharine Flanagan, Laurie Armstrong, Steven Holt, Caitlin Austin, Julie Camp, Laura Barnes, Julie Conover, Jess Clayton, Tia Troy, Tony Herbert, Jennifer Reisfeld, Kirsten Texler, Kate Lessman, Margo Metzger, Molly Brewer, Mike Harrelson, the incredibly helpful Roland Alonzi and Kara Strollo, Jen Elving Asbury, Deborah Park, Liz Biebl, Donnie Sexton, Ashley Johnston, Elizabeth Arnett, Sophie Shafter, Jennifer Thompson, Jody Overstreet (what a bike ride!), and Ken Hill, Jennifer Parnell, Monee Cottmann, Larry Noto, Kendra Borowski, Christine DeCuir and Kelly Schulz, Katerina Scherff, Claire Tucker, Debbie Rizzo, Louise Field of Facilitec, Christian D'Souza of Brübar, David Macbale of Old Town Computers, Elizabeth Pond, L.M.T. And to everyone else I've surely forgotten, thank you.

Glossary

★ ★ ★

3.2 laws: Laws in certain states that only permit beer to be sold when it has an alcohol by weight of 3.2%, equivalent to 4% ABV. Famously applied in Utah, though laws are changing.

22 oz.: aka "bomber." A U.S. standard size for large bottles of beer sold individually.

750ml: aka "wine bottle size." The European standard size for a large bottle of beer, as opposed to 22 oz., which is also becoming more popular in U.S. craft brewing. The "750" is popular with Belgian and Belgian-style brews, and may be closed with a traditional crown cap, cork-and-cap, or cork-and-wire cage combination.

Abbey-style: Refers to malt-forward, typically fruitier beers made with traditional methods of brewing first used by the breweries of Belgian monks, including the Trappist monasteries. Something of a catch-all phrase. See also:Tripel.

Acidity: Level of acid in beer; proportional to the degree of sour/vinegar/lemony taste. A by-product of fermentation adds dimensions of flavor beyond sweet, bitter, and estery notes See also: Esters.

Ale: Formerly, beer without hops; today, beer fermented with ale yeast at warmer temperatures than lagers (which are made with lager yeast), imparting fruitier and more aromatic notes.

Altbier: A style of robust German pale ale that is typically aged, or "conditioned," for longer than standard periods of time, resulting in a smooth brew.

American wild ale: Beer fermented with ambient, naturally-occurring yeast in the United States that is allowed to settle in the beer naturally and begins the fermention spontaneously rather than with the intentional addition of brewers' yeasts. See also: Lambic.

American Pale Ale (APA): Distinguishable by an elevated but still balanced presence of malt and hops, with fruity, floral, and citrus-like flavors.

Attenuation: The degree to which a beer's fermentable sugars have been consumed by yeast or yeasts. See also: Dryness.

Barley wine: Traditionally sweet, nutty, sherry or whiskey-ish beers named for their high alcohol content, which approaches that of wine; often aged in oak barrels.

Barrel-age/aging/aged: Beers aged in wood barrels, resulting in intentional flavors from the wood, of the alcohol formerly aged in the wood (i.e. red wine, Bourbon, Scotch, sherry, rum), or of microorganisms living in the wood.

Bbl (abbrev.): aka "Barrels;" a barrel of beer is 31 gallons and the standard size for a keg is a half-barrel.

Beer engine: A traditionally English device for pumping beer from a cask in a pub's cellar into the drinker's glass.

Belgian-style: A style of brewing that tends to produce beers that are spicier due to the use of certain yeast strains, more intensely flavored and higher in alcohol content than their American counterparts, and often bear the tannins and acids from wood barrels and wild yeasts.

Bière de Garde (France): Literally, "beer to store," which ranges in color from golden to light brown, characterized by a light to medium body, with a slight malt sweetness and slight hop character.

Bierstube (German): A large pub that specializes in beer. Found throughout Germany.

Bitter/Bitterness: The perception of a bitter flavor imparted to beer by hops or malt husks; determined by a sensation on the back of the tongue; measured in International Bitterness Units (IBUs).

BMC: Budweiser, Miller, Coors (casual phrase for major industrial breweries making light lagers on a mass scale).

Body: The heft of a beer, related to its grain content and dryness, or degree of attenuation.

Brettanomyces: A genus of yeast; called "Brett" for short and viewed as a contaminant by most brewers but sometimes used on purpose to create a sour or "barnyard" taste in beer, especially Belgian and Belgian-style beers. Its taste is also described as leathery, funky, and horse-blanket.

Brewhouse: A brewery; a place that houses the equipment used to make beer. Interchangeable with the core equipment itself, which is often clustered.

Brewpub: A pub that makes its own beer and sells it on site.

Cask: A barrel-shaped container for beer, usually made of metal.

Cask-conditioned: Beer that undergoes a secondary fermentation and maturation in the cask; results in light carbonation.

Cicerone: Like a sommelier for beer—a trained expert in selecting and serving beer. The levels are Certified Cicerone and Master Cicerone; both require certification.

Collaboration beers: Beers made when two or more breweries get together to produce one beer.

Craft brewery: A brewery producing six million barrels per year or less using more or less traditional methods of making beer from malted barley, primarily.

Cream ale: Offshoot from the American light lager style; ale that has corn or rice added to it to lighten the body.

Czech-style: Coppery-hued lager heavily hopped with earthy, spicy noble hops from Europe, especially Southeastern Germany and the Czech Republic.

Diacetyl: A natural by-product of fermentation that can give beer unpleasant, butterscotch-like or artificial butter flavors. A common flaw eliminated through careful brewing and sanitation.

Dry, Dryness: Degree to which fermentable sugars have been consumed, or "dried out" from the beer during fermentation and aging.

Dry-hopped: Beer with an addition of dry hops to fermenters and/or aging tanks to punctuate hop aroma without adding high levels of bitterness.

ESB: Extra Special/Strong Bitter; Originally a British style of bitter beers with more aggressive alcohol and hop character and ample malt body.

Esters/Estery: Fruity-smelling, harmless chemical compounds created as a by-product of high-temperature fermentations.

Extreme beer: Catch-all phrase for aggressively hopped ales fermented to a high alcohol percentage, usually around 7% but sometimes nearly double that (most beer hovers between 4% and 6% alcohol, while craft beers average 6%.) Sometimes interchangeable with "Imperial" and "Double." May contain herbs, spices, and fermentable starches other than barley or wheat, fruit, coffee, or other natural additions.

Farmhouse ale: Ale made in a farm setting; a tradition originating in Belgium and northern France and now made on a very small scale in the United States. See also: Saison

Fermenter: Tanks for fermenting beer; can be steel cylindro-conical vessels (CCVs), open stone vessels, or wooden vats.

Filter/Unfiltered: To remove harmless sediments from the brewing and fermentation process from beer; generally unfiltered beer is hazy with yeast cells or grain matter.

Flanders-style: Reddish, sour ales with winelike qualities brewed in Belgium and aged a year or longer in oak barrels, often with Lactobacillus yeast.

Gastropub: A bar or pub that also serves high-quality food.

Geuze (Belgian-style): A type of Belgian beer made from blends of young and old wild yeast beers (aged from three months to three years) that is then bottled with additions of yeast and a small amount of sugar for a second fermentation.

Growler: A half-gallon glass jug (64 oz.), often sold at breweries and brewpubs for beer to go.

Hallertau: The original German lager hop, named after an area in Bavaria that is the largest hop-planting area in the world.

Hefeweizen: Wheat beers that are bottled with the yeast in suspension, creating a cloudy, frothy, and refreshing effect.

Hop/Hops: A perennial vine that produces resinous flowers that impart bitterness and aromas to beer.

IIPA/Double IPA/Imperial IPA: Like an extra-strong IPA; robust and malty with a high hop content; originated in the western United States.

IPA: India Pale Ale; Has a strong bitter taste and a higher hop content than most ales.

Izakaya (Japanese): A Japanese bar that also serves food.

Kellerbier: Literally "cellar beer;" usually German-style lager, served directly from conditioning tanks with a bready, yeasty flavor at the peak of freshness.

Kettle: Meaning brew kettle, in which the brewer boils the ingredients of beer. Often made of stainless steel; occasionally copper-plated.

Kölsch, or Koelsch: A straw-gold, clear, light-bodied beer with a prominent hoppiness locally brewed in Cologne, Germany.

Lager: The beer that results from yeast working at colder fermentation temperatures than ales; typically results in breadier, crisper-tasting beer than ales.

Lambic (Belgian): A typically dry, sour beer created through spontaneous fermentation in a small number of rural breweries in and just outside of Brussels, aged in oak barrels up to three years.

Lupulin: The pollen-like, resinous powdery substance in hop flowers which impart bitterness and aroma to beer.

Macrobrewery: A large industrial brewery making beer on a massive, profit-driven scale.

Malt (ingredient): Barley which has been harvested, wetted, germinated, and dried (or kilned). "Malting" modifies the internal structure of barley to make it ready for brewing.

Malty (descriptor): Tasting like malt sugar, or maltose, which is present in malted barley and other grains that are prominent players in the fermentation of beer.

Märzen-style or Maerzen-style: A style of German lager beer characterized by a reddish brown color, medium to full body, a malty flavor and a clean, dry finish. Traditionally German "Oktoberfest" beer was made in the maerzen-style, but in recent years Oktoberfest beers have gotten more pale.

Mash: (Verb) To release malt sugars by soaking the grains in hot water. (Noun) The liquid that results is called wort, and that is brewed with hops in the brewing kettle.

Michael Jackson, writer: (March 27, 1942 – August 30, 2007). Yorkshire-born journalist whose 1977 book The World Guide to Beer and 16 later titles on beer and whiskey firmly established him as the world's foremost authority on both. Known for his gentlemanly demeanor, dry wit, and warmth, he was also the host of "The Beer Hunter," a two season beer and travel program shown on the U.K.'s Channel 4 and Discovery Channel. A massive image of his face hangs on a banner over the Great American Beer Festival, held in Denver each fall.

Microbrewery: A brewery that produces less than 15,000 barrels per year.

Munich-style: A dark lager with a distinctive taste of malt, produced in Munich since the tenth century.

Nanobrewery: A brewery operating with a system no larger than seven barrels—many have just one or two barrels.

Orval: The beer and company name of one of the most storied breweries in Belgium is in the Notre Dame d'Orval monastery in Villers-devant-Orval, near Florenville in the Belgian province of Luxembourg (not to be confused with the independent duchy of Luxembourg to the east). It is one of the world's six remaining Trappist abbey breweries, owned and occupied by cloistered Trappist monks. The Orval abbey is more than 850 years old.

Oud bruin: Also known as Flanders Brown, a sour tasting beer originating from the Flemish region of Belgium with long aging process that can take up to a year, including secondary fermentation and bottle aging. Often has some residual balancing sweetness.

Pasteurize: To heat beer to a certain degree in order to sterilize it, increasing shelf life.

pH (for brewing): The ideal number is 5.2, which facilitates perfect starch to sugar conversion during the brewing process and before fermentation.

Pils, Pilsner: A pale lager with a strong hoppiness; first brewed in the Bohemian town of Pilsen (Czech: Plzeň).

Porter: A dark-colored ale originated in London brewed with dark malts, possibly named for the street and river porters who popularized it.

Rathskeller (German): A beer hall or restaurant in a basement or underground.

Reinheitsgebot: Also known as the German Purity Law of 1516, which limits beer ingredients in Germany to water, hops, malt and yeast. Though no longer a binding law, it is voluntarily observed in many German breweries, especially in the southern state of Bavaria, and by many German-style breweries outside the country.

Russian Imperial Stout: A stout with high alcohol by volume and a high malt character; tastes like chocolate and burnt or roasted malt.

Saison: Means "season" in French; earthy, unfiltered, low-alcohol pale ales meant to refresh farm workers during the summer; also called "farmhouse ales" and originated in the French-speaking part of Belgium known as Wallonia. Generally 6–8% ABV.

Session beer: An easy-drinking, mild beer with an alcohol content typically less than 4%, intended to be consumed several to a sitting.

Smoky/Smokiness: A taste in beer with a smoke flavor created by using malted barley dried or smoked over wood such as alder, beech, or over peat.

Sour beer: Beers fermented with wild yeasts and bacteria, sometimes but not always utilizing wood. Styles include Flanders Red, Oud Bruin, Lambic (known as American wild ale in the US) with varying degrees of acidity and little or no hop character.

Spontaneous fermentation: Beers made with natural, ambient yeasts in the air ("wild" strains of yeast), rather than yeast being added by the brewer.

Steam beer: A beer made with lager yeasts at the warmer temperatures of ale fermentation; uniquely linked to the Anchor Steam brewery in California. Also called "California Common."

Stout: A dark beer made using roasted malt or barley, hops, water, and yeast; traditionally meant extra strong porter beer.

Tannins: In beer, organic compounds derived from grain husks, non-lupulin hop flower parts, and oak (as in oak barrels) which pucker and dry the mouth, balancing malty sweetness.

Trappist: Refers to beer made by Orval or one of the other six officially authorized Trappist abbeys: Rochefort, Westmalle, Westvleteren, Chimay, and Achel (Belgium); Schaapskooi lies just over the Dutch border at the Koningshoeven monastery. Monks take a vow of silence and live austerely, focused on the contemplative life and some agrarian pursuits such as farming, baking, and brewing.

Tripel: A lighter bodied Belgian-style or Belgian beer with a bright yellow color and a sweet finish; deceivingly alcoholic and good for sipping; named for the brewing process of this type of beer, in which brewers use two to three times the standard amount of malt.

Vienna-style: A lager named for the city in which it originated, brewed using a three-step decoction boiling process; subtle hop taste with residual sweetness.

Wild yeasts/wild ale: Beers fermented with yeast or bacteria strains including Brettanomyces, Lactobacillus, and Pediococcus, microorganisms considered taints in most beers and wine that can have appealing earthy and acidic flavors in beer when wrangled with care.

Yeast: A microorganism added into the raw ingredients of beer in order to facilitate the conversion of malt sugars into alcohol and CO_2.

Zwickelbier: See "Kellerbier".

Zymurgy: The art and science of brewing beer.

Index

★ ★ ★

The Barley Oak	Mandeville	315
The Bulldog	New Orleans	308
The Bulldog Midcity	New Orleans	308
The Maple Leaf	New Orleans	306

Maine
Allagash	Portland	252
Ebenezer's Pub	Lovell	255
Marshall Wharf Brewing Co./Three Tides	Belfast	255
Novare Res Bier Café	Portland	254
The Great Lost Bear	Portland	256
The Lion's Pride	Brunswick	256

Maryland
Alewife	Baltimore	289
Max's Taproom	Baltimore	290
The Brewer's Art	Baltimore	289
The Quarry House Tavern	Silver Spring	291
The Wharf Rat	Baltimore	291

Massachusetts
Boston Beer Company	Jamaica Plain	259
Deep Ellum	Allston	261
Doyle's Café	Jamaica Plain	262
Lord Hobo	Cambridge	261
Redbones	Somerville	261
Sunset Grill & Tap	Allston	261
The Moan & Dove	Amherst	262
The Publick House	Brookline	262

Michigan
Arcadia Brewing	Battle Creek	196
Ashley's Restaurant & Pub	Ann Arbor	196
Bell's Brewery Eccentric Café	Kalamazoo	195
Founders Brewing Company	Grand Rapids	194
HopCat	Grand Rapids	194
Jolly Pumpkin Café & Brewery	Ann Arbor	193

Minnesota
Surly Brewing Co.	Brooklyn	198
The Happy Gnome	St. Paul	197
The Muddy Pig	North Saint Paul	198

Mississippi
| Lazy Magnolia | Kiln | 328 |
| The Keg & Barrell Brew Pub | Hattiesburg | 329 |

Missouri
Boulevard Brewing Company	Kansas City	199
Bridge Tap House & Wine Bar	St. Louis	201
International Tap House	St. Louis	201
Little Yeoman Brewing Co.	Cabool	201
Schlafly Bottleworks	St. Louis	200

Capone's	Norristown	283
Dock Street Brewing Co.	Philadelphia	278
Earth Bread & Brewery	Philadelphia	282
Eulogy	Philadelphia	271
Grace Tavern	Philadelphia	269
Jose Pistola's	Philadelphia	279
Khyber Pass	Philadelphia	269
Local 44	Philadelphia	274
McGillin's Olde Ale House	Philadelphia	278
Memphis Taproom	Philadelphia	273
Midatlantic Restaurant & Tap Room	Philadelphia	270
Monks Café & Belgian Beer Emporium	Philadelphia	274
Resurrection Alehouse	Philadelphia	277
South Philadelphia Tap Room	Philadelphia	278
Stoudt's Brewing Co. & The Black Angus Restaurant & Brewpub	Adamstown	283
Teresa's Next Door	Wayne	281
The 700 Club	Philadelphia	271
The Belgian Café	Philadelphia	272
The Farmhouse	Emmaus	283
The Foodery	Philadelphia	268
The Grey Lodge Public House	Philadelphia	272
The Standard Tap	Philadelphia	268
Tria Café	Philadelphia	282
Tröegs	Harrisburg	283
Victory Brewing Co.	Philadelphia	280
Yard's Brewing Co.	Philadelphia	280
Yuengling	Pottsville	281
South Carolina		
The Community Tap	Greenville	325
Tennessee		
Yazoo Brewing Company	Nashville	326
Texas		
Draught House Pub & Brewery	Austin	164
Jester King Craft Brewery	Austin	164
Live Oak Brewing Co.	Austin	166
Rahr & Sons Brewing Co.	Fort Worth	165
The Flying Saucer Draft Emporium	Austin	166
The Ginger Man	Austin	163
Uncle Billy's Brew & Que	Austin	166
Utah		
Epic Brewing Co.	Salt Lake City	178
Squatters Pub Brewery	Salt Lake City	176
The Bayou	Salt Lake City	178
Uinta Brewing Co.	Salt Lake City	177
Vermont		
Forty Putney Road	Brattleboro	250
Hill Farmstead	Greensboro Bend	249
The Alchemist Pub & Brewery	Waterbury	248

Tasting Notes